CompTIA CASP+ CAS-004 Certification Guide

Develop CASP+ skills and learn all the key topics needed to prepare for the certification exam

Mark Birch

BIRMINGHAM—MUMBAI

CompTIA CASP+ CAS-004 Certification Guide

Group Product Manager: Vijin Boricha

Publishing Product Manager: Rahul Nair

Senior Editor: Sangeeta Purkayastha

Content Development Editor: Nihar Kapadia

Technical Editor: Nithik Cheruvakodan

Copy Editor: Safis Editing

Project Coordinator: Shagun Saini

Proofreader: Safis Editing

Indexer: Hemangini Bari

Production Designer: Nilesh Mohite

Marketing Coordinator: Hemangi Lotlikar

First published: February 2022

Production reference: 4030323

Published by Packt Publishing Ltd.

Livery Place

35 Livery Street

Birmingham

B3 2PB, UK.

ISBN 978-1-80181-677-9

www.packt.com

To all my students, both former and present, who motivate me to help them achieve their learning goals.

– Mark Birch

Contributors

About the author

Mark Birch is an experienced courseware developer and lecturer in information systems and cyber security. Mark has been helping students attain their learning goals for over 25 years. He has been developing content and teaching CompTIA CASP since its inception in 2011 and understands the subject area in depth. He began his career working as an engineer within the aerospace industry for BAE Systems (a major defense contractor), gaining a thorough understanding of industrial controls, CAD/CAM systems, and design principles. Graduating from the University of Central Lancashire with a BSc in Information Technology, Mark has also gained accreditation in the following: Microsoft, CompTIA, Citrix, Novell Networking, and ITIL.

I want to thank all my family for supporting me, understanding that I could not always be "available" during the past year.

About the reviewers

Filip Korngut has over 15 years of experience in information security and systems engineering in the oil and gas, mining, and digital health sectors. He has extensive experience leading the development of major software and digital transformation solutions with primary focus on cybersecurity leadership and technology. Filip has led cybersecurity engagements for the big four consulting firms and has a passion for establishing organizational cybersecurity programs. Filip has two sons with his beautiful wife Erin and a dog named Lily.

Arron Stebbing is a Principal, Sales Acceleration, Technical Trainer at Veeam Software. Arron develops and delivers training programs about modern data protection software.

Arron also contributes to CompTIA as a member of the Technical Advisory Committee and as a subject matter expert for exam development.

Arron is a Certified Facilitator of the LEGO® Serious Play® method. He uses the science-backed process to bring creativity, exuberance, and the inspiration of play to the serious concerns of organizations in the business world.

Arron has extensive experience building and operating cloud service provider environments and has been working in the IT industry for more than 17 years. Arron can communicate with executives about business value and outcomes as well as educate technical teams on how to deliver the business value required to meet the requirements.

Shubham Mishra is India's youngest cyber security expert and a leading name in the field of ethical hacking. He is the founder and CEO of TOAE Security Solutions and has dedicated his life to the robust development of cyber security methods that are being used worldwide. Shubham has worked with some of the largest companies in the world for more than a decade and continues to provide up-to-date and relevant content for the industry.

Table of Contents

2

Integrating Software Applications into the Enterprise

3

Enterprise Data Security, Including Secure Cloud and Virtualization Solutions

4
Deploying Enterprise Authentication and Authorization Controls

Section 2: Security Operations

5

Threat and Vulnerability Management

6

Vulnerability Assessment and Penetration Testing Methods and Tools

7

Risk Mitigation Controls

8

Implementing Incident Response and Forensics Procedures

Section 3: Security Engineering and Cryptography

9

Enterprise Mobility and Endpoint Security Controls

10

Security Considerations Impacting Specific Sectors and Operational Technologies

11

Implementing Cryptographic Protocols and Algorithms

12

Implementing Appropriate PKI Solutions, Cryptographic Protocols, and Algorithms for Business Needs

Section 4: Governance, Risk, and Compliance

13
Applying Appropriate Risk Strategies

14
Compliance Frameworks, Legal Considerations, and Their Organizational Impact

15

Business Continuity and Disaster Recovery Concepts

16

Mock Exam 1

17

Mock Exam 2

Preface

In this book, you will learn how to architect, engineer, integrate, and implement secure solutions across complex environments to support a resilient enterprise. You will find out how to monitor, detect, and implement incident response, and use automation to proactively support ongoing security operations. You will learn how to apply security practices to cloud, on-premises, endpoint, and mobile infrastructure. You will also discover the impact of governance, risk, and compliance requirements throughout the enterprise.

Who this book is for

This book is aimed at CASP+ CAS 004 exam candidates. Many candidates will be using the certification for career enhancement. It will also be of interest to managers who want to gain additional knowledge in the field of cybersecurity and technical implementers who want to understand the operational elements of cybersecurity.

What this book covers

Chapter 1, Designing a Secure Network Architecture, covers designing and understanding both traditional network architectures and complex hybrid networks.

Chapter 2, Integrating Software Applications into the Enterprise, covers the software life cycle, software assurance, and supporting enterprise software applications.

Chapter 3, Enterprise Data Security, Including Secure Cloud and Virtualization Solutions, looks at the challenges facing an enterprise when protecting data in hybrid environments.

Chapter 4, Deploying Enterprise Authentication and Authorization Controls, examines credential management, identity federation, and secure single sign-on. It also covers multi-factor authentication.

Chapter 5, Threat and Vulnerability Management, covers methods used to gather threat intelligence, understand the different threat actors (and adversaries), and prepare appropriate responses.

Chapter 6, Vulnerability Assessment and Penetration Testing Methods and Tools, looks at methods used to help assess an enterprise's security posture, including SCAP scans, penetration testing, and an introduction to a wide range of security tools.

Chapter 7, Risk Mitigation Controls, looks at typical vulnerabilities that may be present within an organization and controls to reduce risk.

Chapter 8, Implementing Incident Response and Forensics Procedures, covers incident response preparation, including the creation of documentation and a **Computer Security Incident Response** (**CSIRT**) team. It also covers forensic concepts and the use of forensic analysis tools.

Chapter 9, Enterprise Mobility and Endpoint Security Controls, examines enterprise mobility management, including mobile device management tools. It also covers endpoint security and host hardening techniques.

Chapter 10, Security Considerations Impacting Specific Sectors and Operational Technologies, looks at regulated business sectors, challenges facing enterprises that must support embedded systems, SCADA systems, and operational technology.

Chapter 11, Implementing Cryptographic Protocols and Algorithms, looks at protecting enterprise data using hashing algorithms and encrypting data using both symmetric and asymmetric algorithms. It also looks at implementing cryptography within security protocols.

Chapter 12, Implementing Appropriate PKI Solutions, Cryptographic Protocols, and Algorithms for Business Needs, covers **Public Key Architecture** (**PKI**), different certificate types, and troubleshooting issues with cryptographic implementations.

Chapter 13, Applying Appropriate Risk Strategies, examines risk assessment types, risk response strategies, including implementing policies, and security best practices.

Chapter 14, Compliance Frameworks and, Legal Considerations, and Their Organizational Impact, covers the challenges of operating within diverse industries, regulatory compliance, and legal regulations.

Chapter 15, Business Continuity and Disaster Recovery Concepts, teaches you how to conduct a business impact analysis and develop business and disaster recovery plans. It also covers high availability and deploying cloud solutions for enterprise resilience.

Chapter 16, Mock Exam 1 and *Chapter 17, Mock Exam 2*, test your knowledge with final assessment tests, comprising accurate CASP+ questions.

To get the most out of this book

CASP+ is an advanced certification building on existing knowledge gathered within a cybersecurity environment. To fully appreciate the concepts covered, it is recommended that you have some baseline cybersecurity practical skills or have gained a baseline security certification such as CompTIA Security+. Candidates who have experience in pen testing and ethical hacking will also have a good base knowledge that is suitable for this book. It would benefit you to have access to a Windows operating system and a recent build of Kali Linux (to practice with tools and commands).

Software/hardware covered in the book	Operating system requirements
Security tools and command-line utilities	Windows and Kali Linux

Additional practical exercises and learning content is available on the companion site: `https://casp.training`.

Download the color images

We also provide a PDF file that has color images of the screenshots and diagrams used in this book. You can download it here: `https://static.packt-cdn.com/downloads/9781801816779_ColorImages.pdf`.

Conventions used

There are a number of text conventions used throughout this book.

`Code in text`: Indicates code words in text, database table names, folder names, filenames, file extensions, pathnames, dummy URLs, user input, and Twitter handles. Here is an example: "A file would be created that would be of interest to the attacker, `Passwords.doc`."

Any command-line input or output is written as follows:

```
dsquery user "ou=it admin,dc=classroom,dc=local"
```

Bold: Indicates a new term, an important word, or words that you see onscreen. For instance, words in menus or dialog boxes appear in **bold**. Here is an example: "The certificate's **Subject Name** value must be valid."

> **Tips or Important Notes**
> Appear like this.

Get in touch

Feedback from our readers is always welcome.

General feedback: If you have questions about any aspect of this book, email us at customercare@packtpub.com and mention the book title in the subject of your message.

Errata: Although we have taken every care to ensure the accuracy of our content, mistakes do happen. If you have found a mistake in this book, we would be grateful if you would report this to us. Please visit www.packtpub.com/support/errata and fill in the form.

Piracy: If you come across any illegal copies of our works in any form on the internet, we would be grateful if you would provide us with the location address or website name. Please contact us at copyright@packt.com with a link to the material.

If you are interested in becoming an author: If there is a topic that you have expertise in and you are interested in either writing or contributing to a book, please visit authors.packtpub.com.

Share Your Thoughts

Once you've read *CompTIA CASP+ CAS-004 Certification Guide*, we'd love to hear your thoughts! Scan the QR code below to go straight to the Amazon review page for this book and share your feedback.

https://packt.link/r/1801816778

Your review is important to us and the tech community and will help us make sure we're delivering excellent quality content.

Section 1: Security Architecture

In this section, you will learn about the challenges that are faced by an enterprise when supporting a large, complex, hybrid network architecture. This section will take you through the design of traditional network architectures up to complex hybrid cloud models. You will also understand the importance of authentication and authorization strategies within complex environments.

This part of the book comprises the following chapters:

- *Chapter 1, Designing a Secure Network Architecture*

- *Chapter 2, Integrating Software Applications into the Enterprise*

- *Chapter 3, Enterprise Data Security, Including Secure Cloud and Virtualization Solutions*

- *Chapter 4, Deploying Enterprise Authentication and Authorization Controls*

1
Designing a Secure Network Architecture

Security professionals need to analyze security requirements and objectives to ensure an appropriate, secure network architecture for a new or existing network and to provide the appropriate authentication and authorization controls.

Designing a modern enterprise network has many practical and security challenges. De-perimeterization means that access to information systems may be made from devices outside of the enterprise network. The types of devices can range from a handheld smartphone used to access a customer record to an **Internet of Things (IoT)** device transmitting telemetry data to a critical monitoring dashboard.

Regulatory or industry compliance may require strict network segmentation between processes and **business units (BUs)**.

It is important to consider all the threat actors when you plan your network—think **Defense in Depth (DiD)**.

This first chapter is an essential building block for the following chapters. It is the information systems on our networks that provide the data and services for an enterprise.

In this chapter, we will cover the following topics:

- Physical and virtual network and security devices
- Application- and protocol-aware technologies
- Advanced network design
- Network management and monitoring tools
- Advanced configuration of network devices
- Security zones

Physical and virtual network and security devices

For the certification exam, it is important that you understand the strengths and weaknesses of all the proposed network devices/appliances, the correct placement of network devices for maximum effect, and the required security configuration.

OSI model

No introduction to networking would be complete without a brief introduction to the **Open Systems Interconnection (OSI)** 7-layer model. As we move through the chapters, you will occasionally see references to layers. This has become a standard reference model and it allows for different vendors to implement services, protocols, and hardware using this reference model. Throughout the book, we will discuss applications, services, protocols, and appliances that sit at different layers within the model. Although the **CompTIA Advanced Security Professional 004 (CASP 004)** exam will not be testing your knowledge specifically (OSI is not a listed objective), it can be useful as a reference aid when we discuss networking subjects. The model is not actually defining a complete working network model—it is a conceptual model. For example, to fully understand the details of the **Simple Mail Transport Protocol (SMTP)**, you would need to gain access to **Internet Engineering Task Force (IETF) Request for Comments (RFC)** documents. Imagine you are looking to manufacture network cables to meet **Category 6 (CAT 6)** standards—you could access **International Organization for Standardization/ International Electrotechnical Commission (ISO/IEC 11801) standards** documentation. See the following screenshot for an overview of the OSI 7-layer model:

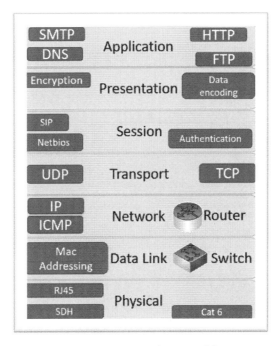

Figure 1.1 – OSI 7-layer model

Vulnerabilities may exist across multiple layers within the OSI model. For example, we may be vulnerable to **Man-in-the-Middle (MITM)** attacks on our layer 2 switch. We will take a look at the many different threats that may impact an enterprise network throughout the book.

Unified threat management

A **unified threat management (UTM)** appliance offers firewall functionality and many additional security functions; it is deployed as a single security appliance or software solution. This security solution offers a comprehensive suite of security features all in a single package. While this is a good solution for small enterprises with limited resources (limited staff and limited budget), it does not offer the DiD required by enterprise customers.

UTMs may include a significant number of converged security features, but not necessarily all of the following:

- **Network firewall**

- **Intrusion detection system (IDS)**

- **Intrusion prevention system (IPS)**

- **Deep packet inspection (DPI)**
- **Data loss prevention (DLP)**
- **Anti-virus capability**
- **Web application firewall (WAF)**
- **Web proxy and content filtering**
- **Spam filtering**
- **Security information and event management (SIEM)**

The following screenshot shows the combined security features supported on a UTM appliance:

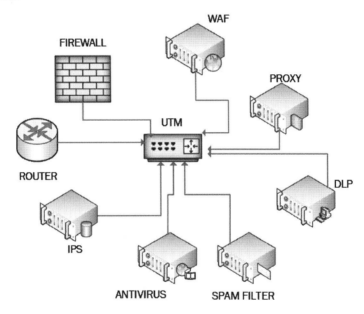

Figure 1.2 – UTM appliance

Advantages

UTM has the following advantages:

- Reduction in management actions (compare the scenario of a small **information technology (IT)** security team managing and monitoring multiple security appliances)
- Reduced footprint in the data center (less hardware)
- Less cost

Disadvantages

UTM has the following disadvantages.

- Risk from a **single point of failure** (**SPOF**) (limited hardware resources are providing many services)

- Negative performance impact on a network due to the workload handled by the device

IDS/IPS

Intrusion detection is an essential security function, typically implemented on the perimeter to protect your organization from incoming threats. It will alert the security team to inbound threats.

Intrusion prevention is the process of performing intrusion detection and then stopping detected incidents. These security measures are available as **IDS** and **IPS**. Active protection is the more commonly adopted approach, meaning a **network intrusion prevention system** (**NIPS**) will be seen protecting most enterprise networks.

IDS and IPS constantly watch your network, identifying possible incidents and logging information about them, stopping incidents, and reporting them to security administrators. In addition, some networks use IDS/IPS for identifying problems with security policies and deterring individuals from violating security policies. IDS/IPS have become a necessary addition to the security infrastructure of most organizations, precisely because they can stop attackers while they are gathering information about your network.

Examples of intrusions

Indicators of compromise (**IOCs**) can be unusual traffic, attacks against protocols (such as high volumes of **Internet Control Message Protocol** (**ICMP**) traffic), and malicious payloads. The result could be excess traffic causing **denial of service** (**DoS**) or compromised systems through unwanted deployments of Trojans and backdoors.

There are two main IDS detection techniques that are routinely used to detect incidents, as outlined here:

- **Signature-based detection** compares known signatures against network events to identify possible incidents. This is regarded as the simplest detection technique as it evaluates attacks based on a database of signatures written by the vendor or operator. In the same way as a first-generation firewall, this approach is limited as it is based on known patterns.

Examples:

A **Secure Shell** (**SSH**) connection using the root account would be in the ruleset.

An email with the subject **password reset** and an attachment with the name passregen.exe would be identified as malicious.

- **Anomaly-based detection** compares definitions of what is considered a normal/benign activity with observed events to identify significant deviations. This detection method can be very effective at spotting previously unknown threats. This type of detection is also known as heuristics-based detection.

Example:

The SMTP messaging server usually contributes to 23% of traffic on the network. If the SMTP server is suddenly generating 70% of the network traffic, this would generate alerts.

Network IDS versus NIPS

The NIPS sits directly behind the firewall (inline) and traffic needs to be forwarded onto the network. The NIPS can block unwanted traffic and payloads. This is illustrated in the following diagram:

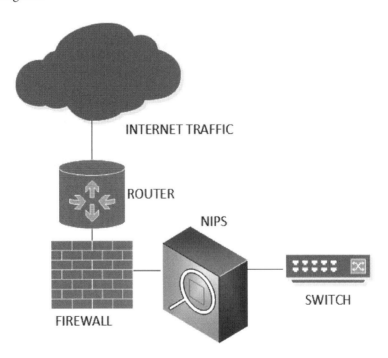

Figure 1.3 – NIPS placement (inline)

Network IDS (NIDS) does not need to be inline; it can monitor traffic but will need to use **port mirroring** or **spanning** on the network switch to be effective, as illustrated in the following diagram:

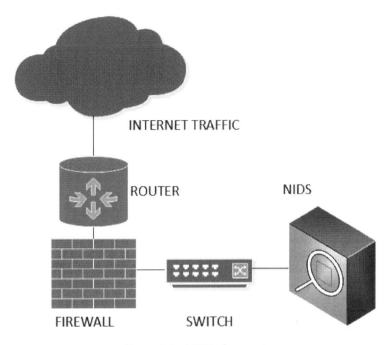

Figure 1.4 – NIDS placement

Wireless IPS

In addition to fixed or wired networks, many organizations may need the flexibility of a Wi-Fi network.

A **wireless IPS (WIPS)** is designed to detect the use of rogue or misconfigured wireless devices. A rogue device can spoof **media access control (MAC)** addresses of trusted network devices. A WIPS can build up a database of known trusted hosts on the network and can also be used to prevent DoS attacks.

An effective WIPS should mitigate the following types of threats:

- **Ad hoc networks**: These use **peer-to-peer (P2P)** connections to evade security controls and risk exposure to malware.

- **Rogue access points (APs)**: These allow attackers to bypass perimeter security.

- **Evil-twin APs**: Users may connect to this *lookalike* network and be vulnerable to sniffing.

- **Misconfigured APs**: These expose a network to possible attacks due to configuration errors.

- **Client misassociation**: This risks infection from connecting to other **service set identifiers** (**SSIDs**) while in range of the authorized AP.

- **MITM attack**: An attacker will route traffic through their network device and sniff the traffic.

- **MAC spoofing**: This may allow the attacker to bypass **access-control lists** (**ACLs**) on the AP or allow them to impersonate another network device.

- **DoS attack**: This happens when a continuous stream of fake requests or messages is sent to the AP.

Inline encryptors

The **High Assurance Internet Protocol Encryptor Interoperability Specification** (**HAIPE-IS**) requires **inline network encryption** (**INE**) devices to be interoperable. For example, **Tactical Local Area Network Encryptor** (**TACLANE**) is a product used by the **United States** (**US**) government and the **Department of Defense** (**DOD**); it is military-grade and meets **National Security Agency** (**NSA**) security requirements. It is manufactured by General Dynamics. This is a device that enables encrypted communication over untrusted networks. Commercial organizations will use site-to-site **virtual private network** (**VPN**) links and not need this technology. The following figure shows a TACLANE INE device:

Figure 1.5 – INE device

This device meets the high assurance required by government and military remote connections.

Network access control

Network access control (**NAC**) enforces a strong, secure posture for devices that connect to our enterprise networks.

A major challenge for many enterprise networks is unmanaged **bring your own device** (**BYOD**) devices and guest devices accessing wireless and switched networks. The goal is to control access to the network, ensuring devices are compliant with baseline security policy. You would want to ensure devices had anti-virus installed and had security patches and firewall functionality.

Devices typically connect through a registration **virtual local area network** (**VLAN**) using a captive portal. If devices are found to be compliant, they could gain network access. Devices found to be uncompliant would be routed through to an isolation VLAN, able to access remediation services. The following diagram shows the components of NAC:

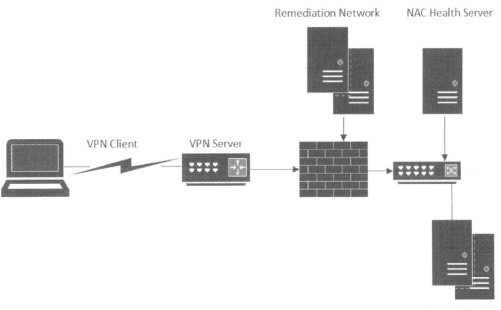

Figure 1.6 – NAC

PacketFence offers a free and open source NAC solution that is distributed under the **General Public License** (**GPL**). The software can be accessed via https://www. packetfence.org/.

SIEM

SIEM allows an organization to centralize security management events, forwarding logs from security appliances to a central system. It provides correlation and normalization for context and alerting, and also provides reporting and alerts based upon real-time logged data inputs. The following diagram shows the architecture of centralized SIEM:

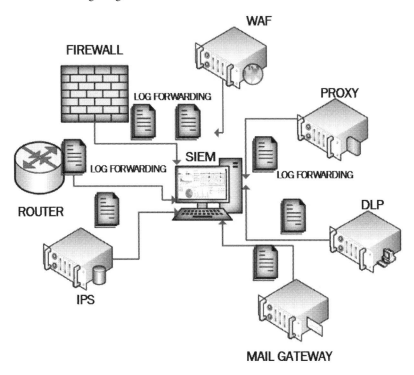

Figure 1.7 – SIEM architecture

Advanced solutions can use behavioral analytics to detect anomalous user behaviors. Privileged user monitoring is a common requirement for compliance reporting. The following screenshot shows a SIEM dashboard:

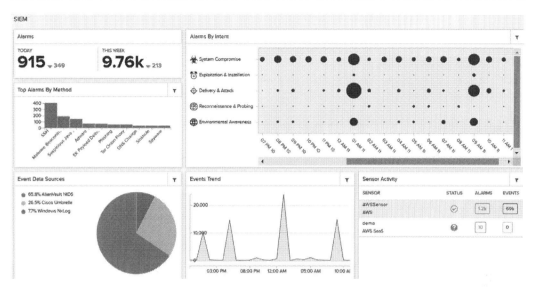

Figure 1.8 – AlienVault/AT&T SIEM dashboard

SIEM threat intelligence can help **security operations center** (**SOC**) teams pinpoint malicious or risk-based events and deliver a response. Analytics and **machine learning** (**ML**) are used to produce insights from huge amounts of collated data; they offer automation to identify hidden threats. Benefits include the following:

- **Real-time monitoring**: Stop threats that can be fast-moving.

- **Incident response**: Quickly identify threats to begin a response.

- **User monitoring**: This will identify unusual user behaviors and risky privilege use.

- **Threat intelligence**: Build up knowledge of security teams.

- **Advanced analytics**: Aid the analysis of large amounts of logged data.

- **Advanced threat detection** : SOC analysts need this advanced toolset to detect and address IOCs.

Switches

A switch is a network device that connects devices on a computer network by receiving and forwarding data to the destination device. Switches use layer 2 MAC addresses to forward data frames at layer 2 of the OSI model. Many enterprise switches will also combine layer 3 functionality in the switch. Layer 3 switches allow for routing traffic between VLANs.

Switches are vulnerable to DOS attacks; the **content-addressable memory** (**CAM**) is typically overloaded/flooded with spoof MAC addresses. Switches can be used for MITM when using **Internet Protocol version 4 (IPV4) Address Resolution Protocol (ARP)** broadcasting. They can also suffer performance degradation due to unwanted looping traffic.

Mitigation would include the following:

- Protect the management interface (use strong passwords).

- Enable **Spanning Tree Protocol** (**STP**) (this will block redundant connections) to prevent looping traffic.

- Connect using SSH (all management traffic is encrypted).

- Provide an **out-of-band** (**OOB**) network (all management is performed on a separate management network).

- Configure 802.1x (require all network connections to be authenticated).

The following screenshot shows what a switch table looks like:

```
Vlan      Mac Address        Type        Ports
----      -----------        --------    -----

   1      0005.5e2e.9319     DYNAMIC     Gig0/1
   1      0060.2f1c.6359     DYNAMIC     Gig0/1
   1      0060.7004.101c     DYNAMIC     Fa0/4
   1      00d0.58b1.3abd     DYNAMIC     Gig0/1
   1      00d0.9719.2339     DYNAMIC     Gig0/1
Switch>|
```

Figure 1.9 – Switch table

Switches provide essential services on enterprise networks and will be responsible for the bulk of all network traffic.

Firewalls

Firewalls are there to block unwanted traffic entering your networks; they can also block outbound traffic. They depend upon rules to block IP addresses, protocols, and ports. More sophisticated firewalls will have more granular rules and may slow down traffic.

Firewall types

Firewalls can be implemented in many different ways; enterprise deployment will have highly capable hardware solutions from vendors such as Cisco or Check Point. Software or host-based firewalls offer additional security with DiD. Data centers and microsegmentation will accelerate the use of virtual firewall deployment. Different types of firewalls are listed here:

- **Hardware firewalls** provide maximum performance. These are typically dedicated appliances with a **central processing unit** (**CPU**) and memory dedicated solely to this function.

- **Software firewalls** generally run on a host operating system, such as **Microsoft Windows Defender Firewall** or **Linux iptables**. They share computing resources with the operating system.

- **Virtual firewalls** are appliances running on a virtual host controlled by a hypervisor. The performance is dependent upon the compute resources allocated by the hypervisor.

Firewall capability

Firewalls have evolved over time, with additional capabilities and functionality.

First-generation firewalls use static packet filtering. They inspect packet headers and implement static rules based upon IP addresses and port addresses. Their big advantage is high performance. A **router** will typically perform as a static packet filter.

Second-generation firewalls also use stateful inspection, in addition to packet filtering. This can monitor **Transmission Control Protocol** (**TCP**) streams (whole stream, not just handshake) and dynamically open ports and track sessions for bi-directional protocols (such as **File Transfer Protocol** (**FTP**)).

Next-generation firewalls (**NGFWs**) have evolved from second-generation firewalls to meet the requirements of a multi-functional security appliance. An NGFW offers all the functionality of the earlier generation, but will typically offer additional functionality in the form of support for VPNs and anti-virus protection. NGFWs have DPI capability, meaning they can offer additional security in the form of DLP and IPS protection. This should not be confused with UTM, although they are similar. NGFWs are designed with performance in mind.

Routers

Routers operate at layer 3 of the OSI model and are interconnection devices (they connect networks together). Routing capability may also be provided by a switch that supports VLANs (it will be called a layer 3 switch).

Routing tables

Routers are only able to forward packets if they have a route for the traffic or a default gateway. Routing tables will comprise a **NETWORK DESTINATION**, **NETMASK**, **GATEWAY**, **INTERFACE**, and **METRIC** value.

Here is a simple routing table:

NETWORK DESTINATION	NETMASK	GATEWAY	INTERFACE	METRIC
0.0.0.0	0.0.0.0	10.0.0.1	10.0.0.254	20
172.16.0.0	255.255.0.0	172.30.0.1	172.30.0.254	30
172.17.0.0	255.255.0.0	172.30.0.1	172.30.0.254	30
172.18.0.0	255.255.0.0	172.30.0.1	172.30.0.254	30

Figure 1.10 – Routing table

Static routing tables may be acceptable for small networks, but we will need to support automated dynamic routing for larger networks.

Dynamic routing

In larger, more complex networks, it is normal to use dynamic routing rather than configuring manual static routes. Within an autonomous network (the network managed by your organization), you will be using interior routing protocols. It would be time-consuming to configure routing tables statically and we would miss the resilience offered by dynamic routing protocols.

The purpose of dynamic routing protocols includes the following:

- Discovering available remote networks
- Maintaining up-to-date routing information
- Choosing the most efficient path to remote networks
- Allocating a new path if a route is unavailable

Routing Information Protocol (**RIP**) is the simplest and easiest routing protocol to configure. It is used for routing over smaller networks (allowing a maximum of 15 hops). It is not considered a secure routing protocol.

Enhanced Interior Gateway Routing Protocol (**EIGRP**) is used on Cisco networks and was developed to work around the drawbacks of using RIP. EIGRP benefits from fast convergence times whenever the network topology is changed.

CISCO devices share their capabilities using **Cisco Discovery Protocol** (**CDP**) with immediate neighbors. This can be disabled on a network.

You can prevent your router from receiving unwanted/poisoned route updates by configuring neighbor router authentication; this uses **Message Digest 5** (**MD5**) authentication.

Open Shortest Path First (**OSPF**) is a good choice for larger networks because it has no restriction on hop counts. OSPF allows routers to communicate securely, and routing information is exchanged through **link-state advertisements** (**LSA**). *RFC 2328* allows for the use of a keyed MD5 identifier to protect OSPF neighbor updates.

Exterior routing

To keep internet working routing tables up to date, edge routers will forward route changes via exterior routing protocols.

Border Gateway Protocol (**BGP**) is the routing protocol used between **internet service providers** (**ISPs**). BGP can also be used to send routing updates between an enterprise and its ISP. BGP can be secured so that only approved routers can exchange data with each other (this uses MD5 authentication).

Proxy

A proxy server acts as a gateway between users and the internet services they access online.

A proxy protects your users from directly connecting with unsafe sites. It can offer **Uniform Resource Locator** (**URL**) filtering and content filtering in addition to performance enhancements. A proxy can be a good choice when protecting our users from threats based upon outbound requests. Firewalls are not designed to deliver this more granular protection. A firewall could block an outbound connection to a port and IP address, but would not offer the same fine-tuning as a proxy server.

Network address translation gateway

Network address translation (**NAT**) is a networking technique commonly used to give an entire private network access to the internet without needing to assign each host a public IPv4 address. The hosts can create connections to the internet and receive responses but will not receive inbound connections initiated from the internet (as they are, in effect, hidden). The following diagram shows a NAT router forwarding traffic to the internet from an internal host:

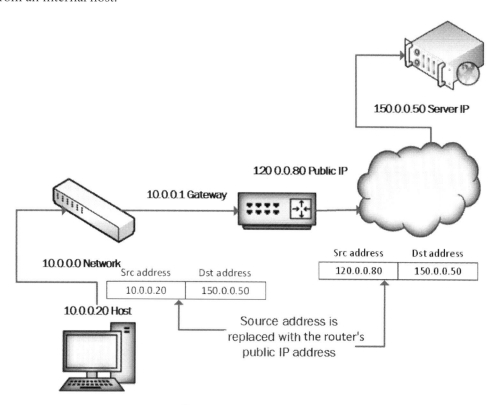

Figure 1.11 – NAT routing

When a host on the internal (private) network sends a request to an external host, the NAT device's public IP address is used as the new source IP address for the outbound traffic. The traffic sent back in reply is returned to the internal host. Most NAT solutions use **port address translation** (**PAT**) to keep track of all the private hosts that have sessions. We can see NAT configuration in the following screenshot:

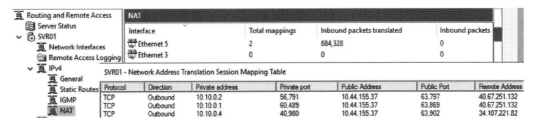

Routing and Remote Access	NAT			
Server Status	Interface	Total mappings	Inbound packets translated	Inbound packets
SVR01	Ethernet 5	2	684,328	0
Network Interfaces	Ethernet 3	0	0	0
Remote Access Logging				

SVR01 - Network Address Translation Session Mapping Table

Protocol	Direction	Private address	Private port	Public Address	Public Port	Remote Address
TCP	Outbound	10.10.0.2	56,791	10.44.155.37	63,797	40.67.251.132
TCP	Outbound	10.10.0.1	60,489	10.44.155.37	63,869	40.67.251.132
TCP	Outbound	10.10.0.4	40,980	10.44.155.37	63,902	34.107.221.82

Figure 1.12 – Microsoft Routing and Remote Access Service (RRAS) with connected clients

NAT is an important service used in both enterprise and small business deployments.

Load balancer

A load balancer will be useful to enterprises that host server farms and would be a key requirement for **high availability** (**HA**) e-commerce sites. When hosting a Citrix server farm supporting remote applications, it is important that the loading on each member is constantly evaluated to ensure new requests are forwarded to a server with the least load.

Hardware security module

A **hardware security module** (**HSM**) is a special *trusted* network computer performing a variety of cryptographic operations: key management, key exchange, encryption, and so on. This device can be a rack-mounted appliance secured in your data center or could be a built-in module for high-end server hardware.

A **trusted platform module** (**TPM**) is typically built into system boards of laptop and desktop computer systems, allowing for the storage of sensitive protected data, including keys and attestation measurements. This is a good example of an HSM incorporated into the system board.

MicroSD HSM is built into a MicroSD form factor. It is useful when you need to extend the functionality of a mobile device and could be used on a cellular phone for secure communications. The HSM would have its own crypto-processing capability, meaning no changes are required on the mobile device. The following screenshot shows a small form-factor HSM:

Figure 1.13 – MicroSD HSM

Many of the security applications mentioned up to this point secure the entire network from threats. In the following section, we will examine more targeted/granular approaches to protect particular services or data types.

Application- and protocol-aware technologies

Some applications will benefit from dedicated security appliances/services operating on sole behalf of those applications. Imagine you wanted to protect your web application server from typical exploits, including **cross-site scripting (XSS)**, **cross-site request forgery (XSRF)**, and **Structured Query Language (SQL)** injection. In that case, you would not want to filter all traffic for these exploits using the network firewall; it would have a huge workload and would slow down traffic for the entire network. Application-aware security appliances process traffic only being forwarded to that service.

The types of security applications that inspect and apply rulesets to application layer traffic are said to be using DPI.

It is important to plan for the placement of these devices to ensure traffic can be inspected before entering or leaving the network and to also minimize latency or delay where inspection and filtering are not required.

In the following section, we will take a look at some examples of application- and protocol-aware security solutions.

DLP

We must ensure the enterprise does not breach legal or regulatory compliance by exfiltration of sensitive data, either knowingly or unknowingly. It is important that intellectual property and customer data are protected, even when compliance is not a factor. Physical restrictions and/or enforceable policy may be used to block data exfiltration to a removable storage medium. DLP can also be implemented on the edge of the network, or as part of a cloud solution. Microsoft is one of many providers offering DLP as part of the **Cloud Access Security Broker** (**CASB**) security suite. In the following screenshot, we are selecting built-in rules to block the exfiltration of financial data:

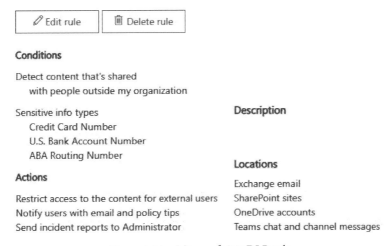

Figure 1.14 – Microsoft 365 DLP rule

There are many built-in templates for regulated industries.

WAF

A WAF is defined as a security solution on the web application level. It allows for **HyperText Transfer Protocol/HTTP Secure** (**HTTP/HTTPS**) traffic to be inspected for anomalies without slowing down the rest of the network traffic. A WAF can be implemented as an appliance, plugin, or filter that applies a set of rules to an HTTP connection.

A WAF helps prevent attacks, such as the following:

- SQL injection attacks
- XSS attacks
- Malicious file execution

- CSRF attacks

- Information leakage

- Broken authentication

- Insecure communications

A WAF can also provide URL encryption and site usage enforcement, as illustrated in the following diagram:

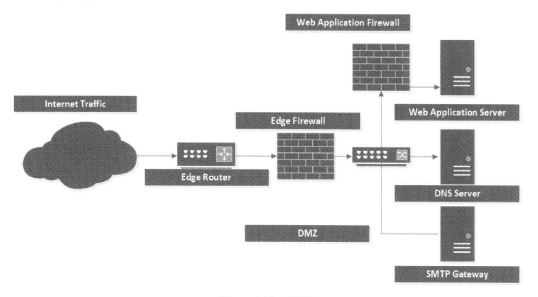

Figure 1.15 – WAF

Advantages

A WAF has the following advantages:

- Allows for the creation of custom rules

- Monitors and blocks malicious traffic

- Can prevent live attacks

- Protects vulnerable web applications

Disadvantages

A WAF has the following disadvantages:

- May slow web traffic
- Could block legitimate traffic
- Requires frequent tuning

Database activity monitoring

Database activity monitoring (**DAM**) tools monitor, capture, and record database activity in near real time and can generate alerts when rules are violated.

DAM can be accomplished by doing the following:

- Network sniffing
- Reading of database logs
- Memory analysis

DAM tools can correlate data and provide the administrator with the tools to detect anomalous database activity and capture a log of events, should this be required for forensics.

As a database is often a critical **line-of-business** (**LOB**) solution, often hosting **enterprise resource planning** (**ERP**), **customer relationship management** (**CRM**), sales order processing, and so on, investing in this additional technology will be worth the cost.

Spam filter

A spam filter typically scans incoming emails to protect your employees from email-borne threats. It can also scan emails leaving the organization (although this is more likely taken care of by a DLP solution). It can be deployed on the **demilitarized zone** (**DMZ**) network, filtering incoming SMTP traffic, and will typically perform additional tasks such as querying **Spamhaus Block List** (**SBL**) providers, such as **Spamhaus**, to drop connections from verified blocked domain names or IP addresses.

Many organizations will deploy this service in a cloud deployment, especially if the ISP hosts the email servers.

The following section covers some of the additional considerations to allow for secure remote working and administration.

Advanced network design

Since the Covid-19 pandemic began to transform the workplace in 2020, there has been a major effect on the way employees access their enterprise's desktop and company data. Enterprises have been forced to accept that the modern workplace will contain a high number of remote working employees. Many enterprises expect a significant proportion of staff to continue with this flexible way of working due to the benefits of work/life balance. What was previously considered the exception, where some workers were able to remotely access the workplace or connect from a temporary location such as a hotel or airport transit lounge, will likely now become the new normal.

There are significant risks in extending the network perimeter to these remote workers, and it is important that all access is secure and identities are verified.

Remote access

This is the term used when accessing systems remotely. We may need to access a desktop to configure settings for a remote worker or configure a network appliance ruleset. In some cases, it may be necessary to assist a remote worker by sharing their desktop. We will compare the main types of remote access in this section.

VPN

A VPN service provides you with a secure, encrypted tunnel when you need to connect across untrusted networks. External threat actors cannot access the tunnel and gain access to your enterprise data.

A VPN can be used for securing remote workers and can also be used to connect sites across untrusted networks.

Enterprise solutions include Microsoft Direct Access, Cisco AnyConnect, and OpenVPN (there are many more). *Figure 1.16* shows a popular VPN client, OpenVPN Connect:

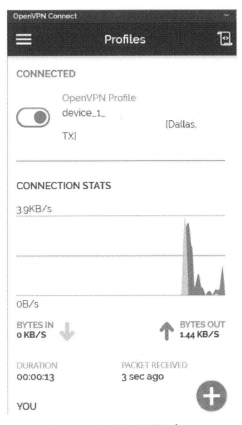

Figure 1.16 – OpenVPN client

Many enterprises will ensure their employees' mobile devices are enabled with an **always-on VPN client**. This ensures that when employees are working outside the corporate network, they will automatically connect over a secure connection, whenever the device is powered on. It is important that all traffic is routed through the VPN connection using a full-tunnel configuration. *Figure 1.17* shows a full-tunnel configuration:

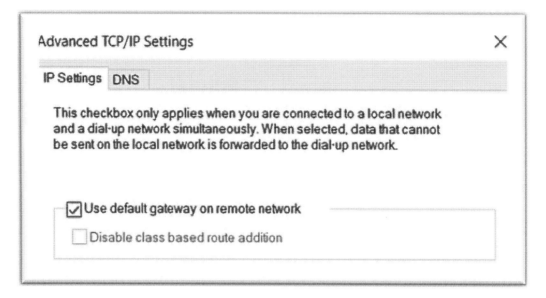

Figure 1.17 – Full-tunnel configuration

When the VPN interface is configured with the default gateway configuration, as shown in *Figure 1.17*, all traffic is routed through the company network, ensuring security policies are enforced.

IPsec

IP Security (**IPsec**) is a suite of protocols deployed in most vendor implementations of IPv4 and is a requirement for **IP version 6** (**IPv6**). When configured, it will protect against replay attacks and ensure the integrity and confidentiality of the data.

Authentication headers (**AHs**) provide authentication, integrity, and protection against replay attacks.

Encapsulating Security Payload (**ESP**) provides authentication, integrity, and confidentiality for your data.

When using **Transport mode**, encryption occurs at the internet layer, protecting all of the layers above the network layer. It is used internally only.

Tunnel mode can be used to create site-to-site VPNs between trusted networks and to connect a host device across an untrusted network. In the following screenshot, we can see that Tunnel mode creates a new IP header:

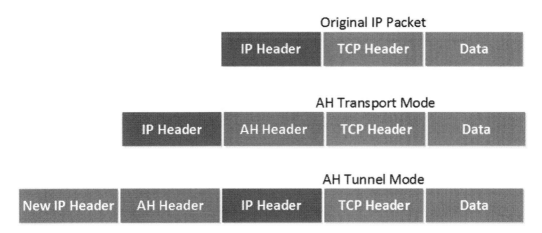

Figure 1.18 – IPsec modes

While IPsec is typically used to protect communications outside the enterprise, it can also be used internally when VLANs cannot offer adequate protection. This is when Transport mode would be appropriate.

SSH

SSH is a standard internet security protocol documented in *RFCs 4251, 4253*, and *4254*. The SSH protocol is a protocol for secure remote login and other secure network services over an insecure network. It is recommended to use SSH in place of Telnet. (Telnet was the main protocol for remote configuration, but it is not encrypted.)

The SSH protocol is typically used across enterprise networks for the following:

- Providing secure access for users and automated processes

- Secure file transfers

- Issuing remote commands

- For admins or technicians to manage network infrastructure

A technician could administer a network switch remotely, without needing to connect a direct cable into the device. The following screenshot offers an overview of the use of SSH:

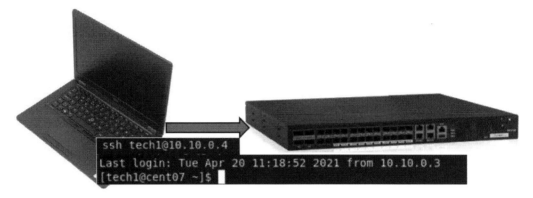

ssh tech1@10.10.0.4
Last login: Tue Apr 20 11:18:52 2021 from 10.10.0.3
[tech1@cent07 ~]$

Figure 1.19 – SSH remote security

SSH has wide support across many hardware vendor platforms and operating systems, including Microsoft (it now comes as an optional feature that can be installed on Windows 10), Linux distributions, and Apple's macOS and iOS.

> Tip
> Make sure you are using SSH 2.0 as earlier implementations use a poor cryptographic suite.

Remote Desktop Protocol

Remote Desktop Protocol (**RDP**) is a proprietary protocol developed by Microsoft that provides a user with a graphical interface to connect to the desktop of a remote computer. An RDP client application must be installed to launch a connection, and the remote computer must run RDP server software. RDP has wide support, and software exists for non-Microsoft operating systems, including Linux, Unix, macOS, iOS, Android, and other operating systems. While RDP servers are built into most Windows operating systems (Home editions of Windows desktop editions are an exception), it is also possible to install RDP server services for Unix and macOS X. The default listening port is TCP 3389 and **User Datagram Protocol** (**UDP**) port 3389. It is important to consider the security implications of enabling RDP services, as this will give a remote user access to the full range of tools and utilities for remote configuration.

> **Tip**
>
> Remember that this connects to a desktop, so it will not be a choice when administering networking hardware appliances.

Virtual Network Computing

Virtual Network Computing (**VNC**) is used for desktop sharing, as opposed to remote control only. It is platform-independent and can be used across many different operating systems. While it is a commercial product and must be licensed for business use, there is a free edition for non-commercial use.

Reverse proxy

A reverse proxy is commonly used when accessing large websites from a public network. Reverse proxies can cache static content (much like a forward proxy), which reduces the load on your web application servers. Reverse proxies can also be used as an extra security layer, allowing for additional analysis of the incoming traffic. The following screenshot shows a client accessing a web application through a reverse proxy:

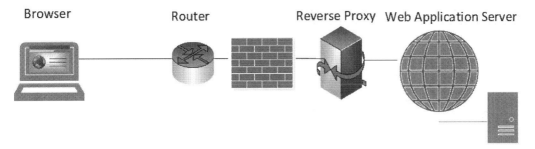

Figure 1.20 – Reverse proxy

HAProxy and `Squid` are open source software implementations used by large internet websites. They will decrypt the incoming HTTPS traffic and apply security rules.

Network authentication methods

It is important to authenticate access onto enterprise networks. The modern approach is to start out with the **Zero Trust model**, which means that no devices are trusted by default. To gain access to a network segment, authentication credentials or some other verification will be required before access is granted. In the past, the priority was always about protecting our systems from threats outside our network. This traffic moving between the internet and our perimeter network is referred to as **North-South traffic**. Traffic moving within our internal network segments is referred to as **East-West traffic**. Due to increased instances of mobility and remote workers accessing multiple networks and Information systems, it is this East-West traffic that must also be secured. We will now take a look at the options to secure access to the network.

802.1x

802.1X is an Ethernet standard using port access protocol for protecting networks via authentication. It was originally intended for use with Ethernet 802.3 switched networks but has become a useful addition to many different network types, including Wi-Fi and VPN. A connecting host or device is authenticated via 802.1X for network access—if authentication is successful, the port is opened; otherwise, it remains closed.

There are three basic pieces to 802.1X authentication, as outlined here:

- **Supplicant**: A software client running on the host
- **Authenticator**: The VPN or switch port
- **Authentication server**: An **Authentication Authorization Accounting** (**AAA**) service, usually a radius server such as Microsoft **Network Policy Server** (**NPS**)

There are many options when it comes to authenticating the supplicant (client device). In the first instance, we have rudimentary (for that, read insecure) methods of authentication.

Password Authentication Protocol (**PAP**) does not secure the authentication request.

Challenge-Handshake Authentication Protocol (**CHAP**) is an improvement over PAP as it supports mutual authentication and uses MD5 hashing to encrypt the challenge.

As CHAP is dependent on MD5, your networks are at risk from **pass-the-hash** exploits.

Extensible Authentication Protocol (**EAP**) is a framework of protocols, allowing for the secure transmission of the supplicant's authentication request. It allows the authentication channel to be encrypted using TLS. The following diagram shows the required components for a client to authenticate onto the wireless network:

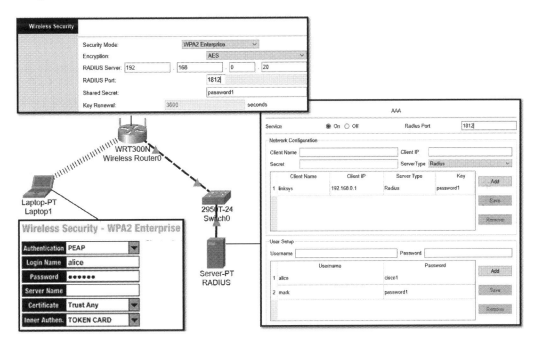

Figure 1.21 – Network authentication

EAP-TLS provides certificate-based mutual authentication of the client onto the network. This requires certificates to be deployed on the supplicant and the AAA server, although it is worth mentioning that devices could be provisioned with **Secure Certificate Enrollment Protocol** (**SCEP**) if you are using a **mobile device management** (**MDM**) tool.

EAP-Tunneled TLS (**EAP-TTLS**) is an extension of EAP-TLS. This can be used for mutual authentication, or certificates can be deployed just on the AAA server.

EAP-Flexible Authentication via Secure Tunneling (**EAP-FAST**) was developed by Cisco. This uses something called a **Protected Access Credential** (**PAC**), which can be managed dynamically by the AAA server.

Lightweight Extensible Authentication Protocol (**LEAP**) is an EAP authentication type, again developed by Cisco. It is used on Wi-Fi networks and uses **Wireless Equivalent Privacy** (**WEP**) keys for mutual authentication. It is no longer considered secure.

Protected Extensible Authentication Protocol (**PEAP**) allows for authentication using passwords, certificates, or smartcards. The authentication traffic between PEAP clients and an authentication server is encrypted using TLS but requires only server-side certificates. PEAP was developed by a consortium of Microsoft, Cisco, and RSA Security.

Placement of hardware and applications

It is important to recognize that many different types of devices may need to be supported on an enterprise network. Some systems may have embedded processing logic that is legacy and vulnerable, or maybe regulatory compliance means certain processes must be isolated from regular business networks. In the following section, we will look at these use case scenarios.

System on a chip

A **system on a chip** (**SoC**) consolidates multiple computer components onto a single, **integrated chip** (**IC**). Components will typically include a **graphical processing unit** (**GPU**), a CPU, and system **random-access memory** (**RAM**).

As an SoC integrates hardware and software, it is designed to draw less power than traditional multi-chip solutions. The Snapdragon processor used in Microsoft Surface X tablets has eight cores plus GPU.

Examples of this SoC technology can also be found in many IoT devices, building automation systems, and Wi-Fi routers. **Raspberry Pi** is a good example of this technology, costing as little as $5 per device. We can see a typical SoC in the following figure:

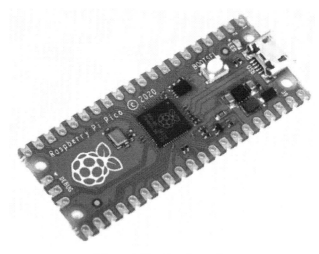

Figure 1.22 – Raspberry Pi

It is important to consider the security implications of using SoC technology. Due to the low cost and nature of embedded logic common to these devices, vulnerabilities are common and can be difficult to mitigate without replacing the device.

In 2018, the NSA was attacked and suffered a significant data breach due to an unauthorized Raspberry Pi device connected to the agency's network. To read more about this published incident, see this link: `https://tinyurl.com/nasapihack`.

Heating, ventilation, and air conditioning controllers

Heating, ventilation, and air conditioning (**HVAC**) is a critical function; sensitive equipment must be placed in an environment that is optimized for temperature and humidity. The monitoring and adjustment for this function need to protect and should be accessed over a segmented/protected network zone. Typical protocols used to communicate and manage these systems use formats such as **Modbus**, **Siemens**, and **BACnet** (there are many others). Modbus does not provide any security, meaning that if these industrial networks were breached, it would be relatively easy to cause outages and disruption on them.

Sensors

Sensors are sophisticated devices that are frequently used to automate the collection of information in automated or industrial environments. A sensor converts the physical parameter (for example, temperature, blood pressure, humidity, and speed) into a signal that can be measured electrically. Examples would include magnetic field sensors, ultrasonic sensors, temperature sensors, flow sensors, and photoelectric sensors, to name but a few. It is essential that the calibration of this equipment and messages sent or received is accurate and controlled. **HVAC**, **engineering production lines**, and **medical equipment** providers are just some of the environments that depend on this technology. The following figure shows a typical monitoring sensor:

Figure 1.23 – Temperature monitoring sensor

Physical access control systems

A **physical access control system** (**PACS**) can be used to grant access to employees and contractors who work at or visit a site by electronically authenticating their **Personal Identity Verification** (**PIV**) credentials.

Examples could include mantraps (now referred to as **access control vestibules**), **radio-frequency identification** (**RFID**) card readers, and biometric identification systems.

Audiovisual systems

Audiovisual (**A/V**) technology systems can be comprised of an assortment of hardware that includes conference telephones, video cameras, interactive whiteboards, digital signage, computers, smartphones, tablets, wireless connectivity, and more. Examples could be video screens distributed throughout a building to broadcast information to employees.

Closed-circuit television systems

A **closed-circuit television** (**CCTV**) system is an important feature for both security and safety on a physical site. In many cases, it is a requirement to meet the needs of regulatory compliance. It is important to safeguard access to CCTV camera feeds and the networks that connect them. Many cameras will now be IP cameras, meaning they can be added directly to Ethernet or Wi-Fi networks. If they are not secured, hackers will discover their location, and you may find that camera IP addresses and locations will be posted onto internet search engines. One such search engine is `https://www.shodan.io`.

The following screenshot shows a listing of unsecured IP cameras worldwide (there are over 4 million):

TOTAL RESULTS

4,184,633

TOP COUNTRIES

United States	642,751
Viet Nam	410,415
China	214,413
United Kingdom	200,968
Korea, Republic of	173,525

More...

Figure 1.24 – Unsecured IP cameras

It is important to place this type of equipment onto segmented networks and change default credentials.

Critical infrastructure

Critical infrastructure is a term to describe assets that are essential for the functioning of a society and economy.

In the US, a new government agency was founded in 2018, offering guidance and helping to build secure and resilient infrastructure: the **Cybersecurity and Infrastructure Security Agency (CISA)**.

CISA lists 16 sectors that are considered of such importance to the US that their incapacitation or destruction would have a major negative effect on security, national economic security, national public health, or safety. You can view which sectors these are in the following list:

- Chemical sector
- Commercial facilities sector
- Communications sector
- Critical manufacturing sector

- Dams sector

- Defense industrial base sector

- Emergency services sector

- Energy sector

- Financial services sector

- Food and agriculture sector

- Government facilities sector

- Healthcare and public health sector

- IT sector

- Nuclear reactors, materials, and waste sector

- Transportation systems sector

- Water and wastewater systems sector

The **European Commission** (**EC**) has launched its own program to reduce the vulnerabilities of critical infrastructures: the **European Program for Critical Infrastructure Protection** (**EPCIP**).

Supervisory control and data acquisition

Supervisory control and data acquisition (**SCADA**) is a system of software and hardware elements that allow industrial organizations to do the following:

- Regulate industrial processes locally or at remote locations

- Display, gather, and process real-time data

- Allow interaction with devices such as pumps, motors, and sensors through **human-machine interface** (**HMI**) software

- Populate events into a log file

SCADA systems are crucial for any organization with an industrial capacity. SCADA allows organizations to maintain efficiency, process data for smarter decisions, and communicate system issues to help mitigate downtime. SCADA has been used in industrial, scientific, and medical environments since the adoption of computers in the 1950s. Some of the equipment was not always designed with security in mind.

The basic SCADA architecture features **programmable logic controllers** (**PLCs**) or **remote terminal units** (**RTUs**). PLCs and RTUs are microcomputers that communicate with an array of objects such as factory machines, HMIs, sensors, and end devices and then carry the information from those objects to computers with SCADA software deployed. The SCADA software processes, distributes, and displays the data, helping operators and other employees analyze the data and make important decisions.

SCADA networks monitor and manage legacy/vulnerable industrial control networks, often using monolithic protocols. They are therefore an easy target to attack; it is vital that guidance is taken and controls put in place to mitigate the risks. In December 2015, 30 Ukrainian electrical substations were *turned off* by hackers. This left around 230,000 homes without power for several hours. Critical infrastructure tools, tactics, and protocols are documented by MITRE (see the following link: `https://tinyurl.com/mitreics`). For more information on the Ukrainian power grid attack, please go to this link: `https://tinyurl.com/icspowerattack`.

NetFlow

NetFlow was originally developed on **Cisco** networking equipment to log traffic. It allows network engineers to gain an understanding of bandwidth usage and types of traffic flow. It now has wide support and is supported on many other kinds of networking equipment, including **Juniper**, **Nokia**, **Huawei**, and **Nortel** (there are many more). It is not intended to replace protocols such as **Simple Network Management Protocol** (**SNMP**). It is useful to establish a baseline and see anomalies on a network. Cisco supports this protocol on most network equipment.

NetFlow consists of three main elements, as outlined here:

- **Flow exporter**: This passes the logs to the collector.
- **Flow collector**: This is where the logged data is stored.
- **Analysis application**: Analyzes received data and reports on the collected data.

Devices that support NetFlow can collect IP traffic statistics on all interfaces where NetFlow is enabled, and later export those statistics as NetFlow records toward at least one NetFlow collector—this is normally a server that does the actual traffic analysis. We can see an overview of the NetFlow process in the following screenshot:

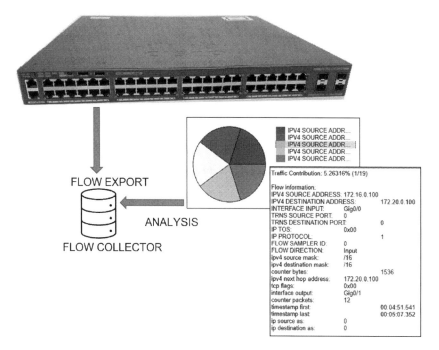

Figure 1.25 – NetFlow

Not all network vendors support NetFlow, but there is an alternative that is also designed for higher-speed networks.

sFlow

The **sFlow** protocol (short for **sampled flow**) is an alternative industry standard for data packets in computer networks. Unlike NetFlow, this is not a proprietary protocol. Its participants include **Hewlett-Packard** (**HP**), Brocade, Alcatel-Lucent, Extreme Networks, Hitachi, and more. This only logs a percentage of the traffic, which is referred to as sampling. sFlow is used on high-speed networks (gigabit-per-second speeds, and higher).

Data flow diagram

A **data flow diagram** (**DFD**) is essential for understanding the flow of information across networks, which may mean interacting with customers, partners, and internal systems. In the following diagram, we can the flow of transactions between different information systems:

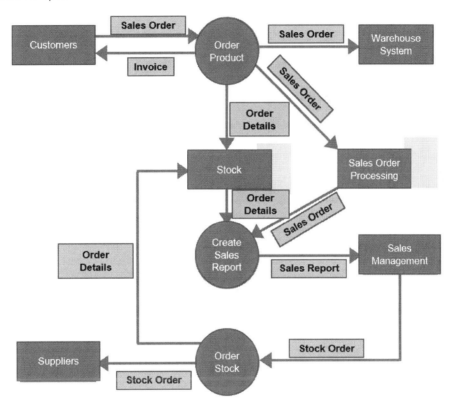

Figure 1.26 – DFD

It is important to see the movement of network traffic between the different information systems in order to place the appropriate security controls in the correct location.

Secure configuration and baselining of networking and security components

It is vitally important that all networking equipment meets a measurable security baseline. For mission-critical switches, DOD uses **secure technical implementation guides** (**STIGs**); there are over 50 security requirements in the *Cisco IOS Switch STIG*. We can see typical configuration items in the following screenshot:

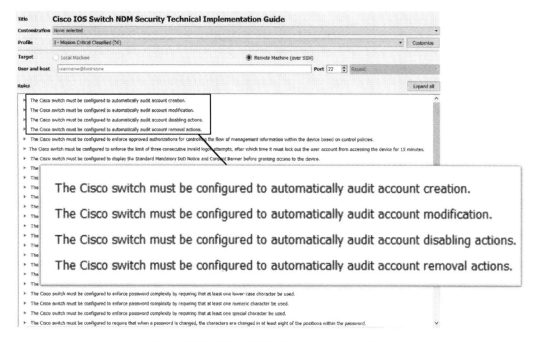

Figure 1.27 – Cisco IOS Switch security baseline

There are configuration guides for many network appliances as well as for operating systems and applications.

Software-defined networking

Software-defined networking (**SDN**) technology is a well-established approach to network management and has been in existence for over 10 years (established around 2011).

It has really come about due to a movement to large, centralized data centers and the virtualization of computer systems. The move to cloud computing has also been a big driver toward the adoption of SDN.

There are many components to move to a true SDN model, and the components shown in *Figure 1.28* are important parts.

SDN has been designed to address the fact that traditional networks are often decentralized and overly complex— think of all those vendor solutions (Cisco, Juniper, HP, Foundry, and so on) with their own hardware and software solutions. SDN allows for a more dynamic, configurable approach. Where the hardware switch (or virtual switch) becomes the data plane and is separated from the management or control plane, **application programming interfaces** (**APIs**) allow for dynamic updates to be controlled by business applications and services.

The following screenshot shows a depiction of SDN:

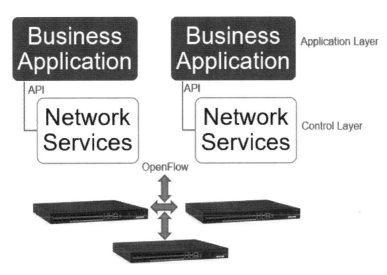

Figure 1.28 – SDN

Network function virtualization (**NFV**) takes the place of dedicated hardware with virtualized software. This means that network services such as firewalls, switches, and routers may now be deployed as software in the data center.

Open SDN

SDN is based upon a set of open standards, allowing for simplified network design and operation because instructions are provided by SDN controllers instead of multiple, vendor-specific devices and protocols.

OpenFlow was the first standard interface for separating network control and data planes.

Open Network Operating System (**ONOS**) is a popular open source SDN controller.

Hybrid SDN

Many enterprise networks still have a significant investment in traditional network infrastructure. While they move toward the goal of SDN, they need to transition and support both technologies. They will need to support a hybrid model.

SDN overlay

This basically moves traffic across physical networking infrastructure. If you compare **Multiprotocol Label Switching** (**MPLS**) links switching customers' VLAN tagged traffic across a **wide-area network** (**WAN**), then this is a similar concept.

The following diagram shows an SDN overlay model:

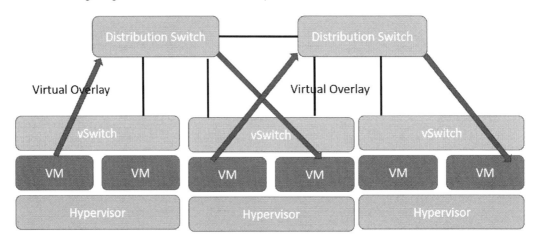

Figure 1.29 – SDN overlay

We're now at the end of this section, and you should have gained an understanding of some challenges that are presented by an enterprise network. Hybrid networks bring fresh challenges all the time and requirements for remote access. Zero Trust networks mean we must ensure all network access is authenticated and authorized. Challenges have arisen from the widespread adoption of cloud and virtualization, meaning the adoption of new technologies is increasing in our data centers. We must be able to monitor and respond to increasing network demands across the enterprise.

Network management and monitoring tools

In this section, we will look at some of the challenges that need to be considered when managing an enterprise network. In particular, we must protect networking services and equipment from unauthorized changes and ensure traffic can flow across our networks.

Alert definitions and rule writing

It is important that rules used by our advanced network protection devices do not cause unnecessary blockages or allow our networks to be overwhelmed by unwanted/malicious traffic. If rules are implemented poorly, then we may see a high number of false positives, meaning the traffic is benign (non-threatening). False negatives will mean the traffic was considered harmless when in fact it is malicious.

Tuning alert thresholds is an important step. An example could be auditing for anomalous file access to a storage device containing a mixture of data with different classification labels. You want to log all read and write access to customer records with an alert being generated for **Move** or **Copy** actions. However, if you set this rule up for all data directories, including non-sensitive data, then you may be overwhelmed by unnecessary alerts.

Eventually, your SOC staff will experience **alert fatigue**, meaning they may well dismiss important security events.

Advanced configuration of network devices

It is important to consider all the current threat actors and future threat actors when designing an enterprise network. Networks are complex and need thorough planning to properly mitigate against known threats and future unknown threats. Advanced tools to detect and mitigate these threats are covered in *Chapter 2, Integrating Software Applications into the Enterprise*, of the book. Baseline configuration guides (government/ DoD networks use STIGs,) are essential, along with a configuration policy. Routers, switches, and other core network components should be compliant before being placed into a production/live environment.

Transport security

It is important when remotely configuring services and hardware over the network that all connections are encrypted and authenticated. Many organizations use the Zero Trust model, ensuring all network connections and actions must be validated.

SSH is recommended for accessing network appliances and services across the network.

Tip

When using SNMP for monitoring and management, it is important to ensure support for **version 3 (v3)**, with full support for encryption and authentication.

Port security

Port security means restricting access to network ports using a combination of disabling unused network ports and deploying ACLs on network appliances.

On a layer 2 device, such as a Wi-Fi AP or switches, we can restrict access based on MAC addresses, and we can enable port security on a per-port basis.

There are two different approaches to restricting access to ports, as outlined here:

- **Dynamic locking**: You can specify the maximum number of MAC addresses that can be associated with a port. After the limit is reached, additional MAC addresses are not added to the CAM table; only the frames with allowable-source MAC addresses are forwarded.

  Cisco refers to these dynamic addresses as **sticky secure MAC addresses**.

- **Static locking**: You can manually specify a list of MAC addresses for a port.

Figure 1.30 shows a MAC filter on a wireless AP:

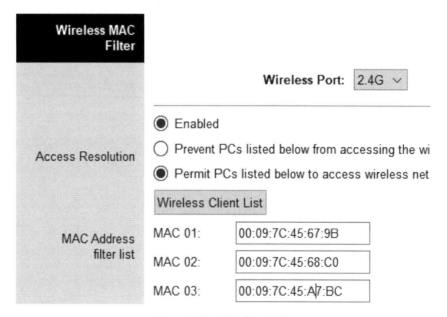

Figure 1.30 – Wireless ACL

Restrictions can be implemented using either the whitelisting or blacklisting of MAC addresses.

Route protection

It is important to ensure network traffic flow is protected. Routers will send neighbors route updates using common dynamic routing protocols. If these routes are poisoned or tampered with, this could allow an attacker to route all traffic through an MITM exploit, sniffing all network traffic. Data could be sent through an endless series of loops, causing a DoS exploit. To prevent these types of attacks, we should ensure we adopt the following practices:

- Network devices are configured using an approved baseline.
- Routing updates should only be accepted after a secure authentication handshake.
- We should avoid the use of less secure routing protocols (such as RIP).
- Disable unnecessary management interfaces.

Distributed DoS protection

Distributed DoS (**DDoS**) attacks can cause major availability issues for an enterprise, often resulting in costly outages and disaffected customers. Recent attacks have seen traffic volumes of over 2.5 **terabytes per second** (**Tbps**) directed at a target organization. In 2017, Google was targeted in an attack that resulted in spoofed **Domain Name System** (**DNS**) requests being sent to 180,000 DNS servers. The resulting traffic was directed at Google infrastructure services. The following screenshot shows high levels of ingress traffic:

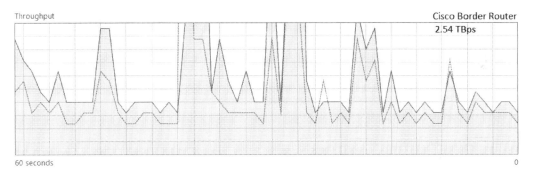

Figure 1.31 – DDoS attack traffic

DDoS mitigation is used to describe the process of guarding applications or networks against a DDoS attack. We can configure rules on our edge routers or work with our ISP to deliver this mitigation.

ISPs will incorporate these services into the services that their customers are using, or this may be an additional chargeable service.

Remotely triggered black hole

Remotely triggered black hole (**RTBH**) is a technique documented in IETF *RFCs 5635* and *3882*. RTBH filtering is a popular and effective technique for the mitigation of DoS attacks.

Often, a DDoS attack will overwhelm security devices on the enterprise perimeter. To thwart this type of attack, the customer will have an arrangement with their ISP. When a threshold is reached, a rule is triggered that sends an authorized route update to the ISP routers. The rule will automatically drop all traffic intended for the customer's internet-facing service. The ISP can then begin to identify the attack and look to block the malicious traffic. When this is done, the normal routing will be put back in place. The process is illustrated in the following diagram:

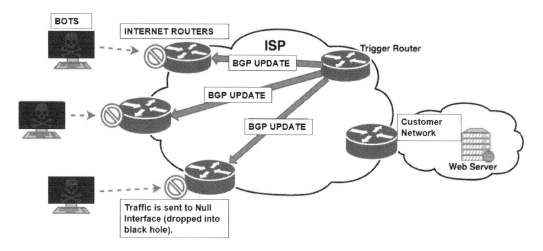

Figure 1.32 – RTBH

Blackhole used for DDOS mititigation can also be referred to as sinkholes.

Security zones

It is important to separate out network assets and services to provide the required levels of security. There will be regulatory requirements for critical infrastructure and SCADA networks. BUs may need to be on separate networks, while internet-facing servers must be placed in perimeter-based networks. Segmentation of networks makes it difficult for an attacker to gain a foothold on one compromised system and use lateral movement through the network.

Consider the following points when segmenting networks:

- Keep critical systems separate from general systems and each other if non-related.

- Limit and monitor access to assets.

- Keep an up-to-date list of personnel authorized to access critical assets.

- Train staff to err on the side of caution when dealing with access to critical assets.

- Consider air gaps when dealing with equipment supporting critical infrastructure (nuclear plant/petrochemical plant).

DMZ

A DMZ is like a border area between two nations where we do not trust our neighbor 100%. You are stopped at a checkpoint and if you are deemed to be a security risk, you are turned away. In the world of networking, we must use a combination of security techniques to implement this untrusted zone. Typically, an enterprise will create a zone using back-to-back firewalls. The assets in the zone will be accessed by users who cannot all be fully vetted or trusted.

The assets in the DMZ must be best prepared for hostile activity, and we may need to place SMTP gateways, DNS servers, and web and FTP servers into this network. It is imperative that these systems are hardened and do not run any unnecessary services.

Figure 1.33 provides an overview of a DMZ:

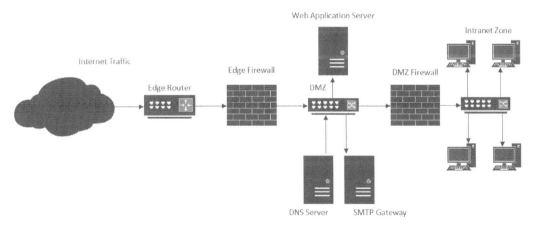

Figure 1.33 – DMZ network zone

A DMZ network can also be referred to as a screened subnet.

Summary

We have gained an understanding of security requirements, to ensure an appropriate, secure network architecture for a new or existing network. We have looked at solutions to provide the appropriate authentication and authorization controls.

We've studied how we can build security layers to allow access to information systems from trusted devices, outside of the enterprise network. You have seen a wide range of devices, including smartphones, laptops, tablets, and IoT devices, that must be secured on a network.

We have gained knowledge and an understanding of regulatory or industry compliance needs for strict network segmentation between processes and BUs

In this chapter, you have gained the following skills:

- Identification of the purpose of physical and virtual network and security devices
- Implementation of application- and protocol-aware technologies
- Planning for advanced network design
- Deploying the most appropriate network management and monitoring tools
- Advanced configuration of network devices
- Planning and implementing appropriate network security zones

These skills will be useful in the following chapters as we look to manage hybrid networks using cloud and virtual data centers.

Questions

Here are a few questions to test your understanding of the chapter:

1. Which is the security module that would store an e-commerce server's private key?

    A. DLP

    B. HSM

    C. DPI

    D. 802.1x

2. How can I mitigate the threat of data leakage?

    A. Through DLP

    B. Through HSM

C. Through DPI

D. Through 802.1x

3. What type of IDS would I be using if I needed to update my definition files?

A. Anomaly

B. Behavior

C. Heuristics

D. Signature

4. What is the purpose of iptables on a host computer?

A. Routing

B. Firewall

C. Switching

D. Encryption

5. Which protocol would be used to manage a router securely from a technician's laptop?

A. Telnet

B. RDP

C. SSH

D. FTP

6. How should I protect my management interface on a switch when I need to configure it remotely? Choose two answers.

A. OSPF

B. OOB management

C. Strong password

D. RIP v2

7. What is an Ethernet standard for port access protocol, used for protecting networks via authentication?

A. 802.11

B. 802.3

C. 802.1x

D. d) 802.5

8. What type of connectivity will allow key personnel to maintain communication with one another and key network resources when the main network is under attack?

    A. Email

    B. OOB

    C. Teams

    D. VNC

9. What is a disadvantage when using a **virtual desktop infrastructure (VDI)**?

    A. Reliance on networks

    B. Better use of hardware resources

    C. Enhanced security

    D. Standard operating environment (SOE)

10. What is used when my contractors use a tablet or thin client to access a Windows 10 desktop in my data center?

    A. OOB

    B. MDM

    C. VDI

    D. SSH

11. What type of routing will help to mitigate a DDoS attack?

    A. OSPF

    B. RTBH

    C. RIP

    D. EIGRP

12. What is it when SOC staff are failing to respond to alerts due to excessive levels of alerts?

    A. False positive

    B. Alert fatigue

    C. False negative

    D. True positive

13. What will I need to support on my network device in order to forward truncated network traffic to a network monitoring tool?

   A. NetFlow

   B. sFlow

   C. SIEM

   D. System Logging Protocol (Syslog)

14. What type of security would I use on my layer 2 switch to isolate the finance network from the development network?

   A. VPN

   B. IPsec

   C. VLAN

   D. RTBH

15. What type of servers would the security team place on the DMZ network?

   A. Web Application server

   B. SMTP Gateway

   C. Intranet File Server

   D. Finance Department Payoll Server

16. What type of security label would CISA assign to the chemical sector and communications sector?

   A. Regulated industry

   B. Protected infrastructure

   C. SCADA

   D. Critical infrastructure

17. What will protect my Wi-Fi network against common threats, including evil-twin/rogue APs and DDoS?

   A. 802.1x

   B. Host-based IPS (HIPS)

   C. Firewall

   D. WIPS

18. What should I configure on mobile users' laptop computers to ensure they will not be vulnerable to sniffing/eavesdropping when accessing the hotel's Wi-Fi network?

    A. Anti-malware

    B. Shielding

    C. Cable locks

    D. VPN

19. Which edge security appliance should be recommended for an organization that has no dedicated security team and needs multiple security protection functions?

    A. Router

    B. WAF

    C. UTM

    D. DLP

20. What should be used to connect a remote government agency across public networks (note that it needs to support the NSA suite of encryption protocols)?

    A. VPN

    B. HAIPE

    C. VLAN

    D. Protected distribution

Case study

You are employed as **chief information security officer** (**CISO**) for MORD Motor Cars U.K. You are meeting with the network team to discuss the proposed plan for the new data center. A new customer-facing e-commerce site will be run from a brand-new office and data center in Coventry, **United Kingdom** (**UK**).

The data center will also allow collaboration with a Chinese manufacturing company, through the addition of **business-to-business** (**B2B**) portals.

Place each device in the position that will offer the best security for the network. For bonus points, which ports need to be opened on the firewall?

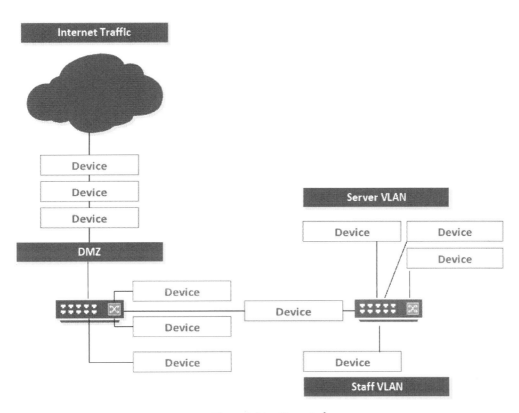

Figure 1.34 – Case study

Answers

1. B
2. A
3. D
4. B
5. C
6. B and C
7. C
8. B
9. A
10. C
11. B
12. B
13. B
14. C
15. A and B
16. D
17. D
18. D
19. C
20. B

Case study answer

The following placement will ensure a strong security posture for our network, although there are additional controls that would further enhance the organization's security, such as DLP, SIEM, and **DNS Security Extensions** (**DNSSEC**):

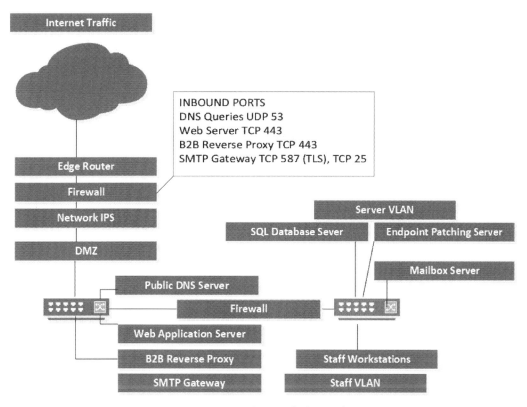

Figure 1.35 – Case study (answer)

2
Integrating Software Applications into the Enterprise

In this chapter, we need to understand the options available for a robust repeatable framework when developing or commissioning new services or software. We must understand how these systems and services can be built securely and validated. As a security professional, it is important to understand how we can provide assurance that products meet the appropriate levels of trust. We need to provide potential customers with the assurance that our services are trustworthy and meet recognized standards.

In this chapter, we will go through the following topics:

- Integrating security into the development life cycle
- Software assurance
- Baselines and templates
- Security implications of integrating enterprise applications
- Supporting enterprise integration enablers

Integrating security into the development life cycle

When considering introducing new systems into an enterprise environment, it is important to adopt a robust repeatable approach. Organizations must incorporate the most stringent standards, consider legal and regulatory requirements, and ensure the system is financially viable.

When developing software, it is important to consider security at every stage of the development process. Some vendors will use a variation called the **Secure Development Lifecycle (SDL)**, which incorporates security requirements at each step of the process.

Systems development life cycle

One of the most well understood and widely implemented approaches to systems development is the **Systems Development Life Cycle (SDLC)**. There are normally 5 stages, although in some models there can be as many as 10 stages. Whichever model you adopt, you should allow for a clearly defined pathway from the initial ideas to a functional working product. *Figure 2.1* shows the SDLC model:

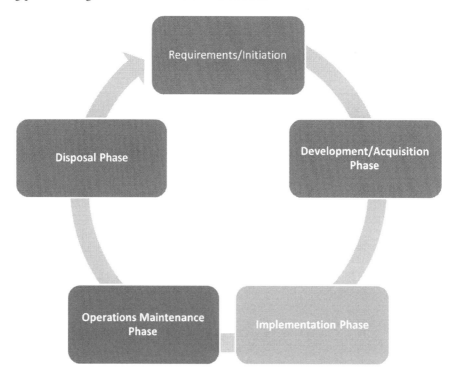

Figure 2.1 – SDLC process

Let's break down each phase of this process.

Requirements analysis/initiation phase

At the beginning of the life cycle, the requirements for the new tool or system are identified, and we can then create the plan. This will include the following:

- Understanding the goals for the system, as well as understanding user expectations and requirements (this involves capturing the user story – what exactly does the customer expect the system to deliver?).
- Identifying project resources, such as available personnel and funding.
- Discovering whether alternative solutions are already available. Is there a more cost-effective solution? (Note that government departments may be required to look toward third parties such as cloud service providers.)
- Performing system and feasibility studies.

Here are some security considerations:

- Will the system host information with particular security constraints?
- Will the system be accessible externally from the internet?
- Ensuring personnel involved in the project have a common understanding of the security considerations. Regulatory compliance would be an important consideration at this stage (such as GDPR or PCI DSS).
- Identifying where security must be implemented in the system.
- Nominating an individual or team responsible for overseeing all security considerations.

The analysis/initiation phase is critical. Proper planning saves time, money, and resources, and it ensures that the rest of the SDLC will be performed correctly.

Development/acquisition phase

Once the development team understands the customer requirements, development can begin. This phase includes design and modeling and will include the following:

- Outlining all features required for the new system
- Considering alternative designs
- Creating **System Design Documents (SDDs)**

Here are some security considerations:

- Must perform risk assessments. SAST, DAST, and penetration testing must be performed.

- Plan the system security testing. This is done with the **Security Requirements Traceability Matrix (SRTM)**.

In *Figure 2.2* we can see an example of an SRTM document:

ID #	Description	Source	Objective	Method
Webapp-01	Ensure all data is encrypted in transit	Design team	Test encryption method used	Data flow analysis using Wireshark
Webapp-02	Ensure all data inputs are validated	Design team	Ensure correct data inputs and exception handling	Fuzzing tool

Figure 2.2 – SRTM

This is a simplified example – in reality, there would be much more testing to be done.

Implementation phase

During this phase, the system is created from the designs in the previous stages:

- Program code is written.

- Infrastructure is configured and provisioned.

- System testing takes place.

- End user/customer training is done.

- Bug tracking and fixing is carried out.

Here are some security considerations:

- Vulnerability scanning against infrastructure, web servers, and database servers is performed.

- Ensure the **SRTM** is now implemented for security testing.

Operations maintenance phase

When the system is live, it will need continuous monitoring and updating to meet operational needs. This may include the following:

- Refreshing hardware
- Performance benchmarking
- Patching/updating certain components to ensure they meet the required standards
- Improving systems when necessary

It is important to continually assess the economic viability of legacy systems to assess whether they meet the operational needs of the business. For example, an expensive IBM mainframe computer may have cost over 1 million dollars in 1980, but the costs to keep it running today may be exorbitant.

Here are some security considerations:

- Hardware and software patching
- Ensuring the system is incorporated into a change management process
- Continuous monitoring

Disposal phase

There must be a plan for the eventual decommissioning of the system:

- Plan for hardware, software, and data disposal.
- Data may need to be migrated to a new system – can we output to a common file format?
- Data will either be purged or archived.

Here are some security considerations:

The business must consider the possibility of any remaining data on storage media. It is also important to consider how we might access archived data generated by the system – is it technically feasible? (Could you recover archived family movies that you found in the attic, stored in Betamax format?)

Development approaches

It is important to focus on a development methodology that fits with the project's needs. There are approaches that focus more on customer engagement throughout the project life cycle. Some approaches allow the customer to have a clear vision of the finished system at the beginning of the process and allow the development to be completed within strict budgets, while other approaches lend themselves to prototyping. Whatever your approach, it must align with the customers' requirements.

Waterfall

The waterfall has been a mainstay of systems development for many years. It is a very rigid approach with little customer involvement after the requirements phase. This model depends upon comprehensive documentation in the early stages.

At the beginning of the project the customer is involved, and they will define their requirements. The development team will capture the customer requirements, and the customer will now not be involved until release for customer acceptance testing.

The design will be done by the software engineers based upon the documentation captured from the customer.

The next stage will be the implementation or coding, there is no opportunity for customer feedback at this stage.

During verification, we will install, test, and debug, and then perform customer acceptance testing. If the customer is not satisfied at this point, we must go right back to the very start.

Figure 2.3 shows the waterfall methodology:

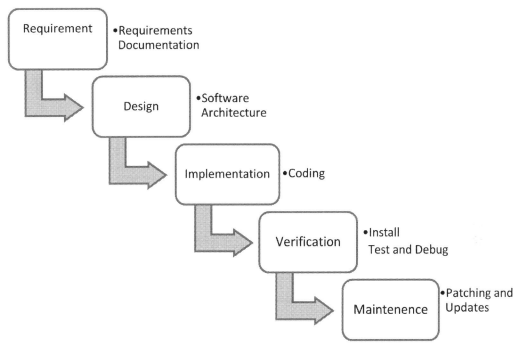

Figure 2.3 – Waterfall Methodology

Like water flowing down a waterfall, there is no going back.

Advantages of the waterfall method

The following points are advantages when using the waterfall method:

- Comprehensive documentation means onboarding new team members is easier.
- Detailed planning and documentation enable budgets and timelines to be met.
- This model scales well.

Disadvantages of the waterfall method

The following points are disadvantages when using the waterfall method:

- We need all requirements and documentation before or at the start of the project.
- No flexibility, change, or modification is possible until the end of the cycle.

- A lack of customer involvement/collaboration after completing the requirements phase.

- Testing is done only at the end of development.

Agile

The Agile methodology is based on plenty of customer engagement. The customer is involved not just in the requirements phase. It is estimated that around 80% of all current development programs use this methodology. When using the Agile method, the entire project is divided into small incremental builds. In *Figure 2.4* we can see the Agile development cycle:

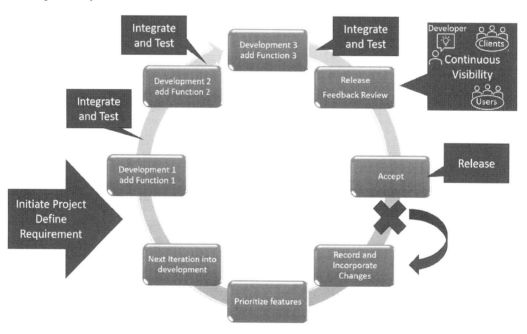

Figure 2.4 – Agile development cycle

The Agile methodology means the customer will have many meetings with the development team. The customer is involved from the start of the project and during the lifetime of the project. They can review software changes and make requests for modifications, which ensures that the result is exactly what the customer wants.

As functionality is added to the build, the customer can review the progress. When the software is released, the customer is more likely to be satisfied, as they have been involved throughout the project.

In the event the customer is not satisfied, we will record the required changes and incorporate this into a fresh development cycle.

Advantages of the Agile method

The following points are advantages when using the Agile method:

- The use of teams means more collaboration.
- Development is more adaptive.
- The testing of code is done within the development phases.
- Satisfied customers, as continuous engagement during development ensures the system meets customer expectations.
- Best for continuous integration.

Disadvantages of the Agile method

The following points are disadvantages when using the Agile method:

- Lack of full documentation
- Not easy to bring in new developers once the project has started
- Project cost overruns
- Not good for large-scale projects

Spiral

The spiral model can be used when there is a prototype. When neither the Agile nor waterfall methods are appropriate, we can combine both approaches.

For this model to be useful, it needs to start with a prototype. We are basically refining a prototype as we go through several iterations. At each stage, we do a risk analysis after we have fine-tuned the prototype – this will be the final iteration that will be used to build through to the final release.

This allows the customer to be involved at regular intervals as each prototype is refined. In *Figure 2.5* we can see the spiral model:

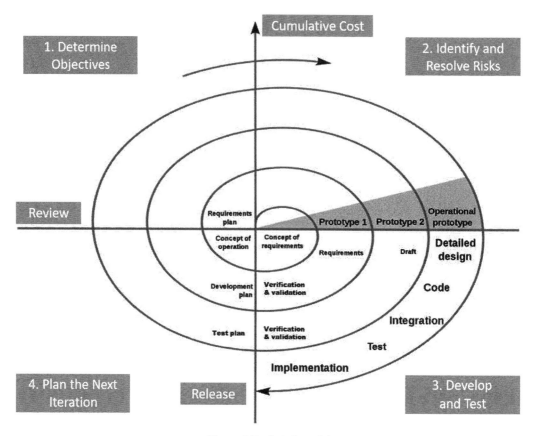

Figure 2.5 – Spiral model

Advantages of the spiral model

The following points are advantages when using the spiral method:

- The use of teams means more collaboration.

- The testing of code is done within the development phases.

- Satisfied customers, as continuous engagement during development ensures the system meets customer expectations.

- Flexibility – the spiral model is more flexible in terms of changing requirements during the development process.

- Reduces risk, as risk identification is carried out during each iteration.

- Good for large-scale projects.

Disadvantages of the spiral model

The following points are disadvantages when using the spiral method:

- Time management – timelines can slip.

- Complexity – this model is very complex compared to Agile or waterfall.

- Cost – this model can be expensive as it has multiple phases and iterations.

Versioning

Version control is of paramount importance. When considering **Continuous Integration/ Continuous Delivery (CI/CD)**, it is important to document build revisions and incorporate this into the change management plan when considering backout plans. For example, Microsoft brings out a major feature release of the Windows 10 operating system bi-annually. The original release was in July 2017 with build number 10240 and version ID 1507. The May 2021 update carries version 21H1 and build 19043. You can check the current build using `winver` on CMD. *Figure 2.6* shows version control:

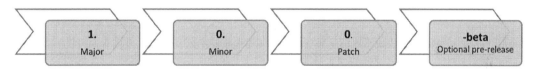

Figure 2.6 – Versioning

It is important to adopt a methodology when approaching systems or software design. A repeatable process means security will not be overlooked, and we are able to adopt a systematic approach.

Choosing the right methodology is also important so the development team can work efficiently, and the customer will be satisfied during and at the end of the process.

Software assurance

It is important that the systems and services that are developed and used by millions of enterprises, businesses, and users are robust and trustworthy. This process of software assurance is achieved using standard design concepts/methodologies, standard coding techniques and tools, and accepted methods of validation. We will take a look at approaches to ensure reliable bug-free code is deployed.

Sandboxing/development environment

It is important to have clearly defined segmentation when developing new systems. Code will be initially written within an **Integrated Development Environment** (**IDE**); testing can be done in an isolated area separate from production systems, often using a development system or network.

Validating third-party libraries

To speed up the development process, it is a common practice to use third-party libraries. Third-party libraries will speed up the development process as developers won't be developing tools or routines that already exist. Examples of popular third-party libraries include **Retrofit**, **Picasso**, **Glide**, and **Zxing**, which are used by **Android** application developers. It is critical that any third-party code that is used can be trusted. The use of third-party libraries might raise some security concerns as vulnerabilities in open source libraries are increasingly targets for hackers. It is important to remain updated with current **Common Vulnerabilities and Exposures** (**CVEs**) relating to third-party libraries.

It is important to consider the potential remediation that may be required if a vulnerability is discovered in a library that is part of your code base. Over 90% of software development includes the use of some third-party code. A vulnerability in the **Apache Struts framework** was reported and classified with **CVE-2017-5638**. Whilst the vulnerability was fixed with a new release of the framework, many customers were impacted. Equifax had 200,000 customer credit card numbers stolen as a result of the vulnerability. The outcome can be very costly in terms of regulatory fines (as with PCI DSS and GDPR, for example), it may also require that applications are re-compiled along with the updated libraries and distributed where necessary.

SecDevOps

The term **DevOps** originates from software development and IT operations. When implemented, it means continuous integration, automated testing, continuous delivery, and continuous deployment. It is a more of a cultural methodology, meaning that development and operations will work as a team.

Over the past few years, it has become commonplace to see Agile development methodology and related DevOps practices being implemented. Adopting these ideas means that the developers improve software incrementally and continuously, rather than offering major updates on annual or bi-annual cycles.

DevOps itself does not deliver cybersecurity. What is needed is **SecDevOps**. The term stresses that an organization treats security with as much importance as development and operations. *Figure 2.7* depicts the close alignment of **Development**, **Operations**, **Application Delivery**, and **Security**:

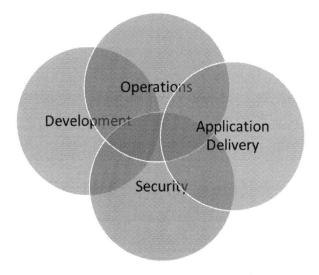

Figure 2.7 – SecDevOps

SecDevOps requires the people involved to take a more comprehensive view of a project. All teams need to focus on security as well as development and maintaining operations. It involves many different elements to automate the deployment of new code and new systems. For SecDevOps to be successful, we must adopt practices that ensure code is secure from the inside out, which means integrating testing tools into the build process and continuously checking code right through to deployment. Automated regression testing is a key process, as we are constantly developing and improving our code modules. Regression testing will focus on the changed code. As this is a cultural approach to deploying software, it is important to champion security efforts from the team. Building a team with a strong focus on security is a very important element.

Defining the DevOps pipeline

A DevOps pipeline ensures that the development and operations teams adopt a set of best practices. A DevOps pipeline will ensure that the building, testing, and deployment of software into the operations environment is streamlined. There are several **components of a DevOps pipeline** as you can see in the following sub-sections.

Continuous integration

CI is the process of combining the code from individual development teams into a shared build/repository. Depending on the size and complexity of the project, this may be done multiple times a day.

Continuous delivery

CD is often used with CI. It will enable the development team to release incremental updates into the operational environment.

Continuous testing

Continuous testing is the process of testing during all the stages of development, the goal being to identify errors before they can be introduced into a production environment.

Testing will identify functional and non-functional errors in the code.

It is important when developing complex systems with large development teams that **integration testing** is run on a daily basis, sometimes several times a day. It is imperative to test all the units of code to ensure they stay within alignment.

When there is a small change of code and this change must be evaluated within the existing environment, we should use **regression testing**.

Continuous operations

The concept of continuous operations ensures the availability of systems and services in an enterprise. The result is that users will be unaware of new code releases and patches, but the systems will be maintained. The goal is to minimize any disruption during the introduction of new code.

Continuous operations will require a high degree of automation across a complex heterogeneous mix of servers, operating systems, applications, virtualization, containers, and so on. This will be best served by an orchestration architecture. In *Figure 2.8* we can see the DevOps cycle.

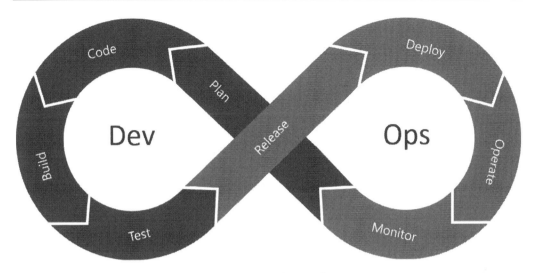

Figure 2.8 – DevOps pipeline

DevOps pipelining is a continuous process.

Code signing

When code has been tested and validated, it should be digitally signed to ensure we have trusted builds of code modules.

It is estimated that over 80% of software breaches are due to vulnerabilities present at the application layer. It is important to eliminate these bugs in the code before the software is released. We will now take a look at three different approaches.

Interactive application security testing

The use of an **Interactive Application Security Tool (IAST)** is a modern approach, addressing the early detection of bugs and security issues. Application code is tested in real time using sensors and deployed agents to detect any potential vulnerabilities. The testing can be automated, which is important when we are looking to incorporate the testing into **CI /CD** environments.

The benefits of IAST are as follows:

- Accurate
- Fast testing
- Easy to deploy
- On-demand feedback

With demand for the rapid development of applications and new functionality, it is important to deploy the correct tools to reduce risk.

Dynamic application security testing

Dynamic Application Security Testing (**DAST**) tools are used against compiled code, but they are done at the end of the development cycle. They have no integration with the code and from the outside in. A **fuzzer** (designed to test input vulnerabilities) is a good example of a DAST tool, and would be part of a **black-box test** where there is no information given about the actual source code. These types of tests require experienced security auditors. DAST tools can be used without credentials, meaning they can also be used by an attacker.

Static application security testing

Static Application Security Testing (**SAST**) tools are used to assess source code in an IDE. The challenge to manually review thousands of lines of code is a huge undertaking, so automated tools are used instead, such as **IBM Rational App Scan**.

SAST tools are run inside the IDE as code is compiled. SAST tools always require direct access to the source code.

SAST tools are known to throw false positives – as they assess code line by line, they are not aware of additional security measures provided by other code modules.

For additional reading on this subject, there is a very useful blog from the **Carnegie Mellon University Software Engineering Institute** at `https://tinyurl.com/seiblog`.

Baseline and templates

It is important for an enterprise to adopt standards and methodologies in order to follow a standard repeatable process when developing new systems or software. It is important to consider interoperability when designing or considering systems supplied by third parties.

The **National Cyber Security Centre** (**NCSC**), a United Kingdom government agency, offers guidance to UK-based enterprises. They have divided each set of principles into five categories, loosely aligned with the stages at which an attack can be mitigated. Here are the five NCSC categories (also available at `https://www.ncsc.gov.uk/collection/cyber-security-design-principles`):

- **Establish the context**

    Determine all the elements that compose your system, so your defensive measures will have no blind spots.

- **Make compromise difficult**

    An attacker can only target the parts of a system they can reach. Make your system as difficult to penetrate as possible.

- **Make disruption difficult**

    Design a system that is resilient to denial-of-service attacks and usage spikes.

- **Make compromise detection easier**

    Design your system so you can spot suspicious activity as it happens and take necessary action.

- **Reduce the impact of compromise**

    If an attacker succeeds in gaining a foothold, they will then move to exploit your system. Make this as difficult as possible.

The **Open Web Application Security Project (OWASP)** is a non-profit foundation created to improve the security of software. There are many community-led open source software projects, and membership runs to tens of thousands of members. The OWASP Foundation is a high-value organization for developers and technology implementors when securing web applications. OWASP offers tools and resources, community and networking groups, as well as education and training events.

When considering security in your application development, there is a very useful source of information in the OWASP Top 10, a list of common threats targeting web applications.

OWASP Top 10 threats (web applications):

- Injection
- Broken authentication
- Sensitive data exposure
- **XML External Entities (XXE)**
- Broken access control
- Security misconfiguration
- **Cross-Site Scripting (XSS)**
- Insecure deserialization
- Using components with known vulnerabilities
- Insufficient logging and monitoring

A PDF document with more detail can be downloaded from the following link: `https://tinyurl.com/owasptoptenpdf`.

Important Note

Specific attack types, including example logs and code, along with mitigation techniques, are covered in *Chapter 7, Risk Mitigation Controls*.

Secure coding standards

Whilst it is important to work toward industry best standards and apply a repeatable security methodology, it is also of critical importance to adopt practices that allow for validation and interoperability with other vendor solutions. This may mean developing applications to work on a particular vendor operating system or maybe to use an available **Software-as-a-Service** (**SaaS**) application hosted on **Amazon Web Services** (**AWS**).

Application vetting processes

Whether your application is for internal use or will be sold commercially, it should go through a **Quality Assurance** (**QA**) process. Microsoft has strict requirements for Universal Windows Platform applications that will be sold through the **Microsoft Store**. The testing process is very stringent, as follows:

- **Security tests**: Your application will be tested to ensure it is malware free.

- **Technical compliance tests**: These are functional tests, to ensure it follows technical compliance requirements. There is a Microsoft-supplied App Certification Kit (which is free to use), ensuring developers can test the code themselves first.

- **Content compliance**: This allows for the complete testing of all the features to make sure it meets content compliance.

- **Release/publishing**: Once an application package has been given the QA *green light*, it will be digitally signed to protect the application against tampering after it has been released.

We will now look at securing our hosting platforms, by adopting a strong security posture on our application web servers.

Hypertext Transfer Protocol (HTTP) headers

It is important when considering the hosting of web applications, to adopt a secure baseline on all your web platforms. Proper **Hypertext Transfer Protocol (HTTP)** headers will help to protect hosted applications.

Whilst secure coding, including input validation, is very important, there are a number of common security configuration settings that should be adopted on the platform hosting the application. Common attacks include **Cross-Site Scripting (XSS)**, **Cross-Site Request Forgery (XSRF)**, **Clickjacking**, and **Man in the Middle (MITM)**, the following security header settings will not prevent all attacks but will add an extra layer of security to your website by ensuring web browsers are connecting in a secure manner.

XSS-Protection

This HTTP security header ensures that the connecting client uses the functionality of the built-in filter on the web browser. It should be configured as follows:

```
X-XSS-Protection "1; mode=block"
```

The **X-Frame-Options (XFO)** security header helps to protect your customers against clickjacking exploits. The following is the correct configuration for the header:

```
X-Frame-Options "SAMEORIGIN"
```

Strict-Transport-Security

The **Strict-Transport-Security (HSTS)** header instructs client browsers to always connect via HTTPS. Without this setting, there may be the opportunity for the transmission of unencrypted traffic, allowing for sniffing or MITM exploits. The following is the suggested configuration for the header:

```
Strict-Transport-Security: max-age=315360000
```

In the preceding example, the time is in seconds, making the time 1 year. (The client browser will always connect using TLS for a period not less than 1 year.)

When the preceding settings are incorporated into your site's `.htaccess` file or your server configuration file, it adds an additional layer of security for web applications.

If you are configuring Microsoft **Internet Information Server** (**IIS**), you can also add these security options through the IIS administration console. In *Figure 2.9* we can see HTTP headers being secured on a Microsoft IIS web application server.

 HTTP Response Headers

Use this feature to configure HTTP headers that are added to responses from the Web server.

Group by:	No Grouping	▼	
Name	**Value**		**Entry Type**
Strict -Transport -Security	max-age=63072000; includeSubDomains; Preload		Local
X-Frame-Options	SAMEORIGIN		Local
X-XSS-Protection	1;mode=block		Local

Figure 2.9 – Securing HTTP response headers

It is important to harden web application servers before deployment.

The **Software Engineering Institute** (**SEI**) CERT Secure Coding Initiative is run from the Software Engineering Institute of Carnegie Mellon University and aims to promote secure coding standards.

In the same way as OWASP publish a top-10 list of vulnerabilities, SEI CERT promotes their top 10 secure coding practices:

- Validate input.
- Heed compiler warnings.
- Architect and design for security policies.
- Keep it simple.
- Default deny.
- Adhere to the principle of least privilege.
- Sanitize data sent to other systems.
- Practice defense in depth.
- Use effective quality assurance techniques.
- Adopt a secure coding standard.

More information about their work and contribution toward secure coding standards can be found at the following link:

```
https://wiki.sei.cmu.edu/confluence/display/seccode/
SEI+CERT+Coding+Standards
```

Microsoft SDL is a methodology that introduces security and privacy considerations throughout all phases of the development process. It is even more important to consider new scenarios, such as the cloud, **Internet of Things** (**IoT**), and **Artificial Intelligence** (**AI**). There are many free tools provided for developers including plugins for Microsoft Visual Studio:

```
https://www.microsoft.com/en-us/securityengineering/sdl/
resources
```

Application Programming Interface (API) management

APIs allow an organization to extend enterprise assets to B2B partners, customers, and other parts of the enterprise. These assets can then be made available through applications in the form of services, data, and applications.

Managing and securing these assets is of critical importance. Data exposure or the theft of intellectual property could be one of many threats. Automation will often be used to provision access to these resources. There are many vendor solutions offered to manage these critical assets. *Figure 2.10* shows customers and partners connecting to services through a management API.

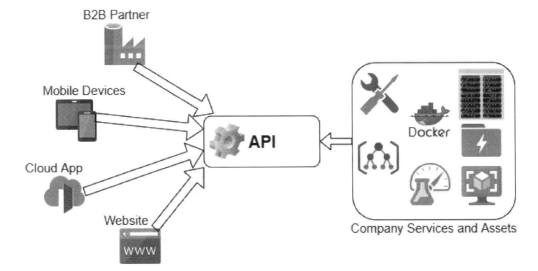

Figure 2.10 – Management API

Examples of popular API management platforms include the following:

- MuleSoft Anypoint Platform
- API Umbrella
- Google Apigee API Management Platform
- CA Technologies
- MuleSoft Anypoint Platform
- WSO2
- Apigee Edge
- Software AG
- Tyk Technologies

Container APIs

Many applications will be virtualized and deployed in containers (for Docker containers, see *Chapter 3, Enterprise Data Security, Including Secure Cloud and Virtualization Solutions*). Containers are an efficient way to scale up the delivery of applications, but when deployed across many hardware compute platforms it can become overly complex. Workloads need to be provisioned and de-provisioned on a large scale. There is a new industry approach to address this need, based on an open source API named **Kubernetes**.

Kubernetes was developed to allow the orchestration of multiple (virtual) servers. Containers are nested into Pods, and Pods can be scaled based upon demand.

An example might be a customer who has purchased an **Enterprise Resource Planning (ERP)** system comprising multiple application modules of code. The SaaS provider has many customers who require these services, and each customer must be isolated from the others. Whilst this could be done manually, automation will be useful to: Deploy, monitor, scale, and when there is an outage the system will be self-healing (it detects the problem and can restart or replicate failed containers). *Figure 2.11* shows an overview of container API management:

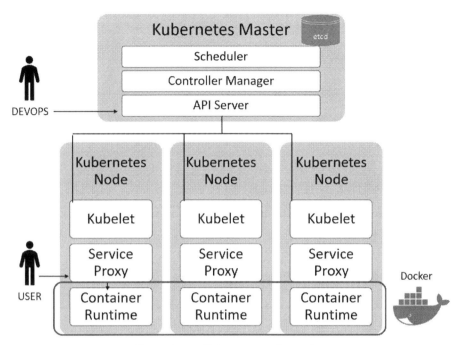

Figure 2.11 – Kubernetes orchestration

When considering developing new systems and services it is important to recognize standard approaches and adopt a baseline for ongoing development. You may be working with B2B partners, selling services to external customers, or hosting web-based applications. You need to make sure the enterprise is using standards and approaches that ensure compatibility and security.

Considerations when integrating enterprise applications

Enterprise application integration is critically important. We have major businesses tools and processes that rely on the integration and communication services provided within an enterprise.

There are many examples of business dependencies within an enterprise. Our sales and marketing efforts would be difficult without the CRM business tools now considered commonplace. Human resources teams would plan employee recruitment using guesswork if not for ERP systems. Project planning could not ensure timely delivery of supply-chain raw materials without ERP systems. There are many more examples of these dependencies. Consider the following business enterprise applications.

Customer relationship management (CRM)

CRM is a category of integrated, data-focused software solutions that improve how an enterprise can engage with their customers. CRM systems help to manage and maintain customer relationships, track sales leads, marketing, and automate required actions.

Without the support of an integrated CRM solution, an enterprise may risk loss of opportunities to competitors.

Just imagine if sales staff lost customer contact information, only to learn that a customer then awarded a multimillion-dollar contract to a competitor. Or perhaps sales teams are chasing the same prospect, creating unfriendly, in-house competition. It is important for these teams to have access to a centralized and automated CRM system. With a properly deployed CRM solution, customers can be allocated to the correct teams (data can be properly segmented) and staff will not lose track of customer interactions and miss business opportunities. In *Figure 2.12* we can see the components of a CRM system:

Figure 2.12 – CRM components

Without this valuable business tool, we will lack efficiency compared to our competitors.

Enterprise resource planning (ERP)

ERP allows an enterprise to manage a complex enterprise, typically combining many business units. A motor manufacturer such as Ford Motors would utilize this system.

ERP allows all the business units to be integrated and all the disparate processes to be managed. The software integrates a company's accounts, procurement, production operations, reporting, manufacturing, sales, and human resources activities.

If Ford Motors gained a government contract to supply 10,000 trucks, they would use an ERP. They would need to work with human resources to plan labor requirements; sales staff would have worked to win this contract using a CRM; the company would use production-planning software to ensure the smooth running of the assembly lines; accounting software would be used to make sure costs are controlled and invoices are paid; and distribution would be used to ensure the customer receives the trucks.

ERP provides integration of core business processes using common databases maintained by a database management system. Some of the well-known vendors in this market include IBM, SAP, Oracle, and Microsoft.

The business importance of this system will mean strict adherence to security, as the data applications that make up the system share data across all the enterprise departments that provide the data. ERP allows information flow between all business functions and manages connections to outside stakeholders. The global ERP software market was calculated to be worth around $40 billion in 2020. *Figure 2.13* shows components of an ERP system:

Figure 2.13 – ERP components

Without having access to this enterprise asset, overall control of end-to-end production processes will be difficult.

Configuration Management Database (CMDB)

A CMDB is a centralized repository that stores information on all the significant entities in your IT environment. The entities, termed as **Configuration Items** (**CIs**), include hardware, the installed software applications, documents, business services, and the people that are part of your IT system. A CMDB is used to support a large IT infrastructure and can be incorporated in endpoint management solutions (such as Microsoft Configuration Manager or Intune), where collections of values and attributes can be automated. This is a very important database for successful service desk delivery in an enterprise. *Figure 2.14* shows the components within a CMDB:

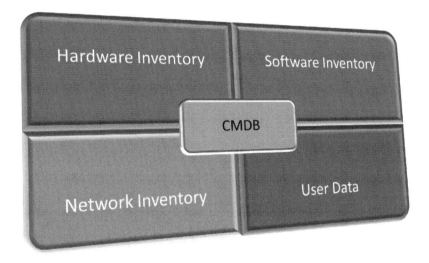

Figure 2.14 – CMDB components

If an enterprise does not have visibility of information systems, including both hardware and software, then it will be difficult to manage.

Content management systems

A **Content Management System** (**CMS**) allows for the management and day-to-day administration of enterprise data using a web portal.

An administrator can delegate responsibility to privileged users who can assist in the management of resources.

The requirements are to add users to access content and where necessary create, edit, and delete content. Version control is important, meaning documents can be checked out for editing but will still be accessible for read access by authorized users of the system.

Microsoft 365 uses SharePoint to allow participants to interact with a web-based portal in an easy-to-use and intuitive way (normally presented to the end user as OneDrive or Microsoft Teams). *Figure 2.15* shows this CMS system:

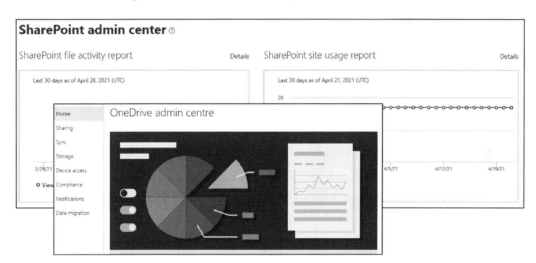

Figure 2.15 – Microsoft SharePoint

Without access to these enterprise applications, an organization might become uncompetitive in their area of operations. Competitors will gain a business advantage using these enterprise toolsets themselves as the organization will be unable to track their resources and assets. Day-to-day management of the enterprise will be difficult and long-term planning goals will become harder to achieve.

Integration enablers

It is important to consider the less glamorous services that provide unseen services, much like the key workers who drive buses, provide healthcare services, deliver freight, and so on. Without these services, staff would not be able to travel to work, remain in good health, or have any inventory to manufacture products. The following sub-sections list the common integration enablers.

Directory services

The **Lightweight Directory Access Protocol (LDAP)** is an internet standard for accessing and managing directory services. LDAPv3 is an internet standard documented in RFC 4511.

There are many vendors who provide directory services, including Microsoft Active Directory, IBM, and Oracle. Directory services are used to share information about applications, users, groups, services, and networks across networks.

Directory services provide organized sets of records, often with a hierarchical structure (based upon X.500 standards), such as a corporate email directory. You can think of directory services like a telephone directory, which is a list of subscribers with their addresses and phone numbers. LDAP uses TCP port 389 and is supported using TLS over TCP port 636.

Domain name system

The **Domain Name System (DNS)** is an important part of the TCP/IP protocol suite. It was implemented in 1984, and on UNIX servers the standard was a daemon named **Berkley Internet Naming Daemon (BIND)**. Common user applications such as web browsers allow the user to type user-friendly domain names, such as www.bbc.com or www.sky.com, but these requests need to be routed across networks using **Internet Protocol (IP)** addresses. DNS translates domain names to IP addresses so applications can connect to services.

DNS is a critical service for any size of organization. Without DNS our enterprise users will not be able to access intranet services, customers will not be able to access e-commerce sites, and partners will not be able to connect to our APIs. To ensure high availability there should be at least one secondary DNS nameserver, and for a large organization there will be many secondary DNS servers.

It is important for name resolution to be a trustworthy process. When DNS lookups result in malicious additions to the DNS server cache or client cache, it is known as **DNS cache poisoning**.

When a computer is re-directed to a malicious website as a result of cache poisoning, it is called **pharming**. To ensure we have secure name resolution, we need to enable **DNSSEC** extensions for all our DNS servers. There is a useful site dedicated to all things related to DNS security at https://www.dnssec.net/.

Authoritative name servers (those that host the DNS for the domain) communicate updates using zone transfers (the zone file is the actual database of records). **Incremental Transfer (IXFR)** describes the incremental transfers of nameserver records, while **All Transfer (AXFR)** describes the transfer of the complete zone file. It is important that this process is restricted to authorized DNS servers using **Access Control Lists (ACLs)**. It is important that any updates to DNS zone files are trustworthy. **RFC2930** defines the use of **Transaction Signatures (TSIG)** for zone file updates. When TSIG is used, two systems will share a secret key (in an Active Directory domain, Kerberos will take care of this). This key is then used to generate a **Hash Message Authentication Code (HMAC)**, which is then applied to all DNS transactions.

Figure 2.16 shows the security configuration for a zone file:

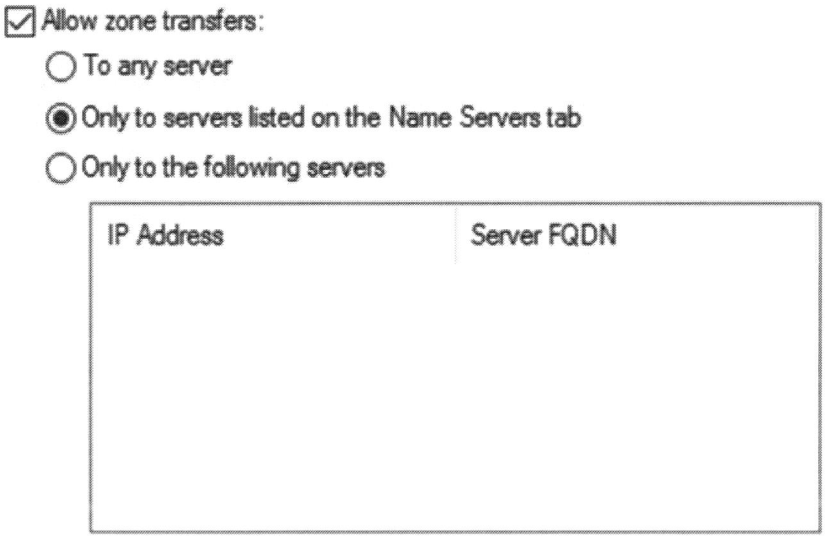

Figure 2.16 – DNS ACL

DNSSEC should be implemented to ensure protection from DNS cache poisoning.

To enable DNSSEC on your forwarding DNS servers, it is a requirement to download and install the root server's public key. On Microsoft DNS, this can be done using `dnscmd` (`dnscmd /RetrieveRootTrustAnchors`). *Figure 2.17* shows a public key record, used to validate DNSSEC responses:

DNS Public Key (DNSKEY)

Name:

(same as parent folder)|

Fully qualified domain name (FQDN):

.

Key Tag: 20326

☑ Zone Key   ☑ Secure Entry Point
Protocol: Algorithm:
DNSSEC   ⌄   RSA/SHA-256   ⌄
Public Key:

AwEAAaz/tAm8yTn4Mfeh5eyI96WSVexTBAvkMgJzkKTOiW1vkIbzxeF3
+/4RgWOq7HrxRixHlFlExOLAJr5emLvN7SWXgnLh4+B5xQlNVz8Og8kvA
rMtNROxVQuCaSnIDdD5LKyWbRd2n9WGe2R8PzgCmr3EgVLrjyBxWezF
0jLHwVN8efS3rCj/EWgvIWgb9tarpVUDK/b58Da+sqqls3eNbuv7pr

☐ Delete this record when it becomes stale

Record time stamp:

Time to live (TTL): |0   :0 :0 :0   (DDDDD:HH.MM.SS)

Figure 2.17 – DNSSEC root public key

Once we have implemented DNNSEC, we can then perform DNS lookups on behalf of our organization with the resulting responses being signed by trusted domains. *Figure 2.18* shows the secure DNS lookup process:

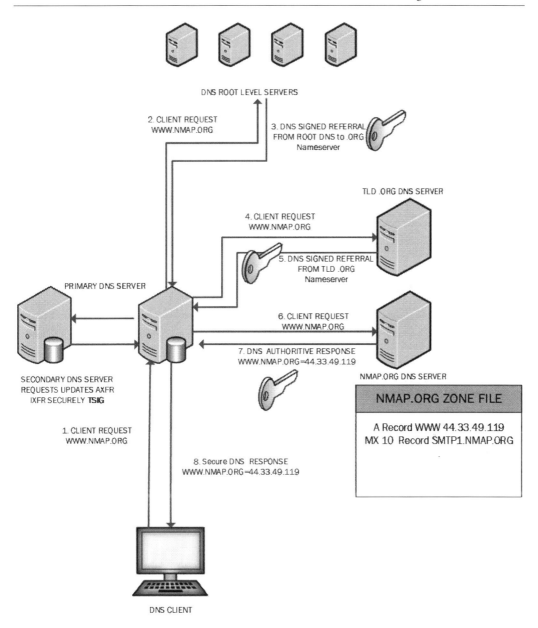

Figure 2.18 – DNSSEC processing

DNSSEC ensures responses from all DNS servers can be validated, and also allows for secure zone transfers between primary and secondary DNS servers. TSIG ensures the updates to the secondary server are trusted.

Service-oriented architecture

Service-Oriented Architecture (SOA) is an architecture developed to support service orientation, as opposed to legacy or monolithic approaches.

Originally, systems were developed with non-reusable units. For example, a customer can buy a complete ERP system, but a smaller customer would like to have only some of the full functionality (perhaps just the human resource and financial elements). In this situation, with legacy or monolithic approaches, the developers could not easily provide these two modules independently.

Using a more modular approach, developers can easily integrate these modules or services packaged up and can provide these services using standards. SOA allows for a communication protocol over a network. The service, which is a single functional unit, can be accessed remotely and offers functionality, such as a customer being able to access order tracking of a purchased item, without needing to access an entire sales order processing application.

Examples of SOA technologies include the following:

- **Simple Object Access Protocol (SOAP)**
- **RESTful HTTP**
- **Remote Procedure Calls written by Google (gRPC)**
- **Apache Thrift** (developed by Facebook)

Enterprise service bus

An **Enterprise Service Bus (ESB)** is used to integrate many different architectures and protocols.

A challenge facing many vendors is integration and competing standards. Legacy information systems such as **IBM Systems Network Architecture (SNA)** (developed for mainframe computers in the 1970s) does not communicate directly on a TCP/IP network, and does not typically host applications that use modern standards-based communication. Without an ESB these systems would be obsolete.

It is possible to implement an SOA without an ESB, but this would be equivalent to building a huge shopping mall with multiple merchants ready for business but without roads, transportation, and utility services. There would be no easy way to access these merchants' services.

The term **middleware** is sometimes used as a term to describe these types of connectivity services. We can see the components of an ESB in *Figure 2.19*:

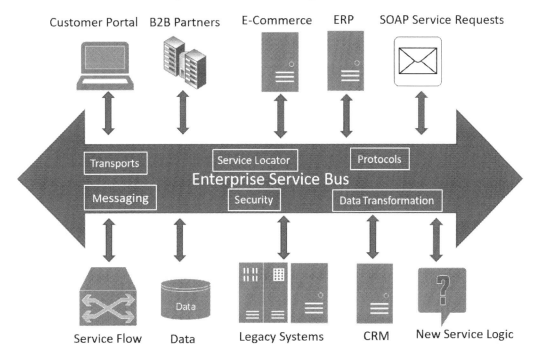

Figure 2.19 – ESB

There is a requirement for this technology in many large enterprises, where complex heterogeneous systems and workloads need this integration enablement.

Summary

In this chapter, we have taken a look at frameworks used for developing or commissioning new services or software (the SDLC and SDL). We have covered how systems and services can be built securely. As a security professional, it is important to understand how we can provide assurance that products meet the appropriate levels of trust. We have learned how to deploy services that can be considered trustworthy and meet recognized standards.

We have looked at the process of automation by deploying DevOps pipelines. We have looked at the cultural aspects of combining development and operations teams (**DevOps**) with a focus on security (**SecDevOps**).

We have examined different development methodologies to understand different approaches to meet customer requirements (**waterfall**, **Agile**, and **spiral**).

We have learned about the importance of testing, including integrated, static, and dynamic testing. We have looked at adopting secure testing environments, including staging and sandboxing. You have learned about the importance of baselines and templates to ensure standards compliance and security are built into new systems and software.

We have looked at guidance and best practices for software development, from government-funded guidance (**NCSC**), to community-based guidance (**OWASP**) and commercial enterprises (**Microsoft SDL**).

We have learned about the security implications of integrating enterprise applications, including **CRM**, **ERP**, **CMDB**, and **CMS**.

Integration enablers are key to any large organization. We should understand the importance of the key services of **DNS**, **Directory Services**, **SOA**, and **ESB**.

In this chapter, you have gained the following skills:

- Learned key concepts of the **SDLC**, including the methodology and security frameworks.

- Gained understanding in DevOps and SecureDevOps

- Learned different development approaches including Agile, waterfall, and spiral

- An understanding of software QA including sandboxing, DevOps pipelines, continuous operations, and static and dynamic testing

- An understanding of the importance of baselines and templates, including NCSC recommended approaches, OWASP industry standards, and Microsoft SDL

- An understanding of the importance of integration enablers including DNS, directory services, SOA, and ESB

These skills learned will be useful during the next chapter, when we take a journey through the available cloud and virtualization platforms.

Questions

Here are a few questions to test your understanding of the chapter:

1. Which of the following is a container API?

    A. VMware

    B. Kubernetes

C. Hyper-V

D. Docker

2. Why would a company adopt secure coding standards? Choose all that apply.

A. To ensure most privilege

B. To adhere to the principle of least privilege

C. To sanitize data sent to other systems

D. To practice defense in depth

E. To deploy effective QA techniques

3. Why does Microsoft have an application-vetting process for Windows Store applications?

A. To ensure products are marketable

B. To ensure applications are stable and secure

C. To make sure patches will be made available

D. To ensure HTTP is used instead of HTTPS

4. What is most important for a development team validating third-party libraries? Choose two.

A. Third-party libraries may have vulnerabilities.

B. Third-party libraries may be incompatible.

C. Third-party libraries may not support DNSSEC.

D. Third-party libraries may have licensing restrictions.

5. What is the advantage of using the DevOps pipeline methodology?

A. Long lead times

B. Extensive pre-deployment testing

C. Continuous delivery

D. Siloed operations and development environments

6. What is the importance of software code signing?

A. Encrypted code modules

B. Software QA

    C. Software integrity

    D. Software agility

7. Which of the following is a common tool used to perform **Dynamic Application Security Testing (DAST)**?

    A. Network enumerator

    B. Sniffer

    C. Fuzzer

    D. Wi-Fi analyzer

8. What type of code must we have to perform **Static Application Security Testing (SAST)**?

    A. Compiled code

    B. Dynamic code

    C. Source code

    D. Binary code

9. What will my sales team use to manage sales opportunities?

    A. CRM

    B. ERP

    C. CMDB

    D. DNS

10. What would be a useful tool to integrate all business functions within an enterprise?

    A. CRM

    B. ERP

    C. CMDB

    D. DNS

11. What would be a useful tool to track all configurable assets within an enterprise?

    A. CRM

    B. ERP

    C. CMDB

    D. DNS

12. How can I ensure content is made accessible to the appropriate users through my web-based portal?

    A. CRM

    B. CMS

    C. CMDB

    D. CCMP

13. How can I protect my DNS servers from cache poisoning?

    A. DMARC

    B. DNSSEC

    C. Strict Transport Security

    D. IPSEC

14. What is it called when software developers break up code into modules, each one being an independently functional unit?

    A. SOA

    B. ESB

    C. Monolithic architecture

    D. Legacy architecture

15. What is the most important consideration when planning for system end of life?

    A. To ensure systems can be re-purposed

    B. To ensure there are no data remnants

    C. To comply with environmental standards

    D. To ensure systems do not become obsolete

16. What type of software testing is used when there has been a change within the existing environment?

    A. Regression testing

    B. Pen testing

    C. Requirements validation

    D. Release testing

17. What is it called when the development and operations teams work together to ensure that code released to the production environment is secure?

    A. DevOps

    B. Team-building exercises

    C. Tabletop exercises

    D. SecDevOps

18. What software development approach would involve regular meetings with the customer and developers throughout the development process?

    A. Agile

    B. Waterfall

    C. Spiral

    D. Build and Fix

19. What software development approach would involve meetings with the customer and developers at the end of a development cycle, allowing for changes to be made for the next iteration?

    A. Agile

    B. Waterfall

    C. Spiral

    D. Build and Fix

20. What software development approach would involve meetings with the customer and developers at the definition stage and then at the end of the development process?

    A. Agile

    B. Waterfall

    C. Spiral

    D. Build and Fix

21. Where will we ensure the proper HTTP headers are configured?

    A. Domain Controller

    B. DNS server

    C. Web server

    D. Mail server

Answers

1. B
2. B, C, D and E
3. B
4. A and D
5. C
6. B
7. C
8. C
9. A
10. B
11. C
12. B
13. B
14. A
15. B
16. A
17. D
18. A
19. C
20. B
21. C

3
Enterprise Data Security, Including Secure Cloud and Virtualization Solutions

An organization must ensure that proper due diligence and due care are exercised when considering the storage and handling of data. Data will be stored and accessed across complex, hybrid networks. Data types may include sensitive data, intellectual property, and trade secrets. Regulatory compliance and legal requirements will need to be carefully considered when planning for the storage and handling of data. Data needs to be labeled and classified according to the business value, controls put in place to prevent data loss, and an alert needs to be raised if these controls have any gaps. We need to plan how to handle data throughout the life cycle, from creation/acquisition to end of life. We must understand the implications of storing our data with third parties, such as B2B partners and cloud providers. We must ensure that appropriate protection is applied to data at rest, in transit, and in use.

In this chapter, we will cover the following topics:

- Implementing data loss prevention
- Implementing data loss detection
- Enabling data protection
- Implementing secure cloud and virtualization solutions
- Investigating cloud deployment models
- Extending appropriate on-premises controls
- Examining cloud storage models

Implementing data loss prevention

It is important to identify sensitive data and put in place preventative controls to control the unwanted exfiltration or leakage of this data. There are many different controls for managing this requirement. We can use policy to ensure that correct data handling and operational procedures are followed. We can use DLP filters at the network egress points, using capability within our **Next Generation Firewall** (**NGFW**) or **Unified Threat Management** (**UTM**) appliance. Your cloud provider may offer **Cloud Access Security Broker** (**CASB**), protecting your organization when users access the cloud. **Microsoft365** offers this protection with a collection of pre-set rules and templates that can be applied. We will look at some additional methods within this section.

Blocking the use of external media

To prevent the local exfiltration of sensitive data, it is important to put in place local controls, also known as **Group Policy** or **Local Policy**, for Windows workstations. **Mobile Device Management** (**MDM**) could be used to disable access to mobile devices' external storage. When considering non-Windows systems (macOS, Linux, Unix, and so on), Group Policy will not be an option, so restrictions could be addressed by scripting or configuration files. *Figure 3.1* shows Group Policy options for the blocking of removable storage:

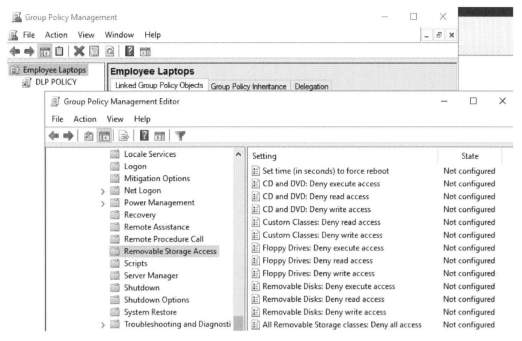

Figure 3.1 – Group Policy for controlling removable storage

Group policy offers a comprehensive range of enhancements and restrictions for Windows operating systems.

Print blocking

It is important to recognize other means of exfiltrating data from systems. Screengrabs and the printing of sensitive information should also be restricted. By way of an experiment, open your mobile banking application and try to use the print screen function. You will not be able to perform this action. To restrict unauthorized printing, **Digital Rights Management** (**DRM**) can be utilized for sensitive documents, as shown in *Figure 3.2*:

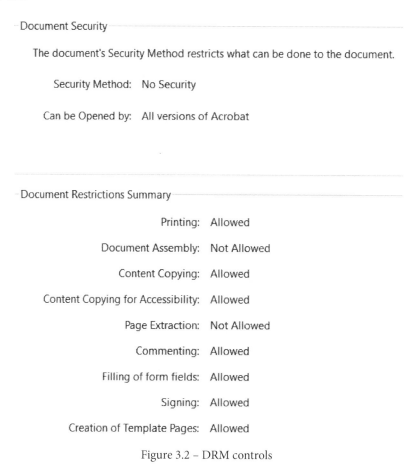

Figure 3.2 – DRM controls

Remote Desktop Protocol blocking

Due to the widespread use of **Virtual Desktop Infrastructure** (**VDI**) and remote support capabilities, this is also an area that requires careful consideration and appropriate security controls. We can use robust authentication and authorization to restrict the use of this technology. *Figure 3.3* shows an example of a remote desktop being disabled:

Remote Desktop

Remote Desktop lets you connect to and control this PC from a remote device by using a Remote Desktop client (available for Windows, Android, iOS and macOS). You'll be able to work from another device as if you were working directly on this PC.

Enable Remote Desktop

 Off

Figure 3.3 – Remote Desktop controls

If it is necessary to make provision for a **Remote Desktop Protocol (RDP)** to access a desktop for administration or business productivity, then controls should be implemented to control functionality within the session. These controls should include the following:

- Clipboard privacy controls

- Remote audio capabilities

- Access to local storage

- Plug and play devices

In *Figure 3.4*, we can some of the restrictions available through Group Policy to control access to resources during a remote session:

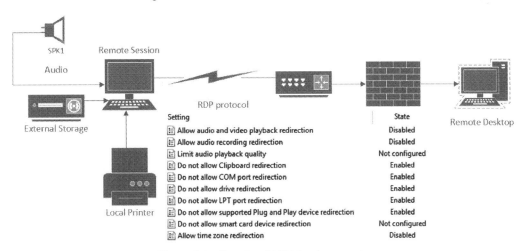

Figure 3.4 – Restricted VDI implementation

RDP configuration allows for granular controls to be applied to the session.

Implementing data loss detection

It is not always possible to implement a 100% **Data Loss Protection** (**DLP**) solution, since a determined insider threat actor may find a workaround. In this case, the objective may be to identify the threat. So, we will now look at methods to detect how the data was exfiltrated from our organization.

Watermarking

If an organization wants to detect the theft or exfiltration of sensitive data, then documents can be checked out from an information system, but an automatic watermark will be applied to the document using the identity of the user who checked out the document, as shown in *Figure 3.5*. If the document is shared or printed, it will clearly show that user's identity.

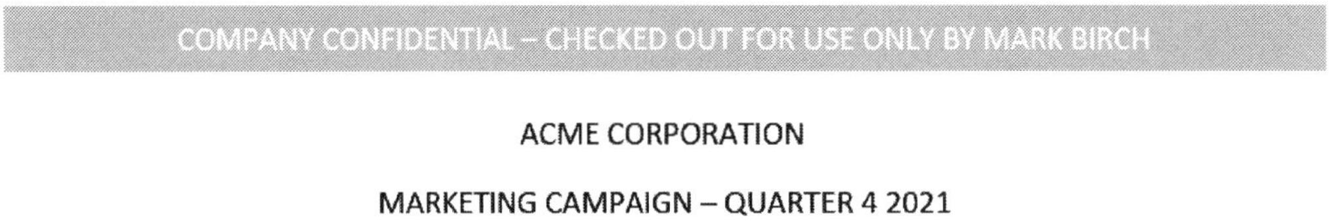

COMPANY CONFIDENTIAL – CHECKED OUT FOR USE ONLY BY MARK BIRCH

ACME CORPORATION

MARKETING CAMPAIGN – QUARTER 4 2021

Figure 3.5 – Watermarking

This type of control is also used to deter the user from distributing protected content.

Digital rights management

Digital rights management (**DRM**) is used to protect digital content, typically copyright material. It can be applied to most digital media types. Examples include video, images, books, music, and software code. Usually, it allows the copyright owner to control the publishing of content and receive payment for their work.

You may have been restricted from printing an Adobe document or found that you are unable to highlight a section of text to copy – this is an example of DRM.

It is also useful within an enterprise for allowing the protection of sensitive document types and can be a useful addition to existing DLP solutions.

Network traffic decryption/deep packet inspection

In some cases, it may be necessary to inspect traffic that has been encrypted. A common deployment is a **Secure Sockets Layer** (**SSL**) decryptor. This allows an organization to decrypt the outgoing packets to apply enterprise DLP rulesets. Careful consideration is required when implementing this technology as our users would not want their employers to monitor connections to their personal bank account sessions. The whitelisting of URLs would be one approach to consider in this regard.

Network traffic analysis

When the detection of data leakage or exfiltration is being considered, one of the common methods is to analyze data flows, in terms of both volume and content. We could use this information to identify unusual user behaviors, such as high volumes of research data being uploaded to **Cloud Data Networks** (**CDNs**).

Enabling data protection

It is important to address all aspects of the **Confidentiality Integrity Availability** (**CIA**) triad. We need to understand the importance of data and label or classify accordingly. We must ensure that data is protected from unauthorized access and that integrity is maintained. Data must also be made available so that business functionality can be maintained.

Data classification

The appropriate data owner needs to be consulted within the enterprise to establish the classification of data to ensure that appropriate controls are implemented.

Due to the amount of data that is typically held by large enterprises, automation is a common approach. For example, keyword or string searches could be utilized to discover documents containing a driver's license number, social security number, debit card numbers, and so on. We have data classification blocking where necessary to prevent data leakage. In *Figure 3.6*, we can see categories that could be used to label data:

☐   EU Debit Card Number

☐   EU Driver's License Number

☐   EU National Identification Number

☐   EU Passport Number

☐   EU Social Security Number (SSN) or Equivalent ID

☐   EU Tax Identification Number (TIN)

Figure 3.6 – Data type tagging

Metadata/attributes

Metadata is the data that describes data. Metadata can be very useful when searching across stores with large files. We can tag data using common attributes or store the data within the file itself. *Figure 3.7* shows metadata data of an image:

📅 27 Apr
Tue, 13:11   GMT+01:00   ✏️

🖼️ 20210427_131125.jpg
12.2 MP   3024 × 4032   3.5 MB

🔆 samsung SM-G950F
ƒ/1.7   1/50   4.2 mm   ISO50

⬆️ Uploaded from an Android device

📍 IKEA Edinburgh   ✏️

Figure 3.7 – Metadata store alongside an image file

Attributes are used with tags; they consist of the identifier followed by a value, as shown in *Figure 3.8*:

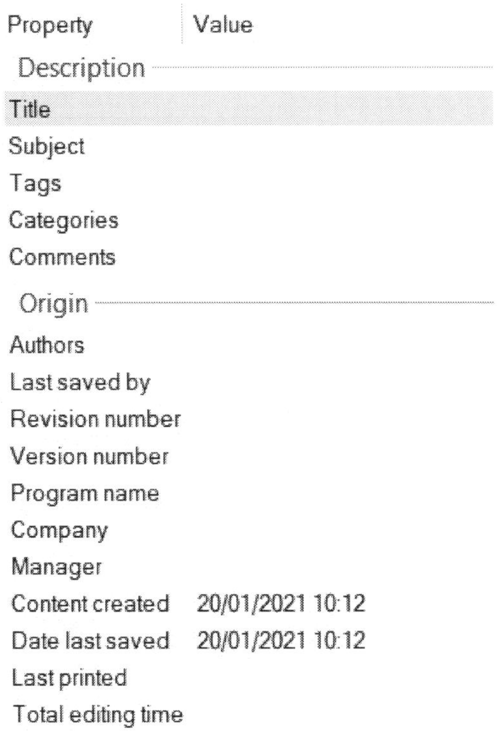

Property	Value
Description	
Title	
Subject	
Tags	
Categories	
Comments	
Origin	
Authors	
Last saved by	
Revision number	
Version number	
Program name	
Company	
Manager	
Content created	20/01/2021 10:12
Date last saved	20/01/2021 10:12
Last printed	
Total editing time	

Figure 3.8 – Document attributes

Data labeling or **tagging** allows data to be handled appropriately according to the importance/value of the data. Once we have established the data type and labeled it accordingly, we can look to automate the management of the data (retention settings, archiving, and so on). In *Figure 3.9*, we can see data classification being applied to a folder within the filesystem:

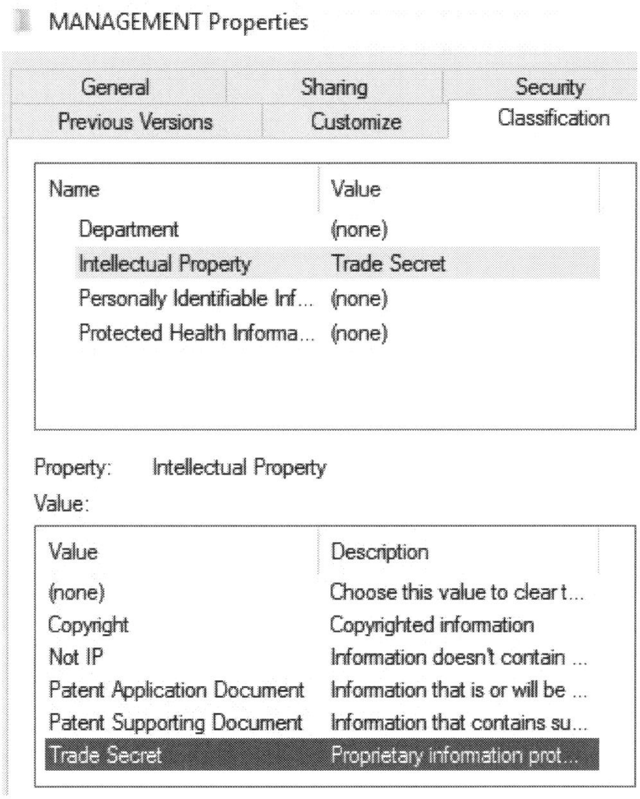

Figure 3.9 – Data labeling

Microsoft file servers allow for classification labels enabled within Directory Services.

Obfuscation

Obfuscation is defined in the Oxford dictionary *as the act of making something less clear and more difficult to understand, usually deliberately.* We can use this approach to protect data.

It is important to protect data in use and data at rest, and there are many ways to achieve this, including strong **Access Control Lists** (**ACLs**) and data encryption. When considering the use of records or processing transactions, certain strings or keys may be hidden from certain parts of the system. Here are some common approaches:

- **Data tokenization**: This is often associated with contactless payments. Your debit card is implemented in the Google Pay app as a token. The bank allocates a unique token to your mobile app but your actual payment details (including the security code on the reverse of the card) are not stored with the token.

- **Data scrubbing**: This can be used to detect or correct any information in a database that has some sort of error. Errors in databases can be the result of human error in entering the data, the merging of two databases, a lack of company-wide or industry-wide data coding standards, or due to old systems that contain inaccurate or outdated data. This term can also be used when data has been removed from log files; the user is likely hiding the evidence.

- **Data masking**: This is a way to create a bogus, but realistic, version of your organizational data. The goal is to protect sensitive data while providing a practical alternative when real data is not needed. This would be used for user training, sales demos, or software testing. The format would remain the same, but, of course, the original data records would not be visible.

The data masking process will change the values of the data while using the same format. The goal is to create a version that cannot be deciphered or reverse engineered.

Anonymization

The use of big data and the use of business intelligence presents significant regulatory challenges. Take, for example, a situation where governments need to track the effectiveness of strategies during a pandemic. A goal may be to publish the fact that 25,000 citizens within the age range of 65-75 years old have been vaccinated within the city of Perth (Scotland). It should not be possible to extract individual **Personally Identifiable Information** (**PII**) records for any of these people. Fraser McCloud, residing at 25 Argyle Avenue, telephone 01738 678654, does not expect his personal details to be part of this published information.

Encrypted versus unencrypted

One method to addressing confidentiality would be to encrypt sensitive data. The overhead, however, means that it is important to identify files or records that meet the criteria for encryption. Data that has no value or sensitivity label should be stored unencrypted. We can use database encryption or file encryption for data at rest. For data in transit, we should use **Transport Layer Security** (**TLS**) or **IPSEC** tunnels.

Data life cycle

It is important to have a plan and organizational policies and procedures to manage data throughout the life cycle, from the initial creation or capture of the data to the point where the data is no longer required. Without knowledge of the data we hold, the importance of the data, and a plan to manage it, we cannot ensure good governance of the data. In *Figure 3.10*, we can see a five-step process depicting the data life cycle:

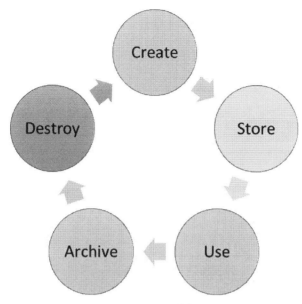

Figure 3.10 – Data life cycle

The following is a detailed explanation of the various stages of the data life cycle shown in *Figure 3.10*:

- **Create**: Phase one of the life cycle is the creation/capture of data. Examples include documents, images, mapping data, and GPS coordinates.

- **Store**: We must store the data within appropriate systems, including file shares, websites, databases, and graph stores.

- **Use**: Once the data is held within our information system, we must ensure that data governance is applied. This means classifying data, protecting data, and retaining it. We must ensure we take care of legal and regulatory compliance.

- **Archive**: Data should be preserved to meet regulatory and legal requirements; this should map across to data retention policies.

- **Destroy**: Data should be purged based upon regulatory and legal requirements. There is no business advantage in retaining data that is not required. When we store data for too long, we may be more exposed as a business in the event of a lawsuit. A legal hold would require a business to make available all records pertaining to the lawsuit.

Data inventory and mapping

Data inventory allows an enterprise to gain visualization of the data that is held and where it is physically located. Any access will be logged and audited. Data mapping can help an organization understand how the data is used and who owns the data.

Data integrity management

The data held by an organization can be critical for business processes to be completed. The data that is held and processed could include sales order processing, records in a CRM database, and financial transactions in a bank.

There are many ways to guarantee the authenticity of data, including **File Integrity Monitoring** (**FIM**). Data could become corrupt, or your organization may be targeted with crypto-malware. Consequently, there must be a plan to recover the data to its previous state.

Data storage, backup, and recovery

Due to the complexities of a modern hybrid computing model, backups and the subsequent restoration of data can be a big challenge. Is the data on-premises or held by a third-party cloud provider? Who is responsible for data backup and restoration?

When planning for data backups, we need to refer to legal and regulatory requirements, as well as operational requirements for the actual routines we will put in place. As regards operational planning, think about **Data Retention Policy** (**DRP**) and **Business Continuity Planning** (**BCP**), especially in relation to **Recovery Point Objectives** (**RPOs**).

It may be cost-effective to back up a directory to cloud storage, often costing a few cents per GB per month.

Types of backups could also be very important. If working with limited time windows to complete full backups every day, then incremental or differential backup types should be considered.

Full backup

A full backup will back up all the files in the backup set every time it is run. Imagine this is a **Network Attached Storage** (**NAS**) array containing 100 terabytes of data. It may take a significant amount of time to back up all the data every day, while also considering the storage overheads.

The advantages are as follows:

- A full backup of the dataset every time
- Quick to restore (only a single backup set is required)

The disadvantages are as follows:

- It is time-consuming.
- Additional storage space is required.

Differential backup

A differential backup is usually run in conjunction with a full backup. The full backup would be run when there is a generous time window, on a Sunday, for example. Each day, the differential backup would back up any changes since Sunday's full backup. So, Monday's backup would be relatively quick, but by the time Friday's differential backup is run, it will have grown to perhaps five times the size of Monday's backup.

The advantages are as follows:

- It is quicker than a full backup.
- It is quicker to restore than an incremental backup (only two backup sets are required – the full differential and the last differential)

The disadvantage is as follows:

- Additional storage space is required (over and above the incremental backup).

Incremental backup

An incremental backup is usually run in conjunction with a full backup. The full backup would be run when there is a generous time window – Sunday, for example. Each day, the incremental backup would back up any changes since the previous backup. So, each daily incremental backup would take approximately the same amount of time, while the volume of data stored would be similar.

The advantages are as follows:

- It is the quickest to back up.
- It requires the least amount of storage space.

The disadvantage is as follows:

- It is the slowest to restore (all the backup datasets will be required)

Redundant array of inexpensive disks

When we need to provide for high availability, with data storage in mind, it is important to consider the **Redundant Array Of Inexpensive Disks** (**RAID**) implementations available. With the majority of the first line enterprise storage residing within **Storage Area Networks** (**SANs**) or hosted on **Network Attached Storage** (**NAS**), it is normally these applications that will host the redundant storage. Here are some of the most popular RAID types:

- **RAID 0**: This is used to aggregate multiple disks across a single volume. It will allow for fast disk I/O operations, and there is no redundancy (hence the **0**). It achieves this performance by spreading the write operations across multiple physical disks. It also speeds up read operations by a similar margin (25-30%). This requires two or more disks, as shown in *Figure 3.11*:

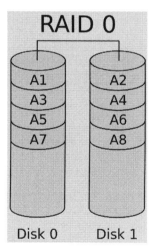

Figure 3.11 – RAID 0 disk striping

The advantages of RAID 0 are as follows:

- Read/write operations are fast.

- Efficient use of available storage (100% of the disks are available for data).

- It is a simple solution to deploy.

The disadvantage of RAID 0 is as follows:

- There is no fault tolerance. If we lose one physical disk, then the volume is unavailable.

- **RAID 1**: This is disk mirroring and uses two disks. The data is written to both disks synchronously, creating a mirror of the data. There is no real performance gain when deploying this RAID level (compared to a single disk). If one of the mirrored disks fails, we can continue to access the storage. *Figure 3.12* shows an example of RAID 1 disk mirroring:

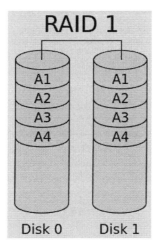

Figure 3.12 – RAID 1 disk mirroring

The advantages of RAID 1 are as follows:

- RAID 1 offers good read and write speed (it is equal to that of a single drive).

- If a drive fails, the data does not have to be rebuilt; it is copied to the replacement drive (which is a quick process).

- RAID 1 is a very simple technology.

The disadvantage of RAID 1 is as follows:

- The effective storage capacity is only half of the total drive capacity because all the data is written twice.

- **RAID 5**: This uses a minimum of three disks. The data is written to all disks synchronously, creating a single logical disk. There is a performance gain for read operations. If one of the RAID 5 disks fails, we can continue to access the storage. This technology uses a single parity stripe to store the redundant data, as shown in *Figure 3.13*:

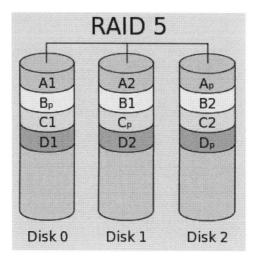

Figure 3.13 – RAID 5 striping with parity

The advantages of RAID 5 are as follows:

- Read operations are very fast, while write data transactions will be slower (due to the parity that must be calculated).

- If one drive fails, you still have access to your data.

The disadvantages of RAID 5 are as follows:

- Write operations can cause latency (in calculating the parity value).

- Drive failures will slow down access (every read operation will require a parity calculation).

- The rebuild time, following a failure, can be lengthy.

- **RAID 6**: This uses a minimum of four disks. The data is written to all disks synchronously, creating a single logical disk. There is a performance gain for read operations. If two of the RAID 6 disks fail, we can continue to access the storage. This technology uses a dual parity stripe to store the redundant data, as shown in *Figure 3.14*:

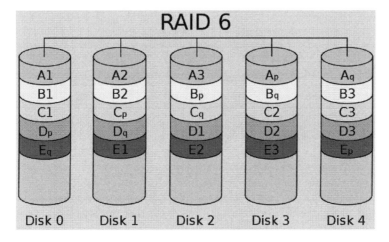

Figure 3.14 – RAID 6 dual stripe with parity

The advantages of RAID 6 are as follows:

- Read operations are very fast, while write data transactions will be slower (due to the parity that must be calculated).

- If two drives fail, you still have access to your data.

The disadvantages of RAID 6 are as follows:

- Write operations can cause latency (in calculating the parity value) that exceeds that of RAID 5 as two parity calculations must be performed during each write operation.

- Drive failures will slow down access (every read operation will require a parity calculation).

- The rebuild time, following a failure, can be lengthy (and longer still if two drives have failed).

- **RAID 10**: This uses a minimum of four disks. It combines RAID 0 and RAID 1 in a single system. It provides security by mirroring all data on secondary drives while using striping across each set of drives to speed up data transfers, as shown in *Figure 3.15*:

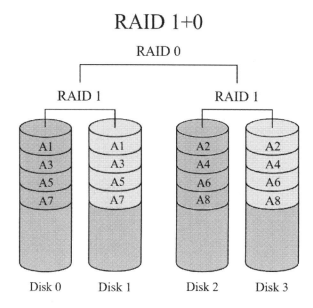

Figure 3.15 – RAID 10 nested raid 1 + 0

The advantages of RAID 10 are as follows:

- Fast read and write operations (no parity calculation to worry about)
- Fast recovery from a failed disk; the rebuild time is quick

The disadvantage of RAID 10 is as follows:

- 50% of the available storage is lost to the mirror (much less cost-effective than striping with parity).

Implementing secure cloud and virtualization solutions

Virtualization allows software to control access to the underlying hardware. It uses a thin layer of code to control access to resources, including networking, CPU, storage, and memory.

Pretty much any compute node can be run virtually on top of a software layer. This software layer is the **hypervisor**. User desktops, email servers, directory servers, switches, firewalls, and routers are just a few examples of **virtual machines** (**VMs**).

Virtualization allows for more flexibility in the data center, rapid provisioning, and scalability as workloads increase. Additional benefits include reducing an organization's footprint in the data center (less hardware, reduced power, and so on). *Figure 3.16* shows resources being allocated to a virtual guest operating system using **Microsoft Hyper-V**:

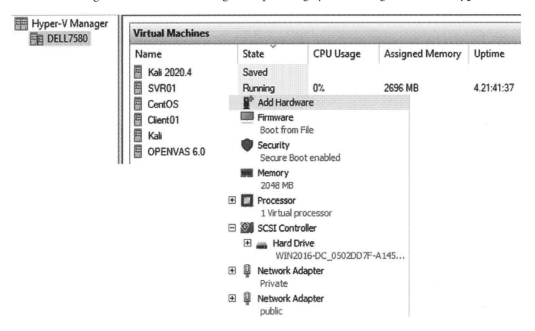

Figure 3.16 – Microsoft Hyper-V

Virtualization strategies

When considering virtualization, an important choice will be the type of hypervisor. If you are planning for the computing requirements of the data center, then you will need to choose a bare-metal hypervisor, also known as **Type 1**. This is going to require minimal overhead, allowing for maximum efficiency of the underlying hardware. Testing and developing may require desktop virtualization tools, where compatibility will be important. If we need to move the development virtual workloads into production, it makes sense to choose compatible models, for example, **VMWare Workstation** for the desktop and **VMWare ESXi** for the production data center. Application virtualization may also be a useful strategy when we have a mixture of desktop users, where compatibility may be an issue. Containers should also be considered for their efficient use of computing resources.

Type 1 hypervisors

In effect, a type 1 hypervisor takes the place of the host operating system. Type 1 tends to be more reliable as they are not dependent on their underlying operating system and have fewer dependencies, which is another advantage. Type 1 hypervisors are the default for data centers. While this approach is highly efficient, it will need management tools to be installed on a separate computer on the network. For security, this management computer will be segmented from regular compute nodes. *Figure 3.17* shows the diagram of Type 1 hypervisors:

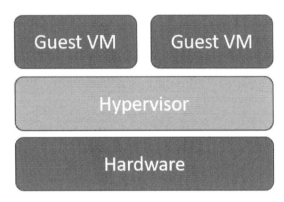

Figure 3.17 – Type 1 hypervisor

Examples of type 1 hypervisors include the following:

- A VMware **Elastic Sky X Integrated** (**ESXi**) hypervisor.

- **Hyper-V** is Microsoft's hypervisor designed for use on Windows systems.

- **Citrix XenServer**, now known as Citrix Hypervisor.

- The **Kernel-Based Virtual Machine** (**KVM**) hypervisor is used on Linux. This hypervisor is built directly into its OS kernel.

- **Oracle VMServer** for x86 incorporates the free and open source Xen hypervisor technology.

Type 2 hypervisors

A type 2 hypervisor requires an installed host operating system. It is installed as an additional software component. It is a useful tool for any job role that requires access to more than one operating system. This type of hypervisor would allow an **Apple Mac** user to run native Microsoft Windows applications using **VMware Fusion**.

The reason type 2 hypervisors are not suitable for the data center is that they are not as efficient as type 1 hypervisors. They must access computing resources from the main installed host operating system. This will cause latency issues when dealing with enterprise workloads. Type 2 is more common when we require virtualization on a desktop computer for testing/development purposes. *Figure 3.18* type 2 hypervisors:

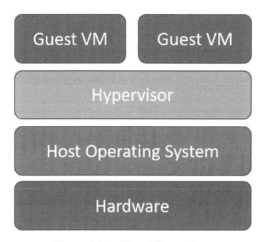

Figure 3.18 – Type 2 hypervisor

Examples of type 2 hypervisors include the following:

- **VMware Fusion**: Allows Mac users to run a large range of guest operating systems.

- **VMware Workstation**: Allows Linux and Windows users to run multiple operating systems on a single PC.

- **VMware Player**: This is free but only supports a single guest OS.

- **Oracle VirtualBox**: Can run on Linux, macOS, and Windows operating systems. It is a free product.

Security considerations for virtualization

VM escape is a term used for an exploit where an attacker uses a guest operating system (VM) to send commands directly to the hypervisor. Vendors such as VMware and Microsoft will pay $250,000 to bounty hunters if they have a workable model, such is the importance associated with this threat. This is not a common type of attack, although there have been a number of instances of compromised hypervisor exploits in the past. In 2008, **CVE-2008-0923** was posted. This documents a vulnerability on **VMware Workstation 6.0.2** and **5.5.4** making a VM escape possible.

VM sprawl Describes unmanaged and unpatched VMs installed on the hypervisor platform. This makes the hypervisor host vulnerable to exploits such as backdoor access or could result in reduced levels of available services.

Containers

Containers are a more efficient way of deploying workloads in the data center. A container is a package containing the software application and all the additional binary files and library dependencies. Because the workload is isolated from the host operating system, any potential bugs or errors thrown by the container-based application will not affect any other applications.

Containers allow for isolation between different applications. It is important to consider the security aspects of containers. If we are using a cloud platform, we need to be sure that we have segmentation from other customers' containers.

Containers allow easy deployment on multiple operating system platforms and make migration an easy process. They have a relatively low overhead as they do not need to run on a VM.

To support containers, you will need a container management system (often called the engine); the most popular product at the moment is Docker. There are versions of Docker that developers can run on their desktops, to then migrate into the data center. *Figure 3.19* shows a container:

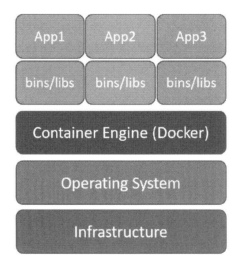

Figure 3.19 – Containers

Emulation

Emulation allows for the running of a program or service that would not run natively on a given platform. Examples could include running legacy arcade games on a modern computer by installing an emulator program. Terminal emulators are used to remote to another device, replacing the need to connect a serial cable direct from a terminal to a network appliance. Linux commands can be used on a Windows 10 desktop computer by emulating the Linux command shell, as shown in *Figure 3.20*:

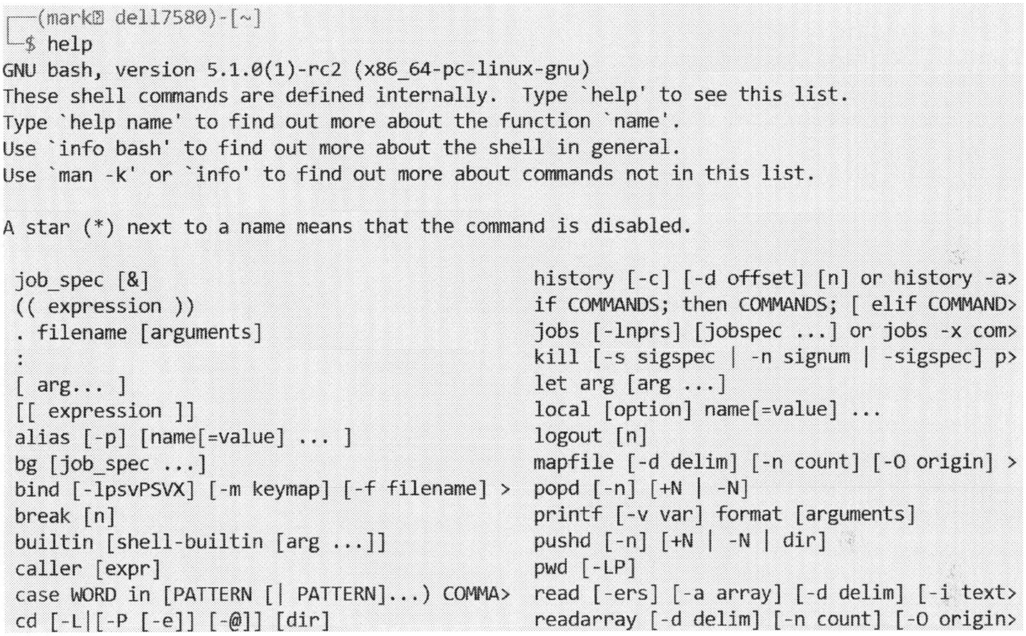

```
┌─(mark☐ dell7580)-[~]
└─$ help
GNU bash, version 5.1.0(1)-rc2 (x86_64-pc-linux-gnu)
These shell commands are defined internally.  Type `help' to see this list.
Type `help name' to find out more about the function `name'.
Use `info bash' to find out more about the shell in general.
Use `man -k' or `info' to find out more about commands not in this list.

A star (*) next to a name means that the command is disabled.

 job_spec [&]                              history [-c] [-d offset] [n] or history -a>
 (( expression ))                         if COMMANDS; then COMMANDS; [ elif COMMAND>
 . filename [arguments]                   jobs [-lnprs] [jobspec ...] or jobs -x com>
 :                                        kill [-s sigspec | -n signum | -sigspec] p>
 [ arg... ]                               let arg [arg ...]
 [[ expression ]]                         local [option] name[=value] ...
 alias [-p] [name[=value] ... ]          logout [n]
 bg [job_spec ...]                        mapfile [-d delim] [-n count] [-O origin] >
 bind [-lpsvPSVX] [-m keymap] [-f filename] >  popd [-n] [+N | -N]
 break [n]                                printf [-v var] format [arguments]
 builtin [shell-builtin [arg ...]]        pushd [-n] [+N | -N | dir]
 caller [expr]                            pwd [-LP]
 case WORD in [PATTERN [| PATTERN]...) COMMA>  read [-ers] [-a array] [-d delim] [-i text>
 cd [-L|[-P [-e]] [-@]] [dir]             readarray [-d delim] [-n count] [-O origin>
```

Figure 3.20 – Windows 10 Linux Bash shell (emulation)

Application virtualization

Application virtualization can be useful when there is a need to support a **Line of Business** (**LOB**) application or a legacy application across multiple platforms. We can publish an application on a Microsoft (Remote Desktop Services) server and host multiple sessions to that single deployed application across an RDP connection. To scale out to an enterprise, we could deploy a server farm. We could, for example, access Windows applications from a Linux host using this deployment model. We also allow the application to be streamed across the network and run locally. Microsoft calls this technology App-V. Citrix has a similar technology, named XenApp. *Figure 3.21* shows application virtualization:

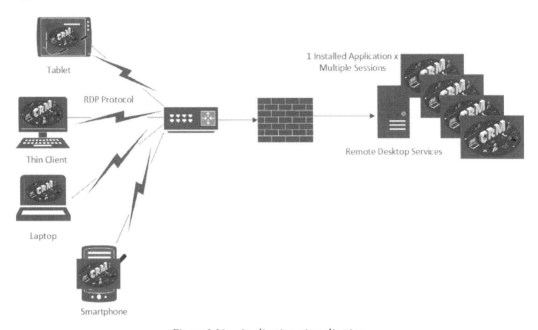

Figure 3.21 – Application virtualization

VDI

VDI allows the provision of compute resources to be controlled from within the data center or cloud. A typical model is an employee using a basic thin client to access a fully functional desktop with all required applications. The user can access their desktop using any device capable of hosting the remote software. Microsoft has an RDP client that can run on most operating systems. The advantages of this approach are resilience, speed of deployment, and security. *Figure 3.22* shows a VDI environment:

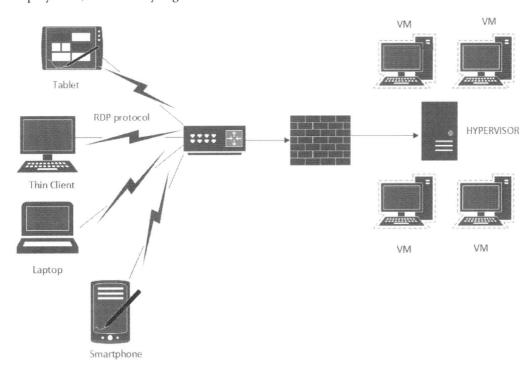

Figure 3.22 – VDI environment

Provisioning and deprovisioning can be automated for VM instances or container deployments. Orchestration tools could be used in an enterprise. For small-scale deployments, templates are created and VMs can be easily built and deployed when needed. *Figure 3.23* shows how you can provision a VM:

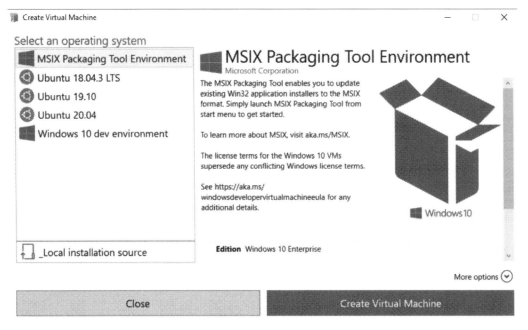

Figure 3.23 – VM provisioning

For more granular and configurable provisioning options, we may use tools such as Microsoft **System Center Virtual Machine Manager** (**SCVMM**) or the **VMware vSphere** suite of tools. To orchestrate the deployment of containers, we would use tools such as **Kubernetes**.

It is important to consider all available options when supporting workloads in data centers, giving business users access to tools, allowing for access to multiple operating systems, or allowing non-compatible applications to be accessed from a desktop. Organizations need to consider the benefits of reducing their footprint in the data center by making better use of computing resources.

Investigating cloud deployment models

Cloud computing has been a mainstay service for many years, becoming more accepted as a serious business model as many enterprises move to more hybrid networks. The power of the cloud is based upon flexibility. There is a much-used phrase, **Elastic Cloud**, which represents cost savings and scalability. It is estimated that around 50% of enterprise workloads are hosted by cloud providers and around 46% of data is hosted in the cloud (based upon estimates for 2021). Growth rates are predicted to remain high. There are many cloud providers; however, the current market leaders are **Amazon Web Services** (**AWS**), **Microsoft Azure**, and **Google**.

Deployment models and considerations

When considering a **Cloud Service Provider** (**CSP**), many considerations will affect this important enterprise decision.

Cybersecurity

The most critical consideration is cybersecurity. When we are storing data, such as intellectual property, PII, PHI, and many other types of data, we must consider all the risks before deploying cloud models.

Business directives

Does the CSP align with our regulatory requirements? Government agencies will only be able to work with providers who meet the FedRAMP criteria. **Federal Risk and Authorization Management Program** (**FedRAMP**) is a US government-wide program that provides a standardized approach to security assessment, authorization, and continuous monitoring for cloud products and services. **Amazon Web Services** (**AWS**) and **Microsoft Azure** cloud offerings have multiple accreditations, including **PCI-DSS**, **FedRAMP**, **ISO27001**, and **ISO27018** to name but a few.

Cost

The cost of operating services in the cloud is one of the most important drivers when choosing a cloud solution. Unfortunately for the **Chief Financial Officer** (**CFO**), the least expensive may not be a workable solution. Certain industries are tied into legal or regulatory compliance, meaning they will need to consider a private cloud or, in some cases, community cloud models.

Scalability

What scalability constraints will there be? It was interesting in early 2020 when organizations were forced to adopt a much more flexible remote working model, which fully tested the scalability of the cloud. Web conferencing products such as Zoom and Microsoft Teams reported a 50% increase in demand from March to April 2020.

Resources

What resources does the CSP have? Many CSPs operate data centers that are completely self-sufficient regarding power, typically powered by renewable energy (wind farms, hydroelectric, and the like). How many countries do they operate in? Do they have data centers close to your business? Do they have a solid financial basis?

Location

The location of the CSP data centers could be critically important. Think about legal issues relating to data sovereignty and jurisdiction. Also, does the provider offer redundancy using **geo-redundancy**. If the New York data center has an environmental disaster, can we host services in the Dallas data center?

Data protection

We must ensure that we can protect customer data with the same level of security as on-premises data stores. We would need to ensure data is protected at rest and in transit.

In *Figure 3.24*, we can see the main options for cloud deployment models:

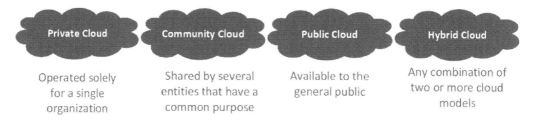

Figure 3.24 – Cloud deployment models

Private cloud

A private cloud allows an enterprise to host their chosen services in a completely isolated data center. Legal or regulatory requirements may be the deciding factor when looking at this model. Economies of scale will often result in a higher cost when implementing this model. Government agencies, such as the **Department of Defense (DoD)**, are prime candidates for the security benefits of this approach. The United Kingdom's **Ministry of Defence (MoD)** has been a user of the private cloud since 2015, awarding a multi-million-pound contract for the use of Microsoft 365 services. In the USA, the DoD has followed suit, also signing up for multi-billion dollar contracts with Microsoft and Amazon.

Government requirements are very strict. Currently, there are two ways to provide cloud services to the United States government. One approach is to go through the **Joint Authorization Board (JAB)** or directly through a government agency, the requirements are strict, and there is a requirement for continuous monitoring. The program is managed as part of The **Federal Risk and Authorization Management Program (FedRAMP)**. To allow a CSP to prepare for this process, there are baseline security audit requirements and additional documentation available through the following link: `https://www.fedramp.gov/documents-templates/`.

Public cloud

Amazon Web Services (AWS), **Microsoft Azure**, and **Google Cloud Platform (GCP)** are examples of public cloud providers. They offer a service in which you can enroll and configure your workloads.

Public cloud providers operate from large geolocated data centers to offer services to a wide range of customers.

Range International Information Group hosts the world's largest data center. It is located in Langfang, China. It covers an area equivalent to 110 football pitches (around 6.3 million square feet). In comparison, Microsoft's main Dublin data center occupies an area of around 10 football pitches.

Millions of global customers are using this model. There is more flexibility and less commitment when using the public cloud.

Most cloud providers' customers will benefit from this shared model, achieving cost savings compared with the private cloud.

Hybrid cloud

A hybrid cloud allows an organization to use more than one cloud model. For example, a utility provider delivering critical infrastructure may be required by regulatory compliance to host critical services in a private cloud. The sales and marketing division of the same enterprise may want to use business productivity tools such as salesforce.com using a cost-effective public cloud model. A hybrid cloud allows an enterprise to meet operational requirements using a blended model.

A community cloud allows organizations operating within the same vertical industry to share costs. They may have the same strict regulatory requirements not suited to a multi-tenant public cloud, but can still look to benefit from a shared cost model. Obviously, they will not achieve the same cost savings as public cloud customers.

Hosting models

When you choose a cloud deployment model, you have, in effect, signed up for either a totally isolated data center or a shared experience. Think of where you live. If you are wealthy, then you can afford to live in a secure compound with your own private security team. If you don't have that sort of money, then maybe you could live in a secure gated community (think community cloud). If you don't want to spend too much of your salary on housing, then maybe you could rent an apartment within a building, sharing common walkways and elevators (think public cloud). However, other options are available.

If you pay the least amount of money possible to host services in a public cloud, then you will most likely be using a multi-tenant model. Your hosted web server will be running as a VM alongside other customers' VMs on the same hypervisor. Maybe your database will be hosted on the same server as the other customers using the same schema.

Many public cloud providers will offer single-tenant services, but at a cost. So, the provider has a public cloud, but allows customers to host services on a separate hardware stack. Obviously, they will want to charge more money for this.

Service models

Once you have chosen the cloud deployment model, you can choose the services that your organization will need. It is important to understand the responsibility of the level of involvement that your employees will need. When buying in services for end users' business productivity, you may want to pay a fixed annual cost without any further involvement, or perhaps you need to host critical infrastructure that enables engineers to have total responsibility for a hosted **Supervisory Control and Data Acquisition (SCADA)** network. *Figure 3.25* shows examples of cloud service models:

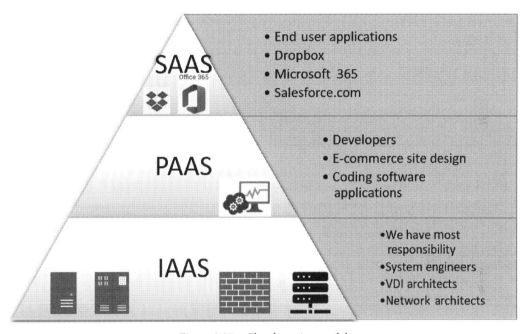

Figure 3.25 – Cloud service model

This simple model helps to define responsibilities when using **Cloud Service Providers (CSPs)**.

Software as a service

Software as a service (SaaS) is where you have the least responsibility. You pay for a license to use a software product or service. Microsoft has a product catalog available for customers to choose from, totaling around 3,000 items.

In a small school, there is no dedicated staff to manage servers and storage or to develop software applications. Instead, the teachers may use Moodle to set work and monitor student progress. They may have Microsoft 365 educational licenses to assign to the students, allowing access to an entire software suite. This is where you would use SaaS. You can see some examples of SaaS applications that can be selected from the Microsoft Azure portal in *Figure 3.26*:

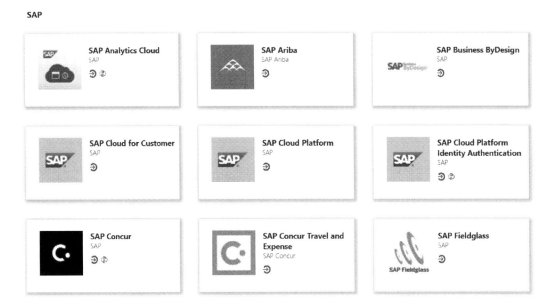

Figure 3.26 – SaaS catalog

With SaaS, you do not perform any development; you just need to pay for licenses for your users.

Platform as a service

When choosing **Platform as a service** (**PaaS**) as a service model, you will be wanting to maintain control of existing enterprise applications while moving the workloads into the cloud. Or you are looking to develop new applications using a **CSP** to host the workloads. The CSP will deploy an environment for your development team, which may consist of a Linux Enterprise Server, Apache Web Server, and MySQL database.

The servers, storage, and networking will be managed by the CSP, while developers will still have control and management of their applications.

Infrastructure as a service

Infrastructure as a service (**IaaS**) offers the best solution to enterprises who need to reduce capital expenditure but access a fully scalable data center. The cloud provider will need to provide power, **Heating, Ventilation, and Air Conditioning** (**HVAC**), and the physical hardware. But we will manage the day-to-day operations using management tools and **application programming interfaces** (**APIs**).

When using IaaS, you will have the most responsibility. You may be managing servers, VDI, access to storage, and controlling network flows. The hardware, however, is managed by the cloud provider.

You would not physically work in the cloud data center, so you cannot install a server in a rack or swap out a disk drive.

It is important to recognize the responsibilities of the CSP and the customer, using the three popular service models. *Figure 3.27* shows the responsibilities each party will have:

Service	Examples	Applications	Middleware	Virtualization	Data	Operating System	Networking	Runtime	Servers	Storage
SAAS	Adobe Connect, CRM, Microsoft 365, Moodle	CSP	CSP	CSP	CSP	CSP	CSP	CSP	CSP	CSP
PAAS	AWS Lambda, Redhat OpenShift, IBM Cloud Foundry	CR	CR	CSP	CSP	CSP	CSP	CSP	CSP	CSP
IAAS	Amazon Web Services (AWS), Microsoft Azure, Oracle Cloud Infrastructure (OCI)	CR	CR	CR	CR	CR	CR	CR	CSP	CSP
Key	CR = Customer's responsibility				CSP = Cloud Service Provider's responsibility					

Figure 3.27 – Cloud shared responsibility matrix

This service model matrix will help you to understand the various responsibilities when adopting a service model.

Cloud provider limitations

Most cloud-based services will make the best use of limited public IP addresses. You will most likely find that your virtual network has a **Network Address Translation** (**NAT**) gateway with a publicly accessible IP address, leaving you free to allocate your own preferred private addressing scheme. However, to facilitate fast low-latency connections between your hosted networks or a partner, it is not necessary to route traffic through a NAT to access other virtual networks hosted by the same CSP. In this instance, we will use **Virtual Private Cloud** (**VPC**) peering.

VPC peering allows connectivity between workloads within a single CSP or allows connectivity with other CSP tenants, such as B2B partners. The advantage of this approach is that traffic is not routed out to the edge of the CSP network and then back to another VPC. It is a much more efficient process whereby a low-latency connection is made directly between the VPCs. This can also be done between different regions. In *Figure 3.28*, we can see an example of VPC peering:

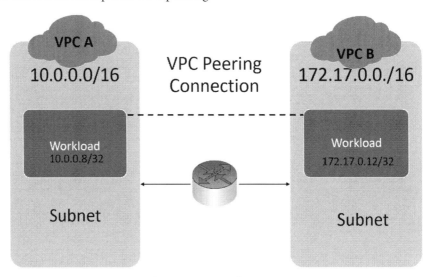

Figure 3.28 – VPC peering

VPC peering is useful for enterprises that need to connect multiple cloud-based workloads.

Extending appropriate on-premises controls

It is important to assess all risks when co-operating with a third-party CSP. Is your data secure? Will it be available? What accreditations does the provider have? Have they been audited by recognized authorities?

Micro-segmentation

Micro-segmentation is used to separate workloads, securely, in your data center or a hosted cloud data center. In practice, this means creating policies that restrict communication between workloads where there is no reason for east-west (server to server) traffic. Network zoning is an important concept and can dynamically restrict communication between the zones when a threat is detected.

Traditional security is based on north-south traffic (data moving through the network perimeter), but now we see thousands of workloads all being hosted within the same data center (inside the perimeter). Virtualization can allow a single hardware compute node to host thousands of VMs. By isolating these workloads using micro-segmentation, we can reduce the attack surface, isolate breaches, and implement more granular policies for given workloads. *Figure 3.29* shows an example of isolated workloads in the data center:

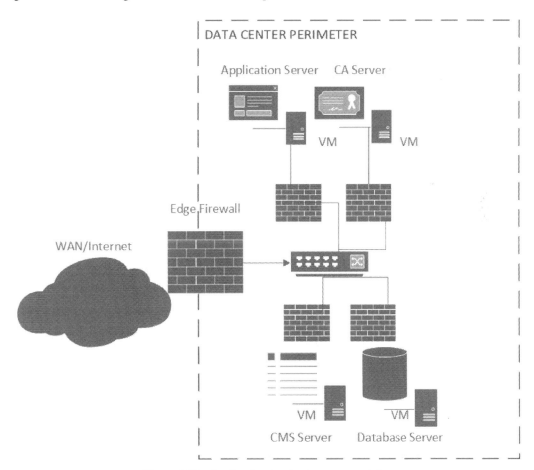

Figure 3.29 – Application-level micro-segmentation

The benefits of this approach is that each individual workload can be secured.

Benefits of micro-segmentation

Organizations that adopt micro-segmentation will gain the following benefits:

- It is a key element of zero-trust architecture.
- A reduced attack surface.
- Improved breach containment.
- Stronger regulatory compliance.
- Streamlined policy management.

Jump box

Remote management is a key requirement when managing on-premises and cloud-based data centers. Network assets will include servers and workloads with valuable data or may host **Industrial Control Systems** (**ICS**). To manage these environments, there is a requirement for highly specialized management tools. It would be difficult for an engineer to manage the SCADA systems and monitor sensitive systems without specialist tools hosted on the SCADA network. Likewise, network engineers may need to remote into the data center to offer 24/7 support on critical systems. One approach is to securely connect to a designated server that has secure access to the data center or ICSes. These servers will have the appropriate management tools already installed and the connection will be made from validated trusted external hosts. *Figure 3.30* shows an example of where a jump box would be deployed:

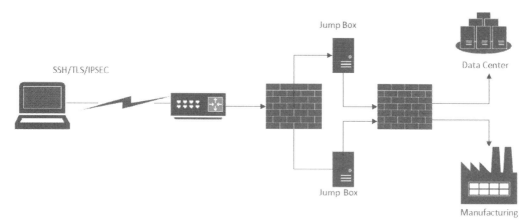

Figure 3.30 – Remote administration using a jump box

A Jump box ensures no code or software can be introduced to vulnerable network systems.

Examining cloud storage models

An enterprise will typically create and manage increasingly large volumes of heterogeneous data. We would expect the finance team to store spreadsheets and use finance databases, marketing may create promotional video clips, while transport and logistics planning will need access to graphing and locational data.

This mix of data types means that a single data store is usually not the most efficient approach. Instead, it's more effective to store different types of data in different data stores, each optimized for a specific workload or usage pattern. Therefore, it's important to understand the main storage models and the pros and cons of each model.

File-based storage

These are regular files that are used in a traditional client-server model. Examples would be user-mapped drives accessing shared folders on a NAS device or a file server. Other file types could be VMs hosted by a hypervisor platform.

Database storage

Databases are described as relational and consist of two-dimensional tables with rows and columns. A common vendor approach is to use **Structured Query Language** (**SQL**) for retrieving and managing data. This ensures that a record is added or updated only when it can be validated (ensuring the integrity of the data).

A **Relational Database Management System** (**RDBMS**) requires a schema, which will consist of *allowed objects* and *attributes*. All read or write operations must use the schema. Examples of relational databases include **Microsoft SQL**, **MySQL**, **PostgreSQL**, and **Oracle SQL**. In *Figure 3.31*, we can see a user object with associated attributes. This schema is used for the Active Directory database.

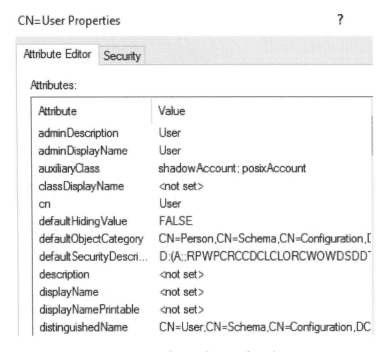

Figure 3.31 – Schema object and attributes

Relational databases support a schema to define objects and attributes allowed within the database.

Block storage

Block storage stores data in fixed-sized chunks called blocks. A block will only store a fragment of the data. This is typically used on a SAN iSCSI or **Fiber Channel** (**FC**). Requests are generated to find the correct address of the blocks; the blocks are then assembled to create the complete file. Block storage does not store any metadata with the blocks. Its primary strength is fast performance, but the application and storage need to be local (ideally on a SAN). Performance will degrade if the application and blocks are farther apart. This storage is typically used by database applications.

Blob storage

Object storage is optimized for storing and retrieving large binary objects (**images, files, video** and **audio streams, large application data objects** and **documents**, and **virtual machine disk images**). To optimize searching through these stores, metadata tags can be linked to a file. These may be customizable by the user (it would be difficult to search through the raw data of a video image). These stores are ideal for large files and large data stores as they will be very scalable.

Key/value pairs

A key/value pair is useful for storing identifiers and values. It is a useful storage type for configuration files or hash lookups, such as rainbow table or any kind of lookup table.

This may be useful when performing a compliance scan. The database could contain a series of identifiers and the actual value it is expecting to be set.

Summary

In this chapter, you have gained an understanding of the security considerations when hosting data on-premises and off-premises. You learned how an enterprise will implement secure resource provisioning and deprovisioning, and the differences between type 1 and type 2 hypervisors. We then looked at containerization and learned how to choose an appropriate cloud deployment model. Then we learned the differences between the different cloud service models and gained an understanding of micro-segmentation and VPC peering, which will help us to select the correct storage model based on the storage technologies offered by cloud providers.

In this chapter, you have acquired the following skills:

- An understanding of how to implement data loss prevention
- An understanding of how to implement data loss detection
- An understanding of what is meant by data protection
- An understanding of how to implement secure cloud and virtualization solutions
- An understanding of the cloud deployment models available
- An understanding of the storage models available in cloud environments

In the next chapter, we will learn about managing identities using authentication and authorization, including **Multi-Factor Authentication (MFA)**, **Single Sign-On (SSO)**, and **Identity Federation**.

8 Enterprise Data Security, Including Secure Cloud and Virtualization Solutions

Questions

Here are a few questions to test your understanding of the chapter:

1. What security setting is it when Group Policy prevents my flash drive from being recognized by my Windows computer?

    A. Watermarking

    B. Blocking the use of external media

    C. Print blocking

    D. Data classification blocking

2. What stops me from capturing bank account details using my mobile banking app?

    A. Watermarking

    B. Blocking the use of external media

    C. Print blocking

    D. Data classification blocking

3. What stops me from printing on my home printer when accessing my work computer using RDP?

    A. Watermarking

    B. Blocking the use of external media

    C. Restricted VDI

    D. Data classification blocking

4. Ben has asked a colleague to collaborate on a project by connecting remotely to his desktop. What would prevent this from happening?

    A. Remote Desktop

    B. Protocol (RDP) blocking

    C. Clipboard privacy controls

    D. Web Application Firewall

5. How can you reduce the risk of administrators installing unauthorized applications during RDP admin sessions?

    A. Remote Desktop

    B. Protocol (RDP) blocking

C. Clipboard privacy controls

D. Web Application Firewall

6. How can I ensure that my sales team can send quotations and business contracts out to customers, but not send confidential company data?

A. Data classification blocking

B. Data loss detection

C. Watermarking

D. Clipboard privacy controls

7. The CISO needs to know who has been sharing *signed-out* company confidential documents on a public web server. How can this be done?

A. Data classification blocking

B. Data loss detection

C. Watermarking

D. Clipboard privacy controls

8. Jenny wants to share a useful business-related video file with her colleague, but when Charles attempts to play it using the same player and codecs it cannot be viewed. What is the most likely cause?

A. DRM

B. Deep packet inspection

C. Network traffic analysis

D. Watermarking

9. What allows a forensics investigator to discover the time and location that a digital image was taken?

A. Metadata

B. Obfuscation

C. Tokenization

D. Scrubbing

10. What may have allowed a rogue administrator to remove evidence from the access logs?

   A. Scrubbing

   B. Metadata

   C. Obfuscation

   D. Tokenization

11. What stops the bank support desk personnel from accessing Ben's 16-digit VISA card number and CVC code?

   A. Metadata

   B. Obfuscation

   C. Key pairs

   D. Masking

12. What ensures that medical researchers cannot unwittingly share PHI data from medical records?

   A. Anonymization

   B. Encryption

   C. Metadata

   D. Obfuscation

13. What allows an organization to manage business data from the moment it is stored to final destruction?

   A. Data life cycle

   B. Containers

   C. Metadata

   D. Storage area network

14. What is another name for a *bare-metal* hypervisor deployed in a data center?

   A. Type 1

   B. Emulation

   C. Type 2

   D. Containers

15. What allows the isolation of workloads, allowing easy migration between vendor platforms?

    A. Type 1

    B. Emulation

    C. Type 2

    D. Containers

16. What allows Amy to play 16-bit Nintendo console games on her Windows desktop computer?

    A. Emulation

    B. Middleware

    C. PaaS

    D. Database storage

17. What allows a legacy Microsoft office application to run on Ben's desktop alongside Microsoft Office 365 applications?

    A. Application virtualization

    B. Database storage

    C. Middleware

    D. PaaS

18. How can we make sure that when a user leaves the organization, we can re-assign their software licenses to the new user?

    A. Deprovisioning

    B. IaaS

    C. Emulation

    D. Off-site backups

19. What type of data is used to provide information about data?

    A. Metadata

    B. Indexes

    C. Emulation

    D. Off-site backups

20. What is the primary reason that a small family coffee shop business would choose a public cloud model?

    A. Cost

    B. Scalability

    C. Resources

    D. Location

21. What type of cloud customer am I likely supporting if I am offering a private cloud and customers require that I have the **Federal Risk and Authorization Management Program** (**FedRAMP**) attestation?

    A. Government

    B. Finance

    C. Utility company

    D. Small online retailer

22. What is used to describe the situation when multiple customers are hosted on a common hardware platform?

    A. Multi-tenant

    B. Platform sharing

    C. Single tenant

    D. Service model

23. What type of cloud service model would be used when buying 50 licenses to access a **customer relationship management** (**CRM**) application?

    A. SaaS

    B. PaaS

    C. IaaS

    D. Security as a service (SecaaS)

24. What type of cloud service model would be used when I need to host my in-house **enterprise resource planning** (**ERP**) suite with a CSP?

    A. SaaS

    B. PaaS)

    C. IaaS

    D. d) SecaaS

25. What type of cloud service model would be used when the Acme corporation needs to deploy and manage 500 VDI instances across four geographical regions?

    A. SaaS

    B. PaaS

    C. IaaS

    D. SecaaS

26. What will my CSP configure so that I have direct communication between multiple instances of VPC?

    A. IPSEC tunnel

    B. VPN

    C. Inter-domain routing

    D. VPC peering

27. What kind of storage model would be best for images, files, video, and audio streams?

    A. File-based storage

    B. Database storage

    C. Block storage

    D. Blob storage

    E. Key/value pairs

28. What kind of storage model would be provided on a **storage area network (SAN)**?

    A. File-based storage

    B. Database storage

    C. Block storage

    D. Blob storage

    E. Key/value pairs

29. What kind of storage model would be useful when performing a compliance scan and the database could contain a series of identifiers and the actual value it is expecting to be set?

    A. File-based storage

    B. Database storage

C. Block storage

D. Blob storage

E. Key/value pairs

30. What is used when a customer is considering their responsibilities when buying in-cloud services.

A. A coud-shared responsibility matrix

B. A cloud-shared cost matrix

C. FedRAMP

D. Platform sharing

Answers

1. B

2. C

3. C

4. B

5. C

6. A

7. C

8. A

9. A

10. A

11. D

12. A

13. A

14. A

15. D

16. A

17. A

18. A

19. A

20. A

21. A

22. A

23. A

24. B

25. C

26. D

27. D

28. C

29. E

30. A

4

Deploying Enterprise Authentication and Authorization Controls

Large enterprises often have very complex environments to manage. There are internal users to manage, there are internal services and external service providers. There are customers to consider, for guest users, within **Business-to-Business (B2B)** relationships. Federation services can be utilized to ensure robust, centralized authentication and access control are addressed in these hybrid environments. To manage all these interactions with information systems, the correct protocols must be chosen to make sure we have secure authentication and authorization. Many modern environments require the use of an additional factor as a single factor, such as just a user password, is known to be weak. In this chapter, you will learn how to effectively select the appropriate solution.

In this chapter, we will go through the following topics:

- Credential management
- Identity federation
- Access control
- Authentication and authorization protocols
- Using **Multi-Factor Authentication** (**MFA**)

Credential management

Credential management is critical for an enterprise. We must consider the day-to-day management of user credentials, including effective management of passwords. We must ensure passwords are created, stored, and destroyed securely. They must always be processed securely as well.

Single Sign-On (SSO)

The goal of SSO is to allow users to use a single account to access many services. This relies on robust authentication so ties in nicely with MFA. The weakness of SSO would be the account credentials being stolen. It is important to protect the account. SSO is very convenient for users. They must only remember one set of credentials.

> **Tip**
> When you sign in to Google to access Gmail, Google Docs, and content on YouTube, you will only need to sign in once with your Google account.

Password repository applications

Organization goals should include the use of SSO wherever possible. This allows a single account to be used for multiple applications or services. This goal, however, is not always achievable as some online service providers may not support SSO and insist upon creating local accounts. To allow users to store these additional accounts with passwords in a safe way, a local secure password repository can be used. Microsoft provides Credential Manager; Apple provides iCloud Keychain. This allows the use of a secure vault to store the required account password and transmit it to the application when required. See *Figure 4.1* for a depiction of Microsoft Credential Manager:

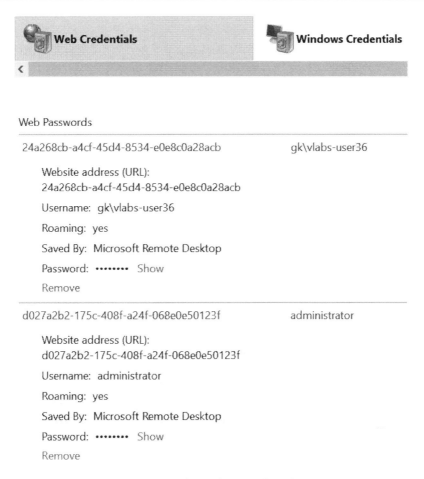

Figure 4.1 – Microsoft Windows Credential Manager

It is important to have a secure, easy-to-use container for authentication credentials.

On-premises versus cloud password repository

As hybrid cloud models become the new normal for a business, they present a challenge for secure credential management. Should passwords be stored with the cloud provider? It is worth considering many cloud providers will have **advanced access control**, **behavioral analytics**, and **continuous validation** as part of their security offering. However, there is often a choice to use federation when accessing cloud-based services. When using Microsoft 365 services, it is possible to manage all identities *on-premises*, including passwords, and gain federated access to cloud portals.

Federation will be covered in detail in the *Identity federation* section.

Hardware key manager

Traditional password management software relies on the local operating system and stores the keys locally. Another option is for a hardware key manager that is quite popular and is relatively low cost but offers additional security just like having a separate smart card. A hardware key will typically support strong encryption algorithms to protect passwords. These devices may include tamper protection, erasing the contents after a number of failed attempts. *Figure 4.2* shows a hardware implementation of a key manager:

Figure 4.2 – Hardware key manager

When we look at the use of multiple accounts that are privileged, there are better-managed solutions to handle this requirement.

Privileged access management

Privilege access management systems are very useful for allowing an employee to log in with their individual account and when necessary, they can check out an elevated credential password. This system will also allow the use of a shared account, but still makes that user accountable because their access to that privileged account will have been logged against their individual user account. This is even more useful nowadays as many organizations have hybrid cloud models, where we need to administrate on-premises and then with multiple cloud providers.

Password policies

Password policies need to be enabled to make sure that users will change their passwords based on the organization's requirements. Passwords can be chosen to have a certain level of complexity and/or meet a minimum character length. Password complexity is used to enforce the use of different character classes (uppercase, lowercase, numbers, and special characters: @ ~ # ! " £ € % &). It is also important to have a password history so that users cannot reuse old passwords. Guidance has changed over recent years. Instead of enforcing *super-complex* passwords, it is accepted that **Two-Factor Authentication** (**2FA**) or MFA is the preferred option to protect identities. A long passphrase is proven to be much more secure overall than a complex password. To enforce password requirements, we could use a policy such as the one shown in *Figure 4.3*:

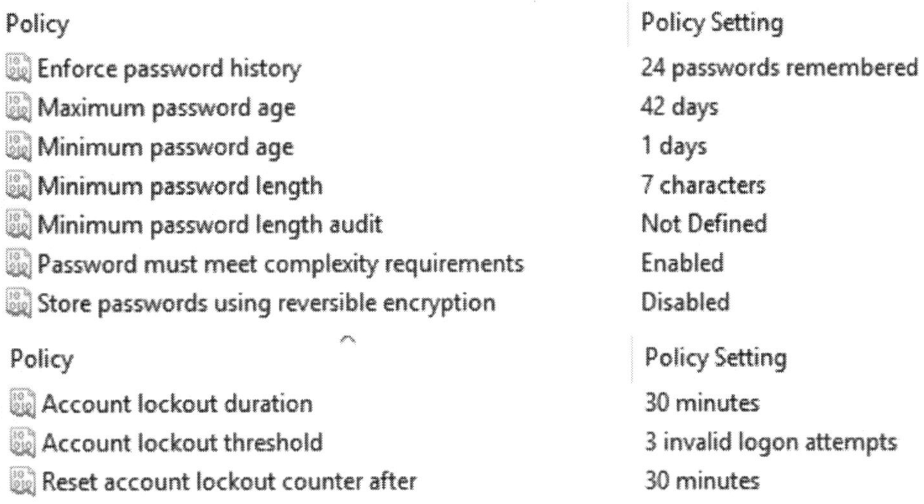

Policy	Policy Setting
Enforce password history	24 passwords remembered
Maximum password age	42 days
Minimum password age	1 days
Minimum password length	7 characters
Minimum password length audit	Not Defined
Password must meet complexity requirements	Enabled
Store passwords using reversible encryption	Disabled

Policy	Policy Setting
Account lockout duration	30 minutes
Account lockout threshold	3 invalid logon attempts
Reset account lockout counter after	30 minutes

Figure 4.3 – Microsoft Group Policy password settings

If we do not have a baseline password requirements policy, users may choose weak passwords.

Password complexity

Password requirements will often have a requirement for complexity. This will require at least three from four character classes: uppercase, lowercase, numbers, and special characters.

Password length

Eight characters is generally recommended as the minimum length of a password; any greater than this and users will adopt bad practices, such as repeating the password to meet this requirement, for example, `Bertie26Bertie26`.

Password history

Password history is important. Without password history, compromised accounts may be reset to the original password, allowing the attackers to gain access to the account again.

Password maximum/minimum age

It is important to have a password minimum age as without a password minimum age, users may reset their passwords multiple times to get back to the original password. A password maximum age, however, is not really recommended anymore. Requiring users to change their password frequently (often every 30, 60, or 90 days) can sometimes mean they choose a weak password by simply incrementing a sequential number at the end of the old password. The passwords that are then chosen are often a poor choice and are vulnerable to attack. Also consider the fact that a compromised password is exploited immediately.

Password auditing

Password auditing is important as it allows the organization to check for weak passwords. Password checking can be done when users reset their passwords. We could use a dictionary word list to generate hashes and check that the users are not using those weak passwords. The **National Cyber Security Center** (**NCSC**) has listed 100,000 passwords taken from `https://haveibeenpwned.com`. The list can be found at the following link: `https://www.ncsc.gov.uk/static-assets/documents/PwnedPasswordsTop100k.txt`. The first 20 words from the list are shown in *Figure 4.4*:

```
123456
123456789
qwerty
password
111111
12345678
abc123
1234567
password1
12345
1234567890
123123
000000
iloveyou
1234
1q2w3e4r5t
qwertyuiop
123
monkey
dragon
```

Figure 4.4 – Password wordlist

If you find any of your passwords that are in use shown in this list, you should change them immediately.

Reversible encryption

Passwords should be stored in a secured format within a password database. They are normally hashed, prior to being written into the database. Password reversible encryption allows passwords to be stored in a plain text format. This is used for some legacy applications (perhaps a remote access management solution). These should never be used. An example would be Microsoft **Remote Access Service** (**RAS**). This allows users to be authenticated using **Challenge Handshake Authentication Protocol** (**CHAP**).

As well as being able to authenticate user accounts within our own sites, it is also important to work with external entities.

Identity federation

Identity federation allows you to use your identity with a third party. Many organizations will use services in the cloud such as software as a service. This allows the user to use SSO in their own enterprise and when accessing these third-party applications. Users only need to remember one identity. Typically, a token will be generated by an identity federation service and passed securely to the third party. Microsoft provides a service called **Active Directory Federation Services (ADFS)**, which allows an authenticated enterprise user to use their credentials on a third-party site. They support many of the standard protocols in use out there including **Security Assertion Markup Language (SAML)**.

Transitive trust

Transitive trust can be very useful within complex enterprise environments. When using directory services, we can create security boundaries referred to as domains or Kerberos realms. It is common to create these boundaries to separate account management geographically. For example, a bicycle manufacturer has a Taiwanese engineering and production plant in Taipei. They have sales, marketing, and distribution in Santa Cruz, US, which is the head office, and the same business function in Morzine, France. Each location has a separate domain, with the US being the root and Taiwan and France being child domains. In *Figure 4.5*, we can see the trust relationships between the domains:

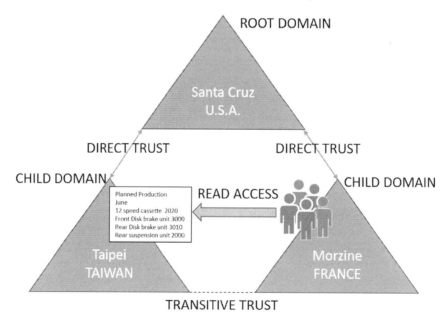

Figure 4.5 – Transitive trust

There are direct trusts between the root domain and the child domains. There is, however, transitive trust between the two child domains. The relationship is similar to the concept of an authenticated **Internet Protocol Security** (**IPsec**) tunnel. An administrator would still need to provision access to resources, but there would be inherent trust between all parts of the organization. The sales team could then be given read privileges to production data from the manufacturing plant.

OpenID

Cloud-based **Identity Providers** (**IdPs**) such as Google, Facebook, and Twitter support a standard called OpenID. This is often used to access third-party services (referred to as the **Relying Party** (**RP**)) who support this standard. The current standard is version 2.0, and it is administered by the OpenID Foundation, a non-profit entity.

Once an identity has been validated by the OpenID provider, a secure token is generated and forwarded to the requesting service provider in the form of a **JavaScript Object Notation Web Token** (**JWT**). *Figure 4.6* shows the OpenID SSO process:

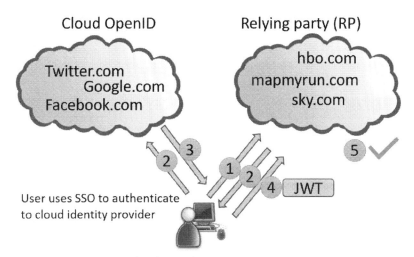

1. User accesses cloud portal
2. Users' browser is redirected back to OpenID provider
3. OpenID provider creates JWT (user is not prompted, they already signed in)
4. Token is sent to relying party (RP)
5. JWT is validated, and access granted

Figure 4.6 – OpenID process

While OpenID is standard for cloud-based identities, there are other options used when enterprise users access third-party corporate portals.

Security Assertion Markup Language (SAML)

SAML is an open standard typically used to access corporate cloud-based portals for access to applications. It requires an IdP. The IdP will typically use directory services internally; the service provider will be the cloud entity. The service provider will require a secure token generated by the IdP. It also makes the experience for the user transparent, makes it easy for them to access third-party services, and supports SSO. Microsoft allows SAML to authenticate identities to Microsoft 365 services. SAML actually creates assertions. It uses the XML language and is secure. Assertions could include authentication attributes and authorization decisions.

The experience will be completely transparent to the user if they have already authenticated with the IdP:

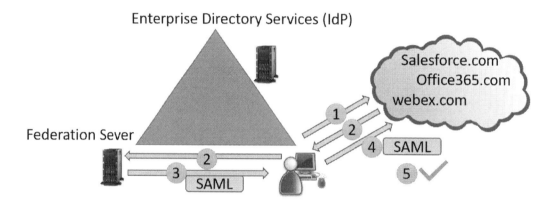

1. User accesses cloud portal   **FEDERATION SERVICES**
2. Users' browser is redirected back to IdP Federation Server
3. Federation Server creates SAML token (user is not prompted, they already signed in)
4. Token is sent to SP (Service Provider)
5. Token is validated and access granted

Figure 4.7 – SAML

SAML is a good choice for accessing third-party corporate portals.

Shibboleth

Shibboleth is similar to SAML. It is, however, used mainly by educational establishments such as colleges and universities. It also allows for SSO by passing a token to the service provider and requires an IdP.

Once we have authenticated accounts, we may give access to resources.

Access control

Access control can be used to control authorization once a user has been authenticated. There may be many different requirements; for example, developers may need to share their code with one another. There may be requirements for very strict access control when there are sensitive documents that must be accessed. There may be a requirement to give privileges and rights to administrative role holders or perhaps to give fine-grained access based upon the location or the country of origin of the account holder. In the following section, we will investigate these choices.

Mandatory Access Control (MAC)

MAC is generally seen as the most secure way of controlling access to assets. It requires clearance levels. It requires the data to be classified or labeled. It can be time-consuming but offers the most security. Government agencies such as the Department of Defense and other such entities will typically use this system. *Figure 4.8* shows the classification options for a filesystem folder:

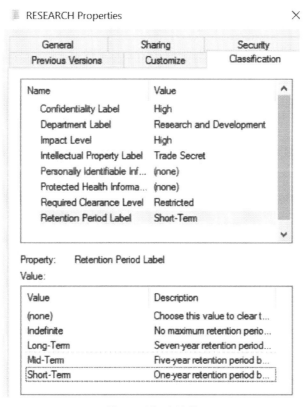

Figure 4.8 – MAC

It is important to ensure strict adherence to a MAC framework; no **write down** and no **read up** (this stops a user with a lower clearance level from seeing data they are not cleared for).

Discretionary Access Control (DAC)

DAC means the authorization to the resource is controlled by the owner. This works well in the Windows NTFS filesystem where the owner of a file or a folder can assign permissions to other users or groups. This allows for decentralization. Another good example could be a SharePoint portal. While ownership is assigned to a team leader, they can then add their co-workers to give them access to the site:

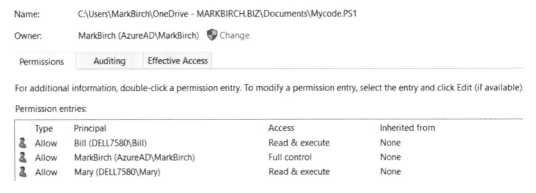

Figure 4.9 – DAC

DAC could work well for smaller integrated teams (such as developers).

Role-based access control

Role-based access control can be used with existing roles, such as administrators, network configuration operators, and backup operators, or groups can be created for business units such as sales, marketing, production, and research. Role-based access control is centralized. It requires the administration to be done centrally. It works well with directory services. In *Figure 4.10*, we can see a list of Microsoft Active Directory groups. There are built-in role groups such as `Cert Publishers` and `DHCP Administrators`. Bill and Ben have been added to the `ITAdmin` group:

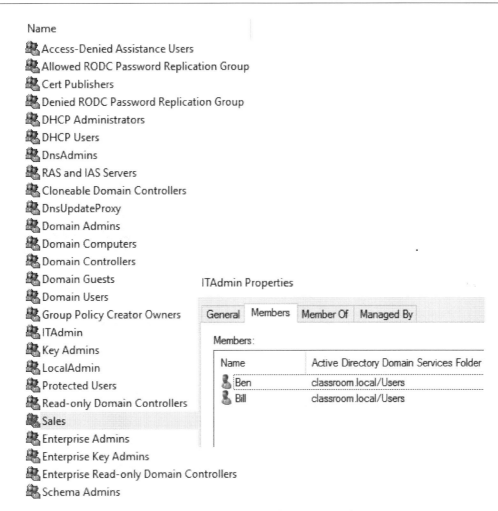

Figure 4.10 – Role-based access control

Roles or groups are commonly used to manage a large enterprise user base and are considered a good way to implement the best practice of least privilege.

Rule-based access control

Rule-based access control can be good for things where we need a common set of controls; for example, a particular department may require all their users to only work within certain hours or the requirement is that certain users can only log on from certain workstations. In *Figure 4.11*, we can see two student accounts have limited logon hours and can only log on from two workstations (`intern01` and `intern02`):

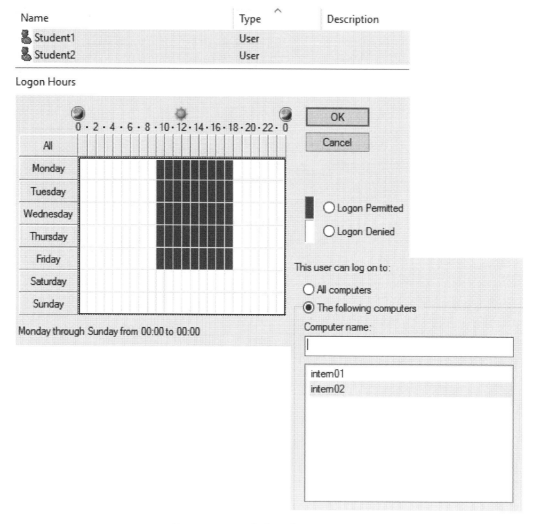

Figure 4.11 – Rule-based access control

Rules can be very useful when we have a set of requirements to assign to multiple accounts.

Attribute-based access control

Attribute-based access control offers another level of granularity. It also works well with directory services. Attributes are associated with objects; for example, a user can have a department or a country attribute associated with their account. These attributes could be used to give more granular access to resources. For example, you may have research data that can only be accessed by scientists in the US. You could put extra controls in place so that members of the **Scientists** group can only access the data if they have **United States** as the country on their Active Directory user account:

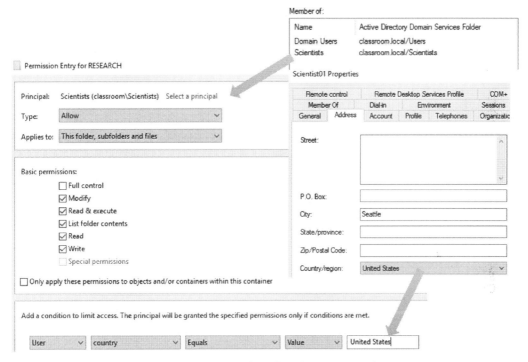

Figure 4.12 – Attribute-based access control

In order to capture user credentials and authorize access to resources, there are industry-standard approaches.

Authentication and authorization protocols

There are many protocols associated with authentication and authorization in an enterprise. A common approach will be to log on within the domain using directory services. This may use Kerberos as an SSO protocol. In other cases, we must look at solutions where this is not possible. Remote access could be an example, or securing access to the network using the new zero-trust approach. In this section, we will take a look at the available protocols.

Remote Authentication Dial-In User Server (RADIUS)

RADIUS is a well-supported **Authentication, Authorization, and Accounting (AAA)** protocol. This is used to gain access to networks, so it could be used to grant access over a **Virtual Private Network (VPN)** or anything that will require remote access. Radius could also be used to gain access to a switch that is **Ethernet 802.1 X**-compliant. This could also be used to gain access to a **Wireless Access Point (WAP)**. AAA allows the RADIUS client (network device) to pass on authentication requests to the AAA server. The server will often pass these requests back to a directory services server, as RADIUS may not actually hold the user account database. RADIUS supports two networking protocols or port numbers. It can operate on UDP port 1812 or UDP port 1645 (this is normally used by Cisco). *Figure 4.13* shows clients (supplicants) accessing networks through 802.1x-compliant RADIUS clients:

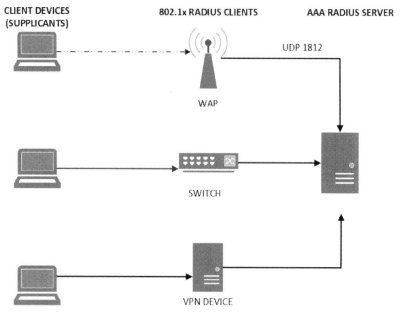

Figure 4.13 – AAA services

While RADIUS is the most widely adopted AAA protocol, there are other solutions.

Terminal Access Controller Access Control System (TACACS)

TACACS was originally developed in 1984 and was very common on UNIX networks for the purpose of authenticating access to a network. It has been further developed by Cisco and the current standard is TACACS+. This has no compatibility with earlier versions. TACACS is like RADIUS but does not have as wide support as RADIUS. It uses TCP ports for AAA, making it more reliable, and it is said to be more secure because it encrypts the entire authentication process (it uses TCP port 49).

Diameter

Diameter is the next version of RADIUS. It is based upon RADIUS but uses TCP ports to make the connection and the authentication more reliable. It has wide support from many vendors. It has been assigned TCP port 3868.

Lightweight Directory Access Protocol (LDAP)

LDAP is a standard for accessing directory services. It was chosen as an alternative to **Directory Access Protocol (DAP)**, as it is more straightforward. LDAP allows for access to directory services and the creation of content, such as user accounts, computer accounts, and other types of objects in directory services. It is usually used to administer directory services. It is defined in RFC 4511. LDAP uses port 389 for regular access. Alternatively, we can use **Transport Layer Security (TLS)**. This uses TCP port 636 and allows for the connection to be secured (LDAPS). *Figure 4.14* shows the typical administration of objects in an LDAP database. In this instance, we are resetting a user password and creating a new user account:

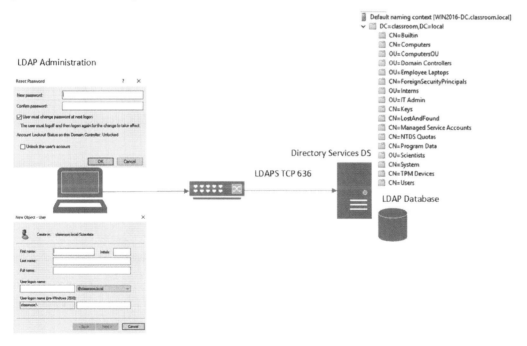

Figure 4.14 – LDAP services

LDAP does not provide the authentication for the user login.

Kerberos

Kerberos is a secure SSO protocol that was developed by the **Massachusetts Institute of Technology** (**MIT**) and is protected by export restrictions to use within the US. This is now supported by the **Internet Engineering Task Force** (**IETF**) and has been assigned several RFCs defining the implementation (RFC 3961, 3962, 4120, and 4121). Kerberos is in widespread use and is supported by many operating system vendors, including Red Hat, Oracle, and IBM. It has been the standard for Microsoft Active Directory services for over 20 years. Kerberos supports encrypted communication and anti-replay. Kerberos is very time-dependent. It is important that the clocks are in synchronization; otherwise, Kerberos authentication will fail. *Figure 4.15* shows the Kerberos SSO mechanism. The server hosting the **Key Distribution Center** (**KDC**) and **Ticket Granting Services** (**TCS**) could be a Windows **Domain Controller** (**DC**) running **Active Directory services**:

1. Client requests a Ticket Granting Ticket (TGT)
2. The KDC verifies the credentials and sends back an encrypted TGT
3. The client sends the TGT to the TGS and requests a Service Ticket (ST)
4. ST is sent to client
5. ST is sent to server hosting services
6. client is able to access service

Key Distribution Center KDC
Ticket Granting Service TGS

1 ben@acme.com

3 TGT

ST 4

2 TGT

Member Server Hosting Data

5 ST

6

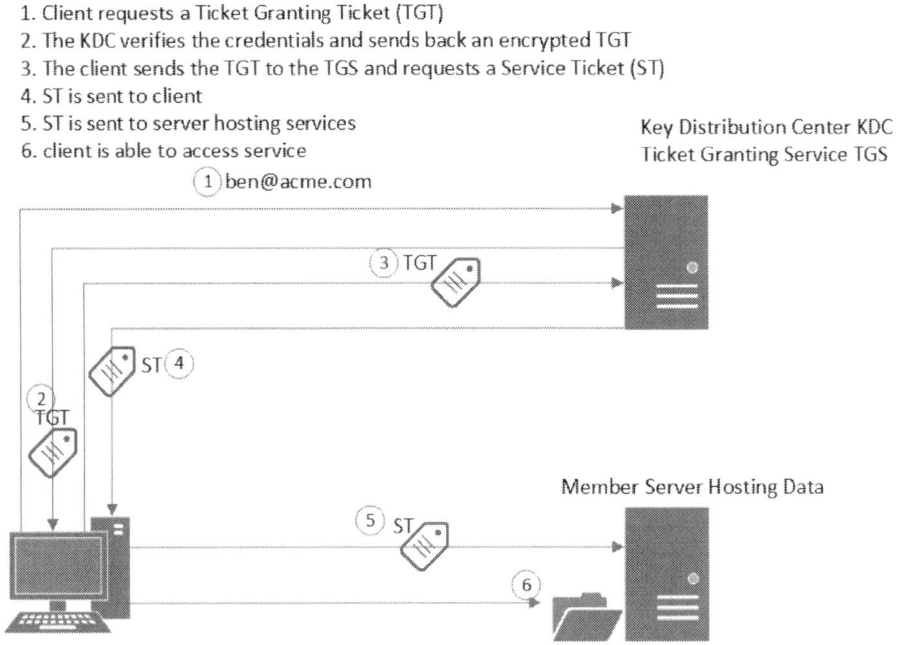

Figure 4.15 – Kerberos authentication

Kerberos is used on enterprise networks but is not used when accessing third-party sites or B2B partners.

OAuth

OAuth allows for SSO. Users can sign in to their **OpenID** provider such as Facebook, Google, or Twitter and they can access third-party services. Users do not need to remember multiple credentials. It is used by many service providers, including Microsoft, Tripadvisor, Hotels.com, and many merchant sites requiring payment authorization. There are currently two versions of **Open Authorization** (**OAuth**): V1 and V2. OAuth V2 is the current standard. PayPal would be a good example of a system we use every day. If you make a payment on a merchant site and you choose to use PayPal, you will end up being prompted to authorize that payment. A token will be securely generated by PayPal and sent to the merchant site. This will authorize the transaction.

Figure 4.16 shows typical sites supporting SSO using OAuth:

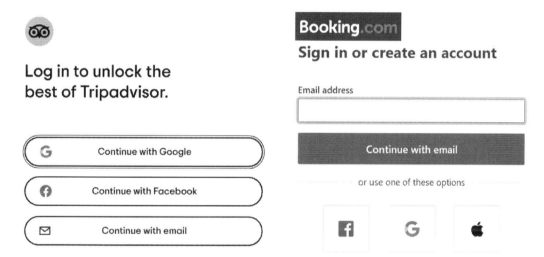

Figure 4.16 – OAuth SSO dialogs

Once you have indicated the account that is to be used, the connection can be transparently made in the future.

> **Important Note**
> OAuth defines the flow of requests and responses to authorize a transaction, while OpenID defines the role of the IdP.

802.1X

802.1X is an Ethernet standard. It defines **Port-Based Access Control** (**PBAC**). It can allow devices or users to be authenticated to a network connection and is supported on switches, remote-access VPNs, and WAPs. It can be easily configured with the use of **Public Key Infrastructure** (**PKI**) certificates. Certificates can be assigned to devices such as computers, mobile devices, IoT devices, and network printers. A wide variety of devices can be connected securely to networks, removing the need for actual credentials to be typed in.

Extensible Authentication Protocol (EAP)

EAP is a framework. This allows more secure authentication methods to be implemented when using PBAC. PBAC is implemented when network devices support **802.1x Ethernet standards**. For more details, see *Chapter 1*, *Designing a Secure Network Architecture*.

Tip

For the certification exam, it is important to recognize the appropriate authentication protocols to provide both security and compatibility within complex enterprise networks.

A single factor for authentication is always a risk. Compromise of a password may be all that is needed for hackers to take control of an account. Having a second factor is the best protection against this threat.

Multi-Factor Authentication (MFA)

MFA is becoming an important consideration for many enterprises as passwords alone are not considered secure enough. Guidance from the NCSC in the United Kingdom recommends that MFA should be used to counter the threat of compromised passwords. Microsoft strongly promotes the use of MFA when accessing their cloud services. It is becoming more and more straightforward to implement multiple factors; for example, Microsoft automatically supports the use of smart cards with Active Directory accounts. There are many third-party solution providers offering mobile authenticator apps. We will take a look at some of the choices in the following sections.

Two-Factor Authentication (2FA)

2FA simply means using two different methods or two different factors during the authentication process. You must combine two different factors. Factors are assigned a unique identifier (there are five factors: Type I through to Type V).

The factors include the following:

- **Type I** – **Something you know**: Password, pin, birthday
- **Type II** – **Something you have**: Token, smart card, RFID card
- **Type III** – **Something you are**: Retina, iris, fingerprint, facial recognition
- **Type IV** – **Somewhere you are** IP address, GPS
- **Type V** – **Something you do**: Gait, handwriting, keystrokes

> Tip
>
> Two factors could be password and smart card, pin and ATM card, or biometrics and a physical token such as an RFID card. One of each type (Type I and Type III, for example) is required.

Additional authentication can be triggered by a change of context; maybe you logged in from a new location, or from a device that you have never logged in from before.

Two-step verification

Two-step verification is supported by many online IdPs. Think about when you log in to Google from a new workstation you have never signed in from before. You would receive a push notification in your Google app on your smartphone and need to respond:

Figure 4.17 – Two-step verification

When using two-step verification, it is preferable to use a second channel. Imagine a fraudster phished the credentials of a user. They would have to gain control of something else as well, such as the user's smartphone.

In-band authentication

In-band authentication would mean doing all the necessary authentication checks using a single channel, such as your internet browser connection to your bank. This would be seen as inferior to other mechanisms. Reliance on in-band authentication makes the possibility of **Cross-Site Request Forgery** (**CSRF/XSRF**) very real. Imagine you are connected to your bank and have logged on with your user account and password. A malicious script could authorize a payment to a criminal.

Out-of-Band Authentication (OOBA)

OOBA would require the use of a secondary channel, such as when you log in to your bank, you receive an SMS message on your smartphone, or when you log in to your Google account, you are asked to verify your identity using your smartphone. Your bank will use OOBA to send you an authorization request, to prevent fraud.

One-Time Password (OTP)

OTPs mean you are prompted for a password that you did not previously know or set; this is typically a password that is generated for you for one-time use where you must enter a strong password for future use to continue.

HMAC-based One-Time Password (HOTP)

HMAC-based systems generate OTPs on demand. The device will have a seed or a key. It will generate codes or passwords based upon an incrementing counter. These passwords do not have to be used immediately, which means this could be less secure. HMAC OTPs do not always have to be used sequentially, which means this system could be exploited.

Time-based One-Time Password (TOTP)

TOTPs are based on the same principle as HMAC-based OTPs. There is a key that will be embedded into your token (or smart app) that creates codes based upon the current time. The password will only be relevant for 30 seconds (although this set time can vary); then, a new password will be generated. This reduces the chances of passwords being compromised. *Figure 4.18* shows an RSA SecurID token device:

Figure 4.18 – RSA SecurID token ("File:RSA SecurID Token Old.jpg" by Alexander Klink is licensed with CC BY 3.0: https://creativecommons.org/licenses/by/3.0)

Time synchronization with the authentication server is important. This type of MFA is very popular and with more and more online digital identities to manage, you need to ensure access is secured to these online portals. When you complete your tax returns, you can secure this with MFA TOTP or connect to your bank to perform electronic banking. *Figure 4.19* shows typical TOTP prompts:

Figure 4.19 – MFA using TOTP

There are many other solutions allowing for secure attestation.

Hardware root of trust

A hardware root of trust is a secure container. A good example would be a hardware implementation of a security module such as the **Trusted Platform Module (TPM)** incorporated into many modern computer systems. This allows for values to be stored that could be used for secure boot, as we can validate the information that is stored in that container. We can use it to store cryptographic keys for **BitLocker Drive Encryption**, providing security while encrypting and decrypting drives.

TPM can store other types of information that can be used to validate or attest that certain conditions or information are correct. It is used for mobile device management, as we can store software and hardware values in a secure container. If we trust that container, we can extract the information from that hardware root of trust. When you enable BitLocker with TPM support, you will need to configure additional settings, as in *Figure 4.20*:

How do you want to back up your recovery key?

ⓘ Some settings are managed by your system administrator.

A recovery key can be used to access your files and folders if you're having problems unlocking your PC. It's a good idea to have more than one and keep each in a safe place other than your PC.

→ Save to your Azure AD account

→ Save to a file

→ Print the recovery key

Figure 4.20 – Hardware root of trust

Users will be able to remember a single set of credentials more easily. Whenever we ask users to authenticate with multiple sets of credentials, we introduce the risk of unsecured user behaviors.

JWT

JWT is based upon an open standard (RFC 7519). It is used for securely sending information between parties where a secure trusted payload is important. The attestation service will validate a piece of information so this could be very useful within a cloud environment where we are not already directly trusting one another. Microsoft could be the attestation provider; they will sign a requestors information package and if the third party trusts Microsoft's attestation service, they will be able to trust the JWT. It is a similar concept to PKI; if you trust the root CA, then you automatically trust certificates generated within that hierarchy. JWTs can be used for both attestation and identity proofing. A common use of JWT is when using federation services such as **OpenID** and **OAuth V2**.

Summary

In this chapter, we have studied the challenges large enterprises face when they must support complex environments, needing to manage internal users and their authentication to external service providers. We have looked at the role of federation services, to ensure robust authentication and access control are addressed in hybrid environments. We have looked at the use of MFA as a single factor is known to be weak. We have studied the options to ensure authentication is needed to gain access to a network.

In this chapter, you have gained the following skills:

- Securely managing credentials
- Understood the situations that require identity federation
- Examined access control models
- Understood authentication and authorization protocols
- Examined the choices for MFA

These core skills will be useful as we move into the next domain: security operations.

Questions

Here are a few questions to test your understanding of the chapter:

1. What is the container on a Windows operating system that allows the secure storage of user credentials and passwords?

    A.   Password repository application

    B.   Credential Manager

    C.   iCloud Keychain

    D.   End user password storage

2. What security would be provided for the storage of passwords in a cloud repository? Choose three.

    A.   Advanced access control

    B.   Behavioral analytics

    C.   Continuous validation

    D.   Reversible encryption

3. What type of device allows the secure retention of user passwords?

    A.   Hardware key manager

    B.   Removable storage

    C.   Password policies

    D.   iCloud Keychain

4. What management solution allows auditing of privileged accounts and *checkout* of these credentials?

    A.   Password policies

    B.   Privileged access management

    C.   Password complexity

    D.   Password auditing

5. What password policy will ensure a password cannot be reused? Choose two.

    A.   Password length

    B.   Password reuse

    C.   Password complexity

    D.   Password history

6. What password policy would most likely force Bill to change his password from flowerpot to F10w€rPot?

    A.   Password length

    B.   Password reuse

    C.   Password complexity

    D.   Password history

7. What password policy will ensure Mary cannot spend her lunch break resetting her password 24 times to make it the original password?

    A.   Minimum password age

    B.   Maximum password age

    C.   Password complexity

    D.   Password history

8. How can you detect the use of a poor password that may match dictionary words?

    A.   Password spraying

    B.   Password auditing

    C.   Password guessing

    D.   Password reset

9. What is required for CHAP authentication, when setting a password requirements policy?

    A.   Strong encryption

    B.   Reversible encryption

    C.   Forward encryption

    D.   Complexity

10. What is the term used when credentials can be used with a third party utilizing SSO?

    A.   Identity proofing

    B.   Identity federation

    C.   Identity cloud

    D.   Identity trust

11. What XML federation service will most like be used to access third-party cloud-based corporate portals?

   A.   Shibboleth

   B.   SAML

   C.   OAuth

   D.   OpenID

12. Which federation service will most like be used to access third-party cloud-based digital services?

   A.   OAuth

   B.   SAML

   C.   Kerberos

   D.   LDAP

13. What access control will offer the most security for a government agency?

   A.   MAC

   B.   DAC

   C.   Role-based access control

   D.   Rule-based access control

14. What access control will offer the most flexibility for de-centralized administration?

   A.   MAC

   B.   DAC

   C.   Role-based access control

   D.   Rule-based access control

15. What access control will allow for access based upon *country* and *department*?

   A.   MAC

   B.   DAC

   C.   Role-based access control

   D.   Attribute-based access control

16. Which AAA service offers the widest support across vendor networking equipment?

   A.   RADIUS

   B.   TACACS+

C.   Circumference

D.   HP proprietary

17. How can I administer my directory services securely?

A.   LDAP using TLS

B.   Kerberos

C.   OAuth

D.   Out-of-band

18. What can I use to authenticate securely to directory services, preventing replay and MITM attacks?

A.   IPsec

B.   Kerberos

C.   CHAP

D.   PAP

19. What Ethernet standard allows networking appliances to authenticate connection attempts?

A.   802.11

B.   802.1X

C.   802.3

D.   802.1s

20. What is the framework that allows many different authentication protocols?

A.   PAP

B.   EAP

C.   CHAP

D.   PEAP

21. What will I need to support if users need to present an RFID card, iris scan, and pin?

A.   MFA

B.   2FA

C.   Two-step verification

D.   In-band authentication

22. What is being used when my bank sends me a confirmation code via SMS?

    A. In-band authentication

    B. OOBA

    C. Bandwidth

    D. Out-of-bounds

23. What type of password is not already known to the user?

    A. Forgotten password

    B. OTP

    C. PIN

    D. KBA question

24. What will I need to support if users need to present a password, memorable secret, and pin?

    A. MFA

    B. 2FA

    C. Two-step verification

    D. Single-factor authentication

25. What type of password will my Microsoft Authenticator application generate?

    A. HOTP

    B. TOTP

    C. Hardware root of trust

    D. JWT

26. What is called it when I sign on to directory services and can use my internal email without being prompted to sign in a second time?

    A. SSO

    B. JWT

    C. Attestation and identity proofing

    D. TPM

Answers

1. B
2. A, B and C
3. A
4. B
5. B and D
6. C
7. A
8. B
9. B
10. B
11. B
12. A
13. A
14. B
15. D
16. A
17. A
18. B
19. B
20. B
21. A
22. B
23. B
24. D
25. B
26. A

Section 2: Security Operations

In this section, you will learn about the many threats that exist for an enterprise, threats that are often highly sophisticated and may be sponsored by state actors. You will learn about the tools and techniques that will enable an enterprise to detect and respond to these threats.

This part of the book comprises the following chapters:

- *Chapter 5, Threat and Vulnerability Management*
- *Chapter 6, Vulnerability Assessment and Penetration Testing Methods and Tools*
- *Chapter 7, Risk Mitigation Controls*
- *Chapter 8, Implementing Incident Response and Forensics Procedures*

5
Threat and Vulnerability Management

In this chapter, we will primarily deal with security operation center activities. Security professionals need to identify different types of threats. **Insider threats** and **Advanced Persistent Threats** (**APT**) are two of the biggest threats currently targeting government departments and commercial organizations. It is important to understand the threat actor skills and motivations, and also the resources that they have available to them – how much time can they afford to spend planning attacks? What is their level of financial backing? How sophisticated are the attackers? Is money an objective of the attack (for example, **ransomware** is nearly always about financial gain)? We need to use threat frameworks to understand how to recognize threats and respond. It is important for security professionals to be able to identify indicators of compromise, and within our security operations center, we also need to respond using a variety of techniques. In this chapter, we will cover the following topics:

- Intelligence types
- Actor types
- Threat actor properties

- Intelligence collection methods
- Frameworks
- Indicators of compromise
- Responses

Intelligence types

Gathering threat intelligence is important as this will allow security professionals to be proactive and equipped to meet the challenges of cyberattacks. We will look at *tactical*, *strategic*, and *operational* intelligence. From a practical point of view, we also need to understand what tools are available to gather this knowledge.

Tactical intelligence

Tactical threat intelligence gathering would be performed primarily by security experts and analysts. It is primarily focused on short-term objectives. This would be the job of the **Security Operations Center** (**SOC**) staff who would analyze feeds from multiple security tools, including **Security Information and Event Management** (**SIEM**) systems. To gather tactical intelligence, we can use threat feeds and open source and closed source/proprietary feeds, depending upon the business. Tactical intelligence will use real-time events and technical analysis to understand adversaries and their tools and tactics. We need the latest tools to identify new and **zero-day** exploits (threats that have no known patches or mitigation). The shorter-term goals will be to identify current threats and emerging threats using technology and automation.

Strategic intelligence

Strategic threat intelligence should be conveyed to senior managers and leaders within an enterprise. It is based on long-term goals – for example, *what are the threats to our industry?* Or *who are the primary threat actors targeting our industry?* An organization would collect historical data and use this to look at trends. You could say strategic intelligence is more about *Who* and *Why*. A military defense contractor should know that China may target them to steal their **intellectual property** (**IP**). Based on this assumption, we must address this risk with the appropriate countermeasures.

Operational intelligence

Operational threat intelligence gathering is often performed by forensics or incident first responders. We need to understand an adversary's techniques and methodologies. We can search through previous data logs looking for signatures from particular activities from known threat actors. We would use this technique to discover previous attacks that were not detected. If you are searching for evidence of nation-state threat actors, you may look at one of the known documented groups, **APT30** (indicators strongly suggest they are sponsored at a government level), and their mode of operation is well documented. Previous attacks have used **spear phishing** as the first step.

See the following link for more intelligence on APT30 activities:

```
https://attack.mitre.org/versions/v9/groups/G0013/
```

Commodity malware

One common form of attack is to use **commodity malware**. This is malware that is cross-platform and has multiple purposes. A good example of commodity malware would be a **remote access trojan**. This could be used against many different operating systems and the end goal can be very different. Effective defenses include patching systems.

Targeted attacks

Targeted attacks may use very specific tools. Examples of targeted attacks include the following:

- **Supply chains**: Attacking software or hardware that is provided by third parties to your organization.

- **Botnets**: This will target your organization with a DDOS (distributed denial of service).

- **Spear phishing attack**: Employees of your organization may receive malicious links within email messages.

Actor types

Organizations must consider threats from many different sources, from the unsophisticated script kiddie to government-sponsored attacks involving nation-state actors. We must also consider attacks from cybercriminals – at present, organized crime is the fastest-growing adversary. In over half of reported cases, major information system breaches can be attributed to insiders. We will highlight these threat actors in the following section.

Advanced persistent threat – nation-state

APTs are persistent in nature and have a strong determination to compromise your systems, typically using advanced techniques, and often have access to high-level resources (nation-states).

As APTs are difficult to detect and highly sophisticated, they may remain unknown for many months or years.

Cybersecurity professionals have labeled all the known adversaries and collected evidence of tools and activities undertaken by these adversaries. There are over 30 known APT groups currently active. For an up-to-date list, follow this URL:

```
https://www.fireeye.com/current-threats/apt-groups.html
```

Massachusetts Institute of Technology Research and Engineering (MITRE) also publishes a list of APT threat actors:

```
https://attack.mitre.org/versions/v9/groups/
```

The goals of APTs are high-level access to intellectual property, government systems, military intelligence, and more. The groups are split between organized crime and nation-state actors.

The goal of nation-state attacks can be to destabilize governments, interfere with the money supply, or attack critical infrastructure.

Insider threat

Insider threats are one of the biggest reasons for security breaches. It is estimated that more than 50% of breaches are attributable to insiders. It could be accidental or it could be a user who has a grudge against the organization (such as a disgruntled employee).

Competitor

A competitor is an entity that works in the same field as your organization. You might be a manufacturer of a very specific and valuable item. Your IP and design plans are therefore very important. There is evidence that foreign powers have sponsored attacks that have actually led to data breaches that allowed those nations to enhance their military manufacturing at the expense of United States defense corporations. There are many instances where commercial enterprises have resorted to underhand tactics to gain access to **Intellectual Property (IP)**

Some best practices to mitigate these threats would include the following:

- Robust screening for new employees
- **Non-Disclosure agreements** (**NDA**s)
- **User behavior analysis** (**UBA**)
- **Data loss Prevention** (**DLP**)

Hacktivist

The **hacktivist** has a political goal. They may have a grudge against banks, governments, and other high-profile targets. Environmentalists may target oil and gas companies. A good example is a group called **Anonymous**. They have launched many successful attacks over the years against big businesses, including **Sony**, **PayPal**, **VISA**, and **Mastercard**. Recently, the group targeted tech billionaire Elon Musk in retaliation for his activity concerning cryptocurrency. See the following link for more information: `https://tinyurl.com/anonymoustarget`

Script kiddie

Script kiddies are often untrained and lack sophistication. However, they can still cause a lot of damage. They download tools and scripts to attack your organization. A goal may be just to vandalize a site or to prove they can gain access. They often do it for the *rush* and the *high* of being a hacker.

Organized crime

Organized crime cybercriminals are a big threat. Their goal is to gain access to finances. They are often sophisticated – they can attack individuals and they can attack big businesses using many different techniques, including **phishing**, **spear-phishing**, and **pharming sites**. The goal is generally to steal money or your valuable information and they will sell the information on the dark web to the highest bidder. Cybercriminals and organized crime actors also launch attacks against your organization using ransomware (this is currently a major source of income for organized crime). Security professionals are now referring to these groups as **Big Game Hunters** (**BGH**).

Individuals may also be targeted through ransomware, where the victim believes they have committed a crime and are willing to pay to avoid further action.

To further understand threats, we need to understand why they are targeting our organization and how.

Threat actor properties

When building up a picture of an adversary, it is important to understand what motivates them, what backing they have, and what approaches they may use.

Resources

The resources available to a threat actor can make a big difference to the effectiveness of the attack. Government-sponsored threat actors working in large teams will have lots of available resources, including sophisticated hardware and software tools. They have access to money, time, skilled people, intelligence, and so on. They can deploy personnel physically to perform reconnaissance missions. They can also access intelligence gathered by other government agencies.

Time

Nation-states or organized crime threat actors are full-time professional hackers (it's their job); they are not doing this as a hobby. Another consideration is the amount of time that they have access to your systems for. APTs may be in place for months or years without an organization's knowledge. This means the amount of information that may have been stolen may also be difficult to assess.

Money

How well funded are the attackers? In many cases, *very well funded*. The potential gains for cybercriminals are enormous. Ransomware alone is believed to have accounted for $20 billion in damages globally in 2020. The FBI has estimated the cost worldwide to be in excess of $4.2 trillion for 2020, and this is predicted to grow to over $10 trillion by 2025, according to reports in this *Cybercrime Magazine* article: `https://tinyurl.com/cybercrimegrowth`

Supply chain access

You must always consider any third-party involvement to be a risk. Your supply chain is where you may be targeted. This could be third-party supplied software or while working with **Business-To-Business (B2B)** partners or contracting out services to third-party suppliers. Anything that you do not directly control could be considered a supply chain attack. The **firmware** in embedded devices or firmware updates on a smartphone could contain malware. When changing part of your network infrastructure, for example, deploying a new firewall may put you at risk of a supply chain threat.

In 2020, **SolarWinds** was attacked by hackers who were able to plant malware into updates destined for SolarWinds customers. There are over 33,000 installed instances of **SolarWinds Orion** and around 18,000 customers installed the patch. The customers included fortune 500 companies, critical infrastructure-related businesses, and government agencies. Hackers were able to access these systems through a backdoor for over nine months before the breach was discovered. By putting our trust in third parties, we run the risk of creating vulnerabilities. For more details, see the following link:

```
https://www.bbc.co.uk/news/technology-55321643
```

Capabilities and sophistication

Mainstream attacks may be more frequent, but the capabilities of the attackers are usually unsophisticated. These are the types of attacks used by script kiddies or hackers using widely distributed tools and techniques. When we are dealing with a more capable and sophisticated adversary, there will be a lower volume of attacks. These attacks, however, will be much more sophisticated. For example, APTs launched by nation-states.

Identifying techniques

Identifying attacks has become very challenging and we must use many tools and techniques, such as advanced analytics, **machine learning** (**ML**), and **artificial intelligence** (**AI**). These are just some of the tools that can help us to detect these types of attacks.

It is vitally important for security professionals to understand the tools and techniques that enable an organization to be well prepared for future attacks.

Intelligence collection methods

There are multiple sources to gather intelligence. Some are automated but, in many cases, there will need to be an investment in time to truly research the available intelligence resources.

Intelligence feeds

There are many sources of intelligence that can be displayed in a dashboard format. We might want to see threat maps from a live feed. A good example would be showing the current activity globally for things like botnets and **command and control (C2)** servers. There is a good example hosted by spamhaus.com, which can be found at the following link: https://www.spamhaus.com/threat-map/. There are many good open source options and many commercial (paid for) options from security organizations such as **Fortinet**, **FireEye**, **Symantec**, and many others. In the United Kingdom, the National Cyber Security Centre (**NCSC**) offers a free threat feed, but only to affiliated government departments.

A good example of an all-round cyber threat feed can be found at the following link:

https://otx.alienvault.com/preview

See *Figure 5.1* for an example threat feed:

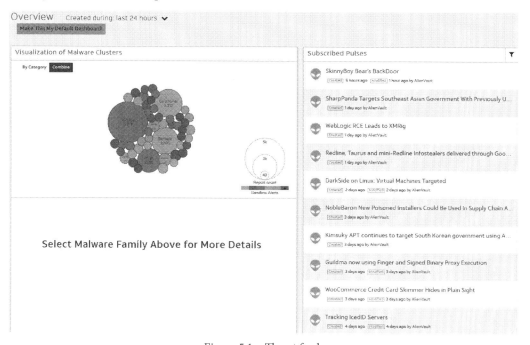

Figure 5.1 – Threat feed

While general cybersecurity threat feeds are very useful in understanding the current threat landscape, more specific feeds are available for different industries, including critical infrastructure. *Figure 5.2* shows options available for different business sectors:

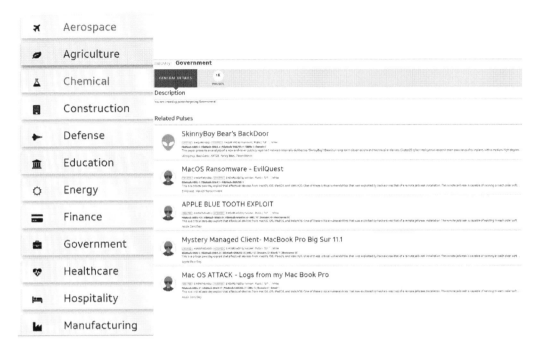

Figure 5.2 – Industry-specific threat feed

There is a supported standard for information sharing of threat feeds. **Trusted Automated eXchange of Indicator Information** (**TAXII**) is a collection of services to support information sharing and **Structured Threat Information eXpression** (**STIX**) is a standard language supported by MITRE.

Deep web

The **deep web**, also known as the **dark web**, is an alternative to the regular internet (also sometimes referred to as the **surface web**). There is no content indexing on the deep web. The deep web is used in countries where personal freedoms are restricted and censorship is in place. But a significant proportion of content on the deep web is generated by criminal activity. Criminals will sell stolen credentials and zero-day exploits to the highest bidders. It is important for law enforcement and cybersecurity professionals to remain aware of the activities and data that criminals are sharing on the deep web. To access sites on the dark web, you will have to gain access to the URL, as it will not be indexed. You will also need to install a browser such as **Tor**. *Figure 5.3* shows the Tor browser, which looks similar to many other regular web browsers. However, you will need to be given access to a site URL, as they cannot be searched:

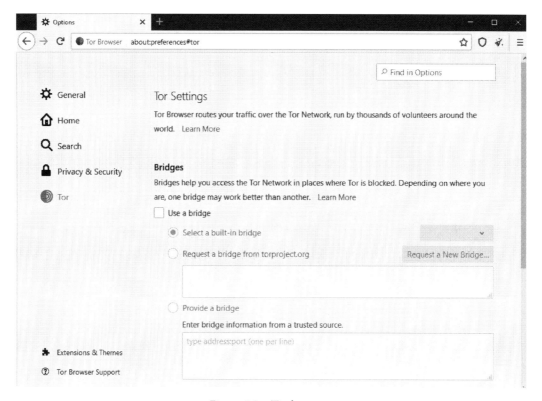

Figure 5.3 – Tor browser

Not all threat intelligence is easy to find and, in some cases, it may require research time and monetary outlay.

Proprietary intelligence

Propriety threat intelligence will only be made available to subscribers. Good examples of this would be certain government threat intelligence that will only be available to certain government agencies. Law enforcement may share information only with certain agencies or related law enforcement departments. Military and classified government intelligence will not be shared and can be considered proprietary.

Open source intelligence

Open source intelligence (**OSINT**) is freely available. It can be used for many different reasons. It is useful to understand this from an attacker's perspective. Email addresses, company information on websites, and DNS records are just some of the pieces of information that are freely available, indexed, and searchable across the internet.

Human intelligence

Human intelligence (**HUMINT**) is intelligence gathered by real people (not machines). This means putting boots on the ground, in a military sense. This could involve physical reconnaissance of a site of interest (perhaps a factory or military site). This skill set will require a certain amount of tradecraft by the intelligence officer. They will be able to read signs and body language, and they will use profiling to understand the motivations and goals of attackers.

To help security professionals understand how to use threat intelligence we can use one of the industry frameworks.

Frameworks

An **attack framework** is very useful to allow us to understand the tools, the tactics, and the techniques attackers will use to launch successful attacks. Security professionals must be able to understand how they plan their attacks right from the initial reconnaissance through to completion of the attack. We will cover some of the industry-accepted approaches in this section.

MITRE adversarial tactics, techniques, and common knowledge (ATT&CK)

MITRE is a not-for-profit organization. It was founded in 1958, primarily as an organization to support government and industry. Many of the current members come from industry (for example, **Microsoft** and **Fujitsu** are current members). MITRE receives government funding to carry out research and is well known for its published attack frameworks and tactics. The matrices are created to understand the tactics and techniques that attackers will use against operating systems, cloud network mobility, and industrial control systems. In *Figure 5.4*, we can see a subset of the *Enterprise* MITRE **ATT&CK** framework:

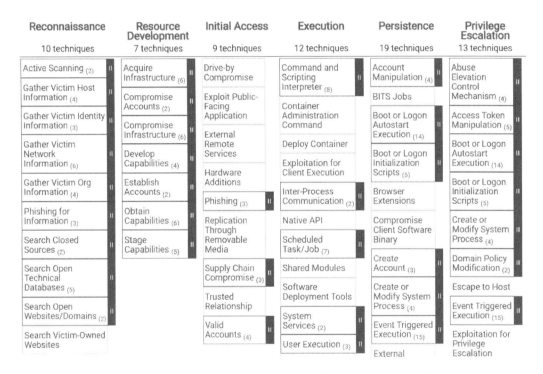

Figure 5.4 – MITRE Att&ck framework (© 2021 The MITRE Corporation. This work is reproduced and distributed with the permission of The MITRE Corporation)

In the Enterprise model, there are 14 headings to give good clear guidance on attack vectors and their impacts. The matrix can be found at the following link:

```
https://attack.mitre.org/versions/v9/matrices/enterprise/
```

ATT&CK for industrial control systems

As **industrial control systems** (**ICS**es) are seen as critical assets, there are government agencies to support these industries in the United States. The **Cybersecurity and Infrastructure Security Agency** (**CISA**) was formed to offer cybersecurity services to the critical industries sectors. CISA has identified 16 sectors that are considered *critical infrastructure*, including energy, food and agriculture, and critical manufacturing. MITRE also publishes an ATT&CK matrix for these ICSes, helping cybersecurity professionals to identify common tactics used. The ICS matrix can be found at the following link:

```
https://collaborate.mitre.org/attackics/index.php/Main_Page
```

MITRE has identified and labeled known attacker groups and their countries of origin. For example, the **Sandworm Team** has been identified as a nation-state-sponsored military intelligence unit. This group has been accused of attacks against the Ukrainian national power grid and was also responsible for the **NotPetya** malware attacks in 2017. For more information, see the following link:

```
https://attack.mitre.org/groups/G0034/
```

The Diamond model of intrusion analysis

The **Diamond model** is very useful when profiling threat actors. You can build up a picture of their capabilities and the target or victims. Forensic analysts can use this model when looking for indicators of compromise, in historical logs. When security professionals understand the exact methods used by the adversary, it can help to speed up the detection process. It is important to understand the capabilities of your adversary. This type of framework is very useful for threat hunting, allowing an organization to understand the motivations and the tools and techniques that will be used for an attack. Shown in *Figure 5.5* is an example of the Diamond model in use:

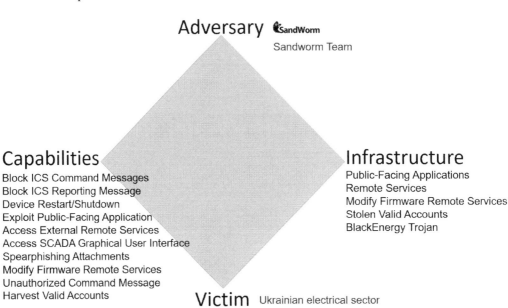

Figure 5.5 – The Diamond model of intrusion analysis

This is a very good approach when focusing on a single attack, maybe during a forensic *hunt*.

Cyber Kill Chain

The **Cyber Kill Chain** is a method developed by **Lockheed Martin**. It is a seven-stage model, which is useful to document each of the steps in the model. If we can break any one of the steps, it can prevent an attack. The seven stages documented by Lockheed Martin are shown in *Figure 5.6*:

```
https://www.lockheedmartin.com/en-us/capabilities/cyber/cyber-
kill-chain.html#Resources
```

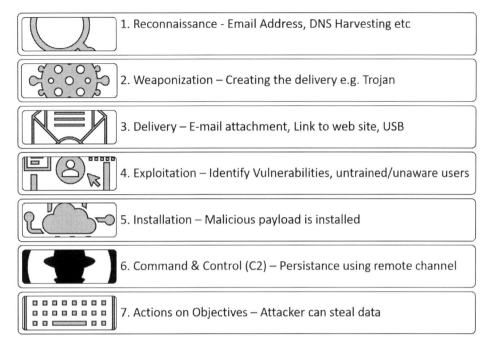

1. Reconnaissance - Email Address, DNS Harvesting etc

2. Weaponization – Creating the delivery e.g. Trojan

3. Delivery – E-mail attachment, Link to web site, USB

4. Exploitation – Identify Vulnerabilities, untrained/unaware users

5. Installation – Malicious payload is installed

6. Command & Control (C2) – Persistence using remote channel

7. Actions on Objectives – Attacker can steal data

Figure 5.6 – Cyber Kill Chain

Frameworks are a very important asset and can be useful for creating incident response playbooks or giving additional context during an investigation.

Threat hunting

Threat hunting can be used within the context of operational intelligence. We need to adopt one of the threat frameworks and search for **Indicators of Compromise** (**IOC**) with a much better understanding of our adversaries' tools and methods. Using this methodology, we are better able to detect APTs.

Threat emulation

Threat emulation allows security professionals to fine-tune their approach to threats using a variety of **Tools, Techniques, and Procedures** (**TTPs**). Team security exercises could be one approach, with the red team using the adversary TTP and the blue team defending the network.

To respond to a threat, we need to recognize what event or series of events is actually threatening.

Indicators of compromise

There are many events that would take place on a busy network. Events can be recorded in logs (where an event is unusual) or coupled with another event that itself appears unusual. This could be an **indicator of compromise** (**IOC**). Another example of an IOC could be several unsuccessful attempts to connect using SSH to a core network appliance, followed by a successful authentication attempt from an unusual or gray-listed IP address. It is important for the security operation center to be able to identify attacks or threats. To identify IOCs, we need inputs in the form of logs and captured network traffic.

Packet capture

Packet capture (**PCAP**) files use a standard log format. They allow us to capture real-time data. Captured data can be analyzed using **Wireshark**, **tcpdump**, or **tshark**. See Wireshark capture in *Figure 5.7*:

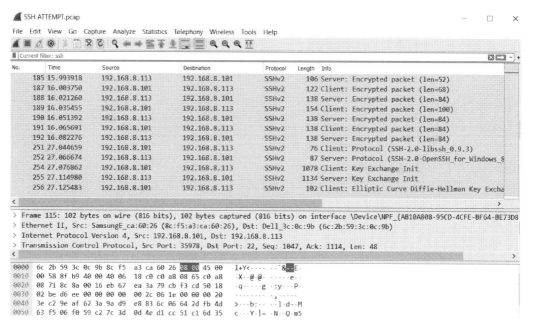

Figure 5.7 – PCAP file

The PCAP format allows logs to be analyzed using different vendor tools and platforms.

Logs

Many different appliances and services will log activities. This could be from applications and services running on a desktop to server-based services. All of this log data can be useful in seeing the big picture. A standard for **Linux/Unix**-based operating systems is **syslog**. This allows for facility codes to be assigned to events. For example, email events would be tagged with a facility code of 2. See *Figure 5.8* for a full list. This is fully documented in **RFC 5424**. Full documentation can be found at the following URL:

```
https://datatracker.ietf.org/doc/html/rfc5424
```

Facility code	Keyword	Description
0	kern	Kernel messages
1	user	User-level messages
2	mail	Mail system
3	daemon	System daemons
4	auth	Security/authentication messages
5	syslog	Messages generated internally by syslogd
6	lpr	Line printer subsystem
7	news	Network news subsystem
8	uucp	UUCP subsystem
9	cron	Cron subsystem
10	authpriv	Security/authentication messages
11	ftp	FTP daemon
12	ntp	NTP subsystem
13	security	Log audit
14	console	Log alert
15	solaris-cron	Scheduling daemon
16–23	local0 – local7	Locally used facilities

Figure 5.8 – Syslog facility codes

Additional logs showing network activity can also be useful.

Network logs

Network logs allow us to capture network traffic activity on switches, routers, firewalls, intrusion detection systems, and many more network appliances. *Figure 5.9* shows an example of a firewall log:

```
#Fields: date time action protocol src-ip dst-ip src-port dst-port size tcpflags tcpsyn tcpack tcpwin icmptype icmpcode info path

2021-06-08 09:53:51 ALLOW UDP 192.168.8.101 224.0.0.251 5353 5353 0 - - - - - - - RECEIVE
2021-06-08 09:53:51 ALLOW UDP 192.168.8.101 224.0.0.251 5353 5353 0 - - - - - - - RECEIVE
2021-06-08 09:54:03 ALLOW UDP 192.168.8.113 192.168.8.1 64254 53 0 - - - - - - - SEND
2021-06-08 09:54:03 ALLOW UDP 192.168.8.113 172.217.16.238 54523 443 0 - - - - - - - SEND
2021-06-08 09:54:06 ALLOW UDP 192.168.8.113 192.168.8.1 58463 53 0 - - - - - - - SEND
2021-06-08 09:54:06 ALLOW TCP 192.168.8.113 52.113.205.4 1746 443 0 - 0 0 0 - - - SEND
2021-06-08 09:54:06 ALLOW TCP 192.168.8.101 192.168.8.113 55978 22 0 - 0 0 0 - - - RECEIVE
2021-06-08 09:54:25 ALLOW UDP 192.168.8.113 192.168.8.1 55181 53 0 - - - - - - - SEND
2021-06-08 09:54:25 ALLOW TCP 192.168.8.113 52.0.218.127 1042 443 0 - 0 0 0 - - - SEND
2021-06-08 09:54:46 ALLOW TCP 192.168.8.113 52.104.18.41 1045 443 0 - 0 0 0 - - - SEND
2021-06-08 09:54:46 ALLOW TCP 192.168.8.113 52.104.18.41 1046 443 0 - 0 0 0 - - - SEND
2021-06-08 09:55:23 ALLOW UDP 192.168.8.113 239.255.255.250 57174 1900 0 - - - - - - - SEND
2021-06-08 09:55:23 ALLOW UDP 192.168.8.113 172.217.16.238 52108 443 0 - - - - - - - SEND
2021-06-08 09:55:32 ALLOW UDP 192.168.8.113 192.168.8.1 49664 53 0 - - - - - - - SEND
2021-06-08 09:55:32 ALLOW UDP 192.168.8.113 216.58.212.227 61629 443 0 - - - - - - - SEND
2021-06-08 09:55:40 ALLOW UDP 192.168.8.113 192.168.8.1 53393 53 0 - - - - - - - SEND
2021-06-08 09:55:40 ALLOW TCP 192.168.8.113 172.217.169.69 1025 443 0 - 0 0 0 - - - SEND
2021-06-08 09:56:11 ALLOW TCP 192.168.8.113 52.97.208.18 1027 443 0 - 0 0 0 - - - SEND
2021-06-08 09:56:19 ALLOW ICMP fe80::2a64:b0ff:fe50:bb7 ff02::1 - - 0 - - - - 134 0 - RECEIVE
2021-06-08 09:56:23 ALLOW UDP 192.168.8.113 172.217.16.238 53097 443 0 - - - - - - - SEND
2021-06-08 09:56:39 ALLOW UDP 192.168.8.113 224.0.0.253 60080 3544 0 - - - - - - - SEND
2021-06-08 09:56:54 ALLOW TCP 192.168.8.113 192.168.8.1 1026 80 0 - 0 0 0 - - - SEND
2021-06-08 09:56:54 ALLOW TCP 192.168.8.113 192.168.8.1 13851 80 0 - 0 0 0 - - - SEND
2021-06-08 09:56:55 ALLOW UDP 192.168.8.113 192.168.8.1 54102 53 0 - - - - - - - SEND
2021-06-08 09:57:15 ALLOW UDP 192.168.8.113 192.168.8.1 57089 53 0 - - - - - - - SEND
2021-06-08 09:57:15 ALLOW UDP 192.168.8.113 142.250.178.3 49312 443 0 - - - - - - - SEND
2021-06-08 09:57:23 ALLOW UDP 192.168.8.113 239.255.255.250 64038 1900 0 - - - - - - - SEND
2021-06-08 09:57:23 ALLOW UDP 192.168.8.113 192.168.8.1 52951 53 0 - - - - - - - SEND
2021-06-08 09:57:23 ALLOW UDP 192.168.8.113 192.168.8.1 52952 53 0 - - - - - - - SEND
2021-06-08 09:57:23 ALLOW TCP 192.168.8.113 51.141.116.70 13853 443 0 - 0 0 0 - - - SEND
2021-06-08 09:57:23 ALLOW TCP 192.168.8.113 51.141.116.70 13852 443 0 - 0 0 0 - - - SEND
2021-06-08 09:57:23 ALLOW UDP 192.168.8.113 192.168.8.1 63436 53 0 - - - - - - - SEND
2021-06-08 09:57:23 ALLOW UDP 192.168.8.113 142.250.180.10 60235 443 0 - - - - - - - SEND
```

Figure 5.9 – Network firewall logs

Network logs can be forwarded to SIEM for more analysis.

Vulnerability logs

Vulnerability logs will be created by vulnerability scanning tools such as **Nessus**, **OpenVAS**, and **Nmap**. It can be useful to consolidate and have a **single pane of glass** to present all of this collected data. Vulnerability logs can be forwarded to SIEM for automation and alerts. *Figure 5.10* shows a log from a vulnerability scan:

```
Starting Nmap 7.91 ( https://nmap.org ) at 2021-06-08
10:06 GMT Summer Time
NSE: Loaded 153 scripts for scanning.
NSE: Script Pre-scanning.
Initiating NSE at 10:06
Completed NSE at 10:06, 0.00s elapsed
Initiating NSE at 10:06
Completed NSE at 10:06, 0.00s elapsed
Initiating NSE at 10:06
Completed NSE at 10:06, 0.00s elapsed
Initiating Ping Scan at 10:06
Scanning www.nmap.org (45.33.49.119) [4 ports]
Completed Ping Scan at 10:06, 0.61s elapsed (1 total
hosts)
Initiating Parallel DNS resolution of 1 host. at 10:06
Completed Parallel DNS resolution of 1 host. at 10:06,
0.16s elapsed
Initiating SYN Stealth Scan at 10:06
Scanning www.nmap.org (45.33.49.119) [1000 ports]
Discovered open port 80/tcp on 45.33.49.119
Discovered open port 25/tcp on 45.33.49.119
Discovered open port 22/tcp on 45.33.49.119
Discovered open port 443/tcp on 45.33.49.119
Discovered open port 2000/tcp on 45.33.49.119
Discovered open port 5060/tcp on 45.33.49.119
Completed SYN Stealth Scan at 10:06, 11.78s elapsed
(1000 total ports)
Initiating Service scan at 10:06
Scanning 6 services on www.nmap.org (45.33.49.119)
Completed Service scan at 10:07, 38.75s elapsed (6
services on 1 host)
Initiating OS detection (try #1) against www.nmap.org
(45.33.49.119)
Retrying OS detection (try #2) against www.nmap.org
(45.33.49.119)
Initiating Traceroute at 10:07
Completed Traceroute at 10:07, 9.08s elapsed
Initiating Parallel DNS resolution of 1 host. at 10:07
Completed Parallel DNS resolution of 1 host. at 10:07,
0.00s elapsed
NSE: Script scanning 45.33.49.119.
Initiating NSE at 10:07
Completed NSE at 10:09, 147.35s elapsed
Initiating NSE at 10:09
Completed NSE at 10:11, 66.03s elapsed
Initiating NSE at 10:11
Completed NSE at 10:11, 0.00s elapsed
Nmap scan report for www.nmap.org (45.33.49.119)
Host is up (0.17s latency).
Other addresses for www.nmap.org (not scanned):
2600:3c01:e000:3e6::6d4e:7061
rDNS record for 45.33.49.119: ack.nmap.org
```

Figure 5.10 – Vulnerability log

When we run a vulnerability scan, it is important to log the results.

Operating system logs

Operating systems will create logged data. This can be useful, as many services may be hosted on an operating system platform. These logs can be uploaded to **endpoint detection and response (EDR)** systems, allowing more granular control and visibility of that data. Logs can include application events, security events, and service logs, such as DNS or DHCP. *Figure 5.11* shows a partial security log from a Windows client:

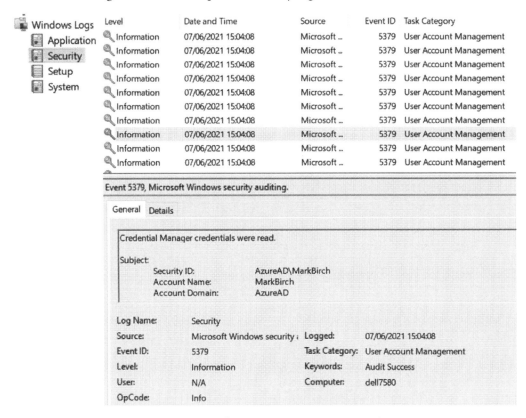

Figure 5.11 – Windows operating system security log

Security logs are very important for accountability and regulatory compliance.

Access logs

Access logs provide an audit trail, when accountability must be established. A security audit may be conducted to establish who accessed an information system through remote access services or who changed permissions on a user's mailbox. We may want to record physical access to a location, such as who gained physical access to the data center at the time when a security breach occurred. Access logs will be important for accountability and may be required to meet regulatory compliance.

NetFlow logs

NetFlow logs are forwarded by network switches, routers, and other network appliances. Logs are gathered by a collector and can be used to baseline the network and visualize the flows and data types. *Figure 5.12* shows a **Cisco NetFlow** log:

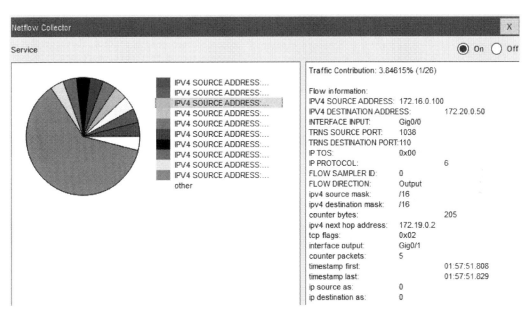

Figure 5.12 – Cisco NetFlow collector

We can also determine where the majority of network traffic originates.

Notifications

Notifications can be sent to an operator console. This could be in the form of an alert or any email message to indicate a threshold value has been hit or a particular event needs some administrator's attention.

File integrity monitoring alerts

File integrity monitoring (**FIM**) systems will alert on modification to key system files or any files that have been identified as important. Specialist products such as **Tripwire** are designed for this task. Windows also has its own system file checker in place to detect any attempts to modify key Windows operating system files. Reporting and alerting are important for real-time protection and may be required for regulatory compliance.

SIEM alerts

SIEM alerts will consolidate events from many sources of log data. We can then use smart analytics machine learning and behavioral analysis on the logged data. SIEM allows for automated alerts on unusual activity or suspicious events.

Data loss prevention alerts

Data loss prevention (**DLP**) systems prevent the exfiltration of sensitive data, intellectual property, and sensitive customer records, such as **personally identifiable information** (**PII**) or **protected health information** (**PHI**). Typically, this is done by using labeling techniques where users label their files with certain classifications to allow the DLP system to understand what level of classification the data is. It is important to monitor this activity, as while the DLP may stop unwanted exfiltration, we need to be aware of these events. *Figure 5.13* shows an event detected by Microsoft DLP:

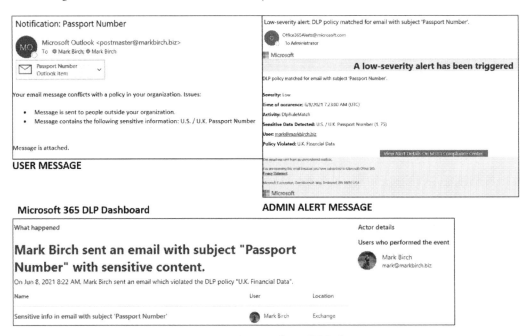

Figure 5.13 – Microsoft 365 DLP alert

DLP is all about threats for data leaving the network. We also need to analyze traffic entering the network.

Intrusion detection system and intrusion prevention system alerts

Intrusion detection systems (**IDS**es) and **intrusion prevention systems** (**IPS**es) offer passive or active approaches respectively. IDSes detect threats but do not take action. IPSes detect and prevent the threat from happening. We need to monitor this activity and be alerted when there is a high number of events or high-importance events. Even though the tool may be doing its job, we still need to be aware of this activity. Threatening and malicious events should be reported either through monitoring alerts or through automated emails.

Antivirus alerts

Antivirus systems are in place to prevent the proliferation of malicious code and programs. Even if the antivirus is successful, we should still log and monitor events to understand the level of this activity. Ideally, this is done from centralized reporting dashboards.

Notification severity and priorities

It is important that severe events are prioritized when considering reporting. It is important to separate the noise in the system if we can filter the logs to highlight severe events, then a quick response can be activated. Any unusual process activity that is automatically remediated should be investigated by security professionals in a timely fashion. It is important to prioritize by **Common Vulnerability Scoring System** (**CVSS**) or impact score, as it will never be possible to fix everything.

Once we have recognized unwanted activity within the enterprise, we need to put controls in place to stop or prevent unwanted activities.

Responses

When we have many security tools to guard our networks, it is important that we use automation to identify events and where possible to provide an automated response. This frees up the **security operation center** (**SOC**) staff to be able to take on board other useful security tasks. **Security Orchestration Automation and Response** (**SOAR**) is a modern approach to respond to real-time threats and alerts. Playbooks can be used to create or provide an automated response. A playbook could be a simple ruleset or a complex set of actions.

Firewall rules

Firewall rules are important to have in place, as they protect your perimeter network services placed in your **Demilitarized Zone (DMZ)**. Firewall rules will also protect your internal resources when deployed as host-based firewalls. Firewall rules may be modified based upon a changing threat landscape and new adversaries. Bad actor IP address ranges may need to be updated on your firewalls.

Intrusion prevention system and intrusion detection system rules

IPSes and IDSes are a very important layer of protection from threats launched from outside your network (see *Chapter 1*, *Designing a Secure Network Architecture*, for more details). As a response to changing threat landscapes and new threats, these rules need to be constantly updated.

Access control list rules

An **access control list** (**ACL**) is quite a generic term. ACLs can comprise permissions on the security tab on a file or a folder. Firewall rules are also often referred to as ACLs. Other examples could be rules created for network devices, for example, a *Layer 2* device such as a wireless access point or a network switch could restrict access based on your MAC address. In response to threats to Layer 2 devices, we can create a whitelist of authorized devices. *Figure 5.14* shows an example of MAC filtering:

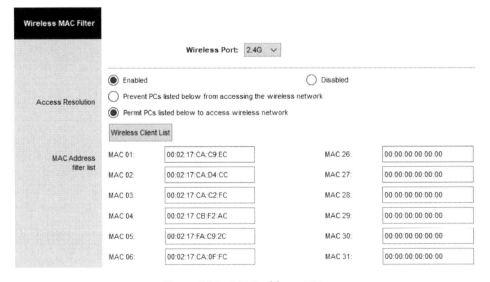

Figure 5.14 – MAC address ACL

Other rules could be based on a known signature or checksum.

Signature rules

Signature rules are normally configured based on what is known, such as a definition file that can be updated as new threats are constantly being detected and are evolving. It is important that signatures are kept up to date and an antivirus engine is very dependent on signatures and updates.

A signature could be a hash match for a known malicious file. For example, the **European Institute for Computer Antivirus Research** (**EICAR**) test file was developed to allow security personnel to check if antivirus software is functional. It uses a well-known string of characters shown here:

```
X5O!P%@AP[4\PZX54(P^)7CC)7}$EICAR-STANDARD-ANTIVIRUS-TEST-FILE!$H+H*
```

Figure 5.15 – EICAR test file

The signature for this string would be as follows:

```
SHA1 3395856ce81f2b7382dee72602f798b642f14140
```

> **Important Note**
> If you try to create the EICAR string and save it as a file, your anti-malware will likely quarantine the file.

Behavior rules

Behavior rules have critical importance when we store so much important data within a modern enterprise. We need systems that detect anomalies based on behavioural analysis. The system would use AI and ML to build rulesets for normal activity. But in the event of an anomaly, for example, a user beginning to transfer a large amount of data to a cloud-based data repository, or a user beginning to delete an unusual number of files within a certain amount of time, the system would generate alerts and notify an administrator. This is typically done by modeling normal user behavior and then comparing the abnormal bahavior against the normal.

The following is an example of a report from **Netwrix Auditor**. More information can be found at `https://tinyurl.com/uebarules`. *Figure 5.16* shows a user behavior report:

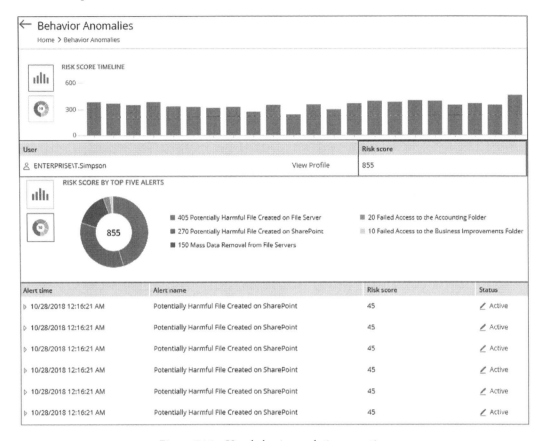

Figure 5.16 – User behavior analytics reporting

We need to put these controls in place to be better prepared for anomalous user activity.

Data loss prevention rules

DLP rules must be constantly updated. Regulatory compliance requirements may change, requiring stricter controls. The search strings that are used to detect PII, PHI, intellectual property, and financial details may need changing and new rulesets will have to be added to your DLP solution. *Figure 5.17* shows a sample DLP ruleset:

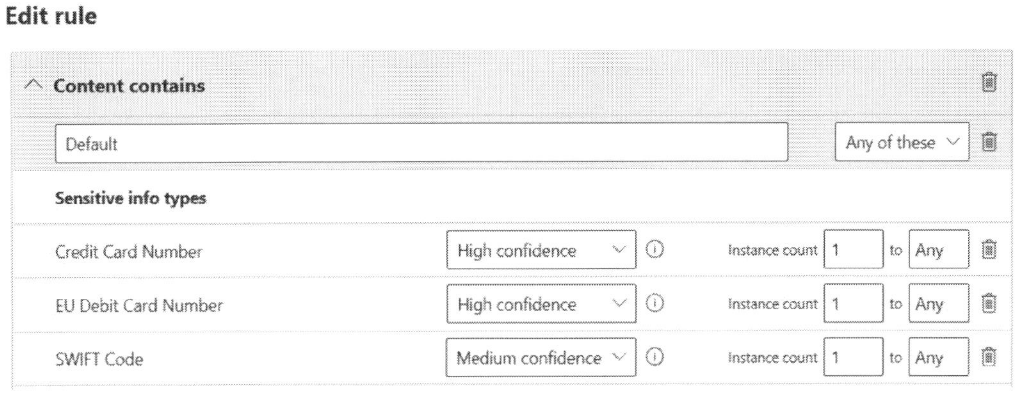

Edit rule

Figure 5.17 – Microsoft 365 DLP rules

Many rules that are implemented are searching for words or particular character sets.

Scripts/regular expressions

Automation could include scripting. Scripts could be created to search for keywords using regular expressions. This may provide protection by scanning captured log data or searching incoming requests to your web server. DLP is a good example of searching outgoing network traffic. We can formulate rules based on these search patterns.

It is vitally important that an organization has identified potential IOCs and has put mitigation in place to respond effectively to these attacks.

Summary

In this chapter, we have looked at the varied tools and techniques that would be used within an enterprise SOC. A security professional will need to identify different types of threats and be able to select the correct approach and framework. We have covered the main industry approaches. We have examined how an organization can identify IOCs and how to respond to a variety of threats.

In this chapter, you have gained the following skills:

- An understanding of the different sources for threat intelligence
- An understanding of the main threat actor types
- An understanding of threat actor properties
- An understanding of intelligence collection methods

- An understanding of frameworks, including MITRE, the Diamond model, and the cyber kill chain model.

- An understanding of how an enterprise detects indicators of compromise.

- How to respond to threats.

This knowledge gained will be very useful as we look into *vulnerability management* and *pen testing* in the next chapter.

Questions

Here are a few questions to test your understanding of the chapter:

1. Which of the following intelligence types focuses on the threat actor and the reason for the attack?

    A. Tactical

    B. Strategic

    C. Targeted

    D. Operational

2. What is used as a common vector to launch a broad range of attacks?

    A. Tactical

    B. Strategic

    C. Commodity malware

    D. Targeted attacks

3. What type of attack would use spear-phishing against engineers in the Ukraine electricity supply industry with the goal of gaining user credentials?

    A. Deep web

    B. Proprietary

    C. Commodity malware

    D. Targeted attacks

4. Which of the following intelligence types focuses on the technical and automated discovery of everyday threats, threat actors, and the reason for the attack?

   A. Tactical

   B. Strategic

   C. Commodity malware

   D. Targeted attacks

5. Which of the following intelligence types uses forensics and historical logs to identity threats?

   A. Tactical

   B. Strategic

   C. Commodity malware

   D. Operational threat intelligence

6. What framework could a forensics team use to document a specific adversary, victim, capabilities, and infrastructure?

   A. Threat emulation

   B. Threat hunting

   C. Diamond model

   D. STIX

7. What is the most likely threat actor if your router firmware has been tampered with over a period of two years, without being detected?

   A. Advanced persistent threat

   B. Competitor

   C. Hacktivist

   D. Script kiddie

8. What is the most likely threat actor if your electrical power delivery capabilities are attacked?

   A. Nation-state

   B. Insider threat

   C. Hacktivist

   D. Script kiddie

9. What threat actor will most likely steal your intellectual property?

    A.   Advanced persistent threat

    B.   Competitor

    C.   Hacktivist

    D.   Script kiddie

10. What is the threat when vulnerabilities are present on your network due to misconfiguration by poorly trained technicians?

    A.   Advanced persistent threat

    B.   Insider threat

    C.   Script kiddie

    D.   Organized crime

11. What is the threat when vulnerabilities are present due to the use of third-party libraries in our code base?

    A.   Advanced persistent threat

    B.   Supply Chain

    C.   Insider threat

    D.   Organized crime

12. What is the likely threat actor when thousands of systems are targeted with crypto malware followed up with a demand for $5,000 in bitcoin?

    A.   Advanced persistent threat

    B.   Supply chain

    C.   Insider threat

    D.   Organized crime

13. What is the public network that hosts unindexed and unsearchable content that may be used for unlawful activities?

    A.   World Wide Web

    B.   Intranet

    C.   Deep web

    D.   Proprietary networks

14. What type of intelligence gathering would involve DNS record harvesting?

    A. Intelligence feeds

    B. Deep web

    C. Open source intelligence (OSINT)

    D. Human intelligence (HUMINT)

15. What type of intelligence gathering would involve physical reconnaissance?

    A. Intelligence feeds

    B. Deep Web

    C. Open source intelligence (OSINT)

    D. Human intelligence (HUMINT)

16. What framework would be the best choice to build up a picture of threat actors and their tactics and techniques for a water treatment plant?

    A. MITRE ATT&CK

    B. ATT&CK for industrial control system (ICS)

    C. Diamond model of intrusion analysis

    D. Cyber kill chain

17. What framework would be used to understand the capabilities of APT29 and how they will target your enterprise information systems?

    A. MITRE (ATT&CK)

    B. ATT&CK for industrial control system (ICS)

    C. Scripts/regular expressions

    D. SRTM

18. What framework uses seven stages, starting with *reconnaissance* and ending in *actions on objectives*?

    A. MITRE (ATT&CK)

    B. ATT&CK for industrial control system (ICS)

    C. Diamond model of intrusion analysis

    D. Cyber kill chain

19. What file type will allow for the analysis of network traffic captured by Wireshark or tcpdump?

   A.   Packet capture (PCAP)

   B.   Vulnerability logs

   C.   Operating system logs

   D.   Portable Data Format (PDF)

20. What can be used to centrally correlate events from multiple sources and raise alerts?

   A.   FIM alerts

   B.   SIEM alerts

   C.   DLP alerts

   D.   IDS/IPS alerts

21. What type of logging can be used for accountability?

   A.   Vulnerability logs

   B.   Operating system logs

   C.   Access logs

   D.   NetFlow logs

22. What type of logging can identify the source of most *noise* on a network?

   A.   Vulnerability logs

   B.   Operating system logs

   C.   Access logs

   D.   NetFlow logs

23. How will I know if my critical files have been tampered with?

   A.   FIM alerts

   B.   SIEM alerts

   C.   DLP alerts

   D.   IDS/IPS alerts

24. George has tried to email his company credit card details to his **Gmail** account. The security team has contacted him and reminded him this is not acceptable use. How were they informed?

   A.   FIM alerts

   B.   SIEM alerts

   C.   DLP alerts

   D.   IDS/IPS alerts

25. An attacker has had their session reset after they successfully logged on to the **Private Branch Exchange (PBX)** after three unsuccessful attempts using SSH. What is the reason for this?

   A.   FIM alerts

   B.   Firewall alerts

   C.   DLP rules

   D.   IPS rules

26. The Acme corporation needs to block the exfiltration of United States medical-related data due to a new regulatory requirement. What is most likely going to get updated?

   A.   ACL rules

   B.   Signature rules

   C.   Behavior rules

   D.   DLP rules

27. Bill the network technician has been tasked with updating security based upon a threat exchange update. Five known bad actor IP addresses must be blocked. What should be updated?

   A.   Firewall rules

   B.   Signature rules

   C.   Behavior rules

   D.   DLP rules

28. What is used to search for character strings in my DLP solution?

    A.   Signature rules

    B.   Behavior rules

    C.   Firewall rules

    D.   Regular expressions

29. What type of rule will alert administrators that Colin is deleting significant amounts of sensitive company data?

    A.   Signature rules

    B.   Behavior rules

    C.   Firewall rules

    D.   Regular expressions

30. What will alert the SOC team to IOCs detected in logs of multiple network appliances?

    A.   SIEM alerts

    B.   Behavior alerts

    C.   DLP alerts

    D.   Syslogs

31. What type of rule will alert administrators about a known malware variant that has the following checksum:

    sha1 checksum 29386154B7F99B05A23DC9D04421AC8B0534CBE1?

    A.   ACL rules

    B.   Signature rules

    C.   Behavior rules

    D.   DLP rules

32. Charles notices several endpoints have been infected by a recently discovered malware variant. What has allowed Charles to receive this information?

    A.   SIEM alerts

    B.   Antivirus alerts

    C.   DLP alerts

    D.   Syslogs

Answers

1. A
2. C
3. D
4. A
5. D
6. C
7. A
8. A
9. B
10. B
11. B
12. D
13. C
14. C
15. D
16. B
17. A
18. D
19. A
20. B
21. C
22. D
23. A
24. C
25. D
26. D
27. A
28. D
29. B
30. A
31. B
32. B

6
Vulnerability Assessment and Penetration Testing Methods and Tools

Security professionals must constantly assess the security posture of operating systems, networks, industrial control systems, end user devices, and user behaviors (to name but a few). We must constantly assess the security of our systems by utilizing vulnerability scanning. We should use industry-standard tools and protocols, to ensure compatibility across the enterprise. Security professionals should be aware of information sources where current threats and vulnerabilities are published. We may need independent verification of our security posture; this will involve enlisting third parties to assess our systems. Independent audits may be required for regulatory, legal, or industry compliance.

In this chapter, we will cover the following topics:

- Vulnerability scans
- **Security Content Automation Protocol (SCAP)**
- Information sources

- Testing methods
- Penetration testing
- Security tools

Vulnerability scans

Vulnerability scans are important as they allow security professionals to understand when systems are lacking important security configuration or are missing important patches. Vulnerability scanning will be done by security professionals in the enterprise to discover systems that require remediation. Vulnerability scanning may also be performed by malicious actors who wish to discover systems that are missing critical security patches and configuration. They will then attempt to exploit these weaknesses.

Credentialed versus non-credentialed scans

When performing vulnerability assessments, it is important to understand the capabilities of the assessment tool. In some cases, credentials will be required to give useful, accurate information on the systems that are being scanned. In some cases, some tools do not require credentials and the scans can be done anonymously. If we want to get an accurate security assessment of an operating system, it is important we supply credentials that are privileged. This will allow the vulnerability report to list settings such as the following:

- Installed software version
- Local services
- Vulnerabilities in registry files
- Local filesystem information
- Patch levels

Tenable Nessus is a popular vulnerability scanner, used by government agencies and commercial organizations. In their configuration requirements, they stipulate the use of an administrator account or root (for non-Windows).

If we run a scan without credentials, we will see the report from an attacker's perspective. It will lack detail, as there is no local logon available.

Agent-based/server-based

There are some vulnerability assessment solutions that require an agent to be installed on the end devices. This approach allows for pull technology solutions, meaning the scan can be done on the end device and the results can be pushed back to the server-based management console. There are also solutions where there are no agents deployed (agentless scanning). This means the server must push out requests to gather information from the end devices. In most cases, agent-based assessments will take some of the workload off the server and potentially take some traffic off the network.

Criticality ranking

When we run a vulnerability assessment and we look at the output report, it is important to present the reports in a meaningful language that allows us to assess the most critical vulnerabilities and be able to respond accordingly. *Figure 6.1* shows two vulnerability scans. In the first instance, there are highly critical vulnerabilities related to Wireshark installation. The report indicates they can be remediated with a software update. The second scan shows these vulnerabilities have been remediated:

SCAN 1. Report

Vulnerability		Score
Windows IExpress Untrusted Search Path Vulnerability		9.3 (High)
Wireshark Security Updates (wnpa-sec-2017-43_wnpa-sec-2017-42)-Windows		7.8 (High)
Wireshark Security Updates (wnpa-sec-2018-34_wnpa-sec-2018-41) Windows		7.8 (High)
Microsoft Windows SMB/NETBIOS NULL Session Authentication Bypass Vulnerability		7.5 (High)
Wireshark Denial of Service Vulnerability (Windows)		7.5 (High)
MS Windows HID Functionality (Over USB) Code Execution Vulnerability		6.9 (Medium)
Wireshark Security Updates (wnpa-sec-2018-05 to -14) Windows		5.0 (Medium)

SCAN 2. Report

Vulnerability		Score
Windows IExpress Untrusted Search Path Vulnerability		9.3 (High)
Microsoft Windows SMB/NETBIOS NULL Session Authentication Bypass Vulnerability		7.5 (High)
MS Windows HID Functionality (Over USB) Code Execution Vulnerability		6.9 (Medium)

Figure 6.1 – Critical ranked vulnerabilities

Other remediation requires configuration workarounds and the removal of applications/ services.

Active versus passive scans

Active scanning will require interaction between the reporting/management station and the endpoints. Passive scanning can collect logged data and perform analysis on this data. On certain networks, such as **Operational Technology** (**OT**), we may not want to overwhelm the network or endpoints with additional reporting and subsequent network traffic. With passive scanning, the goal is to connect to a read-only (span) port and perform analysis on network traffic without injecting any data.

An alternative approach is to use active scanning, in an effort to generate more accurate reporting. A good example of active scanning would be SCAP.

Security Content Automation Protocol (SCAP)

SCAP is an open standard and is used by many vendors within the industry to support a common security reporting language. It is supported by the **National Vulnerability Database** (**NVD**), which is a US government-funded organization that produces content that can be used within a SCAP scanner.

It is used extensively within US government departments, including the **Department of Defence** (**DoD**), and meets **Federal Information Security Management Act** (**FISMA**) requirements.

Extensible Configuration Checklist Description Format (XCCDF)

XCCDF specifies a format for configuration files. These are the checklists that the SCAP scanner (the vulnerability assessment tool) will use. They are written in an XML format. Within the US government and DoD, these files are more commonly known as **Secure Technical Implementation Guide** (**STIG**). More information can be obtained from the following public site: `https://public.cyber.mil/stigs/`.

> **Important Note**
> XCCDF does not contain commands to perform a scan but relies on the **Open Vulnerability and Assessment Language** (**OVAL**) to process the requirements.

Open Vulnerability and Assessment Language (OVAL)

OVAL is an open international standard and is free for public use. It enables vendors to create output that is consistent. If I view a report that has been run using the Nessus tool, it will match the output created by another vendor's OVAL-compliant tool.

Common Platform Enumeration (CPE)

CPE is used to identify different operating system types, devices, and applications. This can then allow the vulnerability scanning tool to make automated decisions about which vulnerabilities to search for. An example would be if the system is identified as Linux running a common web application service, it will only need to check for vulnerabilities against those installed products.

Figure 6.2 shows a recent scan that has discovered 16 CPE items:

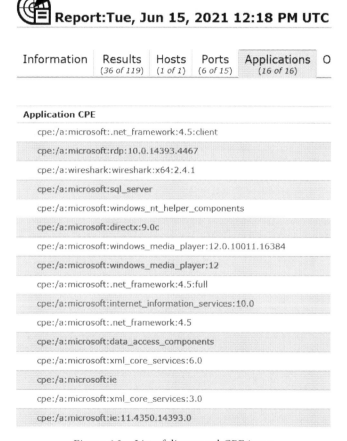

Figure 6.2 – List of discovered CPE items

When you begin a SCAP scan, the scanner will use this information to apply the correct templates/audit input for the scan. In the *Figure 6.2* example, the tool will now look for any vulnerabilities associated with the Windows Server operating system with services including **Remote Desktop Protocol** (**RDP**), Wireshark, and Internet Explorer 11 (there are more services).

Common Vulnerabilities and Exposures (CVE)

CVEs are published by the NVD and MITRE. They give information about the vulnerability; this includes the severity or importance of the vulnerability and how to remediate the vulnerability. This will often be a link to a vendor site for a patch or resolution.

Common Vulnerability Scoring System (CVSS)

CVSS is used to calculate the severity of vulnerabilities by using qualitative risk scoring. The current scoring system is version 3.1. There is a CVSS calculator available at the following link, `https://www.first.org/cvss/calculator/3.1`, to enable security professionals to view the metrics that are used. See *Figure 6.3* for an example CVSS calculator:

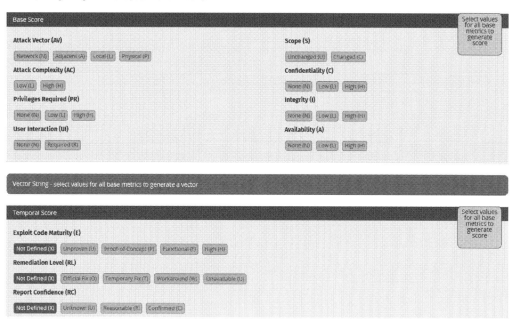

Figure 6.3 – CVSS calculator

An example of a critically rated vulnerability is shown in *Figure 6.4*:

VMware Guest to Host Escape Vulnerability (CVE-2012-1516)
Vulnerability

Due to a flaw in the handler function for Remote Procedure Call (RPC) commands, it is possible to manipulate data pointers within the Virtual Machine Executable (VMX) process. This vulnerability may allow a user in a Guest Virtual Machine to crash the VMX process resulting in a Denial of Service (DoS) on the host or potentially execute code on the host.

Attack

A successful exploit requires an attacker to have access to a Guest Virtual Machine (VM). The Guest VM needs to be configured to have 4GB or more of memory. The attacker would then have to construct a specially crafted remote RPC call to exploit the VMX process.

The VMX process runs in the VMkernel that is responsible for handling input/output to devices that are not critical to performance. It is also responsible for communicating with user interfaces, snapshot managers, and remote console. Each virtual machine has its own VMX process which interacts with the host processes via the VMkernel.

The attacker can exploit the vulnerability to crash the VMX process resulting in a DoS of the host or potentially execute code on the host operating system.

CVSS v3.1 Base Score: 9.9

Metric	Value	Comments
Attack Vector	Network	VMX process is bound to the network stack and the attacker can send RPC commands remotely.
Attack Complexity	Low	The only required condition for this attack is for virtual machines to have 4GB of memory. Virtual machines that have less than 4GB of memory are not affected.
Privileges Required	Low	The attacker must have access to the guest virtual machine. This is easy in a tenant environment.
User Interaction	None	The attacker requires no user interaction to successfully exploit the vulnerability. RPC commands can be sent anytime.
Scope	Changed	The vulnerable component is a VMX process that can only be accessed from the guest virtual machine. The impacted component is the host operating system which has separate authorization authority from the guest virtual machine.
Confidentiality	High	Full compromise of the host operating system via remote code execution.
Integrity	High	Full compromise of the host operating system via remote code execution.
Availability	High	Full compromise of the host operating system via remote code execution.

Figure 6.4 – Critical vulnerability

> **Important Note**
>
> CVE02012-1516 documents a VM escape vulnerability, which could severely impact a modern data center. This would be a top priority to remediate.

The accepted approach is to deal with critically rated vulnerabilities first.

Common Configuration Enumeration (CCE)

This is a set of identifiers to allow configuration items to be easily verified. Currently, the standard is designed only for software-configurable items. This standard allows for templates to be created using a standard format. A common set of identifiers is published for the Microsoft Windows operating system. This allows for the creation of template files to be used with SCAP scanners.

Asset Reporting Format (ARF)

ARF is a standard report format, based on XML templates. It allows for the results of a scan to be formatted in a SCAP-compliant way.

Now that we are aware of the standards and tools available, we should consider who will be responsible for the security assessment.

Self-assessment versus third-party vendor assessment

Self-assessments may be acceptable in certain situations where internal reporting is important. In all cases, governance and risk compliance should be a continuous assessment but sometimes we may need third-party verification; for example, to operate as a **Certificate Authority** (**CA**), you would require third-party auditing reports. To operate as a cloud data center, you would typically require third-party verification, as your customers may only be able to work with suppliers who have accreditation (US government agencies only work with cloud providers who meet FedRAMP requirements). PCI DSS compliance requires an external party to perform a yearly penetration test, where they would likely perform a vulnerability scan. This yearly test cannot be performed internally.

Patch management

Patch management is critical in an enterprise. End devices, servers, and appliances all require constant updating. We have operating systems running services and applications and embedded firmware. Patches offer functionality improvements on the system and, more importantly, security mitigation. Vulnerabilities in a system can ultimately cause availability issues to operations. Patches are first tested by the vendor; they can then be made available to the customer. Occasionally, patches can break working systems, and then the benefit of the patch is largely outweighed by the need to have the system functioning properly. Therefore, an enterprise should thoroughly test patches in a non-production environment before deploying them into a production environment.

There are many other sources for security-related information.

Information sources

While it is important to use automation where possible to produce reports and generate reporting dashboards, it is also important to consider alternative resources to maintain a positive security posture. These resources will provide additional vendor-specific information and industry-related information.

Advisories

It is important for an organization to monitor security advisories; this is information published by vendors or third parties. The information is security-related and will be posted as an update when a new vulnerability is discovered, such as a zero-day exploit. This would be an important mechanism, allowing security professionals to be informed about new threats. We can use advisories to access advice and mitigation for new and existing threats. Some example site URLs are listed as follows:

- **Cisco**: `https://tools.cisco.com/security/center/publicationListing.x`

- **VMware**: `https://www.vmware.com/security/advisories.html`

- **Microsoft**: `https://www.microsoft.com/en-us/msrc/technical-security-notifications?rtc=1`

- **Hewlett Packard**: `https://www.hpe.com/us/en/services/security-vulnerability.html`

> **Tip**
> This would be a good choice for recent vulnerabilities that may not have a CVE assigned to them, such as a zero-day exploit.

Bulletins

Bulletins are another way for vendors to publish security-related issues and vulnerabilities that may affect their customers. Many vendors will support subscriptions through a **Remote Syndicate Service** (**RSS**) feed. Examples of vendor security bulletins are listed as follows:

- **Amazon Web Services** (**AWS**): `https://tinyurl.com/awsbulletins`

- **Google Cloud**: `https://cloud.google.com/compute/docs/security-bulletins`

Vendor websites

Vendor websites can be useful resources for security-related information. In addition to the previously mentioned (advisories and bulletins), additional security-related information, tools, whitepapers, and configuration guides may be available. Microsoft is one of many vendors who offer their customers access to extensive security guidance and best practices: `https://docs.microsoft.com/en-us/security/`.

Information Sharing and Analysis Centers (ISACs)

ISACs allow the sharing of security information or cyber threats by organizations that provide critical infrastructure; it is a global initiative. This initiative also allows the sharing of information between public and private organizations. For more information concerning this initiative, go to `https://www.nationalisacs.org/`.

News reports

News reports can be a useful resource to heighten people's awareness of current threat levels and threat actors. In May/June 2021, there were prominent news reports about recent outbreaks of crypto-malware and ransomware. The following cases made headline news:

- 14 May 2021: The US fuel pipeline Colonial paid criminals $5 million to regain access to systems and resume fuel deliveries. See details at the following link: `https://tinyurl.com/colonialransomware`.

- 10 June 2021: JBS, the world's largest meat processing company, paid out $11 million in bitcoin to regain control of their IT services. Follow the story at this link: `https://tinyurl.com/jcbransomware`.

It is important to be aware that ransomware is still one of the biggest threats facing an organization's information systems.

Testing methods

There are various methods to search for vulnerabilities within an enterprise, depending on the scope of the assignment. Vulnerability assessments are performed by both security professionals, searching for vulnerabilities, and attackers threatening our networks (searching for the same vulnerabilities).

Static analysis

Static analysis is generally used against source code or uncompiled program code. It requires access to the source code so it is more difficult for an attacker to gain access. During a penetration test, the tester would be given the source code to carry out this type of analysis. **Static Application Security Testing** (**SAST**) is an important process to mitigate the risks of vulnerable code.

Dynamic analysis

Dynamic analysis can be done against systems that are operating. If this is software, this will mean the code is already compiled and we assess it using dynamic tools.

Side-channel analysis

Side-channel analysis is targeted against measurable outputs. It is not an attack against the code itself or the actual encryption technology. It requires the monitoring of signals, such as CPU cycles, power spikes, and noise going across a network. The electromagnetic signals can be analyzed using powerful computing technologies and artificial intelligence. Using these techniques, it may be possible to generate the encryption key that is being used in the transmission. An early example of attacks using side-channel analysis was in the 1980s, where IBM equipment was targeted by the Soviet Union. Listening devices were placed inside electronic typewriters. The goal seems to have been to monitor the electrical noise as the carriage struck the paper, with each character having a particular distinctive signature. See the following URL for more information: `https://tinyurl.com/ibmgolfball`.

Reverse engineering may be necessary when we are attempting to understand what a system or piece of code is doing. If we do not have the original source code, it is possible to run an executable in a sandbox environment and monitor its actions. Some code can be decompiled; an example would be Java. There are many available online tools to reverse-engineer Java code. One example is `https://devtoolzone.com/decompiler/java`. Other coding languages do not readily support decompiling.

If the code is embedded on a chip, then we may need to monitor activities in a sandbox environment. Monitor inputs and outputs on the network and compile logs of activity.

Wireless vulnerability scan

Wireless vulnerability scanning is very important as many organizations have a wireless capability. Vulnerabilities may be related to the signal strength, meaning it is visible outside the network boundary.

Security professionals need to secure wireless networks to ensure we are not vulnerable to unwanted intruders. Unsecured protocols must not be used on our wireless networks, ensuring credentials cannot be seen in clear text. We need to ensure administration is not happening across wireless networks in an unsecured format. Older networks may have been configured to use **Wireless Encryption Privacy** (**WEP**) encryption, which is easily crackable, so hackers look for WEP systems so they can crack the key.

Software Composition Analysis (SCA)

It is estimated that around 90% of software developed contains open source software (this was around 10% in 2000). Open source software may be included in developed software by code reuse, it can also be included when a company purchases **Commercial Off-the-Shelf** (**COTS**) products. Third-party development, third-party libraries, and developers accessing code repositories may be other sources of open source software.

SCA is a tool that can analyze all open source code in use in your environment. It is important to have visibility of any third-party code that is included in your production systems. SCA tools can detect all use of third-party code.

As well as searching for third-party code artifacts, SCA will also report on any licensing issues. It is important to understand the restrictions that may affect the distribution or use of software that contains open source code. It may only allow use for non-commercial projects or have strict requirements to distribute your developed software freely.

One of the biggest risks is introducing vulnerabilities through the use of third-party code. SCA can produce reports, allowing for remediation. For more information, see the following link: `https://tinyurl.com/scaTools/`.

Fuzz testing

Fuzz testing will be used to ensure input validation and error handling are tested on the compiled software. Fuzzing will send pseudo-random inputs to the application, in an attempt to create errors within the running code. A fuzzer needs a certain amount of expertise to program and interpret the errors that may be generated. It is common now to incorporate automated fuzz testing into the DevOps pipeline. **Google** uses a tool called **ClusterFuzz** to ensure automated testing of its infrastructure is maintained and errors are logged.

While it is vitally important to perform regular vulnerability assessments against enterprise networks and systems, it will be important to obtain independent verification of the security posture of networks, systems, software, and users.

Penetration testing

Penetration testing can be performed by in-house teams, but regulatory compliance may dictate that independent verification is obtained. It is important you choose a pen testing team that is qualified and trustworthy. The **National Cyber Security Center** (**NCSC**) recommends that United Kingdom government agencies choose a penetration tester that holds one of the following accreditations:

- **CREST**: https://www.crest-approved.org/
- **Tigerscheme**: https://www.tigerscheme.org/
- **Cyber Scheme**: https://www.thecyberscheme.org/

It is important that penetration testers use an industry-standard framework. There are many to choose from. One very useful resource is **Open Web Application Security Project** (**OWASP**). They offer guidance, allowing organizations to select testing criteria to meet regulatory compliance. More information can be found at the following link: http://www.pentest-standard.org/index.php/Exploitation.

One of the popular standards is the **Penetration Testing Execution Standard** (**PTES**). This standard covers seven steps:

1. Pre-engagement interactions
2. Intelligence gathering
3. Threat modeling
4. Vulnerability analysis
5. Exploitation
6. Post-exploitation
7. Reporting

The first step is pre-engagement, where discussions need to be held between the penetration testing representative and the customer representative.

Requirements

When an organization is preparing for security testing, for the report to have value, it is important to understand the exact reasons for the engagement. Are we looking to prepare for regulatory compliance? Perhaps we are testing the security awareness of our employees?

Box testing

When considering the requirements of the assessment, it is worth considering how realistic the assessment will be in terms of simulating an external attack from a highly skilled and motivated adversary.

White box

White box testing is when the attackers have access to all information that is relevant to the engagement. So, if the penetration testers are testing a web application and the customer wants quick results, they would provide the source code and the system design documentation. This is also known as a **full-knowledge test**.

Gray box

Gray box testing sits between white and black and may be a good choice when we don't have an abundance of time. We could eliminate reconnaissance and footprinting, by making available physical and logical network diagrams. This is also known as a **partial-knowledge test**.

Black box

In black box testing, the testers would be given no information, apart from what is publicly available. This is also known as a **zero-knowledge test**. The customer's goal may be to gain a real insight into how secure the company is with a test that simulates a real-world external attacker.

Scope of work

When preparing for penetration testing, it is important to create a scope of work. This should involve stakeholders in the organization, IT professionals managing the target systems, and representation from the penetration testers. This is all about what will be tested. Some of the issues to be discussed would include the following:

- What is the testing environment?
- Is the test for some type of regulatory compliance?
- How long will the testing take? A clear indication of timelines and costs is important.
- How many systems are involved? It is important to have a clear idea of assets to be tested.
- How should the team proceed after initial exploitation?

- Data handling: Will the team need to actually access sensitive documents (PHI, PII, or IP), or simply prove that it is possible?

- Physical testing: Are we testing physical access?

- What level of access will be required? What permissions are needed?

It is important to agree upon how the testing will proceed.

Rules of engagement

It is important to set clear rules about how the testing will proceed. While the scope is all about what is included in the testing, this is more about the process to deliver the test results. Here are some of the typical issues covered within the rules of engagement:

- **Timeline**: A clear understanding of when and how long the entire process will take is important.

- **Locations**: The customer may have multiple physical locations; do we need to gain physical access to all locations, or can we perform remote testing? Is the testing impacted by laws within a specific country?

- **Evidence handling**: Ensure all customer data is secured.

- **Status meetings**: Regular meetings to keep the customer informed of progress is important.

- **Time of day of testing**: It is important to clarify when testing will take place. The customer may want to minimize disruption during regular business hours.

- **Invasive versus non-invasive testing**: How much disruption is the customer prepared to accept?

- **Permission to test**: Do not proceed until the documentation is signed off. This may also be necessary when dealing with cloud providers.

- **Policy**: Will the testing violate any corporate or third-party policies?

- **Legal**: Is the type of testing proposed legal within the country?

Once the rules of engagement are agreed upon and documented, the test can begin. If the rules of engagement are not properly signed off, there could be legal ramifications as you could be considered to be hacking a system.

Post-exploitation

Post-exploitation will involve gathering as much information as possible from compromised systems. This phase will also involve persistence. It is important to adhere to the rules of engagement already defined with the customer. Common activities could include privilege escalation, data exfiltration, and **Denial of Service** (**DOS**). For a comprehensive list of activities, follow this URL: `http://www.pentest-standard.org/index.php/Post_Exploitation#Purpose`.

Persistence

Persistence is the goal for attacks that are long term, for instance, **Advanced Persistent Threats** (**APTs**) are long-term compromises on the organizations' network. **MITRE** lists 19 techniques, used for peristence, in the **ATT&CK Matrix for Enterprise**. The full list can be found at the following link: `https://attack.mitre.org/tactics/TA0003/`. Here are a few of the techniques that are listed:

- Account Manipulation
- **Background Intelligent Transfer Service** (**BITS**) Jobs
- Boot or Logon AutoStart Execution
- Boot or Logon Initialization Scripts
- Browser Extensions
- Compromise Client Software Binary
- Create Accounts

Pivoting

Pivoting is when an attacker gains an initial foothold on a compromised system and then moves laterally through the network to bigger and more important areas. This will typically be achieved by using an existing backdoor, such as a known built-in account. The **MITRE ATT&CK Matrix for Enterprise** lists nine techniques for lateral movement. The following is a list of typical tactics used for pivoting:

- Exploitation of Remote Services
- Internal SpearPhishing
- Lateral Tool Transfer
- Remote Service Session Hijacking
- Remote Services

- Replication Through Removable Media

- Software Deployment Tools

- Taint Shared Content

- Use Alternate Authentication Material

For more detail on these nine methods, follow this URL: `https://attack.mitre.org/versions/v9/matrices/enterprise/`.

Pivoting allows the tester to move laterally through networks and is an important process for gaining insights into systems on other network segments.

Rescanning for corrections/changes

It is important for management and security professionals to act on the results of penetration testing. Controls should be put in place to remediate issues with the highest criticalities being prioritized. We can run further tests to assess the controls.

Security professionals and penetration testing teams will use a variety of tools to test the security posture of networks, systems, and users.

Security tools

There are many tools available to identify and collect security vulnerabilities or to provide a deeper analysis of interactions between systems and services. When penetration testing is being conducted, the scope of the test may mean the team is given zero knowledge of the network. This would be referred to as black box testing. The team would need to deploy tools to enumerate networks and services and use reverse engineering techniques against applications. We will take a look at these tools.

SCAP scanner

A SCAP scanner will be used to report on deviations from a baseline, using input files such as STIGs or other XML baseline configuration files. The SCAP scan will also search for vulnerabilities present, by detecting the operating system and software installed using the CPE standard. Once the information is gathered about installed products, the SCAP scan can now search for known vulnerabilities related to CVEs.

Figure 6.5 shows the results of a SCAP scan with critical vulnerabilities listed first (OpenVAS is an OVAL-compliant SCAP scanner):

Figure 6.5 – OpenVAS SCAP scan

To remediate one of the critically rated vulnerabilities, there is a vendor fix, in the form of a software update; *see Figure 6.6*:

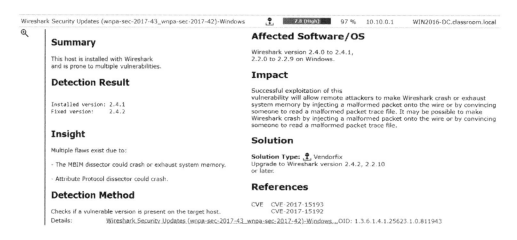

Figure 6.6 – Vendor fix

For each identified vulnerability, there will be a course of action, patch to be downloaded, configuration change, workaround, or uninstallation.

Network traffic analyzer

It is important for baseline traffic to be gathered. This allows professionals to understand normal traffic patterns and be alerted to anomalies. These tools can be useful for capacity planning as we can detect trends. *Figure 6.7* shows the network traffic flow breakdown:

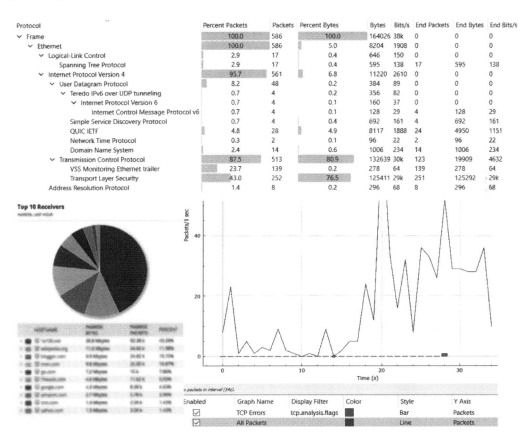

Figure 6.7 – Network traffic flow

As well as understanding the traffic patterns on the network, it is important to consider the security posture of the devices connected to the network.

Vulnerability scanner

A vulnerability scanner can be used to detect open listening ports, misconfigured applications, missing security patches, poor security on a web application, and many other types of vulnerability. *Figure 6.8* shows a vulnerability scan against a website:

10.10.0.1 / 10.10.0.1 port 80	
Target IP	10.10.0.1
Target hostname	10.10.0.1
Target Port	80
HTTP Server	Microsoft-IIS/10.0
Site Link (Name)	http://10.10.0.1:80/
Site Link (IP)	http://10.10.0.1:80/

URI	/
HTTP Method	GET
Description	Retrieved x-powered-by header: ASP.NET
Test Links	http://10.10.0.1:80/ http://10.10.0.1:80/
OSVDB Entries	OSVDB-0
URI	/
HTTP Method	GET
Description	Uncommon header 'strict -transport -security' found, with contents: max-age=63072000; includeSubDomains; Preload
Test Links	http://10.10.0.1:80/ http://10.10.0.1:80/
URI	/
HTTP Method	GET
Description	Uncommon header 'strict -transport -security' found, with contents: max-age=63072000; includeSubDomains; Preload
Test Links	http://10.10.0.1:80/ http://10.10.0.1:80/
OSVDB Entries	OSVDB-0
URI	/
HTTP Method	GET
Description	The X-Content-Type-Options header is not set. This could allow the user agent to render the content of the site in a different fashion to the MIME type
Test Links	http://10.10.0.1:80/ http://10.10.0.1:80/
OSVDB Entries	OSVDB-0

Host Summary	
Start Time	2021-06-17 10:53:08
End Time	2021-06-17 10:54:42
Elapsed Time	94 seconds
Statistics	8041 requests, 0 errors, 6 findings

Scan Summary	
Software Details	Nikto 2.1.6
CLI Options	-host 10.10.0.1 -Format html -output /home/mark/Documents/vreport.htm
Hosts Tested	1
Start Time	Thu Jun 17 10:53:07 2021
End Time	Thu Jun 17 10:54:42 2021
Elapsed Time	95 seconds

Figure 6.8 – Vulnerability scanner

A vulnerability scan is very important but may not reveal additional information contained within network traffic protocols and payloads.

Protocol analyzer

A protocol analyzer is useful when we need to perform **Deep Packet Inspection** (**DPI**) on network traffic. tcpdump, TShark, and Wireshark would be common implementations of this technology. It is possible to capture network traffic using a common file format, to then analyze within the tool at a later time. We could use this tool to confirm the use of unsecure protocols or data exfiltration. *Figure 6.9* shows Wireshark in use, with a capture of unsecured FTP traffic:

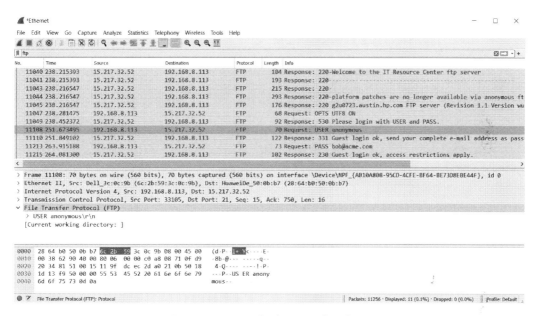

Figure 6.9 – Wireshark protocol analyzer

When the network needs to be enumerated or mapped, a protocol analyzer will not be the most efficient tool. An active scan may be a better choice.

Port scanner

A port scanner will typically perform a ping sweep in the first instance, to identify all the live network hosts on a network. Each host will then be probed to establish the TCP and UDP listening ports. Port scans can be done to identify unnecessary applications present on a network. They can also be used by hackers to enumerate services on a network segment. A port scan performed by NMAP is shown in *Figure 6.10*:

```
nmap -T4 -A -v 192.168.0.0/24

Initiating SYN Stealth Scan at 11:15
Scanning 192.168.0.8 [1000 ports]
Discovered open port 139/tcp on 192.168.0.8
Discovered open port 445/tcp on 192.168.0.8
Discovered open port 135/tcp on 192.168.0.8
Discovered open port 2179/tcp on 192.168.0.8
Discovered open port 808/tcp on 192.168.0.8
Discovered open port 5357/tcp on 192.168.0.8
Completed SYN Stealth Scan at 11:15, 0.06s elapsed (1000 total ports)
Initiating Service scan at 11:15
Scanning 6 services on 192.168.0.8
Completed Service scan at 11:15, 21.06s elapsed (6 services on 1 host)
Initiating OS detection (try #1) against 192.168.0.8
NSE: Script scanning 192.168.0.8.
Initiating NSE at 11:15
Completed NSE at 11:15, 14.34s elapsed
Initiating NSE at 11:15
Completed NSE at 11:15, 0.01s elapsed
Initiating NSE at 11:15
Completed NSE at 11:15, 0.00s elapsed
Nmap scan report for 192.168.0.8
Host is up (0.00020s latency).
Not shown: 994 closed ports
PORT      STATE SERVICE          VERSION
135/tcp   open  msrpc            Microsoft Windows RPC
139/tcp   open  netbios-ssn      Microsoft Windows netbios-ssn
445/tcp   open  microsoft-ds?
808/tcp   open  mc-nmf           .NET Message Framing
2179/tcp  open  vmrdp?
5357/tcp  open  http             Microsoft HTTPAPI httpd 2.0 (SSDP/UPnP)
|_http-server-header: Microsoft-HTTPAPI/2.0
|_http-title: Service Unavailable
Device type: general purpose
Running: Microsoft Windows 10
OS CPE: cpe:/o:microsoft:windows_10
OS details: Microsoft Windows 10 1809 - 1909
Network Distance: 0 hops
TCP Sequence Prediction: Difficulty=261 (Good luck!)
IP ID Sequence Generation: Incremental
Service Info: OS: Windows; CPE: cpe:/o:microsoft:windows
```

Figure 6.10 – NMAP scan

Once an attacker or penetration tester has identified available hosts and services, they can attempt to gather more information, using additional tools.

HTTP interceptor

HTTP interceptors are used by security analysts and pen testers. When we need to assess the security posture of a web application without being given access to the source code, this tool is useful. *Figure 6.11* shows **Burp Suite**, a popular HTTP interceptor. It is provided as a default application on **Kali Linux**:

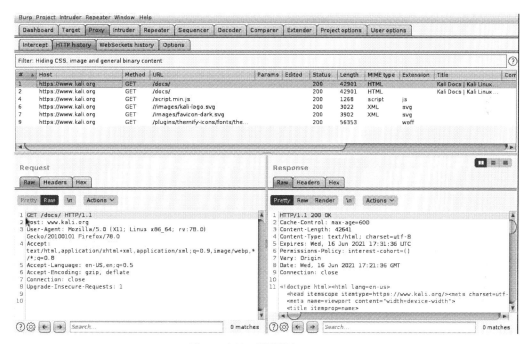

Figure 6.11 – HTTP interceptor

The HTTP interceptor is installed as a proxy directly on the host workstation. All browser requests and web server responses can be viewed in raw HTML, allowing the tester to gain valuable information about the application. See *Figure 6.12* for the interceptor traffic flow:

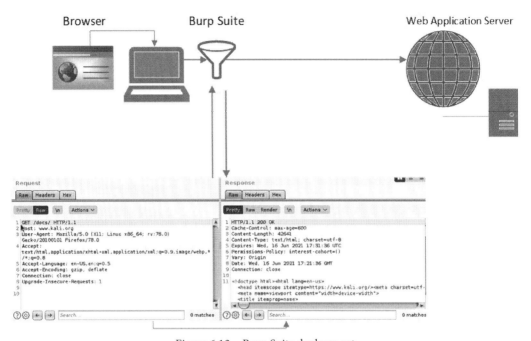

Figure 6.12 – Burp Suite deployment

The use of this tool would require some developer/coding knowledge, to interpret the captured payloads.

Exploit framework

Penetration testers can use an exploitation framework to transmit payloads to hosts on a network. Typically, this is done through vulnerabilities that have been identified. Popular frameworks include **Sn1per**, **Core Impact**, **Canvas**, and **Metasploit**. Exploit frameworks must be kept up to date to make sure all vulnerabilities are discovered and tested. Once a scan has detected hosts on the network and identified operating systems, the attack can begin. *Figure 6.13* shows a Linux host about to be tested by Metasploit:

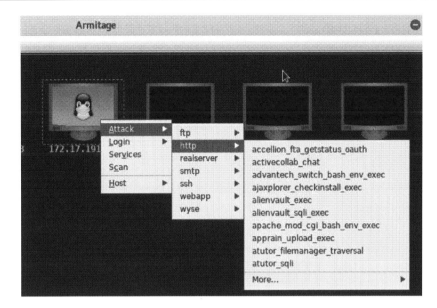

Figure 6.13 – Exploitation framework

Exploitation frameworks can be quite complex, requiring expertise in a pen testing environment.

Password crackers

Password crackers are useful to determine whether weak passwords are being used in the organization. Common password crackers are **Ophcrack**, **John the Ripper**, and **Brutus** (there are many more examples). There are many online resources as well, including dictionary and rainbow tables.

Figure 6.14 shows the use of John the Ripper against a Linux password database:

User account

```
(root💀kali2020)-[/etc]
# john --format=sha512crypt mypasswd -show
root:toor:0:0:root:/root:/usr/bin/zsh
tech01:security:1001:1001::/home/tech01:/bin/sh
tech02:strong:1002:1002::/home/tech02:/bin/sh

3 password hashes cracked, 1 left
```

User password

Figure 6.14 – John the Ripper password cracking

In the output for *Figure 6.14*, the first column is for the user account and the second value is the *cracked* password. So, user `tech02` has set their password to be `strong` (which is just a plain text dictionary word).

> **Important Note**
>
> While *toor* is not a common dictionary word, it is a poor choice of password for the root account.

Dependency management tools

Dependency management is important when planning to build large and often complex applications. Many software builds will incorporate third-party libraries and additional code modules. These tools will ensure we are using the correct library version or code version and can also keep track of any security issues with all code bases.

Popular tools include **NuGet** (for Microsoft .NET development) and **Composer** (for PHP developers), but there are many more.

Summary

In this chapter, we have looked at a variety of tools and frameworks to protect information systems.

We have identified the appropriate tools used to assess the security posture of operating systems, networks, and end user devices. We have also learned how to secure our systems using vulnerability scanning. We have identified industry-standard tools and protocols, to ensure compatibility across the enterprise (such as SCAP, CVE, CPE, and OVAL), and examined information sources where current threats and vulnerabilities are published. We have also looked at the requirements for managing third-party engagements, to assess our systems, and learned about the tools used for internal and external penetration testing.

These skills will be important as we learn about incident response and forensic analysis in the next chapter.

Questions

Here are a few questions to test your understanding of the chapter:

1. When performing a SCAP scan on a system, which of the following types of scans will be most useful?

    A. Credentialed

    B. Non-credentialed

    C. Agent-based

    D. Intrusive

2. What would be most important when monitoring security on ICS networks, where latency must be minimized?

    A. Group Policy

    B. Active scanning

    C. Passive scanning

    D. Continuous integration

3. What is the protocol that allows for the automation of security compliance scans?

    A. SCAP

    B. CVSS

    C. CVE

    D. ARF

4. What standard would support the creation of XML-format configuration templates?

    A. XCCDF

    B. CVE

    C. CPE

    D. NMAP

5. What standard allows a vulnerability scanner to detect the host operating system and installed applications?

    A. XCCDF

    B. CVE

    C. CPE

    D. SCAP

6. What standard supports a common reporting standard for vulnerability scanning?

    A. XCCDF

    B. CVE

    C. OVAL

    D. STIG

7. What information type can be found at MITRE and NIST NVD that describes a known vulnerability and gives information regarding remediation?

    A. CVE

    B. CPE

    C. CVSS

    D. OVAL

8. What is used to calculate the criticality of a known vulnerability?

    A. CVE

    B. CPE

    C. CVSS

    D. OVAL

9. If my organization is preparing to host publicly available SaaS services in the data center, what kind of assessment would be best?

    A. Self-assessment

    B. Third-party assessment

    C. PCI compliance

    D. Internal assessment

10. When we download patches from Microsoft, where should they be tested *first*?

    A. Staging network

    B. Production network

    C. DMZ network

    D. IT administration network

11. Where can security professionals go to remain aware of vendor-published security updates and guidance? (Choose all that apply.)

    A. Advisories

    B. Bulletins

    C. Vendor websites

    D. MITRE

12. What allows European critical infrastructure providers to share security-related information?

    A. ISACs

    B. NIST

    C. SCAP

    D. CISA

13. What kind of testing would be performed against uncompiled code?

    A. Static analysis

    B. Dynamic analysis

    C. Fuzzing

    D. Reverse engineering

14. What type of analysis would allow researchers to measure power usage to predict the encryption keys generated by a crypto-processor?

    A. Side-channel analysis

    B. Frequency analysis

    C. Network analysis

    D. Hacking

15. What type of analysis would most likely be used when researchers need to study third-party compiled code?

    A. Static analysis

    B. Side-channel analysis

    C. Input validation

    D. Reverse engineering

16. What automated tool would developers use to report on any outdated software libraries and licensing requirements?

    A. Software composition analysis

    B. Side-channel analysis

    C. Input validation

    D. Reverse engineering

17. What is it called when we send pseudo-random inputs to an application, in an attempt to find flaws in the code?

    A. Fuzz testing

    B. Input validation

    C. Reverse engineering

    D. Pivoting

18. What is the term for lateral movement from a compromised host system?

    A. Pivoting

    B. Reverse engineering

    C. Persistence

    D. Requirements

19. When would a penetration tester use a privilege escalation exploit?

    A. Post-exploitation

    B. OSINT

    C. Reconnaissance

    D. Foot printing

20. What is the correct term for a penetration tester manipulating the registry in order to launch a binary file during the boot sequence?

    A. Pivoting

    B. Reverse engineering

    C. Persistence

    D. Requirements

21. What tool would allow network analysts to report on network utilization levels?

    A. Network traffic analyzer

    B. Vulnerability scanner

    C. Protocol analyzer

    D. Port scanner

22. What would be the *best* tool to test the security configuration settings for a web application server?

    A. Network traffic analyzer

    B. Vulnerability scanner

    C. Protocol analyzer

    D. Port scanner

23. With what tool would penetration testers discover live hosts and application services on a network segment?

    A. Network traffic analyzer

    B. Vulnerability scanner

    C. Protocol analyzer

    D. Port scanner

24. What type of tool would perform uncredentialed scans?

    A. Network traffic analyzer

    B. Vulnerability scanner

    C. Protocol analyzer

    D. Port scanner

25. What could be used to reverse engineer a web server API when conducting a zero-knowledge (black box) test?

   A. Exploitation framework

   B. Port scanner

   C. HTTP interceptor

   D. Password cracker

26. What tool could be used by hackers to discover unpatched systems using automated scripts?

   A. Exploitation framework

   B. Port scanner

   C. HTTP interceptor

   D. Password cracker

27. What would allow system administrators to discover weak passwords stored on the server?

   A. Exploitation framework

   B. Port scanner

   C. HTTP interceptor

   D. Password cracker

28. What documentation would mitigate the risk of pen testers testing the security posture of all regional data centers when the requirement was only for the e-commerce operation center?

   A. Requirements

   B. Scope of work

   C. Rules of engagement

   D. Asset inventory

29. What documentation would mitigate the risk of pen testers unintentionally causing an outage on the network during business hours?

   A. Requirements

   B. Scope of work

   C. Rules of engagement

   D. Asset inventory

30. What type of security assessment is taking place if the tester needs to perform badge skimming *first*?

    A. Network security assessment

    B. Corporate policy considerations

    C. Facility considerations

    D. Physical security assessment

Answers

1. A
2. C
3. A
4. A
5. C
6. C
7. A
8. C
9. B
10. A
11. A, B and C
12. A
13. A
14. A
15. D
16. A
17. A
18. A
19. A
20. C
21. A
22. B
23. D

24. D
25. C
26. A
27. D
28. B
29. C
30. D

7
Risk Mitigation Controls

A large enterprise providing information services or critical infrastructure presents a large attack surface. We must consider all aspects of security, including application vulnerabilities and the likelihood that we will be attacked (always think worst-case scenario). We must be aware of the kind of attacks to expect and, most importantly, how to mitigate these threats. We must be proactive in our approach, using the latest tools and techniques to best protect our assets. We must also consider physical security. But most importantly, we should deploy **defense in depth**.

In this chapter, we will go over the following topics:

- Understanding application vulnerabilities
- Assessing inherently vulnerable systems/applications
- Recognizing common attacks
- Proactive and detective risk reduction
- Applying preventative risk reduction

Understanding application vulnerabilities

Information systems offer many options to interact with business users and customers. We have public-facing web application servers, **business-to-business** (**B2B**) API connectivity requirements, and mobile devices, to name a few. It is important that we eliminate vulnerabilities during the design and development process when rolling out new systems and services. We must also consider the security of legacy applications that may still be required by the business. It is useful to refer to industry best practices when considering application vulnerabilities and the **Open Web Application Security Project** (**OWASP**) is a recommended resource:

```
https://owasp.org/www-project-top-ten/
```

We will see the various vulnerabilities in the following section.

Race conditions

A *race condition*, also known as **time of check time of use** (**TOCTOU**), is usually associated with a stored value and the use of that stored value. It is a time-related vulnerability that can cause unexpected or unwanted results. For example, an application stores a shopping basket with a total value of $500. Another thread (within the code module) commits the total as a sales transaction and charges the customer account. This process takes 800 ms before reading in the total value. Meanwhile, the customer has been able to change the stored value of $500 to $1. These flaws are difficult to test for.

Buffer overflows

A *memory buffer* is used to store a value. An attacker can target the memory location by inputting too many characters and can cause unwanted results. If the buffer has a 16-byte limit and the actual data sent is for 17 bytes, then the outcome will be an overflow, where the extra byte may have access to a memory location for unwanted processing. This result of a buffer overflow can be a **denial of service** (**DoS**) condition or the goal may be to run an arbitrary command. It is important for developers to perform input validation within the code.

Integer overflows

Integer overflows target a memory location storing a numerical value. If the appropriate input validation checks are not present in the code, then a value may be accepted that is outside of the range declared for the memory location. This can cause errors and unwanted results.

Broken authentication

Broken authentication is one of the OWASP top-10 risks. Attackers will target applications using **credential stuffing** (lists of valid accounts and passwords), brute-force password attacks, unexpired session cookies, and many more. Protection against these types of attacks would include the elimination of weak passwords and the use of **multi-factor authentication** (**MFA**). For more details, see `https://tinyurl.com/OWASPA2`.

Insecure references

This vulnerability now comes under the OWASP heading of *broken access control* and is number 5 in the *web at-risk* categories. It means a user can gain access to a part of the system that they have no authorization for. It is made possible by privilege escalation, bypassing access control validation, or reusing another user's session ID. For more information, see `https://tinyurl.com/OWASPA5`.

Poor exception handling

Poor exception handling may cause system outages or give attackers additional information about the system. Imagine an attacker is logging into a web portal and, after entering the wrong data into the password field, the web portal throws the standard MySQL error message along with the information that the password string for the user is wrong. The attacker now knows the version of the backend database application and also knows that they have a valid user ID.

Security misconfiguration

Security misconfiguration could affect many parts of a system providing customer-focused web applications. The network environment could be poorly configured, or a misconfigured firewall may allow access over an insecure port. The operating system, libraries, applications, storage, and HTTP improper headers should all be considered when assessing organizational security.

Information disclosure

Information disclosure could allow an attacker to view data that is covered by regulatory compliance, laws, intellectual property, and more. This vulnerability can be present due to a number of factors, including weak encryption algorithms, no encryption, insecure protocols, and unsecured data storage, to list a few. For more information, see `https://tinyurl.com/OWASPA3`.

Certificate errors

It is important to allow for secure transport of internet application protocols. Certificates must meet certain criteria in order to be trusted by the client-side application. *Figure 7.1* shows typical fields on a standard X.509 certificate:

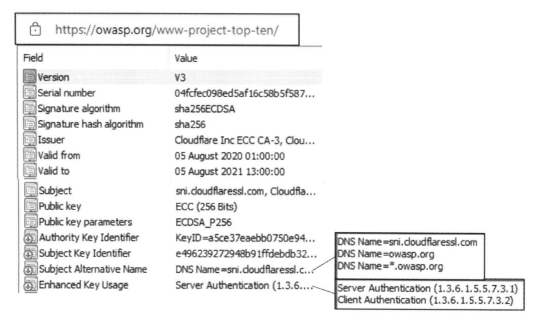

Figure 7.1 – Certificate fields

The following requirements must be met for the application server to be trusted:

- The client must trust the **certificate authority (CA)**.

- The certificate **Subject Name** value must be valid.

- The certificate **Validity date** value must be valid.

- The certificate **Enhanced Key Usage** field must be present.

- The certificate is not on the **Certificate Revocation List (CRL)**.

If the certificate will be used for multiple sites, it will need to support **wildcards** or **Subject Alternate Names (SANs)**.

To assess the security posture of a hosted application accessed over SSL/TLS, a vulnerability assessment tool will also check for all the common vulnerabilities associated with certificates.

Figure 7.2 shows a connection to a web page that is not trusted:

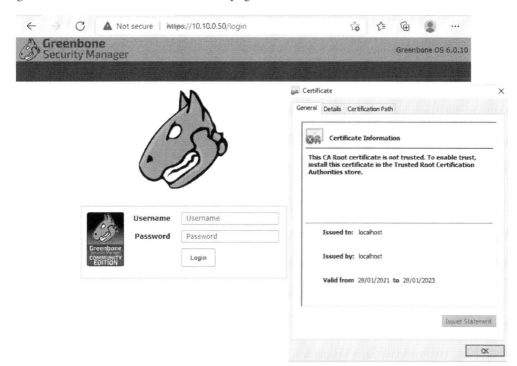

Figure 7.2 – Untrusted web browser connection

If the certificate authority is not trusted, then the certificate provided by the site will show an error.

Weak cryptography implementations

When using TLS, the use of SSL has been deprecated, as it is now considered less secure. *Figure 7.3* shows the output from a vulnerability testing tool against a banking website:

Protocols	
TLS 1.3	Yes
TLS 1.2	Yes
TLS 1.1	No
TLS 1.0	No
SSL 3	No
SSL 2	No

Figure 7.3 – Secure Transport Layer Security (TLS)

The current industry standard is *TLS 1.2*. Some sites may also support *TLS 1.3*. SSL is not used anymore as it is considered insecure. As we can see in *Figure 7.3*, older, un-secure standards are not supported. It is a cat and mouse game where better encryption standards get released and the push is on for people to upgrade their systems to the stronger and more secure standards.

Weak ciphers

A *cipher* is the combination of a unique key and a method to encrypt the data. The **Data Encryption Standard** (**DES**) was developed in the 1970s and would definitely meet the criteria for a weak cipher. It has a maximum key size of 64 bits, but in reality, the actual key size used is only 56 bits.

Weak cipher suite implementations

A *cipher suite* is a combination of encryption types. For a secure session with a website, we will use a combination of *symmetric*, *asymmetric*, and *hashing encryption*. In *Figure 7.4*, we can see the acceptable cipher suites supported by our banking website:

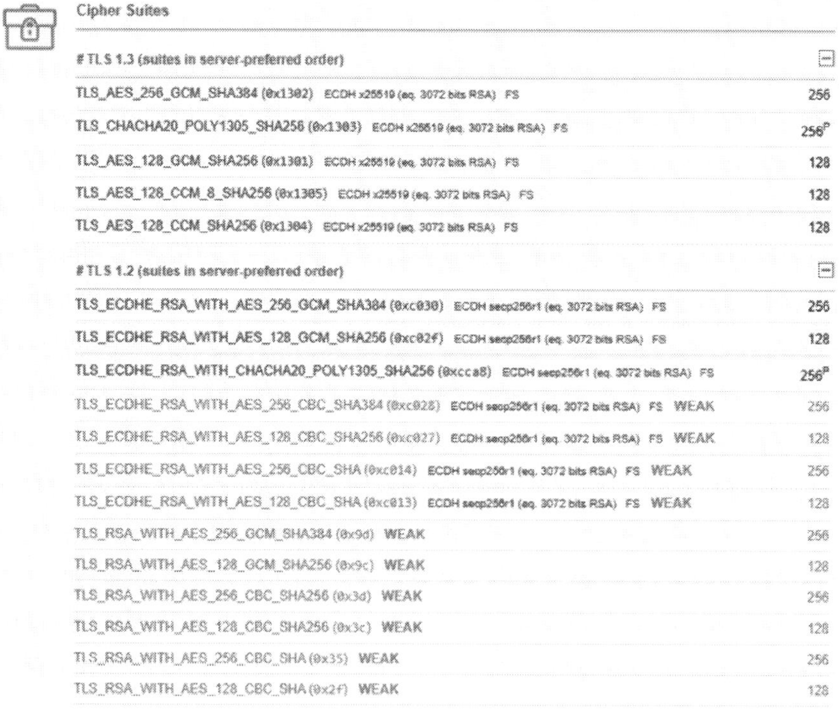

Figure 7.4 – Output from the Qualys SSL Labs vulnerability testing tool

In the scan results, the weakest detected cipher suites are considered to be acceptable, as the site received an *A+* security rating.

Software composition analysis

It is important to identify all code bases and libraries used to host web application services. **Software composition analysis (SCA)** can automate the process of checking for vulnerabilities within these code bases and also check for licensing infringements (easily overlooked when using third-party libraries).

Use of vulnerable frameworks and software modules

Any system development that does not adhere to a structured framework with a repeatable secure project-managed process presents risks. There are many frameworks that ensure a secure framework and can lead to robust, secure systems. The **National Institute of Standards and Technology (NIST)** guidance would advocate for the use of a **secure software development framework (SSDF)**. NIST published a whitepaper with guidance for implementing this framework (`https://tinyurl.com/nistSSDF`). **Microsoft** also advocates the use of a secure framework called the **Security Development Lifecycle (SDL)**. Microsoft uses a 12-step approach to ensure that secure coding/development is maintained. *Figure 7.5* shows the 12 steps:

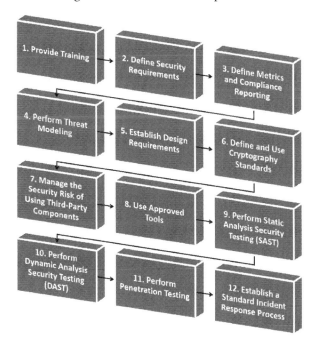

Figure 7.5 – Microsoft SDL framework

For more details, use the following link:

```
https://tinyurl.com/MicrosoftSDLFramework
```

Use of unsafe functions

There are certain development languages that are vulnerable to the use of deprecated, unsafe functions. Examples include **C**, **C++**, and **Assembly**. Some functions make the likelihood of a buffer overflow or other such processes a real possibility.

One example is the `strcpy()` function. It is used to copy data and doesn't check the data size to ensure it will fit into a memory buffer. This can result in buffer overflow exploits. There is a replacement function, `strcpy_s()`, that should now be used.

The MITRE Corporation has published **CWE-676** to document the use of dangerous functions that can lead to exploits. See the following link for more information:

```
https://tinyurl.com/MITRECWE-676
```

OWASP also provides a very good resource called **cheat sheets**. These document many examples of unsafe functions and ways to mitigate their use:

```
https://cheatsheetseries.owasp.org/index.html
```

Third-party libraries

When we use third-party libraries, we need to ensure vulnerabilities are not present and that we are not infringing on any licensing restrictions.

Dependencies

It is important to ensure dependencies are in place so software can be deployed and functions reliably without error. For example, a program written in **Java** needs a Java **virtual machine** (**VM**) to be available, and without this dependency, it cannot run. Another example would be an application that will use location services provided by the **Google Maps API**. Many applications will now use online services, and if that service is withdrawn, your code will not function.

End-of-support and end-of-life

Many systems will reach a point when the original developer or manufacturer stops developing patches or offering support for their product. At this point, you run the risk of supporting a vulnerable system that hackers will know cannot be patched. **End-of-life** (**EOL**) is one of the greatest risks in cybersecurity. The mitigation for these systems is *segmentation* and *controlled access*.

Regression issues

When a software component has previously worked well, but now proves to be slow or unresponsive, it is known as a *software regression bug*. It is important we test all software modules to ensure they are still functioning whenever other parts of the system are changed. The testing is known as *regression testing*.

Assessing inherently vulnerable systems and applications

A good example of where we have inherent vulnerabilities would be when considering critical infrastructure. Many power plants and other such industries may rely on technology that was developed and installed decades ago. The main criteria were about reliability and availability, not security. This has proven to be the case with fresh attacks on critical infrastructure being a weekly occurrence. Applications used in these industries may also lack security controls, with the main goal being reliability. When we consider web application servers, there are always inherent risks due to the hosting of public-facing applications and services. We will now consider some of these issues.

Client-side processing and server-side processing

Client-side processing runs on the client and server-side runs on the server. Client-side processing is performed using dynamic runtime code – it is not compiled into binary files. Server-side code is compiled and will be coded in languages such as C+, C++, **Rust**, and **Microsoft C#**. Uncompiled code running on a client browser should be considered untrustworthy, as it is more easily manipulated and can easily become the target of code injections, allowing malicious changes to be forwarded to the web application server. Uncompiled code can be referred to as *byte code*, whereas compiled code is referred to as *machine code*. Another common way to describe the code that will run on the client browser is *interpreted code*, which needs an interpreter to process the code (such as **Python** or **Perl**).

JSON and representational state transfer

Web applications use APIs to make services available to other computers and applications across networks. A popular standards-based approach is to use **representational state transfer** (**RESTful**) architectures, where there is support for secure TLS (using the HTTPS protocol), as well as support for standard message formats, such as **XML** and **JSON**.

JSON is an extension of **JavaScript**. It allows for the transmission and storage of data and is a lightweight, low-overhead mechanism. It is based on key-value pairs, where there is a field name followed by a value. An example of a JSON key pair would look like the following:

```
{"firstName": "John","lastName":"Jones"}
```

Browser extensions

A *browser extension* adds additional functionality to a web browser. A useful addition to allow playing media-rich content is **Adobe Flash** – once installed, it is important to keep this up to date with patches, as there are many instances of vulnerabilities on older versions of Flash. **ActiveX** is a supported browser extension within the **Microsoft Internet Explorer** browser. ActiveX allows functionality such as spell checkers, language translators, and location services to be available within the browser. It is important to validate the source for any downloaded browser extensions and to ensure they are updated/patched. The **Microsoft Edge** browser will only allow the addition of browser extensions from the **Windows Store**. See *Figure 7.6* for an example of Microsoft Edge extensions:

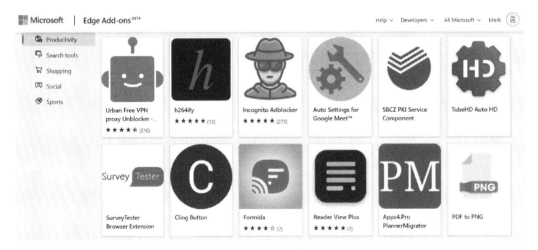

Figure 7.6 – Microsoft Edge extensions

Access to these extensions can be restricted by policy restrictions.

Hypertext Markup Language 5 (HTML5)

HTLM5 is the latest implementation of a format that describes how to display web documents. It uses semantics and tags to allow the rich display of web pages. It also allows for dynamic content such as streaming media and as such offers an alternative for Adobe Flash.

Asynchronous JavaScript and XML (AJAX)

Asynchronous JavaScript and XML (**AJAX**) allows requests to be sent from the client browser to the web application server. It is able to send XML requests over HTTP and display the results using the JavaScript and HTML **Direct Object Model** (**DOM**). It is useful when you do not need to refresh the entire page. **Google Maps** uses this technology.

Simple Object Access Protocol (SOAP)

Simple Object Access Protocol (**SOAP**) is a standard message format based on XML that can be used to pass information between a client and a server-based web application.

Recognizing common attacks

Attacks against systems and software are a real threat, based on the fact that systems need to be made accessible to business users and customers. For web applications, the typical scenario is a customer-facing application server behind a firewall, able to communicate with intranet-based services. A typical deployment can be seen in *Figure 7.7*, where the inputs will be through web-based forms run on the client browser and the results forwarded to the web application server:

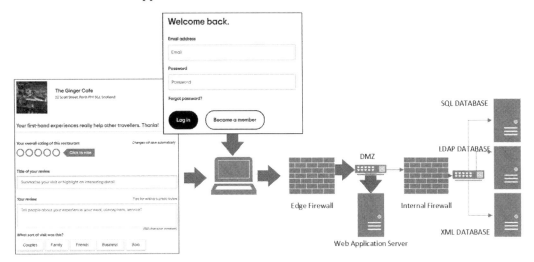

Figure 7.7 – Web application server located in DMZ

When we secure our networks using secured firewalls, it is difficult to attack the intranet services directly, so it is the web application server that is targeted. This is where the attacker will direct the attacks. In this section, we will focus on attacks that use the model shown in *Figure 7.7*.

Directory traversal

Directory traversal is when an attacker can input syntax that allows them to move through the filesystem of the target web server. The goal of this is to access directories and files that should be restricted. *Figure 7.8* shows a typical string that attempts to move into the root directory and then switch into the etc folder and display the password file:

The Ginger Cafe
22 Scott Street, Perth PH15EJ, Scotland

Your first-hand experiences really help other travellers. Thanks!

```
mark:x:1000:1000:mark,,,:/home/mark:/usr/bin/zsh
systemd-coredump:x:999:999:systemd Core Dumper:/:/usr/sbin/nologin
tech01:x:1001:1001::/home/tech01:/bin/sh
tech02:x:1002:1002::/home/tech02:/bin/sh
```

Figure 7.8 – Directory traversal

In the preceding example, there are no passwords stored, but we have still gained access to user accounts.

Cross-site scripting

Cross-site scripting (**XSS**) is an attack where the hacker will embed a script into a web page, then once the script is added to the web page, it will be loaded whenever the page is rendered in a user's web browser. The target could be a travel site where you can leave reviews. In *Figure 7.9*, we can see a script that has been added to a website that will run a script from the attacker's site:

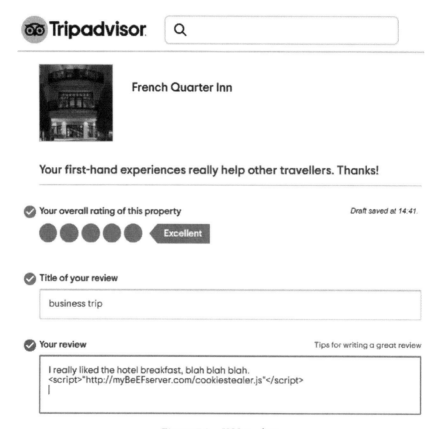

Figure 7.9 – XSS exploit

In the XSS example, the script will run when the page is rendered in the victim's browser and the attacker's script will steal the session cookie.

Cross-site request forgery

A **cross-site request forgery** (**CSRF**) happens when a user already has a trusted connection to a website, authenticated over HTTPS. The goal of the attacker is to run a script that would authorize some kind of transaction. An example could be to make a payment using online banking. In *Figure 7.10*, a victim will load the web page and the script will make a payment into another customer's account:

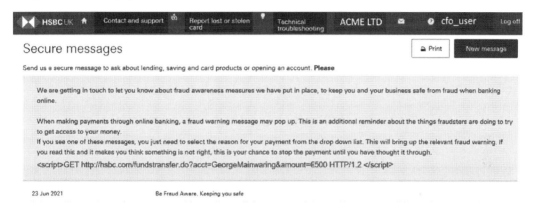

Figure 7.10 – CSRF example

The example script at the bottom of the bank customer's message is shown in the following snippet:

```
<script>GET http://hsbc.com/fundstransfer.
do?acct=GeorgeMainwaring&amount=€500 HTTP/1.2</script>
```

This kind of attack is, however, highly unlikely to succeed on a banking website.

Injection attacks

Injection attacks will use the customer-facing web application server as the go-between. The commands will target the input fields of the application and the web application will forward the requests to the backend server.

XML

XML is a common language for exchanging data and facilitating communication between web applications. The goal is to access content or manipulate transactions.

LDAP

LDAP command verbs allow searching, creating, or modifying accounts stored in directory services. Some examples using command-line syntax for **Microsoft Active Directory** services are shown as follows. In the first example, we are searching for all users in the `itadmin` container:

Input:

```
dsquery user "ou=it admin,dc=classroom,dc=local"
```

Result:

```
"CN=Mark Birch,OU=IT Admin,DC=classroom,DC=local"
```

In the second example, we are creating a new user account in the `users` container:

Input:

```
dsadd user "cn=sqlsystem,cn=users,dc=classroom,dc=local" -pwd
Pa$$w0rd1
```

Result:

```
dsadd succeeded:cn=sqlsystem,cn=users,dc=classroom,dc=local
```

Structured Query Language

Structured Query Language (**SQL**) is commonly used to store user accounts for web applications. It is a very powerful language allowing queries and record retrievals. SQL databases can be used to store many different record types. SQL databases are used for **enterprise resource planning** (**ERP**), sales order processing, and many other lines of business applications. The range of commands is large, allowing everything from retrieval of records to entire table deletions. During a logon through a web application, we can use a valid user account and password, which will result in the following SQL string:

```
SELECT id FROM users WHERE username = 'jack' AND password =
'patch'
```

Then, using that command logic, we could submit the following command:

```
SELECT * FROM users WHERE username = 'user1' AND password =
'mypass1' OR 1=1
```

In this example the AND condition is evaluated before the OR operator, making the WHERE clause true. If the application does not perform the appropriate string checks, then the application will select the first record in the user's table as the command logic will make the statement true (1=1 is always true). This would result in an authentication bypass exploit. *Figure 7.11* shows how this could be input into a login screen:

Figure 7.11 – SQL injection attempt

This type of exploit allows the attacker to access the first account in the table of users. *Figure 7.12* shows a successful login attempt:

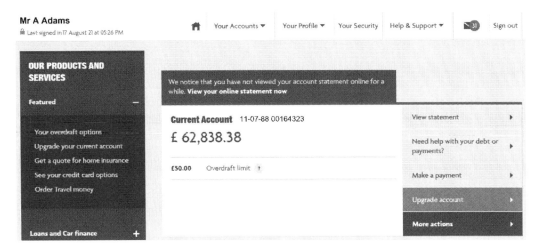

Figure 7.12 – SQL injection login

Now, the hacker can attempt to manipulate account details.

Sandbox escape

There are many examples of code running in a secure sandbox with no insecure interactions with the local operating system or filesystem allowed, with **Chrome** and Edge browsers being examples of this technology. A vulnerability was reported in November 2020 that allowed code to be run using Chrome outside of the sandbox. This allowed attackers to target this flaw (**CVE-2020-6573**). Google released an update for Chrome to mitigate the threat. Security researchers who discovered the flaw were paid $20,000.

VM hopping

When **VMs** are hosted on the same hypervisor or are accessible over the same virtual network, there is the possibility for an attacker to gain access to another virtual host. This attack can succeed if security is not addressed properly. Attacks can be launched through the switch. A DoS could cause the switch to forward packets to all ports.

VM escape

When access to the underlying hypervisor is possible, then the attacker has broken out of their isolated VM. The attacker may access the filesystem, re-route traffic, or re-configure networking devices. It is the same as an attacker having access to your physical data center with all the cabinets and racks unlocked. There are over 50 documented vulnerabilities associated with this exploit. **CVE-2020-3962** lists a vulnerability within **VMware** products that allows for *VM escape*.

Border Gateway Protocol and route hijacking

Border Gateway Protocol (**BGP**) allows routing information to be exchanged between external routers. **Internet exchange points** (**IXPs**) (they are the main ISPs) share routing information with each other using IP address prefixes and **autonomous system numbers** (**ASNs**). **IBM** has been allocated `ASN17390` and has 20 **IPV4** prefixes. They will share this information with other BGP peers. Attackers may gain access to an internet BGP router and announce fake routes. In most cases, the outcome will be a DoS, resulting in *blackouts* for parts of the internet. In April 2021, **Vodafone** was targeted, and attackers were able to hijack 30,000 IP prefixes, causing massive problems for Google, Microsoft, and **Cloudflare**. For more information on this attack, see the following link:

```
https://tinyurl.com/BGPattack
```

Interception attacks

These types of attacks allow a third party to gain access to our intellectual property, customer records, or anything that we would consider confidential. The means of attack will typically use a **man-in-the-middle** (**MITM**) to access the data. *Figure 7.13* shows the user's browser accessing an e-commerce application:

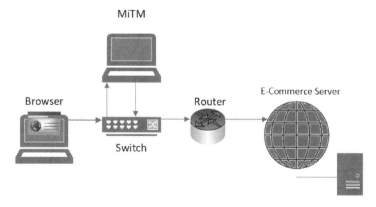

Figure 7.13 – MITM attack

All the data will be accessed by the attacker before it is sent to the router and also before it is returned to the client browser.

Denial of service and distributed denial of service

DoS attacks are targeted at a service or resource where the resources are totally consumed and thereby denying access to legitimate users. This type of attack can be launched from a single-host system. When the attack is launched from large numbers of systems or endpoints, the amount of traffic can quickly escalate. This type of attack is a **distributed denial of service** (**DDOS**). Often the attackers are unaware they are part of the attack. Botnets can be used, making use of compromised computers or **Internet of Things** (**IoT**) devices. **OVH** (a web hosting provider) was the target of a DDOS attack in September 2016. Around 990 Gbs of traffic was sent from over 140,000 IoT devices. The malware responsible was identified as **Mirai**. See *Figure 7.14* for an example of an IoT IP camera:

Figure 7.14 – IoT camera

Most of the IoT devices used in the attack were IP cameras. Vulnerable, internet-accessible IoT devices can be found using search tools such as **Shodan** (`https://www.shodan.io/`).

Social engineering

This is still a highly successful attack variant targeting humans. As many of these exploits appear to be genuine and believable, they stand a good chance of success. There are many:

- **Email-based phishing**: Typically, there is a link in an email to recover your locked account or reset a compromised credential.

- **Instant messaging smishing**: Typically, there is a link in an **SMS** message to recover your locked account or reset a compromised credential.

- **Phone or VOIP vishing**: The caller will have a cover story that will convey a sense of urgency – your bank account has been accessed, or your identity has been stolen.

- **Dumpster diving**: This is where an attacker can search through discarded company documents thrown into the trash. If we do not sanitize these documents, then useful company information may be stolen. Documents could include calendars, organizational charts, and sensitive data. This can be used to gain intelligence on an organization's employees and may play a part in active reconnaissance.

- **Shoulder surfing**: Gaining access to credentials by being in close proximity to a user who is logging in to a system. They could be looking over someone's shoulder to see their password.

- **Card or credential skimming**: Used to gain access to token-based credentials by cloning **radio-frequency identification** (**RFID**) cards.

Networks can be targeted where we have not hardened network appliances.

VLAN hopping

This exploit allows an attacker to gain access to traffic on a protected network segment (**VLAN**) that should be securely segmented. There are two well-known attack vectors that are commonly used.

Double tagging

The attacker crafts a VLAN frame with two tags: one tag for the valid VLAN, and a second tag for the protected segment. When the frame is passed between switches across a trunk port, the original tag will be removed by the receiving switch to reveal a VLAN ID that matches one of the supported VLANs on the switch. When we allow ports to be associated with the default VLAN, this is possible, as the sending switch does not perform the check for the VLAN ID.

Switch spoofing

The attacker will connect a device to a switch port that is set up to auto-negotiate as a trunk port. This is targeting the **Dynamic Trunking Protocol** (**DTP**) feature, and if the switch is not secured, then the attacker can forward all VLAN traffic to their device. It is important to disable this configuration as a default option. To remediate this vulnerability, we would set all ports as access-only ports, and for the ports that are used for trunking, we would use the following command:

```
switch(config-if)# switchport nonegotiate
```

This would stop an attacker connecting to a port and setting up a trunk to their device.

It is important to be vigilant and proactive in the face of increasing numbers of security incidents.

Proactive and detective risk reduction

When an organization faces many potential adversaries and advanced threats, it is important to have sophisticated tools, techniques, and trained personnel to protect our information systems. **Advanced persistent threats** (**APTs**) may mean we missed initial **indicators of compromise** (**IOCs**) and continue to be targeted by adversaries. We need to identify where attacks are originating, what systems may have been compromised, and prepare appropriate responses. It is common to deploy teams of security professionals, both internal and external, to combat the ever-increasing number and complex attacks. To aid investigators using forensic techniques, it is also common to use automation. **Big data** techniques and **machine learning** (**ML**) are now commonly used to process raw logged data. We will take a look at these technologies in the following section.

Hunts

A *hunt team* will be tasked with discovering IOCs and APTs. The goal will be to discover previous attacks and attacks in progress and prevent future attacks by gathering threat intelligence. Forensics techniques and access to historical logged data can be used.

Developing countermeasures

Once security professionals have identified **tactics, techniques, and procedures** (**TTPs**), we can use this information to build better defenses. Known blocks of *bad actor IP addresses* can be blocked, rules can be updated on **Network Intrusion Prevention** (**NIP**), **Remote Triggered Blackhole** (**RTBH**) rules can be created, as well as many other countermeasures.

Deceptive technologies

There are tools and technologies that can be used to delay or divert attackers while at the same time gathering useful threat intelligence. This includes the following techniques.

Honeynet

A *honeynet* is a collection of systems and services set up to simulate a vulnerable network. The goal will be to divert the attackers from the real network and to identify the attackers and their tools and techniques. The goal of the honeynet is to simulate a real network. With honeynets mainly deployed as virtual instances running on hypervisors, we can also use the power of *dynamic network configurations* to provide for changing configurations and responses to activity.

Honeypot

A *honeypot* has the same goals as a honeynet but is a single system, such as a vulnerable web application server.

Decoy files

A *decoy file* can be used to discover the whereabouts of attackers and both internal and external threats. A file would be created that would be of interest to the attacker, for example, `passwords.doc`. The file would contain a hidden image, and when the file is opened the image will be accessed from the web server. All access will be logged, including the IP address of the system opening the file. This would generate a *beacon*.

Security data analytics

It is important to be able to gather intelligence by the analysis of logs and other data types. By analyzing data flows and data contents, we can filter out the unnecessary data and concentrate on the useful data.

Processing pipelines

Processing pipelines are used to read or capture raw data, process the data, and store the output in data lakes or warehouses for further analysis. When we apply this technique to building automation into our security, we can use **artificial intelligence (AI)** and ML to better protect information systems. The data is unstructured, raw data at the start of the process. *Figure 7.15* shows the steps of the processing pipeline:

Figure 7.15 – Processing pipeline

The processing steps are shown as follows:

1. **Capture data**: Capture raw data from existing data records or live data streams.
2. **Process data**: Formatting from many different data types into a usable format.
3. **Store data**: Typical storage is a data lake. It is still raw data.
4. **Analyze data**: Now we try to make sense of all the captured data.
5. **Use data**: Build rules for our security appliances.

Other techniques to make the best use of large pools of data are discussed in the following subsections.

Indexing and search

When we need to store large repositories of data, it is important that we can gain quick access to the relevant information, whatever the file format. To make this a quick process, we can add keywords to an index that offers fast search capabilities, much like an index in a book or a table of contents in a report. Microsoft operating systems provide a built-in indexing service for quick search of the filesystem. See *Figure 7.16* for an example of **Microsoft Indexing Service**:

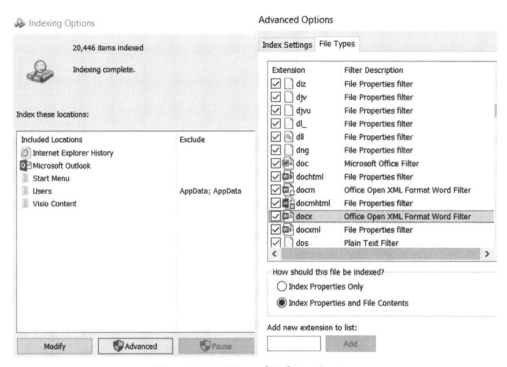

Figure 7.16 – Microsoft Indexing Service

It is useful to index large repositories of data for quick searches.

Log collection and curation

Raw logs are the starting point for effective auditing and further analysis. It is important to filter out the noise and present the most interesting information for further analysis. This is similar to the way a curator in a museum will ensure the audience (visitors) are presented with interesting exhibits to view. The curation of logs is important to make sure analysis is focused on the important events.

Database activity monitoring

Database activity monitoring (DAM) is an extra security layer protecting your database applications. This can provide more granular rules and enforcement policies to protect important information stored in transaction-based databases. DAM can monitor database logs, transactions in memory, and traffic forwarded to the database application. The additional reporting and protection offered by this tool can be useful when considering regulatory compliance.

Applying preventative risk reduction

Wherever it is possible, we will look to use prevention to protect our data and information systems. Preventative technologies will offer a solid base that we can build on. In most cases, a **standard operating environment** (**SOE**) will offer many security benefits. SOE allows us to deploy operating system images that can be measured against a baseline and then further enhanced with additional security add-ons. In this section, we will look at some preventative technologies.

Antivirus

Antivirus tools are an important preventative solution. They can be deployed on end devices and on network gateways, such as **next-generation firewalls** (**NGFWs**) and **unified threat management** (**UTM**). The latest antivirus tools will use smart detection techniques, including *heuristic analysis*, and centralized control and monitoring.

Immutable systems

Immutable systems allow systems to be deployed easily from a validated image. This relies on strict version control. When a change is required, updates and patches can be tested in a non-production environment and signed off. The build image is then created and assigned a version identifier, and production images can then be replaced. When we adopt this process, there is less likelihood that we will have systems that do not align with a strict security posture.

Hardening

To ensure systems and services are protected when in use, there should be a checklist or baseline, to ensure only the required applications and services are available. By adopting this approach, we can minimize our security footprint. If we disable or uninstall unnecessary services and applications, then we avoid the risk of service or listening ports being compromised. *Vendor hardening* guides and baseline configuration compliance tools can be very useful. *Figure 7.17* shows a configuration compliance scan for **Red Hat Linux 7**. This will allow the configuration to be enforced through remediation:

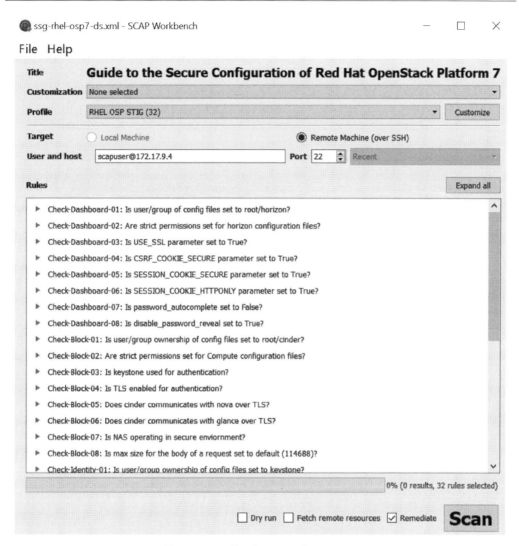

Figure 7.17 – Baseline compliance scan

See the **Center for Internet Security (CIS)** *benchmarks* for hardening guides:

https://workbench.cisecurity.org/benchmarks

Sandbox detonation

If an unknown file or attachment cannot be validated as genuine, then the safest way to understand its purpose or logic is to observe behaviors in a secure environment where there will be no adverse impacts to other systems. The analysis will allow files, scripts, macros, and URL behaviors to be determined. The sandbox will emulate the operating system but isolate access to the physical hardware. **Microsoft Windows 10** supports a secure sandbox (see *Figure 7.18*):

Figure 7.18 – Windows Sandbox

Other examples include cloud-based solutions to test suspicious files automatically.

Application control

It is important to protect networks and information systems by ensuring we restrict the applications that are installed to a set that are considered safe and vulnerability-free. It is important that any applications used by the enterprise are covered by software licenses.

License technologies

Licensing can be complex in a large organization with multiple sites, business units, and devices. It is important to have global oversight of the licenses that are available and in use. Unexpected licensing costs or legal actions are best avoided. There are many tools available to provide the appropriate information and reporting to ensure we are compliant.

Comparing allow lists versus block lists

We can control code that can be installed and executed by using *application whitelisting* or *application blacklisting*. This can be achieved using **Mobile Application Management (MAM)**, **Microsoft Group Policy**, or via third-party tools. *Figure 7.19* shows **Microsoft Application Control Policy** options:

Figure 7.19 – Microsoft Application Control Policy

In *Figure 7.19*, we can see an application whitelist. Everyone has access to Windows default locations, but administrators can run all application files. In the example, the `ITAdmin` group can run an application in the `tools` folder. We also see an example of a block list, where the sales group is blocked from running `REGEDIT.EXE` (the Windows Registry Editor).

Group Policy allows an enterprise to control update files, application executables, scripts, and Windows Store applications.

Atomic execution

An *atomic execution* of a transaction means all or nothing. Examples could include a write or move operation within the filesystem. When we move a file onto a new disk partition, the original will be deleted. Therefore, a successful write operation must be accomplished before the original can be deleted. This would ensure that a sudden loss of power would not result in missing data. Also, the thread of execution, moving the file, would be isolated from any other running process.

With other transactions, such as committing a payment operation to a database, this process would ensure the process could not be manipulated by a race condition (or TOCTOU).

Security automation

Within large, complex enterprises, the challenge is to maintain a strong security posture while supporting a diverse, heterogeneous environment. It is not uncommon to see a mixture of Windows, **Linux**, **Unix**, and specialist operating systems supported within the enterprise. To maintain a secure, stable environment, we must look at *automating* security tasks.

Cron and scheduled tasks

A common method for automating tasks on Linux systems is to use **Cron**. It is the built-in task scheduler. The configuration for the tasks is held in a `crontab` file, and there is a default `crontab` file in the `/etc` directory, as shown in *Figure 7.20*:

```
# /etc/crontab: system-wide crontab
# Unlike any other crontab you don't have to run the `crontab'
# command to install the new version when you edit this file
# and files in /etc/cron.d. These files also have username fields,
# that none of the other crontabs do.

SHELL=/bin/sh
PATH=/usr/local/sbin:/usr/local/bin:/sbin:/bin:/usr/sbin:/usr/bin

# Example of job definition:
# .---------------- minute (0 - 59)
# |  .------------- hour (0 - 23)
# |  |  .---------- day of month (1 - 31)
# |  |  |  .------- month (1 - 12) OR jan,feb,mar,apr ...
# |  |  |  |  .---- day of week (0 - 6) (Sunday=0 or 7) OR sun,mon,tue,wed,thu,fri,sat
# |  |  |  |  |
# *  *  *  *  * user-name command to be executed
17 *    * * *   root    cd / && run-parts --report /etc/cron.hourly
25 6    * * *   root    test -x /usr/sbin/anacron || ( cd / && run-parts --report /etc/cron.daily )
47 6    * * 7   root    test -x /usr/sbin/anacron || ( cd / && run-parts --report /etc/cron.weekly )
52 6    1 * *   root    test -x /usr/sbin/anacron || ( cd / && run-parts --report /etc/cron.monthly )
```

Figure 7.20 – Sample crontab configuration file

This allows for the automation of any repetitive tasks. The following example would run a backup job at midnight every Sunday:

```
* 0 * * 0 /bin/sh backup.sh
```

There is an interesting **graphical user interface** (**GUI**) utility, allowing for the creation of `crontab` lines, at the following link:

`https://crontab-generator.org/`

Bash

Bash is a common shell that is now included with many common operating systems, including Unix, Linux, and **macOS**, and can be added as a feature on Microsoft Windows. It allows commands to be executed from within the shell and also supports automation through shell scripts. It is important to install the latest version and to apply any updates, as there are vulnerabilities on older versions. There are many commands available and `help` will display the range of commands. To view help on specific commands, we use `man <command name>` or `<command name> --help`.

PowerShell

PowerShell is the current Microsoft command shell. It is open source and can also be installed on Linux and macOS operating systems. It is very powerful and includes extra functionality that is not available through the GUI. Commands are executed by combining a *verb* and a *noun*. Examples of verbs are get, set, start, and stop, which are the actions, and the noun will refer to the object, such as vm or service. An example command to obtain a list of all available VMs and display the output is shown in *Figure 7.21*:

```
PS C:\Windows\system32> get-vm

Name          State    CPUUsage(%) MemoryAssigned(M) Uptime                Status             Version
----          -----    ----------- ----------------- ------                ------             -------
CentOS        Saved    0           0                 00:00:00              Operating normally 9.0
Client01      Running  0           3914              1.00:19:50.0350000    Operating normally 9.0
Kali          Off      0           0                 00:00:00              Operating normally 9.0
Kali 2020.4   Running  0           4096              1.00:19:50.7100000    Operating normally 9.0
OPENVAS 6.0   Running  0           4096              1.00:19:51.4140000    Operating normally 9.0
SVR01         Running  0           2346              1.00:19:50.3290000    Operating normally 9.0
```

Figure 7.21 – get-vm displaying a list of VMs

To perform an action, we can use Start-VM, and we will then need an identifier for the action. This will be the name CentOS. See *Figure 7.22* for the command and the outcome:

```
PS C:\Windows\system32> Start-VM CentOS
PS C:\Windows\system32> get-vm CentOS

Name    State    CPUUsage(%) MemoryAssigned(M) Uptime                Status             Version
----    -----    ----------- ----------------- ------                ------             -------
CentOS  Running  0           4096              00:00:22.4810000      Operating normally 9.0
```

Figure 7.22 – PowerShell Start-VM

To see a list of all available PowerShell commands (**cmdlets**), type `Get-Command`. To display help for a particular command, use `Get-Help <command name>`. Commands can be combined within scripts; these are then saved as `.ps1` files. For creating and testing PowerShell scripts, Microsoft provides an extra tool called the **Integrated Scripting Environment** (**ISE**). See *Figure 7.23* for an example of the ISE:

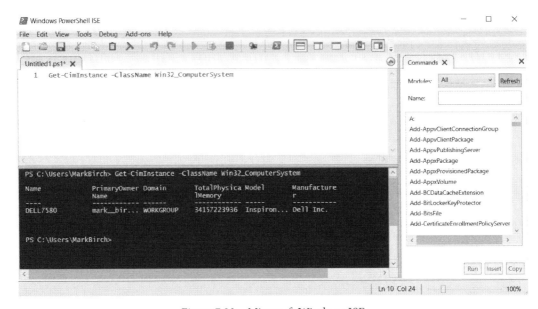

Figure 7.23 – Microsoft Windows ISE

Microsoft provides comprehensive help and documentation for PowerShell and this can be found at the following link:

`https://docs.microsoft.com/en-us/powershell/`

Python

Python is an open source interpreted programming language. It is supported on many operating systems and can be used to automate administrative tasks. One of the benefits of using Python is that it is relatively easy for new users to understand. For additional information, including downloads and help, see the following link:

`https://www.python.org/`

Physical security

To ensure our organization is fully protected from all threats, including physical threat actors, we must ensure we have defense in depth. Information systems may be hosted within our own managed data centers, with third parties and also cloud providers. To ensure we meet expected industry and regulatory standards for security, there are audits that can be performed. When planning for the security of a data center, there are recognized international standards such as the **American National Standards Institute/ Telecommunications Industry Association (ANSI/TIA-942)**. This standard focuses on physical security controls. Regulatory compliance standards, such as the **Payment Card Industry Data Security Standard (PCI DSS)** or the **Sarbanes-Oxley Act**, have certain requirements for physical security controls. The **Statement on Standards for Attestation Engagements No. 16 (SSAE 16)** is a compliance audit that focuses on controls implemented by service organizations.

Review of lighting

ANSI/TIA-942 has requirements for occupied space, entry points, and unoccupied space within a data center. For entry points and unoccupied spaces, it is a requirement that motion sensors are deployed and will automatically activate lighting. The lighting should be of a standard that safe passage is possible, and identification is possible using video cameras. In all occupied zones, lighting must be provided at a minimum intensity of 200 lux.

Review of visitor logs

To meet SSAE 16 standards, a service organization must restrict access to operating sites to personnel who have a legitimate business need. Any visitors to a site must be accompanied and physical access must be logged.

Camera reviews

It is important to review available tools and technologies when choosing systems, such as IP video. Cameras can be used for facial recognition and vehicle license plate recognition, as well as detecting intrusions within a facility, so systems supporting high definition or **Infrared (IR)** may also need to be considered. To ensure high-quality images are recorded, it may be necessary to have high-capacity network infrastructure and storage.

Comparing open spaces versus confined spaces

The health and safety of our employees, customers, and visitors should always be a high priority. There are laws and regulations that may differ between countries and also between industries. In the United Kingdom, the **Health and Safety Executive (HSE)** is a government department overseeing safety in the workplace. Laws are put in place to ensure personnel safety is maintained. Appropriate risk assessments should be completed whenever considering work of a hazardous nature. Open spaces are generally safer for employees, as the risks from poor ventilation or other such limitations are removed.

The **Confined Spaces Regulations 1997** define *confined space* as the following:

> *"confined space means any place, including any chamber, tank, vat, silo, pit, trench, pipe, sewer, flue, well or other similar space in which, by virtue of its enclosed nature, there arises a reasonably foreseeable specified risk."*

An organization must pay close attention to health and safety. Regulations and laws concerning health and safety can be very strict. Policies, procedures, and adequate training must be made mandatory.

Where an employer has been shown to have not performed due care, penalties can result in fines and prison sentences.

Summary

In this chapter, we have assessed enterprise risk using many applicable methods. We have studied options to mitigate risks. Enterprises will host information services or critical infrastructure, and this presents a large attack surface. We have considered all aspects of security, including application vulnerabilities and the likelihood that we will be attacked. We have learned about many common application vulnerabilities. We have understood the importance of inherently vulnerable systems and applications. In this chapter, we have investigated common attacks against applications and learned about the benefits of proactive and detective risk controls. You have learned about effective preventative risk reduction. This knowledge will be useful when planning for incident response and the use of forensic analysis in the next chapter.

In the next chapter, we will take a look at planning an effective incident response policy. We will understand the importance of forensics to identify and provide evidence in the event of a breach. We will also learn which tools are appropriate during the forensics process.

Questions

Here are a few questions to test your understanding of the chapter:

1. Attackers find a vulnerability on a website that allows them to select items from a shopping basket. When the authorize payment button is selected, there is a 500 ms delay. The attackers run a script that takes 200 ms and allows the final payment to be altered. What is the vulnerability that has been targeted?

    A. Buffer overflow

    B. Integer overflow

    C. Broken authentication

    D. Race condition

2. Attackers find a vulnerability on a website that allows them to select items from a shopping basket. There is a running total value for the basket. When items are added beyond a total of $9,999, the total displays a value starting from $0.00. What is the vulnerability that has been targeted?

    A. Buffer overflow

    B. Integer overflow

    C. Broken authentication

    D. Weak ciphers

3. What allows attackers to sniff traffic on a network and capture cookies sent over HTTP?

    A. Improper headers

    B. Poor exception handling

    C. Certificate errors

    D. Race condition

4. What allows developers to maintain an inventory of all code libraries and licenses used in their applications?

    A. Weak cryptography implementations

    B. Weak ciphers

    C. Weak cipher suite implementations

    D. Software composition analysis

5. Developers are reviewing legacy applications written in the C programming language. This is due to a number of recent buffer overflow attacks against the application. They have replaced instances of `gets()` with `fgets()` and `strcpy()` with `strcpy_s()`. What has prompted this activity?

   A. Use of unsafe functions

   B. Third-party libraries

   C. Dependencies

   D. Regression

6. What is it called when developers no longer release security patches for their software applications?

   A. End-of-support/end-of-life

   B. Regression issues

   C. Dependencies

   D. Bankruptcy

7. What is an example of code that is not developed by a development team but is incorporated into many software builds?

   A. Use of unsafe functions

   B. Third-party libraries

   C. Dependencies

   D. Regression

8. What is it called when developers rely on a cloud provider API for full functionality of their software applications?

   A. Use of unsafe functions

   B. Third-party libraries

   C. Dependencies

   D. Regression

9. When a software component has previously worked well but now proves to be slow or unresponsive, what is it known as?

    A. Unsafe functions

    B. Unsafe third-party libraries

    C. Software dependencies

    D. Software regression bug

10. When considering input validation for your web application, where should the validation take place?

    A. Client-side

    B. Flash

    C. Server-side

    D. ActiveX

11. What is runtime or interpreted code that can provide media-rich web content within a web browser?

    A. REST

    B. Browser extensions

    C. ActiveX

    D. HTML5

12. What is runtime or interpreted code that can provide partial page updates (therefore saving bandwidth) when repositioning a map on screen?

    A. AJAX

    B. SOAP

    C. Flash

    D. ActiveX

13. Security professionals have found **IOCs** while reviewing **Security Incident and Event Management** (**SIEM**) logs. The following commands were found from the application server logs:

```
../../../../../etc/password
```

What type of activity did they see?

A. Directory traversal

B. XSS

C. CSRF

D. SQL injection

14. Security professionals have found IOCs while reviewing SIEM logs. The following commands were found in the application server logs:

```
GET http://acmebank.com/transferfunds.
do?acct=bobjones&amount=$400 HTTP/1.1
```

What type of activity did they see?

A. Injection

B. XML

C. LDAP

D. XSRF

15. While reviewing web application firewall logs, security professionals have found IOCs. The following commands were found in the logs:

```
SELECT * FROM users WHERE username = ''OR 1=1 -' AND
password = 'mypass1'
```

What type of activity did they see?

A. Injection

B. XML

C. LDAP

D. SQL

16. While executing malware in an isolated environment, malware has been found on previously unaffected systems. What is the likely cause?

A. Sandbox escape

B. VM hopping

C. VM escape

D. Sandbox detonation

17. Internet traffic has been rerouted causing outages for many large internet providers. Attackers have used default accounts to configure ISP routers. What technology or vector of attack has been used?

    A. BGP

    B. VLAN hopping

    C. LDAP

    D. DDoS

18. What type of attack will most likely be effective when untrained users are targeted?

    A. Social engineering

    B. VLAN hopping

    C. Hunts

    D. DDoS

19. Security researchers need to understand APT bad actors by observing their tools, tactics, and procedures. What would be the best tool for this?

    A. Honeynet

    B. Honeypot

    C. Decoy files

    D. Antivirus

20. Security researchers place a `password.txt` file in an unsecured location on a publicly accessible server. They are going to map all the IP addresses that attempt to access the file. What is the best description for the `password.txt` file?

    A. Honeynet

    B. Honeypot

    C. Decoy files

    D. Logic bomb

21. Microsoft security researchers need to understand APT bad actors by observing their tools, tactics, and procedures. They gather massive amounts of raw security data every day from customer endpoints. What would be the best approach to identify IOCs?

    A. Processing pipelines

    B. Indexing and search

C. Log collection and curation

D. Database activity monitoring

22. What allows an organization to deploy server operating systems that must be replaced when there is an updated version?

A. Immutable systems

B. Hardening

C. Sandbox detonation

D. License technologies

23. What is it when my organization only allows a core set of applications to be supported on end user devices?

A. Application whitelisting

B. Application hardening

C. Application blacklisting

D. Atomic execution

24. What is it when my application will process a transaction in an isolated space, allowing rollback if the write cannot be performed?

A. Application whitelisting

B. Application hardening

C. TOCTOU

D. Atomic execution

25. Linux systems need to run a scheduled backup at midnight every day. What would allow administrators to automate the process?

A. Cron

B. Bash

C. PowerShell

D. Python

26. Linux system administrators need to execute common shell commands. What should they use?

A. Cron

B. Bash

C. PowerShell

D. Python

27. Microsoft administrators need to run powerful command-line utilities and create scripts to automate everyday system tasks. Scripts will also be created using .PS1 extensions. What will they use?

A. Cron

B. Bash

C. PowerShell

D. Python

28. Acme Corporation needs to support a common programming language that will function across different vendor operating systems. What should they choose?

A. Cron

B. Bash

C. PowerShell

D. Python

Answers

1. D
2. B
3. A
4. D
5. A
6. A
7. B
8. C
9. D
10. C
11. D
12. A
13. A

14. C

15. D

16. A

17. A

18. A

19. A

20. C

21. A

22. A

23. A

24. D

25. A

26. B

27. C

28. D

8
Implementing Incident Response and Forensics Procedures

When considering all the threats that can impact an organization, it is important to ensure there are policies and procedures in place to deal with unplanned security-related events. To ensure timely responses to security incidents, we should implement detailed planning to provide controls and mitigation. It is important, given the nature of sophisticated, well-funded adversaries, that we use a holistic approach when deploying appropriate threat detection capabilities. Some approaches may involve automation, which can lead to occasional mistakes (false positives and false negatives), so it is important that we also ensure we include humans in the loop. The ever-increasing complexity of attacks and a large security footprint add to these challenges. There is also evidence that **Advanced Persistent Threat** (**APT**) actors are likely to target vulnerable organizations. Countering APTs may require that we use advanced forensics to detect **Indicators of Compromise** (**IOCs**) and, where necessary, collect evidence to formulate a response.

In this chapter, we will cover the following topics:

- Understanding incident response planning

- Understanding the incident response process

- Understanding forensic concepts

- Using forensic analysis tools

Understanding incident response planning

An organization of any size much have effective cyber-security **Incident Response Plans** (**IRPs**). In the case of regulated industries, it may be a regulatory requirement that they have appropriate plans and procedures to mitigate the damage caused by security-related incidents. The **Federal Information Security Management Act** (**FISMA**) has very strict requirements for appropriate plans to be in place for federal agencies and contractors. These requirements include providing at least two points of contact with the **United States Computer Emergency Readiness Team** (**US-CERT**) for reporting purposes. A **NIST SP800-61** publication titled **Computer Security Incident Handling Guide** offers guidance on effective incident response planning for federal agencies and commercial enterprises. When developing a plan, it is important to identify team members, team leaders, and an escalation process. It is important to ensure there are team members available 24/7 as we cannot predict when an incident will occur. Stakeholder involvement is important while developing the plan. Legal counsel will be important, as well as working with parts of the business such as human resources, as they will offer advice about the feasibility of the plan concerning employee discipline. There is comprehensive guidance available within the **NIST SP800-61** documentation on this, which is available at `https://tinyurl.com/NIST80061R2`. For organizations in the United Kingdom, there are very useful resources available from the **National Cyber Security Centre** (**NCSC**); see the following URL: `https://tinyurl.com/ncscirt`.

Event classifications

There are many ways to identify anomalous or malicious events. We can take advantage of automated tools such as **Intrusion Detection Systems** (**IDS**) and **Security Incident and Event Monitoring** (**SIEM**). We can also rely on manual detection and effective security awareness training for our staff, which can help in detecting threats early. Service desk technicians and first responders can also be effective in detecting malicious activity. **Common Attack Pattern Enumeration and Classification** (**CAPEC**) was established by the US Department of Homeland Security to provide the public with a documented database of attack patterns. This database contains hundreds of references to different vectors of attack. More information can be found at `http://capec.mitre.org/data/index.html`.

Triage event

It is important to assess the type and severity of the incident that has occurred. You can think of triage as the work that's been done to identify what has happened. This term is borrowed from emergency room procedures when a patient in the ER is triaged to determine what needs to be fixed. This enables the appropriate response to be made concerning the urgency, as well as the team members that are required to respond. It is important to understand systems that are critical to enterprise operations as these need to be prioritized. This information is generally available if **Business Impact Analysis** (**BIA**) has been undertaken. BIA will identify mission-essential services and their importance to the enterprise. BIA will be covered in detail in *Chapter 15*, *Business Continuity and Disaster Recovery Concepts*. As there will be a finite number of resources to deal with the incident, it is important not to focus on the first-come, first-served approach.

Understanding the incident response process

The incident response process is broken down into six distinct phases. Each of these phases is important and must be completed before moving forward. The following diagram shows these distinct phases:

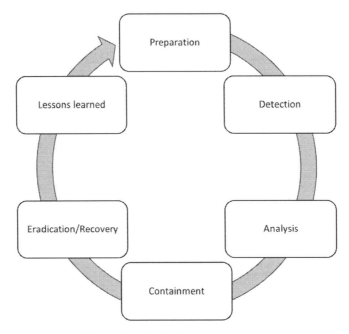

Figure 8.1 – Incident response process

Now, let's discuss these six phases.

Preparation

While preparing for an IRP, it is a good practice to harden systems and mitigate security vulnerabilities to ensure a strong security posture is in place. In the preparation phase, it is normal to increase the enterprise's resilience by focusing on all the likely attack vectors. Some of the tasks that should be addressed to prepare your organization for attacks include the following:

- Perform risk assessments
- Harden host systems
- Secure networks
- Deploy anti-malware
- Implement user awareness training

It is important to identify common attack vectors. While it is almost impossible to foresee all possible attack vectors, common ones can be documented and incorporated into playbooks.

The following diagram shows some common attack vectors to consider:

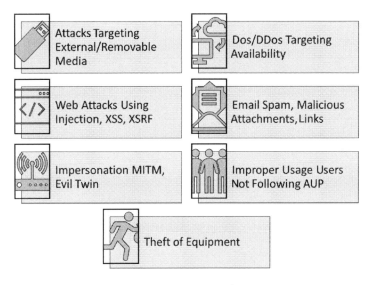

Figure 8.2 – Common attack vectors

Although the preparation phase will increase the security posture, we must also have the means to detect security incidents.

Detection

To respond to a security incident, we must detect anomalous activity. The vector that's used for an attack can be varied in that it can include unauthorized software, external media, email attachments, DoS, theft of equipment, and impersonation, to name a few. We must have the means to identify new and emerging threats. Common methods include *IDP, SIEM, antivirus, AntiSpam, FIM software, data loss prevention technology*, and *third-party monitoring services*. Logs from key services and network flows (**NetFlow** and **sFlow**) can also help detect unusual activity. First responders, such as service desk technicians, may also be able to confirm IOCs when responding to user calls.

Once we have detected such security-related events, we must analyze the activity to prepare a response.

Analysis

Not every reported security event or automatic alert is necessarily going to be malicious; unexpected user behavior or errors may result in false reporting. It is important to discard normal/non-malicious events at this stage. When a security-related event is incorrectly reported, it can result in the following:

- **False positives**: This is where an event is treated as a malicious or threatening activity but turns out to be benign.

- **False negatives**: This is when a malicious event is considered non-threatening and no subsequent action is taken when there is a threat.

When the correct tools and investigative practices are followed, then the correct diagnosis should be made, resulting in the following:

- **True positives**: This means that the event has been identified as malicious and the appropriate action can be taken.

- **True negatives**: This means that an event has been correctly identified as non-threatening and no remedial action needs to be taken.

It is important to document the incident response process using issue tracking systems, which should be readily available for IRT members. The following diagram shows information that should be recorded in this application database:

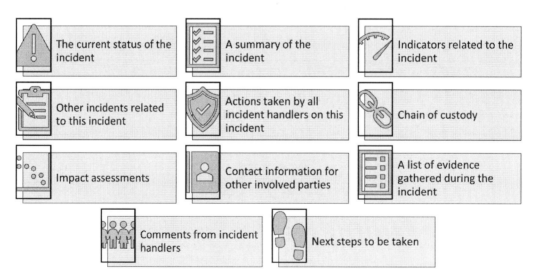

Figure 8.3 – Incident documentation

Security and confidentiality must be maintained for this information.

Containment

It is important to devise containment strategies for different types of incidents. If the incident is a *crypto-malware attack* or *fast-spreading worm*, then the response will normally involve quickly isolating the affected systems or network segment. If the attack is a *DoS* or *DDoS* that's been launched against internet-facing application servers, then the approach may involve implementing a **Remote Triggered Black Hole** (**RTBH**) or working with an ISP offering **DDoS mitigation services**.

The following diagram shows the criteria that should be considered when planning containment strategies:

Potential damage or theft of resources

Requirements for evidence preservation

Service availability (For example, network connectivity services provided to Third parties)

Time and resources to implement the strategy

Effectiveness of the strategy (example, full containment or partial containment)

Duration of the solution (example, emergency workaround suitable for 5 hours)

Figure 8.4 – Containment strategy

Some containment strategies may involve further analysis of the attack by containing the activity within a sandbox.

Eradication and recovery

Once the incident has been contained, it may be necessary to eradicate malware or delete malicious accounts before the recovery process can begin. Recovery may require replacing damaged hardware, reconfiguring the hardware and software, and restoring from backups. It is important to have access to documentation, including implementation guides, configuration guides, and hardening checklists. This information is typically available within the **Disaster Recovery Plan** (**DRP**).

Lessons learned

An important part of the incident response process is the after-action report, which allows improvements to be made to the process. What went well or not well should be addressed at this point. The team should perform this part of the exercise within days of the incident. The following diagram highlights some of the issues that may arise from a lessons learned exercise:

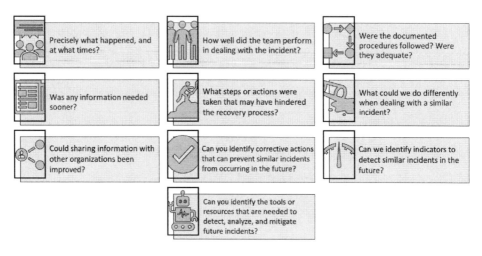

Figure 8.5 – Lessons learned

Lessons learned will allow us to understand what improvements are necessary for the IRP.

Specific response playbooks/processes

It is important to plan for as many scenarios as possible. Typical scenarios could include *ransomware*, *data exfiltration*, *social engineering*, and *DDoS*, to name a few.

Many available resources are available that an organization can use to prepare for common scenarios. For example, NIST includes an appendix in **NIST SP800-61** documenting multiple incident handling scenarios. This document can be found at the following URL: `https://tinyurl.com/SP80061`.

When considering response actions, we will need to create manual and automated responses.

Non-automated response methods

If manual intervention is required, there should be clear documentation, including CMDB, network diagrams, escalation procedures, and contact lists. If the incident type has not been seen before, all the actions must be captured and documented to create a playbook for the future.

Playbooks

Playbooks can be used to respond to an incident by giving security professionals a set of checks and actions to work through common security scenarios. This can be very beneficial in reducing response times and containing the incident. The following diagram shows a playbook that's been created to help handle a malware incident:

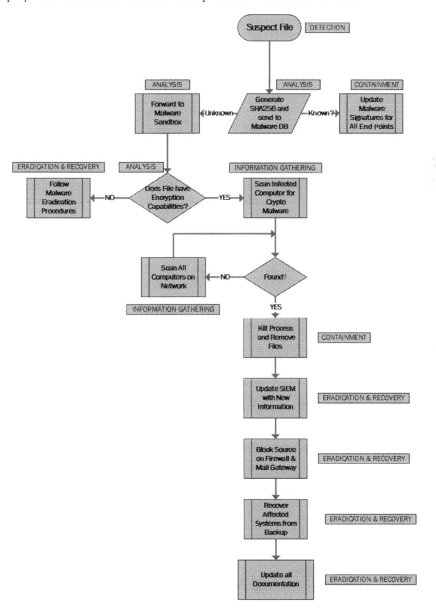

Figure 8.6 – Playbook for a malware incident

Playbooks can be very useful as they provide a step-by-step set of actions to handle typical incident scenarios.

Automated response methods

Automated responses can be triggered by a human-in-the-loop, who may need to activate a response or have a fully automated one. Let's look at some examples of these approaches.

Runbooks

A **runbook** will allow first responders and other **Incident Response Team** (**IRT**) members to recognize common scenarios and document steps to contain and recover from the incident. It could be a set of discrete instructions to add a rule to a firewall or to restart a web server during the recovery phase within incident response. Runbooks do not include multiple decision points (this is what playbooks are used for), so they are ideal for automated responses and will work well when integrated within **Security Orchestration and Response** (**SOAR**).

Security Orchestration and Response (SOAR)

SOAR allows an organization to use advanced detection capabilities to identify threats and then harness orchestration to respond to these threats. Using tools such as SIEM, we can easily detect IOCs and prepare a response. The response may include semi-automation using runbooks or be able to fully automate responses. Orchestration allows for complex tasks to be defined using visual tools and scripting. The following diagram shows the workflow for a SOAR:

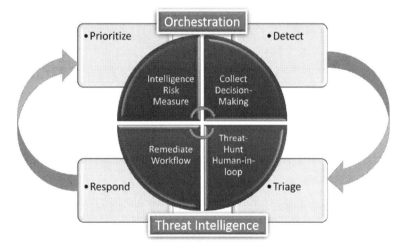

Figure 8.7 – SOAR workflow

There are many vendor solutions currently being offered to orchestrate security responses.

Communication plan

It is important to have effective communication plan stakeholder management.

The IRT may need to communicate with many external entities, and it is important to document these entities within the IRP. Some examples of these parties are shown in the following diagram:

Figure 8.8 – Communication plan

It is important to consider how an organization will communicate with media outlets. Rules of engagement should be established before the need arises to deal with reporting to news outlets.

Within incident response, there is a need for investigative tools to understand whether an incident is actually taking place and also to collect evidence for a legal response. The tools and techniques that are used will involve the use of computer forensics.

Understanding forensic concepts

An organization must be prepared to undertake computer forensics to support both legal investigations and internal corporate purposes. When considering different scenarios, it will be important to understand where external agencies or law enforcement need to be involved. If the investigation is to be performed by internal staff, then they should have the appropriate training and tools. Guidance for integrating forensic techniques into incident response is covered in **NIST SP800-86**. More information can be found here: `https://tinyurl.com/nistsp80086`.

Forensic process

It is important to follow the correct forensic process. This can be broken down into four steps, as shown in the following diagram:

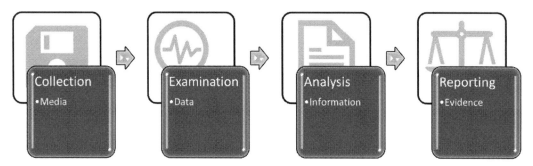

Figure 8.9 – Forensic process

These four steps are covered in the following list. We will discuss the appropriate tools to be used in more detail later in this chapter:

1. Data collection involves identifying sources of data and the feasibility of accessing data. For data that's held outside the organization, a court order may be required to gain access to it. It is important to use validated forensic tools and procedures if the outcome is going to be a legal process.

2. Once we have collected the data, we can examine the raw data. Such data could include extensive log files or thousands of emails from a messaging server; we can filter out the logs and messages that are not relevant.

3. Data analysis can be performed on the data to correlate events and patterns. Automated tools can be used to search through the logged data and look for IOCs.

4. During the reporting phase, decisions will be made as to what further action is applicable. Law enforcement will need detailed evidence to construct a legal case. Senior management, however, will require reports in a more business-orientated format to formulate a business response.

It is important to adhere to strict forensics procedures such as the order of volatility, so as not to miss crucial evidence. Also, a chain of custody should be created as the evidence is collected.

Chain of custody

A chain of custody form must begin when the evidence is collected. It is important to document relevant information about where and how the evidence was obtained. When the evidence changes hands, it is important that documentary evidence is recorded, detailing the transaction.

The following diagram shows a typical chain of custody form:

EVIDENCE CHAIN OF CUSTODY FORM				
Acme Corp				
Case Name:		Reason Evidence Obtained:		
Case Number:				
Item No.	Evidence Type	Model No.	Serial No.	
Content Owner		Description		
Forensic Investigator	Creation	Hash Value	Date/Time	
CHAIN OF CUSTODY				
Date/Time	Released By:	Received By	Reason for Change	

Figure 8.10 – Chain of custody form

Without this important documentation, a legal or disciplinary process may be difficult.

Order of volatility

When you're undertaking computer forensics, it is important to follow standards and accepted practices. Failure to do so may result in a lack of evidence or evidence that is inadmissible. **RFC 3227** is the **Internet Engineering Taskforce (IETF)** standard for capturing data that will be used to investigate data breaches or provide evidence of IOCs. The volatile data is held in a CPU cache that contains data that is constantly being overwritten, while archived media is long term and is stored on paper, a backup tape, or WORM storage. The following screenshot shows some of the storage locations that should be addressed:

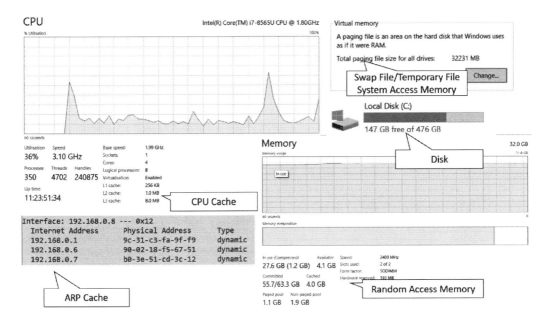

Figure 8.11 – Evidence locations

Specialist forensics tools will be required to capture this data.

The order in which efforts are made to safeguard the evidence is important. Allowing the computer to enter hibernation or sleep mode will alter the memory's characteristics and result in missing forensic artifacts. The following diagram shows the correct order of volatility:

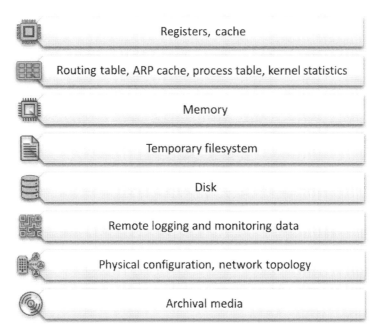

Figure 8.12 – Order of volatility

It is important that this order is followed, as failure to do so will likely result in missing evidence.

The list is to be followed in a top-down fashion, with registers and the cache being the most volatile and archived media being the least volatile. Let's look at some common tools that we can use to collect such evidence.

Memory snapshots

Memory snapshots allow forensic investigators to search for artifacts that are loaded into volatile memory. It is important to consider volatile memory as an anomalous activity that may be found that does not get written to storage or logs.

Images

For investigators to analyze information systems while looking for forensic artifacts, the original *image/disk* mustn't be used (it will be stored securely as the control copy). The image must be an identical bit-by-bit copy, including allocated space, unallocated space, and free and slack space.

Evidence preservation

Once the evidence has been obtained, it is important to store the evidence in a secure location and maintain the chain of custody. We must be able to demonstrate that the evidence has not been tampered with. *Hashing* the files or images is performed to create a verifiable checksum. Logs can be stored on **Write Once Read Many** (**WORM**) to preserve the evidence.

Cryptanalysis

Cryptography may have been used to hide evidence or to render filesystems that were unreadable during a ransomware attack. In these cases, *cryptanalysis* may be deployed to detect the techniques that were used, as well as the likely attacker.

Steganalysis

Steganography is a technology that's used to hide information inside another file, often referred to as the carrier file. Steganalysis is the technology that's used to discover hidden payloads in carrier files. Digital image files are often used to hide text-based data, such as JPEGs. When text is hidden in a compressed digital image file, it can distort the pixels in the image. These distortions are then identified by the Steganalysis tool.

Using forensic analysis tools

Now that we have a good understanding of the types of evidence that can be collected and the analysis that can be performed, we must assemble a forensic tool kit. We must ensure that the tools that we are using are recognized as valid tools and make sure that they are used correctly. For example, to capture a forensic image of a storage device, we need a tool that performs a bit-by-bit copy. We would not use the same tool that allows us to prepare images/templates for distributing an operating system. In this section, we will identify common tools that are used for forensics analysis.

File carving tools

These tools allow a forensics investigator to search a live system or a forensic image for hidden or deleted files, file fragments, and their contents. Two tools are suitable for this process, shown as follows.

foremost

foremost allows you to retrieve various file types that have been deleted from the filesystem. It will search for file fragments in many different formats, including documents, image formats, and binary files. It can retrieve deleted files from the live file system or a forensics image.

The following screenshot shows help for the foremost command:

```
└─# foremost -h
foremost version 1.5.7 by Jesse Kornblum, Kris Kendall, and Nick Mikus.
$ foremost [-v|-V|-h|-T|-Q|-q|-a|-w-d] [-t <type>] [-s <blocks>] [-k <size>]
         [-b <size>] [-c <file>] [-o <dir>] [-i <file]

-V  - display copyright information and exit
-t  - specify file type.  (-t jpeg,pdf ...)
-d  - turn on indirect block detection (for UNIX file-systems)
-i  - specify input file (default is stdin)
-a  - Write all headers, perform no error detection (corrupted files)
-w  - Only write the audit file, do not write any detected files to the disk
-o  - set output directory (defaults to output)
-c  - set configuration file to use (defaults to foremost.conf)
-q  - enables quick mode. Search are performed on 512 byte boundaries.
-Q  - enables quiet mode. Suppress output messages.
-v  - verbose mode. Logs all messages to screen
```

Figure 8.13 – The foremost command

Here is an example of using the foremost command:

```
foremost -t pdf,png -v -i /dev/sda
```

In this example, we are searching the fixed drive for the .pdf and .png file types.

strings

This is a useful forensics tool for searching through an image file or a memory dump for *ASCII* or *Unicode* strings. It is a built-in tool that's included with most Linux/Unix distributions.

The following screenshot shows the options for the `strings` command:

```
└─# strings -h
Usage: strings [option(s)] [file(s)]
 Display printable strings in [file(s)] (stdin by default)
 The options are:
  -a - --all                Scan the entire file, not just the data section [default]
  -d --data                 Only scan the data sections in the file
  -f --print-file-name      Print the name of the file before each string
  -n --bytes=[number]       Locate & print any NUL-terminated sequence of at
  -<number>                   least [number] characters (default 4).
  -t --radix={o,d,x}        Print the location of the string in base 8, 10 or 16
  -w --include-all-whitespace Include all whitespace as valid string characters
  -o                        An alias for --radix=o
  -T --target=<BFDNAME>     Specify the binary file format
  -e --encoding={s,S,b,l,B,L} Select character size and endianness:
                              s = 7-bit, S = 8-bit, {b,l} = 16-bit, {B,L} = 32-bit
  -s --output-separator=<string> String used to separate strings in output.
  @<file>                   Read options from <file>
  -h --help                 Display this information
  -v -V --version           Print the program's version number
 strings: supported targets: elf64-x86-64 elf32-i386 elf32-iamcu elf32-x86-64 pei-i386 pei-x86-64 elf64-l1om
  elf64-k1om elf64-little elf64-big elf32-little elf32-big pe-x86-64 pe-bigobj-x86-64 pe-i386 srec symbolsre
 c verilog tekhex binary ihex plugin
 Report bugs to <http://www.sourceware.org/bugzilla/>
```

Figure 8.14 – The strings command

In this example, we are searching within a binary file, where we need to see if there are any embedded `copyright` strings:

```
strings python3 | grep copyright
```

We are using the `strings` command to search for all the strings within `python3` and piping the output to the `grep` command, to only display strings containing `copyright` characters.

Binary analysis tools

There are many tools in a forensic toolkit that can be used to identify the content and logic that's used within binary files. As these files are compiled, we cannot analyze the source code, so instead, we must use analysis tools to attempt to see links to other code modules and libraries. We can use reverse engineering techniques to break down the logic of binary files. There are many examples of binary analysis tools, some of which we will look at now.

Hex dump

A hex dump allows us to capture and analyze the data that's stored in flash memory. It is commonly used when we need to extract data from a smartphone or other mobile device. It will require a connection between the forensics workstation and the mobile device. A hex dump may also reveal deleted data, such as SMS messages, contacts, and stored photos that have not been overwritten.

Binwalk

Binwalk is a useful tool in computer forensics as it will search binary images for embedded files and executable code. When running the tool, the results can be placed in a folder for further analysis. It can also be used to compare files for common elements. We may be able to detect signatures from a known malicious file in a newly discovered suspicious file. The output will display the contents and the offsets in decimal and hex of the payloads. The following screenshot shows the output of the `binwalk` command:

```
└─$ binwalk x86_64-linux-gnu-c++filt

DECIMAL        HEXADECIMAL       DESCRIPTION
--------------------------------------------------------------------------------
0              0x0               ELF, 64-bit LSB shared object, AMD x86-64, version 1 (SYSV)
106640         0x1A090           Copyright string: "Copyright (C) 2020 Free Software Foundation, Inc."
127280         0x1F130           Unix path: /usr/lib/debug/.dwz/x86_64-linux-gnu/binutils-x86-64-linux-gnu.debug
```

Figure 8.15 – Binwalk

In the preceding output, the file is an **Executable Linking Format** (**ELF**) system file comprising a text string and a path to an executable file.

Ghidra

Ghidra is a tool developed by the **National Security Agency** (**NSA**) for reverse engineering. It includes software analysis tools that are capable of reverse engineering compiled code. It is a powerful tool that can be automated and also supports many common operating system platforms. It is designed to search out malicious processes embedded within binary files.

GNU Project debugger (GDB)

Debugging tools allow developers to find and fix faults when executing compiled code. It can be helpful to capture information about bugs in the code that cause unexpected outcomes or cause code to become unresponsive. Debuggers can also show other running code modules that may affect the stability of your code. GDB runs on many common operating systems and supports common development languages.

OllyDbg

Another popular reverse engineering tool is OllyDbg. It can be useful for developers to troubleshoot their compiled code and can also be used for malware analysis. OllyDbg may also be used by adversaries to steal **Intellectual Property** (**IP**) by cracking the software code.

Readelf

Readelf allows you to display the content of ELF files. ELF files are system files that are used in Linux and Unix operating systems. ELF files can contain executable programs and libraries. In the following example, we are reading all the fields contained within the `ssh` executable program file:

```
readelf -a ssh
```

Objdump

This is a similar tool to Readelf in that it can display the contents of operating system files on Unix-like operating systems.

Strace

Strace is a tool for tracing system calls made by a command or binary executable file. The following screenshot shows the Strace output for `hostname`. The actual output for `hostname` would be the local system's hostname (`dell7580`):

```
└─$ strace hostname
execve("/usr/bin/hostname", ["hostname"], 0x7fffd46d3210 /* 23 vars */) = 0
brk(NULL)                               = 0x7fffba4f8000
access("/etc/ld.so.preload", R_OK)      = -1 ENOENT (No such file or directory)
openat(AT_FDCWD, "/etc/ld.so.cache", O_RDONLY|O_CLOEXEC) = 3
fstat(3, {st_mode=S_IFREG|0644, st_size=42342, ...}) = 0
mmap(NULL, 42342, PROT_READ, MAP_PRIVATE, 3, 0) = 0x7f51f94ad000
close(3)                                = 0
openat(AT_FDCWD, "/lib/x86_64-linux-gnu/libc.so.6", O_RDONLY|O_CLOEXEC) = 3
read(3, "\177ELF\2\1\1\3\0\0\0\0\0\0\0\0\3\0>\0\1\0\0\0@\2\0\0\0\0\0\0"..., 832) = 832
fstat(3, {st_mode=S_IFREG|0755, st_size=1839792, ...}) = 0
mmap(NULL, 8192, PROT_READ|PROT_WRITE, MAP_PRIVATE|MAP_ANONYMOUS, -1, 0) = 0x7f51f9470000
mmap(NULL, 1852680, PROT_READ, MAP_PRIVATE|MAP_DENYWRITE, 3, 0) = 0x7f51f92a0000
mprotect(0x7f51f92c5000, 1662976, PROT_NONE) = 0
mmap(0x7f51f92c5000, 1355776, PROT_READ|PROT_EXEC, MAP_PRIVATE|MAP_FIXED|MAP_DENYWRITE, 3, 0x25000) = 0x7f51f92c5000
mmap(0x7f51f9410000, 303104, PROT_READ, MAP_PRIVATE|MAP_FIXED|MAP_DENYWRITE, 3, 0x170000) = 0x7f51f9410000
mmap(0x7f51f945b000, 24576, PROT_READ|PROT_WRITE, MAP_PRIVATE|MAP_FIXED|MAP_DENYWRITE, 3, 0x1ba000) = 0x7f51f945b000
mmap(0x7f51f9461000, 13576, PROT_READ|PROT_WRITE, MAP_PRIVATE|MAP_FIXED|MAP_ANONYMOUS, -1, 0) = 0x7f51f9461000
close(3)                                = 0
arch_prctl(ARCH_SET_FS, 0x7f51f9471580) = 0
mprotect(0x7f51f945b000, 12288, PROT_READ) = 0
mprotect(0x7f51f94bd000, 4096, PROT_READ) = 0
mprotect(0x7f51f94aa000, 4096, PROT_READ) = 0
munmap(0x7f51f94ad000, 42342)           = 0
brk(NULL)                               = 0x7fffba4f8000
brk(0x7fffba519000)                     = 0x7fffba519000
uname({sysname="Linux", nodename="dell7580", ...}) = 0
fstat(1, {st_mode=S_IFCHR|0660, st_rdev=makedev(0x4, 0x1), ...}) = 0
ioctl(1, TCGETS, {B38400 opost isig icanon echo ...}) = 0
write(1, "dell7580\n", 9dell7580
)                                       = 9
exit_group(0)                           = ?
+++ exited with 0 +++
```

Figure 8.16 – The strace command

Here, we can see a very detailed output showing all the system operations that are required to deliver the resultant computer hostname.

ldd

To display dependencies for binary files, we can use the `ldd` command. This tool is included in most distributions of Linux operating systems and will show any dependent third-party libraries.

The following screenshot shows `ldd` searching for dependencies in the `ssh` binary file:

```
ldd ssh
    linux-vdso.so.1 (0x00007fffe6585000)
    libselinux.so.1 => /lib/x86_64-linux-gnu/libselinux.so.1 (0x00007f2ebc4b0000)
    libcrypto.so.1.1 => /lib/x86_64-linux-gnu/libcrypto.so.1.1 (0x00007f2ebc1b0000)
    libdl.so.2 => /lib/x86_64-linux-gnu/libdl.so.2 (0x00007f2ebc1a0000)
    libz.so.1 => /lib/x86_64-linux-gnu/libz.so.1 (0x00007f2ebc180000)
    libresolv.so.2 => /lib/x86_64-linux-gnu/libresolv.so.2 (0x00007f2ebc160000)
    libgssapi_krb5.so.2 => /lib/x86_64-linux-gnu/libgssapi_krb5.so.2 (0x00007f2ebc110000)
    libc.so.6 => /lib/x86_64-linux-gnu/libc.so.6 (0x00007f2ebbf30000)
    libpcre2-8.so.0 => /lib/x86_64-linux-gnu/libpcre2-8.so.0 (0x00007f2ebbea0000)
    /lib64/ld-linux-x86-64.so.2 (0x00007f2ebc5bb000)
    libpthread.so.0 => /lib/x86_64-linux-gnu/libpthread.so.0 (0x00007f2ebbe7e000)
    libkrb5.so.3 => /lib/x86_64-linux-gnu/libkrb5.so.3 (0x00007f2ebbd90000)
    libk5crypto.so.3 => /lib/x86_64-linux-gnu/libk5crypto.so.3 (0x00007f2ebbd60000)
    libcom_err.so.2 => /lib/x86_64-linux-gnu/libcom_err.so.2 (0x00007f2ebbe70000)
    libkrb5support.so.0 => /lib/x86_64-linux-gnu/libkrb5support.so.0 (0x00007f2ebbd40000)
    libkeyutils.so.1 => /lib/x86_64-linux-gnu/libkeyutils.so.1 (0x00007f2ebbd30000)
```

Figure 8.17 – The ldd command

After running the `ldd` tool for the `ssh` command, we can see that there are multiple dependencies.

file

The `file` command is used to determine the file type of a given file. Often, the extension of a file, such as `csv`, `pdf`, `doc`, or `exe`, will indicate the type. However, many files in Linux do not have extensions. In an attempt to evade detection, attackers may change the extension to make an executable appear to be a harmless document. `file` will also work on compressed or zipped archives. The following screenshot demonstrates the use of the `file` command:

```
└─# file mydoc.pdf
mydoc.pdf: ELF 64-bit LSB shared object, x86-64, version 1 (SYSV), dynamically linked, in
terpreter /lib64/ld-linux-x86-64.so.2, BuildID[sha1]=5917ff8fa041d4cb54c7846799e32a9e4191
75e2, for GNU/Linux 3.2.0, stripped
```

Figure 8.18 – The file command

In the preceding example, we can see that a file has been disguised to look like a PDF document but is, in fact, a binary executable.

Analysis tools

Forensic toolkits are comprised of tools that can analyze filesystems, metadata, running operating systems, and filesystems. We need advanced tools to detect the APTs and IOCs that are hidden within our information systems. Let's look at some examples of analysis tools.

ExifTool

To view or edit a file's metadata, we will need a specific analysis tool. **ExifTool** supports many different image formats, including JPEG, MPEG, MP4, and many more popular image and media formats.

The following command is used to extract metadata from an image that's been downloaded from a website:

```
exiftool nasa.jpg
```

The following screenshot shows the output of the preceding command:

```
ExifTool Version Number         : 12.16
File Name                       : nasa.jpg
Directory                       : .
File Size                       : 78 KiB
File Modification Date/Time     : 2021:07:07 17:04:33+01:00
File Access Date/Time           : 2021:07:07 17:04:33+01:00
File Inode Change Date/Time     : 2021:07:07 17:04:33+01:00
File Permissions                : rw-r--r--
File Type                       : JPEG
File Type Extension             : jpg
MIME Type                       : image/jpeg
JFIF Version                    : 1.01
Resolution Unit                 : None
X Resolution                    : 1
Y Resolution                    : 1
Exif Byte Order                 : Little-endian (Intel, II)
Image Description               : Photo Date: 2020-01-10Location: Teague AuditoriumSubject: Graduation ceremony of the 2017
 class of Astronaut Candidates.Photographer: James Blair
Software                        : Picasa
Artist                          : JAMES BLAIR
Copyright                       : NASA
XMP Toolkit                     : XMP Core 5.5.0
Description                     : Photo Date: 2020-01-10Location: Teague AuditoriumSubject: Graduation ceremony of the 2017
 class of Astronaut Candidates.Photographer: James Blair
Rights                          : NASA
Creator                         : JAMES BLAIR, James Blair - NASA - JSC
Profile CMM Type                : Linotronic
Profile Version                 : 2.1.0
Profile Class                   : Display Device Profile
Color Space Data                : RGB
Profile Connection Space        : XYZ
Profile Date Time               : 1998:02:09 06:49:00
Profile File Signature          : acsp
Primary Platform                : Microsoft Corporation
```

Figure 8.19 – ExifTool metadata

This information is very interesting as it displays details of the photographer, their location, and many other details.

Nmap

Nmap can be used during analysis to fingerprint operating systems and services. This will aid security professionals in determining the operating system's build version and the exact versions of the hosted services, such as DNS, SMTP, SQL, and so on.

Aircrack-ng

When we need to assess the security of wireless networks, we can use **Aircrack-ng**. This tool allows you to monitor wireless traffic, as well as attack (via packet injection) and crack WEP and WPA **Pre-Shared Keys** (**PSKs**).

Volatility

The Volatility tool is used during forensic analysis to identify memory-resident artifacts. It supports memory dumps from most major 32-bit and 64-bit operating systems, including Windows, Linux, macOS, and Android. It is extremely useful if the data is in the form of a Windows crash dump, Hibernation file, or VM snapshot.

Sleuth Kit

This tool is a collection of tools that are run from the command line to analyze forensic images. It is usually incorporated in graphical forensic toolkits such as Autopsy. The forensic capture will be performed using imaging tools such as dd. **Sleuth Kit** also supports dynamically linked storage, meaning it can be used with live operating systems as well as with static images. When it is dynamically linked to operating system drives, it can be useful as a real-time tool, such as when responding to incidents.

Imaging tools

When considering the use of imaging tools to be used in forensic investigation, one of the primary goals is to choose a tool that has acceptance when presenting evidence to a court. Not all tools guarantee that the imaging process will leave the original completely intact, so additional tools such as a hardware write blocker are also important. The following tools are commonly used when the evidence will need to be presented to a court of law.

Forensic Toolkit (FTK) Imager

FTK Imager is an easy-to-use graphical tool that runs on Windows operating systems. It can create images in standard formats such as E01, SMART, and dd raw. It lets you hash image files, which is important for integrity, and also logs the complete imaging process. *Figure 8.20* shows FTK Imager:

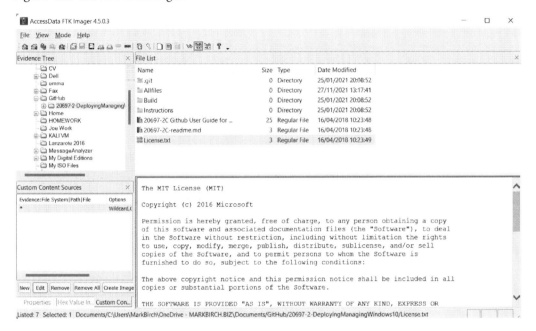

Figure 8.20 – FTK Imager

dd command

The dd command is available on many Linux distributions as a built-in tool. It is known commonly as **data duplicator** or **disk dump**. Although on older builds of Linux the tool also allowed for the acquisition of memory dumps, it is not possible to take a complete dump of memory on a modern distribution.

The format of the command is dd if=/dev/sda of=/dev/sdb <options>, where if is the input field and of is the output field. In this case, we are copying from the first physical disk to the second forensics attached disk.

Hashing utilities

When we are working with files and images, it is important to use hashing tools so that we can identify files or images that have been altered from the original. A hash is a checksum for a piece of data. We can use a hash value to record the current state of an image before a cloning process, after which we can hash the cloned image to prove it is the same. During forensic analysis, we can use a database of known hashes for our operating system and application software to spot anomalies. Many hashing utilities are included with operating systems.

Sha<keylength>sum is included with most Linux distributions, allowing for the checksum of a file to be calculated using sha160, 224, 256, 384, and 512. In the following example, a sha256 is being calculated for the Linux grep command:

```
sha256sum grep
605aaf67445e899a9a59c66446fa0bb15fb11f2901ea33386b3325596b3c8
423 grep
```

The resulting checksum (also called a digest) is displayed as a 64-character hexadecimal string.

ssdeep can be used to identify similarities in files; it is referred to as a fuzzy hashing program. It can be used to compare a known malicious file with a suspicious file that may be a zero-day threat. It will highlight blocks of similar code and is used within many antivirus products.

Using live collection and post-mortem tools

During forensic analysis, we must closely follow the guidelines for the order of volatility to capture evidence that will be lost or overwritten. Once we have recorded or logged the data, we can analyze and investigate it using a variety of tools.

netstat allows a live report to be created on listening ports, connected ports, and the status of connections for local and remote network interfaces. If you need to capture this output for further analysis, it can be piped to a file using the `netstat <options> filename` syntax. The following screenshot shows the output of the `netstat` command, saved as a text file:

```
[SupportAssistAgent.exe]
  TCP     192.168.8.113:1040      51.140.84.251:https       CLOSE_WAIT
[SupportAssistAgent.exe]
  TCP     192.168.8.113:1044      40.78.128.150:https       ESTABLISHED
[SearchApp.exe]
  TCP     192.168.8.113:1045      a-0001:https              ESTABLISHED
[SearchApp.exe]
  TCP     192.168.8.113:1046      204.79.197.222:https      ESTABLISHED
[SearchApp.exe]
  TCP     192.168.8.113:1047      13.107.18.254:https       ESTABLISHED
[SearchApp.exe]
  TCP     192.168.8.113:1048      131.253.33.254:https      ESTABLISHED
[SearchApp.exe]
  TCP     192.168.8.113:1049      13.107.138.9:https        ESTABLISHED
[WINWORD.EXE]
  TCP     192.168.8.113:1050      52.97.212.66:https        ESTABLISHED
[SearchApp.exe]
  TCP     192.168.8.113:1055      52.97.208.2:https         ESTABLISHED
[WINWORD.EXE]
  TCP     192.168.8.113:1070      52.97.133.162:https       ESTABLISHED
[OUTLOOK.EXE]
  TCP     192.168.8.113:1072      52.109.8.21:https         ESTABLISHED
[OfficeClickToRun.exe]
  TCP     192.168.8.113:1073      40.97.164.146:https       CLOSE_WAIT
[dirmngr.exe]
  TCP     192.168.8.113:1074      52.98.145.98:https        ESTABLISHED
[OUTLOOK.EXE]
  TCP     192.168.8.113:1075      40.97.164.146:https       CLOSE_WAIT
[dirmngr.exe]
  TCP     192.168.8.113:1076      87.237.18.210:http        TIME_WAIT
  TCP     192.168.8.113:1077      87.237.18.210:http        TIME_WAIT
  TCP     192.168.8.113:1078      52.97.133.226:https       ESTABLISHED
```

Figure 8.21 – netstat output

Here, we can see all the connected interfaces and ports, as well as information about the application or service that is using the port.

ps can be used to view running processes on Linux and Unix operating systems. Each process is allocated a process ID, which can be used if the process is to be terminated with the `kill` command.

The following screenshot shows the output of `ps -A` (shows all processes) when run on Kali Linux:

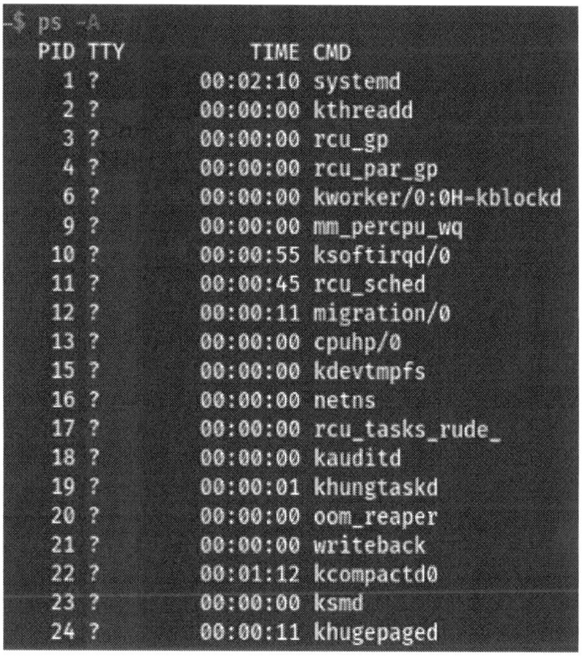

```
$ ps -A
  PID TTY          TIME CMD
    1 ?        00:02:10 systemd
    2 ?        00:00:00 kthreadd
    3 ?        00:00:00 rcu_gp
    4 ?        00:00:00 rcu_par_gp
    6 ?        00:00:00 kworker/0:0H-kblockd
    9 ?        00:00:00 mm_percpu_wq
   10 ?        00:00:55 ksoftirqd/0
   11 ?        00:00:45 rcu_sched
   12 ?        00:00:11 migration/0
   13 ?        00:00:00 cpuhp/0
   15 ?        00:00:00 kdevtmpfs
   16 ?        00:00:00 netns
   17 ?        00:00:00 rcu_tasks_rude_
   18 ?        00:00:00 kauditd
   19 ?        00:00:01 khungtaskd
   20 ?        00:00:00 oom_reaper
   21 ?        00:00:00 writeback
   22 ?        00:01:12 kcompactd0
   23 ?        00:00:00 ksmd
   24 ?        00:00:11 khugepaged
```

Figure 8.22 – The ps command

We can pipe Linux or Windows commands into a file using the pipe, >, operator.

vmstat can be used to show the number of available computing resources and currently used resources. The resources are *proc* (running processes), *memory* (used and available), *swap* (virtual memory on disk), *I/O* (shows blocks sent and received from disk), *system* (interrupts per second, hardware calls), and *CPU* (processor activity). The `vmstat` command with no options will show the average values since the system was booted. The following screenshot shows an example where there is a 5-second update for the display:

```
└$ vmstat 5
procs -----------memory---------- ---swap-- -----io---- -system-- ------cpu-----
 r  b   swpd   free   buff  cache   si   so    bi    bo   in   cs us sy id wa st
 0  0  32924 158228 567508 1705680    0    0     1    12    0    4  1  1 99  0  0
 0  0  32924 157976 567508 1705680    0    0     0     3    0  157  2  3 95  0  0
 0  0  32924 157976 567508 1705680    0    0     0     0    0  273  3  6 91  0  0
 0  0  32924 158228 567508 1705680    0    0     0     0    0  105  2  2 96  0  0
 0  0  32924 158228 567508 1705680    0    0     0     0    0  123  1  3 96  0  0
 0  0  32924 158228 567508 1705680    0    0     0     0    0  117  1  3 96  0  0
 0  0  32924 157220 567508 1705680    0    0     0    17    0  163  2  2 96  0  0
 0  0  32924 157220 567512 1705680    0    0     0    14    0  138  1  4 95  0  0
 0  0  32924 157220 567512 1705680    0    0     0     0    0  109  1  4 95  0  0
 0  0  32924 156716 567512 1705680    0    0     0     0    0   96  1  2 97  0  0
 0  0  32924 156716 567512 1705680    0    0     0     7    0  129  2  3 95  0  0
 0  0  32924 156716 567512 1705680    0    0     0     0    0  105  1  3 96  0  0
 0  0  32924 156716 567512 1705680    0    0     0     0    0   78  1  1 98  0  0
 0  0  32924 156716 567516 1705680    0    0     0    14    0  154  2  3 95  0  0
 0  0  32924 156716 567516 1705680    0    0     0     0    0  107  1  4 95  0  0
 0  0  32924 156716 567516 1705680    0    0     0     0    0   84  1  2 97  0  0
```

Figure 8.23 – The vmstat command

As the system is relatively idle, there are no obvious big changes in the reported values. It is important to understand that updates every few seconds may cause unnecessary processing in the host system.

lsof allows you to list all opened files, the process that was used to open them, and the user account associated with this. The following screenshot shows all the opened files associated with the user mark:

```
COMMAND      PID USER    FD   TYPE     DEVICE  SIZE/OFF      NODE NAME
systemd     1011 mark    cwd  DIR         8,2      4096         2 /
systemd     1011 mark    rtd  DIR         8,2      4096         2 /
systemd     1011 mark    txt  REG         8,2   1669568   2101277 /usr/lib/systemd/systemd
systemd     1011 mark    mem  REG         8,2   1321344   2097650 /usr/lib/x86_64-linux-gnu/libm-2.31.so
systemd     1011 mark    mem  REG         8,2    153808   2100470 /usr/lib/x86_64-linux-gnu/libudev.so.1.6.18
systemd     1011 mark    mem  REG         8,2   1574952   2100478 /usr/lib/x86_64-linux-gnu/libunistring.so.2.1.0
systemd     1011 mark    mem  REG         8,2    149576   2097437 /usr/lib/x86_64-linux-gnu/libgpg-error.so.0.29.0
systemd     1011 mark    mem  REG         8,2     71896   2101097 /usr/lib/x86_64-linux-gnu/libjson-c.so.5.1.0
systemd     1011 mark    mem  REG         8,2     34904   2101096 /usr/lib/x86_64-linux-gnu/libargon2.so.1
systemd     1011 mark    mem  REG         8,2    438568   2099513 /usr/lib/x86_64-linux-gnu/libdevmapper.so.1.02.1
systemd     1011 mark    mem  REG         8,2     30776   2100498 /usr/lib/x86_64-linux-gnu/libuuid.so.1.3.0
systemd     1011 mark    mem  REG         8,2   3044192   2097655 /usr/lib/x86_64-linux-gnu/libcrypto.so.1.1
systemd     1011 mark    mem  REG         8,2     26976   2097229 /usr/lib/x86_64-linux-gnu/libcap-ng.so.0.0.0
systemd     1011 mark    mem  REG         8,2    584360   2099174 /usr/lib/x86_64-linux-gnu/libpcre2-8.so.0.9.0
systemd     1011 mark    mem  REG         8,2    149608   2099628 /usr/lib/x86_64-linux-gnu/libpthread-2.31.so
systemd     1011 mark    mem  REG         8,2     18688   2097649 /usr/lib/x86_64-linux-gnu/libdl-2.31.so
systemd     1011 mark    mem  REG         8,2    162496   2097199 /usr/lib/x86_64-linux-gnu/liblzma.so.5.2.4
systemd     1011 mark    mem  REG         8,2    845744   2100462 /usr/lib/x86_64-linux-gnu/libzstd.so.1.4.5
systemd     1011 mark    mem  REG         8,2    133464   2097977 /usr/lib/x86_64-linux-gnu/liblz4.so.1.9.2
systemd     1011 mark    mem  REG         8,2     35280   2101102 /usr/lib/x86_64-linux-gnu/libip4tc.so.2.0.0
systemd     1011 mark    mem  REG         8,2    128944   2098073 /usr/lib/x86_64-linux-gnu/libidn2.so.0.3.7
systemd     1011 mark    mem  REG         8,2   1168056   2097453 /usr/lib/x86_64-linux-gnu/libgcrypt.so.20.2.6
```

Figure 8.24 – The lsof command

In the preceding example, FD is the file descriptor and TYPE is the file type, such as REG, which means that it is a regular file.

netcat

To execute commands on a remote computer, we can install **netcat** (**nc**). netcat can be launched as a listener or a compromised computer to give remote access to attackers. It may also be used in forensics to gather data with a minimum footprint on the system under investigation.

To set up a listening port on the system under investigation, we can type the following command:

```
nc -l -p 12345
```

To connect from the forensics workstation, we can use the following command:

```
nc 10.10.0.3 12345
```

This will allow us to run commands on the system under investigation to reflect all the outputs on the forensics workstation.

To transfer a file for investigation, we can use the following commands. On the system under investigation, we will wait for 180 seconds on port 12345 to transfer vreport.htm:

```
nc -w 180 -p 12345 -l < vreport.htm
```

To transfer the report file to the forensics workstation, we can use the following command:

```
nc 10.10.0.51 12345 > vreport.htm
```

We now have a copy of the report on the forensics workstation (the report is a vulnerability scan that was performed with a different tool).

tcpdump can be used to capture real-time network traffic and also to open captured traffic using common capture formats, such as **pcap**. tcpdump is included by default on most Linux distributions. It is the Linux version of Wireshark.

To capture all the traffic on the eth0 network interface, we can use the following command:

```
tcpdump -I eth0
```

The following screenshot shows the traffic that was captured on eth0:

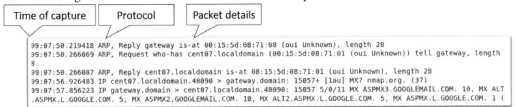

Figure 8.25 – The tcpdump capture

The preceding screenshot shows the command line's tcpdump output, which can also be saved for later analysis.

Conntrack is used by security professionals to view the details of the **IPTABLES** (firewall) state tables. It is a very powerful command-line tool, but in this instance, it will be of interest to see extra details about the firewall's state table. It allows for detailed tracking of firewall connections. To see a list of all the current connections and their state, we can use the following command:

```
conntrack -L
```

The output can be seen in the following screenshot:

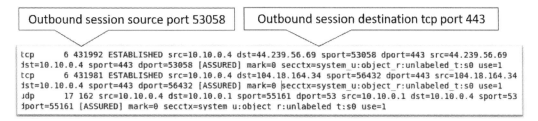

```
tcp      6 431992 ESTABLISHED src=10.10.0.4 dst=44.239.56.69 sport=53058 dport=443 src=44.239.56.69
dst=10.10.0.4 sport=443 dport=53058 [ASSURED] mark=0 secctx=system_u:object_r:unlabeled_t:s0 use=1
tcp      6 431981 ESTABLISHED src=10.10.0.4 dst=104.18.164.34 sport=443 dport=56432 src=104.18.164.34
dst=10.10.0.4 sport=443 dport=56432 [ASSURED] mark=0 secctx=system_u:object_r:unlabeled_t:s0 use=1
udp     17 162 src=10.10.0.4 dst=10.10.0.1 sport=55161 dport=53 src=10.10.0.1 dst=10.10.0.4 sport=53
dport=55161 [ASSURED] mark=0 secctx=system_u:object_r:unlabeled_t:s0 use=1
```

Figure 8.26 – Conntrack output

The preceding screenshot shows the detailed output from the firewall state table, including all current connections. The fine detail for this tool is beyond the scope for CompTIA CAS students, though more details can be found at `https://conntrack-tools.netfilter.org/manual.html`.

Wireshark

One of the most well-known protocol analyzers is **Wireshark**. It is available for many operating system platforms and presents the security professional with a **Graphical User Interface** (**GUI**). Using Wireshark, we can capture traffic in real time to understand normal traffic patterns and protocols. We can also load up packet capture files for detailed analysis. It also has a command-line version called **TShark**. The following screenshot shows a packet capture using Wireshark:

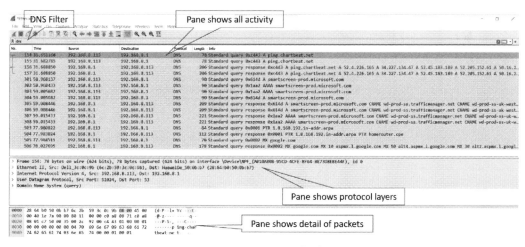

Figure 8.27 – Wireshark

In the example, we have filtered the displayed packets to show only DNS activity. Wireshark is a very powerful tool. For further examples and comprehensive documentation, go to `https://www.wireshark.org/docs/`.

Summary

In this chapter, we have considered many threats that can impact an enterprise and identified policies and procedures to deal with unplanned security-related events. We learned about the importance of timely responses to security incidents. Knowledge has been gained on deploying the appropriate threat detection capabilities. We have studied automation, including orchestration and SOAR, also taking care to include a human in the loop. Ever-increasing evidence of APTs means that we need to rely on forensics to detect IOCs and, where necessary, collect the evidence to formulate a response. You should now be familiar with incident response planning and have a good understanding of forensic concepts. After completing the previous section, you should now be familiar with using forensic analysis tools.

Cybersecurity professionals must be able to recognize and use common security tools as these will be important for many day-to-day security activities. **Nmap**, **dd**, **hashing utilities**, **netstat**, **vmstat**, **Wireshark**, and **tcpdump** are tools that will feature in the CASP 004 certification exam's questions. Specialist binary analysis tools are not as commonly used outside of specialist job roles.

These skills will be useful when we move on to the next chapter, where we will cover securing enterprise mobility and endpoint security.

Questions

Answer the following questions to test your knowledge of this chapter:

1. During a security incident, a team member was able to refer to known documentation and databases of attack vectors to aid the response. What is this an example of?

    A.   Event classification

    B.   A false positive

    C.   A false negative

    D.   A true positive

2. During a security incident, a team member responded to a SIEM alert and successfully stopped an attempted data exfiltration. What can be said about the SIEM alert?

    A. It's a false positive.

    B. It's a false negative.

    C. It's a true positive.

    D. It's a true negative.

3. During a security incident, a senior team leader coordinated with members already dealing with a breach. They were told to concentrate their efforts on a new threat. What process led to the team leader's actions?

    A. Preparation

    B. Analysis

    C. Triage event

    D. Pre-escalation tasks

4. A CSIRT team needs to be identified, including leadership with a clear reporting and escalation process. At what stage of the incident response process should this be done?

    A. Preparation

    B. Detection

    C. Analysis

    D. Containment

5. During a security incident, a team member responded to a SIEM alert stating that multiple workstations on a network segment have been infected with crypto-malware. what part of the incident response process should be followed?

    A. Preparation

    B. Detection

    C. Analysis

    D. Containment

6. After a security incident, workstations that were previously infected with crypto-malware were placed in quarantine, wiped, and successfully scanned with an updated antivirus. what part of the incident response process should be followed?

    A. Analysis

    B. Containment

    C. Recovery

    D. Lessons learned

7. During a security incident, multiple systems were impacted by a DDoS attack. To mitigate the effect of the attack, a CSIRT team member follows procedures to trigger a BGP route update. This deflects the attack and the systems remain operational. What documentation did the CSIRT team member refer to?

    A. Communication plan

    B. Runbooks

    C. Configuration guides

    D. Vendor documentation

8. Critical infrastructure has been targeted by attackers who demand large payments in bitcoin to reveal the technology and keys needed to access the encrypted data. To avoid paying the ransom, analysts have been tasked to crack the cipher. What technique will they use?

    A. Ransomware

    B. Data exfiltration

    C. Cryptanalysis

    D. Steganalysis

9. During a security incident, multiple systems were impacted by a DDoS attack. A security professional working in the SOC can view the events on a reporting dashboard and call up automated scripts to mitigate the attack. What system was used to respond to the attack?

    A. Containment

    B. SOAR

    C. Communication plan

    D. Configuration guides

10. A technician who is part of the IRT is called to take a forensic copy of a hard drive on the CEO's laptop. He takes notes of the step-by-step process and stores the evidence in a locked cabinet in the CISO's office. What will make this evidence inadmissible?

    A.   Evidence collection

    B.   Lack of chain of custody

    C.   Missing order of volatility

    D.   Missing memory snapshots

11. A forensic investigator is called to capture all the possible evidence from a compromised laptop. To save battery life, the system is put into sleep mode. What important forensic process has been overlooked?

    A.   Cloning

    B.   Evidence preservation

    C.   Secure storage

    D.   Backups

12. A forensic investigator is called to capture all possible evidence from a compromised computer that has been switched off. They gain access to the hard drive and connect a write blocker, before recording the current hash value of the hard drive image. What important forensic process has been followed?

    A.   Integrity preservation

    B.   Hashing

    C.   Cryptanalysis

    D.   Steganalysis

13. Law enforcement needs to retrieve graphics image files that have been deleted or hidden in unallocated space on a hacker's hard drive. What tools should they use when analyzing the captured forensic image?

    A.   File carving tools

    B.   `objdump`

    C.   `strace`

    D.   `netstat`

14. FBI forensics experts are investigating a new variant of APT that has replaced Linux operating system files on government computers. What tools should they use to understand the behavior and logic of these files?

    A. Runbooks

    B. Binary analysis tools

    C. Imaging tools

    D. `vmstat`

15. A forensic investigator suspects stolen data is hidden within JPEG images on a suspect's computer. After capturing a forensic image, what techniques should they use when analyzing the JPEG image files?

    A. Integrity preservation

    B. Hashing

    C. Cryptanalysis

    D. Steganalysis

16. Attackers have managed to install additional services on a company's DMZ network. Security personnel need to identify all the systems in the DMZ and all the services that are currently running. What command-line tool best gathers this information?

    A. `Nmap`

    B. `Aircrack-ng`

    C. Volatility

    D. The Sleuth Kit

17. A forensic investigator is called to capture all possible evidence from a compromised computer that has been switched off. They gain access to the hard drive and connect a write blocker. What tool should be used to create a bit-by-bit forensic copy?

    A. `dd`

    B. Hashing utilities

    C. `sha256sum`

    D. `ssdeep`

18. To stop a running process on a Red Hat Linux server, an investigator needs to see all the currently running processes and their current process IDs. What command-line tool will allow the investigator to view this information?

   A.   netstat -a

   B.   ps -A

   C.   tcpdump -i

   D.   sha1sum <filename>

19. While analyzing a running Red Hat Linux server, an investigator needs to show the number of available computing resources and currently used resources. The requirements are for the running processor, memory, and swap space on the disk. What tool should be used?

   A.   vmstat

   B.   ldd

   C.   lsof

   D.   tcpdump

20. During a live investigation on a Fedora Linux server, a forensic analyst needs to view a listing of all opened files, the process that was used to open them, and the user account associated with the open files. What would be the best command-line tool to use?

   A.   vmstat

   B.   ldd

   C.   lsof

   D.   tcpdump

21. While analyzing a running Red Hat Linux server, an investigator needs to run commands on the system under investigation to reflect all the outputs on the forensics workstation. The analyst also needs to transfer a file for investigation using minimum interactions. What command-line tool should be used?

   A.   netcat

   B.   tcpdump

   C.   conntrack

   D.   Wireshark

22. Security professionals need to assess the security of wireless networks. A tool needs to be identified that allows wireless traffic to be monitored, and the WEP and WPA security to be attacked (via packet injection) and cracked. What would be the best command-line tool to use here?

    A.   `netcat`

    B.   `tcpdump`

    C.   `Aircrack-ng`

    D.   Wireshark

23. A forensic investigator needs to search through a network capture saved as a `pcap` file. They are looking for evidence of data exfiltration from a suspect host computer. To minimize disruption, they need to identify a command-line tool that will provide this functionality. What should they choose?

    A.   `netcat`

    B.   `tcpdump`

    C.   `Aircrack-ng`

    D.   Wireshark

24. A forensic investigator is performing analysis on syslog files. They are looking for evidence of unusual activity based upon reports from **User Behavior Analytics (UBA)**. Several packets show signs of unusual activity. Which of the following requires further investigation?

    A.   `nc -w 180 -p 12345 -l < shadow.txt`

    B.   `tcpdump -I eth0`

    C.   `conntrack -L`

    D.   `Exiftool nasa.jpg`

25. Recent activity has led to an investigation being launched against a recent hire in the research team. Intellectual property has been identified as part of code now being sold by a competitor. UBA has identified a significant amount of JPEG image uploads to a social networking site. The payloads are now being analyzed by forensics. What techniques will allow them to search for evidence in the JPEG files?

    A.   The Steganalysis tool

    B.   The Cryptanalysis tool

    C.   The Binary Analysis tool

    D.   The Memory Analysis tool

Answers

The following are the answers to this chapter's questions:

1. A
2. C
3. C
4. A
5. D
6. C
7. B
8. C
9. B
10. B
11. B
12. A
13. A
14. B
15. D
16. A
17. A
18. B
19. A
20. C
21. A
22. C
23. B
24. A
25. A

Section 3: Security Engineering and Cryptography

In this section, you will learn how to deploy various controls to protect enterprise data and systems. You will learn how to protect end devices using a variety of different technologies and learn the importance of cryptography and PKI when protecting enterprise data.

This part of the book comprises the following chapters:

- *Chapter 9, Enterprise Mobility and Endpoint Security Controls*

- *Chapter 10, Security Considerations Impacting Specific Sectors and Operational Technologies*

- *Chapter 11, Implementing Cryptographic Protocols and Algorithms*

- *Chapter 12, Implementing Appropriate PKI Solutions, Cryptographic Protocols, and Algorithms for Business Needs*

9
Enterprise Mobility and Endpoint Security Controls

In a large enterprise, there is a business need for flexibility and mobility, but it is vitally important to address the risks, in terms of cybersecurity. Many business solutions comprise heterogeneous workloads on the server side and have to deal with a large number of end devices. These can include traditional desktop computers, laptops, tablets, handheld devices, and wearable technology. We need to assess the security of these devices, choose the appropriate technologies that the enterprise should adopt, and ensure that we can provide the necessary attestation that they do not present unacceptable business risks. There are security requirements to ensure that deployed system images are built from a validated secure template. Services should only be enabled if there is a business need for them. There is also the challenge of providing network access to a variety of mobile devices, including personal devices that are Wi-Fi enabled. **Compensating controls** should be deployed to offer additional protection – for example, **Firewalls**, **Endpoint Detection and Response** (**EDR**) plans, and **antivirus** tools.

In this chapter, we will learn about the tools and techniques needed to secure our endpoint devices. We will study the following topics:

- Implementing enterprise mobility management
- Security considerations for mobility management
- Implementing endpoint security controls
- Deploying host hardening
- Understanding endpoint security software

Implementing enterprise mobility management

One of the challenges of supporting devices in a hybrid network is the fact that the traditional network perimeter has been moved, so there is no longer a fixed enterprise boundary – in other words, users are accessing information systems from outside the enterprise. In many cases, information systems can be managed by third parties such as cloud providers. We call this phenomenon **de-perimeterization**.

Enterprise mobility management is the process of ensuring that mobile devices comply with the enterprise security policy. An enterprise will have the challenge of supporting mobile users, home/remote working setups, and personal computing devices that are not managed using traditional on-premises controls. We must accept that the business will have a need for this hybrid approach, but we also must understand the controls needed to protect the business from the loss, theft, and exfiltration of valuable business data. To ease the administration of security controls, we should choose vendor solutions that allow enterprise-owned and personal devices to be managed with a single-enterprise toolset, often referred to as a **single pane of glass**. In this section, we will look at the security features that need to be managed in this situation.

Managed configurations

There are many configuration settings available on the typical operating system, no matter who the vendor is. Without the proper management of these settings, devices that access corporate data will present a security risk. In the following subsections, we will take a look at some of the available configuration options.

Application control

It is important that we can control applications that are installed in the enterprise workspace – that is, every application should be justified by a business need. When users have access to the **Google Play Store**, **Apple App Store**, or **Microsoft Store**, they have the option to install hundreds of applications. Applications often have multiple configuration options, such as access to contacts information or access to location data. These settings can be controlled by using **mobile application management** (**MAM**) tools, deployment scripts, or **Microsoft Group Policy Objects** (**GPOs**). To allow for some flexibility in our application control, we can enable **containerization** for enterprise applications and data. Many vendors offer solutions that allow an organization to host a customized or restricted list of applications on their own company-branded portal. *Figure 9.1* shows a user view of the Microsoft Store with **Trainingpartners** company branding:

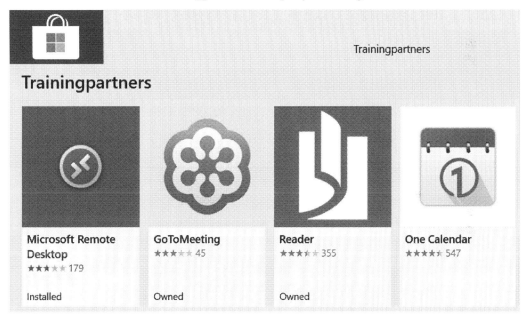

Figure 9.1 – A restricted Microsoft Store application

Normally, a **Windows** user can choose from hundreds of available applications to install on their devices. But with the restricted view, this can be controlled. If we only allow devices to have access to an approved subset of application store programs, we can reduce our security footprint.

Passwords

At a minimum, we should enable screen locks and a minimum password length (based on company standards). This is to ensure that the data on the device will not be accessible if the device is lost or stolen.

Multi-factor authentication requirements

Passwords alone are not always considered to be adequate security for enterprise mobile devices. We may choose to enable additional authentication factors, such as **one-time passwords** (**OTPs**) using hardware tokens or mobile authenticator applications. Another useful authentication option for mobile devices is to use built-in biometric readers. Biometric authentication can include reading fingerprints, facial recognition, voice authentication, and iris scans. Many devices come with card reader functionality, making it easier to implement smart cards for **multi-factor authentication** (**MFA**). Microsoft also supports secure tokens in the form of a secure USB key, which provides the same functionality as a smart card. Smart cards and USB keys are considered a form of **token-based authentication**.

Figure 9.2 displays some additional sign-in options for Windows:

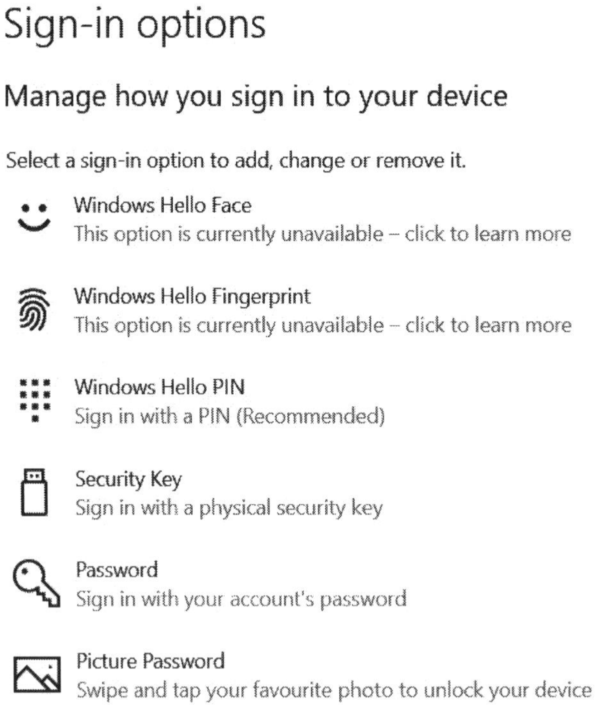

Sign-in options

Manage how you sign in to your device

Select a sign-in option to add, change or remove it.

Windows Hello Face
This option is currently unavailable – click to learn more

Windows Hello Fingerprint
This option is currently unavailable – click to learn more

Windows Hello PIN
Sign in with a PIN (Recommended)

Security Key
Sign in with a physical security key

Password
Sign in with your account's password

Picture Password
Swipe and tap your favourite photo to unlock your device

Figure 9.2 – MFA authentication methods on Windows

MFA adds another line of defense in cases where a password could be compromised.

Patch repositories

In order to offer the best levels of protection, it is important to access the latest patches for supported end devices and ensure that they are deployed in a timely fashion. Failure to implement patches will result in vulnerabilities that could have been mitigated. Additionally, not installing the latest patches may render a device non-compliant, and the user may not be able to access company resources until the device is updated and made compliant.

Firmware over-the-air (FOTA)

For mobile operating systems such as **Android** and **Apple iOS**, it is important that firmware updates are downloaded and installed when they become available. These updates add functionality to the device, but more importantly, they add security features and updates. It is important to control this process by allowing updates only over approved cellular networks.

Remote wipe options

It is important to render enterprise data unrecoverable by initiating a remote wipe process, when a device has been reported as missing or stolen. It is possible that this instruction will not be received by the **mobile device management** (**MDM**) agent due to a lack of cellular or network signal. *Figure 9.3* shows some of the remote wipe options available for a lost or stolen mobile device:

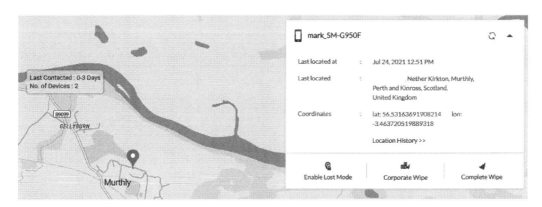

Figure 9.3 – Remote wipe options

For personal devices, we may only need the option for a corporate wipe. In *Figure 9.3* we see the options to secure an Android smartphone.

Wi-Fi

Wi-Fi is the primary connection type for most mobile devices, although it is also commonplace to access 4G+ and 5G cellular networks at high speed with limitless data plans. In both instances, we should look to secure these links.

Wi-Fi protected access (WPA2/3)

WPA2 offers increased security over the older options of **Wireless Encryption Privacy (WEP)** and the **Wireless Protected Access (WPA) Temporal Key Integrity Protocol (TKIP)**. It supports the **Advanced Encryption Standard (AES)**, offering a greater level of security than the older protocols. **WPA3** was introduced in 2018 and offers additional levels of security. WPA3 supports the use of 256 bit AES encryption and also secures access to the network if we cannot use **802.1x** and **RADIUS**. The previous Wi-Fi implementations use **pre-shared keys (PSKs)**, which are vulnerable to password cracking and brute force attacks. WPA3 uses **Simultaneous Authentication of Equals (SAE)** instead of PSKs – this limits the number allowed of password attempts and uses additional security protection methods.

Device certificates

It is common for security certificates to be distributed to users and devices for a variety of purposes. We can use certificates to gain trusted access to the network using **802.1X security**. There are many security applications that also require the use of certificates, such as IPsec-based **virtual private networks (VPNs)**, the **S/MIME** standard, and **Pretty Good Privacy (PGP)**.

To automate the deployment of certificates, we can use the **Simple Certificate Enrolment Protocol (SCEP)**. This is supported in most MDM solutions. *Figure 9.4* shows the SCEP enrolment process:

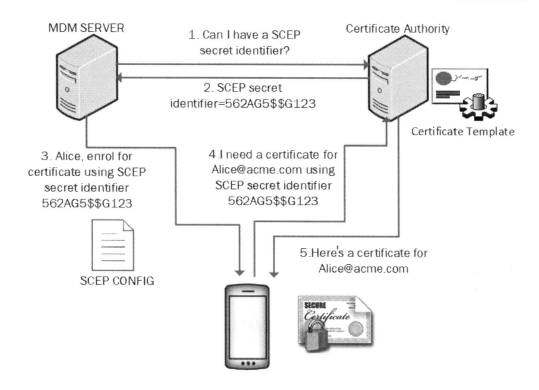

Figure 9.4 – The SCEP enrolment process

If we control the deployment of certificates, it is less likely that users will be able to install certificates from untrustworthy certificate authorities.

Device profiles

To automate common settings on mobile devices, a profile with a set of configuration objects can be deployed to the devices. Common profiles can include settings for Wi-Fi, VPNs, and many more. *Figure 9.5* displays some available settings when deploying device configuration profiles:

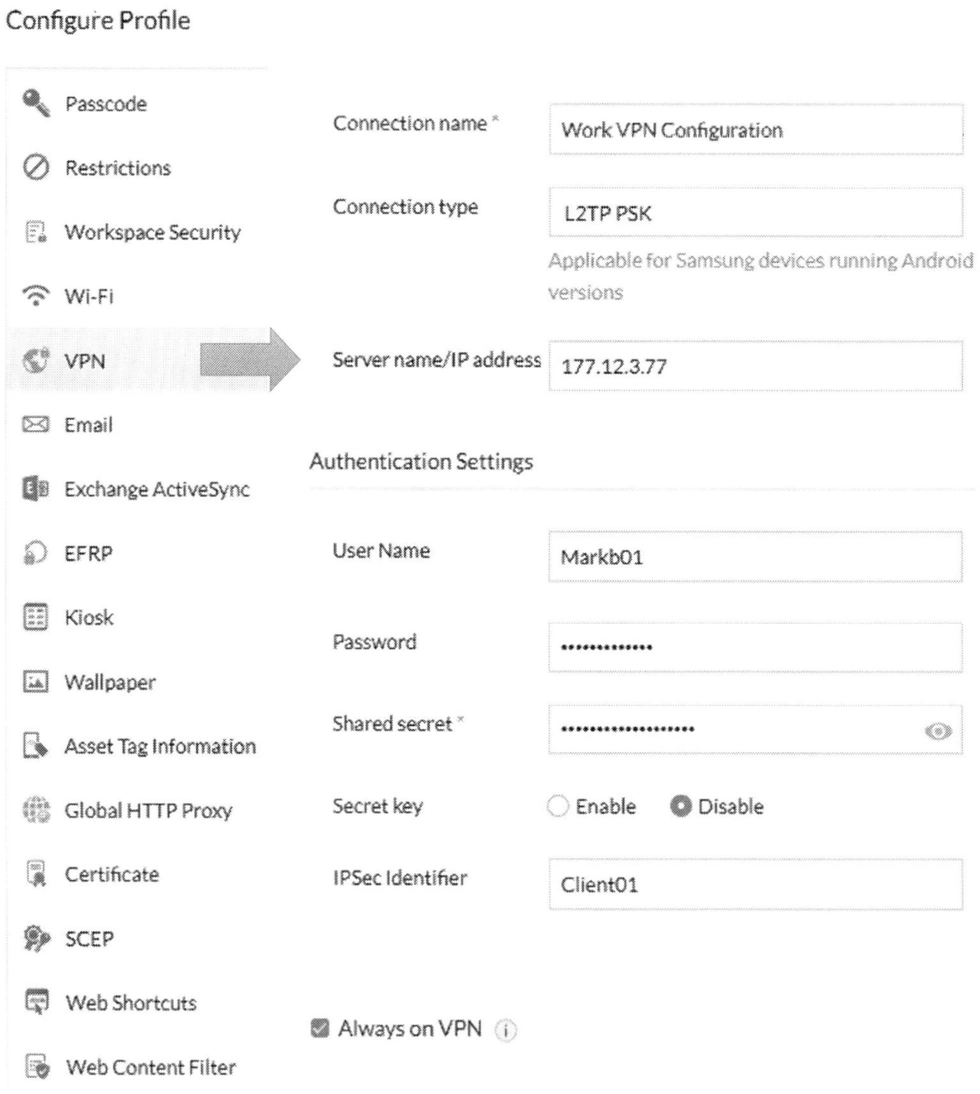

Configure Profile

Passcode

Restrictions

Workspace Security

Wi-Fi

VPN

Email

Exchange ActiveSync

EFRP

Kiosk

Wallpaper

Asset Tag Information

Global HTTP Proxy

Certificate

SCEP

Web Shortcuts

Web Content Filter

Connection name *   Work VPN Configuration

Connection type   L2TP PSK

Applicable for Samsung devices running Android versions

Server name/IP address   177.12.3.77

Authentication Settings

User Name   Markb01

Password   ●●●●●●●●●●●●

Shared secret *   ●●●●●●●●●●●●●●●●●●   👁

Secret key   ○ Enable   ● Disable

IPSec Identifier   Client01

☑ Always on VPN ⓘ

Figure 9.5 – An example VPN device configuration profile

When there are many settings to manage, a profile is a convenient way to deploy custom configuration settings. In *Figure 9.5* we are deploying a VPN profile to Android devices.

Bluetooth

Bluetooth is a relatively short-range radio frequency. **Class 2 Bluetooth** (which is most common for consumer devices) transmits at 2.5 mW and has a range of around 10 meters. It allows data to be sent wirelessly with no encryption. This means wireless headsets could allow users to attend a secure web conference but a wireless listening device could be used to eavesdrop on the conference. It is common to restrict the use of Bluetooth in these situations.

Near-field communication

Near-field communication (**NFC**) operates at low speeds over short distances (up to 4 cm). It can be used to transfer data – such as configuration data or print jobs – to an NFC-enabled printer. It is commonly used in the wireless payment systems for **Apple Pay** and **Google Pay**. Once a user has unlocked a mobile device, then NFC-enabled applications may transfer data without any user verification. This function could lead to fraudulent payment transactions (currently the United Kingdom allows up to £100 to be transferred using contactless payment). It could also allow confidential data to be transferred.

Peripherals

Mobile devices can support extensibility through **SD** and **MicroSD** cards or **USB On-The-Go** (**OTG**). This allows for data transfer and connectivity using USB devices.

Geofencing

One effective way to control the functionality of mobile devices is to use **GPS** tracking to locate devices and restrict functions based upon the proximity of the device to a site of interest. So, we could map out the coordinates of a secure site and create a **geofence**. When devices are inside the geofence, we can disable the devices' cameras and any recording capability, and when devices are outside the geofence, normal service can be restored. In case a company device is stolen, we can create conditions where the device is wiped of all its enterprise data when it is taken outside the geofence.

VPN settings

VPN settings can be configured by deploying a **VPN profile** to a mobile device. It is important to ensure confidentiality of business data when company employees are outside the workplace. An *always-on* profile ensures that the device will always connect through the secure VPN. Implementing a full tunnel configuration will ensure all applications and browser activity is routed through the company network. This configuration will make sure all security protocols can be applied. *Figure 9.6* shows an example of a VPN client using a full tunnel VPN:

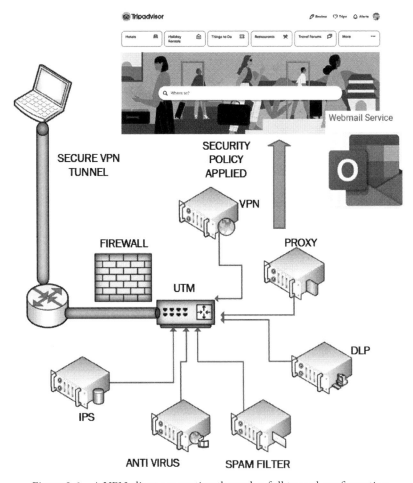

Figure 9.6 – A VPN client connecting through a full tunnel configuration

Without this configuration, the device can connect directly to external applications without the appropriate security policies being applied.

Geotagging

An organization should consider the security of applications that use **geotagging**. For example, users could install a fitness application on a mobile phone that automatically uploads their activity (complete with maps) to social media. This is quite common when you look at applications such as **Strava** or **MapMyRun**. In *Figure 9.7*, we can see the mapping feature on the Strava application:

Figure 9.7 – The Strava mapping feature

If you allow other users to view your activities, then you may reveal sensitive details about your movements or reveal information regarding sensitive locations.

Full device encryption

It is important to secure enterprise data stored on mobile devices. At a minimum, we should enforce the use of **screen lock** and **storage encryption** (including for SD cards). If a password-enabled screen lock is not required, then access to the data may still be possible if the device is lost or stolen. If the mobile device contains removable storage, it should be encrypted, as the media may otherwise be readable when mounted on another piece of hardware.

It is important that the device is hardened against tampering so that any attempt to change the boot process will result in the data being unrecoverable.

Tethering

Because mobile data plans can be very affordable on cellular networks, it is common for users to use their mobile phones as a **hotspot** for their laptops. This presents a security risk when a laptop is plugged into the enterprise **local area network** (**LAN**), as the laptop can now bridge two networks.

Airplane mode

Mobile devices commonly have a setting that turns off all radio frequency channels (for example, **airplane mode**). This could be a useful configuration option to invoke when location-based security is a priority. Disabling radio frequency channels protects the device from network based threats. It also means the device cannot download security updates or be managed using **Mobile Device Management** (**MDM**).

Location services

Mobile operating systems often have privacy options associated with **location services**. If location services are enabled, then content providers can deliver more tailored information for users. Microsoft now includes a feature on Windows operating systems called **News and Interests** that delivers traffic reports, weather forecasts, and local news to devices based on their location. You may not want this location information to be available for all applications. We can restrict these features in the Microsoft privacy settings seen in *Figure 9.8*:

Location

Allow desktop apps to access your location

Some apps and Windows features need to access your location to work as intended. Turning off this setting here might limit what desktop apps and Windows can do.

⬤ On

Some desktop apps might not appear in the following list or are not affected by this setting. Find out why

Microsoft Defender Application Guard Manager
Last accessed 09/07/2021 07:56:35

Microsoft Edge
Last accessed 09/07/2021 17:03:18

Microsoft Teams
Last accessed 09/07/2021 08:08:10

Geofencing

Geofencing means using your location to see when you cross in or out of a boundary drawn around a place of interest.

None of your apps are currently using geofencing.

Choose which apps can access your precise location

3D Viewer	⬤	Off
Camera	⬤	Off
Desktop App Web Viewer	⬤	Off
Mail and Calendar	⬤	Off
Maps	⬤	Off
Skype	⬤	On
Weather	⬤	On

Figure 9.8 – The Microsoft location services privacy settings

Location sevices can also be useful when enforcing context based authentication. **User and Entity Behavior Analytics UEBA** can block suspicious authentication attempts from unusual locations. **Impossible Time Travel** can also be detected, where separate login attempts are not feasable based upon the time duration and location of the attempts.

DNS over HTTPS (DoH)

When using traditional **Domain Name Services** (**DNS**) for name queries, we are sending requests to a designated DNS server with no security – this means that every request and reply is sent in plaintext. This may reveal useful intelligence to an eavesdropper on a network segment. Many web browsers, including Edge and Chrome, allow configuration settings to be updated, allowing for secure **TLS** connections to be made to public DoH servers. In *Figure 9.9*, we can see the security settings for the **Microsoft Edge** browser:

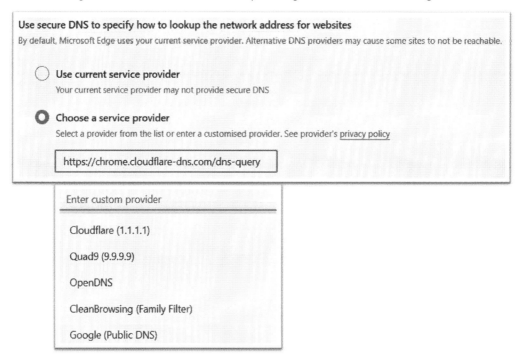

Figure 9.9 – The Microsoft Edge browser DoH settings

Another alternative is to use a secure VPN connection back to the enterprise network where we can safely send DNS queries to the enterprise DNS servers.

Custom DNS settings

Many ISPs may limit their customers' access to content by restricting and filtering DNS queries. This can also be an effective control for enterprise users by blocking name resolutions for certain websites. Users may find a workaround to these restrictions by using a custom DNS server that does not log any activity or block name resolution requests. By restricting access to these settings, we can ensure that all internet activity is controlled.

Deployment scenarios

There are many different scenarios that an organization may consider when deploying mobility management. For example, costs can be a driving factor and support issues may be important. But security and management will always be the priority when implementing MDM.

Bring your own device challenges

When users access enterprise data on a personal device, it can present many challenges for the organization. There is the issue of what devices the organization is willing to support. There are also many different versions of operating systems to support and also different hardware platforms. It is important to define a secure encrypted container on the device to hold corporate applications and data. We will need to define policies to secure any sensitive company data. It is also important to identify MDM tools that will enable the management of all the personal device types that will be supported.

Corporate-owned devices

When an organization is responsible for purchasing the mobile devices that will be used by employees, there can be much more control in selecting the operating systems and devices that best suit the organization's business needs.

Corporate-owned, personally enabled (COPE) devices

When a company allows users to access personal data using its devices, it is important to separate the business data and applications from the personal data. In the same way that we protect business data with **bring your own device (BYOD)** policies, we must use the same strategy with **corporate-owned, personally enabled (COPE)** devices. This means separating business data and personal data. MDM will be used to ensure that containerization is implemented.

Choose your own device (CYOD) challenges

Often, enterprise users are familiar with a particular technology and will be more engaged with the technology if it is a device or operating system that they find easy to use. The challenge for the enterprise is to allow users to have a degree of choice in the devices they use but to restrict the list of available devices to a manageable number. This will ensure that we only have to support a small number of hardware devices and operating systems. **Android fragmentation** is a term used to describe the proliferation of devices running many different versions of the Android operating system. There have been numerous versions of Android operating system releases (currently 19 versions at the end of 2021). The goal of the organization is to restrict the handsets and the operating systems that will be allowed to connect to the business network. This will help to reduce support complexity and will reduce the security footprint.

With mobility being a major consideration for most organizations, it is important to recognize the possible security implications when supporting end devices, operating systems, and applications. We will now investigate some of the security features and configurations that we can manage for mobile devices.

Security considerations for mobility management

Many security considerations arise when an enterprise wants to support a mobile workforce. Devices offer a wide range of features and functions that may represent a risk to the organization.

The unauthorized remote activation and deactivation of devices or features

While many devices support an array of security features, many of these can be deactivated – for example, the user may inadvertently disable or deactivate a security feature such as a daemon supporting an anti-malware application. This risk should be mitigated by using secure operating systems (such as **Security-Enhanced Linux** (**SELinux**) or **Security-Enhanced Android** (**SEAndroid**)) along with MDM.

Encrypted and unencrypted communication concerns

When we are supporting mobility, we should always identify the weakest links in a network. This means that if we harden the device using **full device encryption (FDE)**, screen locks, and application whitelisting, we also need to ensure that network communication is secured. We should restrict the use of Bluetooth and also restrict Wi-Fi access to trusted WLANs.

Physical reconnaissance

Mobile devices can be used to gather intelligence. If we allow the use of camera, video, audio, and GPS functionality on mobile devices, a malicious user could capture accurate data about a site that could later be used in an attack. This device may belong to an insider threat actor or the data could be stolen from an unsecured mobile device.

Personal data theft

While the main focus of MDM is to protect business data, it is also important to protect a user's personal data. **Personal data** may include **protected health information (PHI)**, **personally identifiable information (PII)**, and other types of confidential data.

Health privacy

Many devices will support fitness applications that can store the medical records of users. Due to the COVID-19 pandemic, public health service tracking applications are also commonplace. In the United Kingdom, there are **National Health Service (NHS)** applications that can store a citizen's COVID-19 status and records of their immunization history. This data would be referred to as PHI in the United States. It is important that this type of data is held securely.

The implications of wearable devices

Wearable devices may have GPS tracking capabilities and they frequently store detailed personal information, including heart rates and blood pressure readings. The synchronization of data between the wearable device and an application on another system may also be a vulnerability. Many wearable devices may use low-powered Bluetooth or NFC to transfer data. Senitive data may be exposed as a result of unsecured data transmission.

The digital forensics of collected data

It is important to keep forensic toolkits and techniques updated, as new technologies, such as wearable technology, may be the target of attacks. It is important that we can access the storage and memory of mobile devices to search for **indicators of compromise** (**IOCs**).

Unauthorized application stores

The default settings on most mobile operating systems block access to sideloading applications. **Sideloading** involves the acquisition of an installation package from sources that are not approved – for example, **Android APK** or **iOS IPA** files can be installed directly, without the need to download them from the approved online store. This restriction can be circumvented by **jailbreaking** an iOS device or **rooting** an Android device.

When you *jailbreak* or *root* a device, you are modifying the vendor operating system to break away from the secure restricted settings that are in place by default. For example, on iOS, it is not possible to install applications from outside of the Apple App Store, so installing jailbreaking software will allow users to install applications and themes that have not been officially approved by Apple. Apple also provides developer licenses that allow the use of sideloading applications on an iOS device (this developer license currently costs $99 per year). There is also a free Apple Store application called **Xcode** that allows for sideloading when you have the application source code of the unapproved application.

Containerization

When we allow the personal use of mobile devices that will also access or store business data, we need to implement **segmentation**. Segmenting applications and data on mobile devices is referred to as **containerization**. On **Samsung** devices, there is a vendor-created container called **Secure Folder**. This can be managed using the **Samsung Knox** security tools, or it can be managed using third-party MDM tools. Currently, Knox is supported by **Microsoft Endpoint Manager** (previously **Microsoft Intune**), **VMware AirWatch**, **Ivanti MobileIron**, and many more. *Figure 9.10* shows the Secure Folder application on a **Samsung 9.0** device:

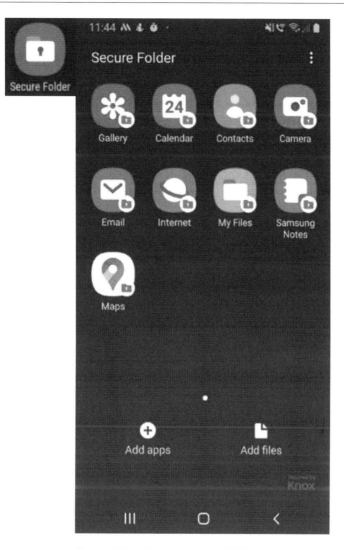

Figure 9.10 – Samsung Secure Folder

These applications and any business data are stored completely separately from the personal space on the device.

Original equipment manufacturer (OEM) and carrier differences

Many cellular operators will provide their customers with customized versions of popular operating systems and will lock the mobile device into their network offerings. When you purchase a device that is not locked into a cellular provider, the user has more flexibility to choose between providers simply by changing the **subscriber identity module (SIM)** card. This offers the opportunity for the user to use any cellular operator, including operators in other countries. For example if a company buys cellular handsets from T-Mobile, then they will only allow the handsets to work on T-Mobile cellular networks.

Supply chain issues

There have been many instances of security breaches due to the installation of default applications by vendors that turned out to be malicious. **Adups** (software used to monitor user behavior) was installed, by default, on a variety of devices using the Android operating system. This software allowed for backdoor access to call logs, contact lists, SMS messages, and location tracking. For more information, see the report at `https://tinyurl.com/adupshack`.

The use of an eFuse

An **eFuse** can be useful when for protecting the integrity of a mobile device. An eFuse will trip under certain conditions. The main reasons for the tripping of an eFuse are normally an unsigned bootloader, an unsigned kernel, or unsigned scripts that might be running. In these circumstances, the eFuse will disable access to the secure container. This also updates the security status of the device from **official** to **untrusted**. An eFuse is like a regular electrical fuse that protects electrical devices. In this case it is embedded directly into the firmware. For more details on eFuse, see the following URL: `https://tinyurl.com/samsungefuse`.

Implementing endpoint security controls

It is important to understand all the risks that endpoints pose to an organization and implement the appropriate controls to mitigate these risks. These controls can include choosing trusted hardware and software platforms and utilizing attestation services to ensure the platforms have a strong security posture. We must also protect our systems from unauthorized changes using tools such as **host intrusion detection systems (HIDSes)** and **host intrusion prevention systems (HIPSes)**. In addition, **endpoint detection and response (EDR)** software can help an organization where there are threats that are sophisticated and currently undocumented (such as zero day exploits). Now, we will investigate a number of techniques to secure endpoint devices.

Hardening techniques

It is important to recognize that there are many ways to strengthen the security posture of devices. In this section, we will investigate some of the **hardening techniques** available.

Removing unneeded services

Running unneeded services on a computer system offers additional connection opportunities for malicious actors such as malware (**remote access trojans (RATs)** and **worms**). To reduce the overall security footprint of a system we should disable these services based on the business needs of the system. For example, an internet-facing public web server will not need to run file and print sharing services, although this might be a requirement when the server is deployed as a departmental internal server.

Disabling unused accounts

It is important to identify built-in system or user accounts that may present a security risk. Examples of risks could include guest accounts and vendor-created support accounts. There should be a security policy that ensures this becomes an automated process. In *Figure 9.11*, we can see which default local accounts have been disabled on a Windows 10 host computer.

Figure 9.11 – Disabled default Windows accounts

When an account does not need to be used in an information system, it should be disabled.

Images and templates

To assist with the goal of implementing a strong security posture for end devices, a customized hardened operating system image is a good building block for security. On United States **Department of Defense (DoD)** networks, there is a Windows operating system build image called the **Windows Secure Host Baseline (SHB)**. This ensures the deployment is hardened by default. In this instance, there are over 200 specific security requirements that must be enabled by default. All the tools needed to create an operating system build image and verify it can be found in the **GitHub** repository at `https://tinyurl.com/windowsDoDshb`.

Removing end-of-life devices (obsolescence management)

When a device is no longer considered serviceable or represents too big a risk to the enterprise, it should be decommissioned. It is important to ensure, when removing a device, that this action does not weaken the security posture of the network. If it is a security appliance, then it should be replaced.

Removing end-of-support devices

When a device can no longer be protected through vendor support and patching then it will become a vulnerability. For example, Microsoft withdrew support for the **Windows 7** operating system in January 2020. In July 2021, there were 135 vulnerabilities listed as **Common Vulnerabilities and Exposures (CVEs)** affecting Windows 7. As there is no automated patching offered for end-of-support devices or operating systems, vulnerabilities often remain unmitigated.

Local drive encryption

Managed FDE will provide protection for valuable business data in the case of the loss or theft of mobile devices. **BitLocker** is the built-in FDE option for Windows operating systems.

Enabling no execute (NX)/execute never (XN) bit

For any system hosting applications that may be vulnerable to attacks against the system memory (**Random Access Memory (RAM)**), it is important to ensure that built-in security is enabled to offer protection against this attack vector. **No execute** (**NX**) is a security feature supported by 64 bit **AMD** CPUs, while **execute never** (**XN**) is supported by 64 bit **Intel** CPUs. These features are designed to prevent the execution of code in areas of memory assigned for the storage of data. It is a design that makes it difficult for an attacker to cause a **buffer overflow** when trying to re-purpose the memory location for the execution of arbitrary commands. *Figure 9.12* shows how this setting is enabled by default on Windows in a security feature called **Data Execution Protection** (**DEP**).

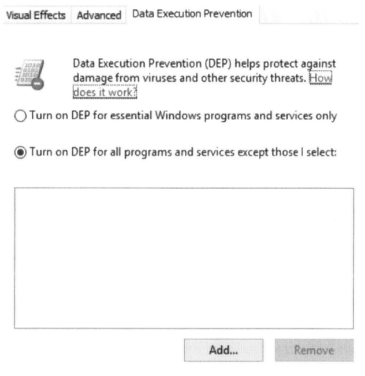

Figure 9.12 – The Microsoft DEP feature

On Windows servers, this setting is enabled for all Windows applications and services. **ARM RISC** processor chips support the XN bit. For more information see the following URL: `https://tinyurl.com/nxdep`.

Disabling central processing unit (CPU) virtualization support

The setting for **virtualization support** is normally found in the firmware settings of the endpoint device. If this is enabled, it allows for virtual images to be launched in a hypervisor. This is not something that is normally required for the majority of user desktops. If enabled, it may allow a user to run unauthorized applications on a virtual machine.

Secure encrypted enclaves and AMD Secure Memory Encryption

Many processors now have built-in support for the encryption of memory in use. This means that the contents of the RAM and the CPU memory itself can be secured. AMD CPUs support a feature called **Secure Memory Encryption** (**SME**). This uses AES 128 bit encryption and creates an ephemeral key at boot time. When support is enabled in the system firmware/BIOS, the feature can run transparently with most operating systems (there is no additional requirement for any coding within the operating system). Software applications can use this support to encrypt and decrypt pages of memory.

Shell restrictions

To limit the ability of a user to access command shell tools and utilities, it is common to block access to the shell itself or to limit the commands that can be accessed within the shell. On Windows operating systems, it is common practice to block access to the **Command Prompt** (**CMD**) and **PowerShell** interfaces for standard users. This is not really an option for **Linux** and **Unix** systems because most of the functionality of these operating systems is accessed outside of the **graphical user interface** (**GUI**). Common shells used on Linux include **Bash** and **KornShell**. In *Figure 9.13*, we have created a new user account with a restricted shell by using the -s switch command:

```
[root@cent07 ~]# useradd henry -s /bin/rbash
[root@cent07 ~]# passwd henry
```

Figure 9.13 – Implementing a restricted shell

There are a limited number of commands available within the restricted shell. The user cannot call up any commands that exist in other directories or use powerful administrator utilities.

Address space layout randomization

Address space layout randomization (**ASLR**) is designed to protect computer systems from attacks against memory. By enabling this feature, it prevents an attacker from being able to use memory addressing to predict where applications will be located. For example, an attacker may attempt to launch a buffer overflow attack followed by a call to a memory location where they expect a shell to be running. In ASLR, the running applications will always be allocated random memory locations, so this mitigates this type of attack.

In *Figure 9.14*, we can see the default settings for a **Windows 10** client:

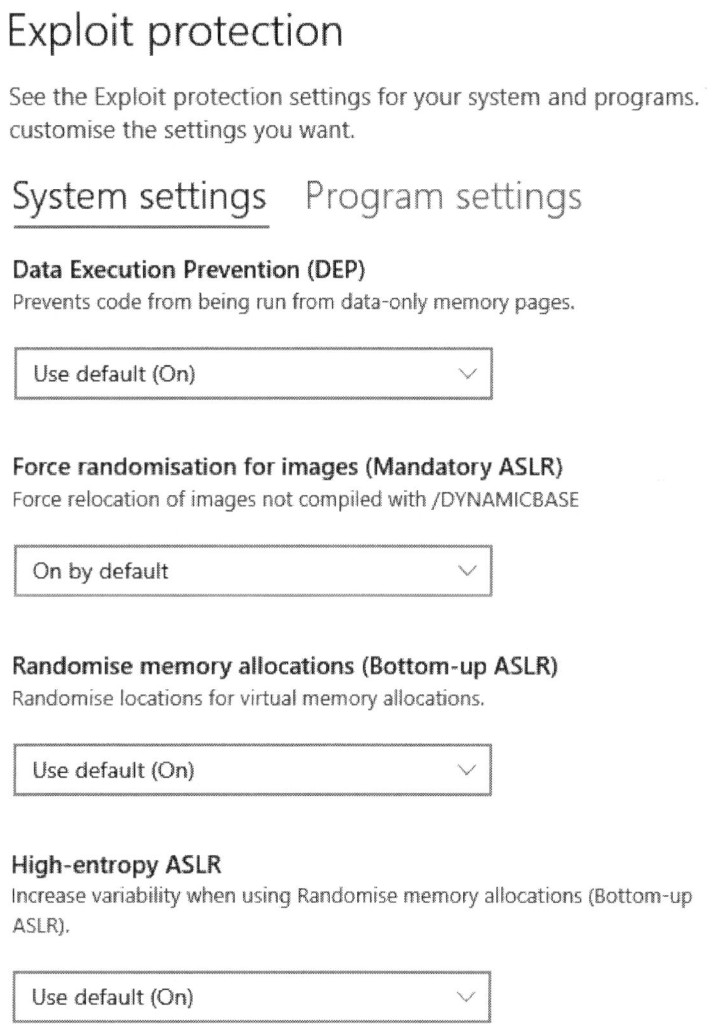

Exploit protection

See the Exploit protection settings for your system and programs. customise the settings you want.

System settings   Program settings

Data Execution Prevention (DEP)
Prevents code from being run from data-only memory pages.

Use default (On)   ∨

Force randomisation for images (Mandatory ASLR)
Force relocation of images not compiled with /DYNAMICBASE

On by default   ∨

Randomise memory allocations (Bottom-up ASLR)
Randomise locations for virtual memory allocations.

Use default (On)   ∨

High-entropy ASLR
Increase variability when using Randomise memory allocations (Bottom-up ASLR).

Use default (On)   ∨

Figure 9.14 – Microsoft Windows ASLR settings

This feature is supported on most operating systems, including Linux, Microsoft Windows, and **macOS**.

Patching

It is important to identify all of our assets and ensure we have the automated patching of these devices enabled. If we cannot deploy vendor patches, we risk the possibility of vulnerabilities leading to data loss or we might encounter availability issues. Patching should be planned to avoid the potential of these disruptions and availability issues. Ideally, we would fully test the effects of operating system or software application patches in a test/staging area before deploying them into production. *Figure 9.15* shows a screenshot from **ManageEngine Patch Manager Plus**:

	Computer Name	Logged On Users	Operating System	Domain	Missing Patches	Failed Patches	Installed Patches	Service Pack
☐	DESKTOP-T8ENG57	administrator	Windows 10 Enterprise Edition (x64)	classroom	0	0	10	Windows 10 Version 21H1 (x64)
☐	WIN2016-DC	administrator	Windows Server 2016 Datacenter Edition (x64)	classroom	0	0	13	Windows Server 2016 Gold (x64)
☐	cent07	root	CentOS Linux release 7.9.2009 (Core)	linuxosgroup	0	0	121	--

Figure 9.15 – ManageEngine Patch Manager Plus

It is important to choose patch management products that support heterogeneous environments (mixture of host operating systems). For more details on the ManageEngine product see the following URL: `https://tinyurl.com/MEpatchmanager`.

Firmware

It is important to update embedded operating system code, as this could be vulnerable to attacks if not kept up to date. For example, **Cisco IOS** has several vulnerabilities posted for potential attacks against its **Session Initiation Protocol** (**SIP**) that can cause a **Denial of Service** (**DoS**) condition. *CVE-2008-3799* documents a cybersecurity vulnerability, where an attack can cause a memory leak, eventually resulting in resource exhaustion. **SIP** is used with **Voice over Internet Protocol** (**VOIP**), it is used to place a call to another subscriber. As many business-based telephony solutions have adopted this technology it is important to secure this important functionality.

Logging and monitoring of endpoint devices

The continuous monitoring of endpoint devices allows security professionals to be alerted to any discrepancies in configuration changes or anomalous activities relating to the devices. *Figure 9.16* shows the health status for monitored endpoint devices using the **ManageEngine** MDM platform:

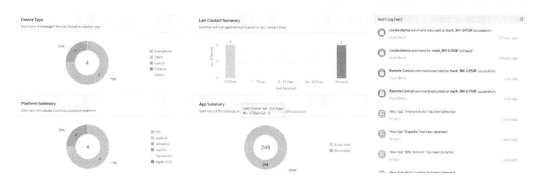

Figure 9.16 – Endpoint device monitoring

It is important to be alerted when devices do not comply with security policies or have been targeted by malware.

Mandatory access control

When we are looking for a high level of protection for operating systems, **mandatory access control** (**MAC**) can be used. Using this results in additional security controls being available to the operating systems. The controls, once enabled, enforce security settings. There are two examples of operating systems that support **MAC**, which we detail in the following subsections.

SELinux

SELinux was originally developed as a series of Linux security modules that were added as patches to the Linux operating systems. It was originally developed by the U.S. **National Security Agency** (**NSA**) but is now open source. It is incorporated into most Linux distributions. With most operating systems, file ownership is controlled through **discretionary access control** (**DAC**), which means the owner can set or change permissions on files and folders that they own. The root account normally also has the right to change the permissions on other users' files and folders, however, SELinux enforces MAC, which means changing other users' permissions will not work (as the system will override these changes).

SELinux has three main settings:

- **Enforcing**: In this setting, the SELinux security policy is enforced.

- **Permissive**: In this setting, SELinux prints warning messages instead of enforcing the security policy.

- **Disabled**: In this setting, no SELinux policy is loaded.

There are hundreds of possible enforcement settings. These are delivered via Boolean settings (that is, on/off options). To view all of the currently enforced settings, you can run `getsebool -a` from the Linux command shell.

Figure 9.17 shows the partial output of the preceding command for some SELinux enforcable settings:

```
httpd_anon_write --> off
httpd_builtin_scripting --> on
httpd_can_check_spam --> off
httpd_can_connect_ftp --> off
httpd_can_connect_ldap --> off
httpd_can_connect_mythtv --> off
httpd_can_connect_zabbix --> off
httpd_can_network_connect --> off
httpd_can_network_connect_cobbler --> off
httpd_can_network_connect_db --> off
httpd_can_network_memcache --> off
httpd_can_network_relay --> off
httpd_can_sendmail --> off
httpd_dbus_avahi --> off
httpd_dbus_sssd --> off
httpd_dontaudit_search_dirs --> off
httpd_enable_cgi --> on
httpd_enable_ftp_server --> off
httpd_enable_homedirs --> off
httpd_execmem --> off
httpd_graceful_shutdown --> on
httpd_manage_ipa --> off
httpd_mod_auth_ntlm_winbind --> off
httpd_mod_auth_pam --> off
httpd_read_user_content --> off
httpd_run_ipa --> off
httpd_run_preupgrade --> off
httpd_run_stickshift --> off
httpd_serve_cobbler_files --> off
httpd_setrlimit --> off
httpd_ssi_exec --> off
httpd_sys_script_anon_write --> off
```

Figure 9.17 – SELinux enforcable settings

The output displayed in *Figure 9.17* shows a subset of an SELinux security policy, this just lists some of the web application server settings.

Next, we will look at how Android uses **Security-Enhanced Linux** (**SELinux**) to enforce MAC on Android mobile devices.

Android Security-Enhanced Linux

The Android operating system adds security extensions by incorporating SELinux into the Android mobile operating system (sometimes referred to as **SEAndroid**). It was incorporated into Android version 4.4 and is based on the same security model as SELinux. There are many security controls available, including protecting privileged services/daemons from misuse. Applications must be run in a sandbox and there is an extensible policy available to add additional restrictions. Much of the security is included within the Kernel, but the use of **middleware mandatory access control** (**MMAC**) allows application privileges to be assigned during installation and at runtime. SEAndroid uses the *enforcing* mode as a default.

Many additional security enhancements for SEAndroid rely on hardware support to store measurements or certificates securely.

Trusted Platform Module technology

Many system boards have built-in support for a specific **hardware security module** (**HSM**) called a **Trusted Platform Module** (**TPM**). This secure module has crypto-processing capabilities and also provides for the secure storage of measurements or values. The TPM standard is a recognized standard (*ISO/IEC 11889*) and is supported by many hardware and software vendors. A TPM is typically used to ensure the integrity of an operating system platform. In the case of Microsoft BitLocker, if the recorded values are not consistent at boot time, then the boot process will halt. The values that are stored are called **platform configuration registers** (**PCRs**), and around six of these PCRs are normally used to *attest* that the platform has not been tampered with.

Figure 9.18 shows some of the typical values that can be stored. These values are stored as a cryptographic hash:

PCT Number	Allocation
0	BIOS
1	BIOS configuration
2	Option ROMs
3	Option ROM configuration
4	MBR (master boot record)
5	MBR configuration

Figure 9.18 – PCR values

There are many additional value types that can be stored, such as software application versions or the current status of anti-virus updates.

Secure Boot

To ensure the integrity of operating systems, it has become a standard procedure to check the integrity of the **bootloader** needed to launch the installed operating system. Windows operating systems from **Windows 8.0** onward have supported this feature. This requires a supported firmware interface (that is, one following the **Unified Extensible Firmware Interface** (**UEFI**) specification) that comes with a pre-loaded security key. The boot files are signed using the pre-loaded key and then validated during the boot sequence. Systems sold with Microsoft Windows 10 pre-installed have **Secure Boot** enabled by default. *Figure 9.19* shows the components required for Secure Boot:

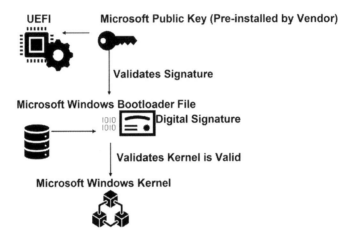

Figure 9.19 – The Microsoft Windows Secure Boot components

To add support for Linux Secure Boot, we would need to ensure there is a signed Linux bootloader. To do this, we could add the operating system vendor's public key into UEFI.

UEFI

UEFI has been the standard firmware to support PC systems since Windows 8.0 was released, in 2008. It offers many advantages over the previous option (the **Basic Input Output System** (**BIOS**)), including a mouse-driven graphical environment. UEFI allows for system checks and security processing to be carried out before launching the operating system. As operating systems launch quickly when installed on **solid-state drives** (**SSDs**), it is hard to press the correct function key quickly enough to access the menu. It is common to access the UEFI settings through the Windows Advanced Recovery options menu, within the operating system. *Figure 9.20* shows the Windows menu used to access the UEFI settings:

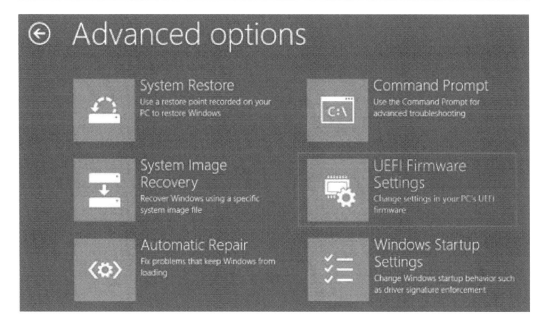

Figure 9.20 – The Windows UEFI menu

All modern business computers now support the UEFI firmware.

BIOS protection

The BIOS component has been standard within computing systems since the 1980s. It allows for a series of **power-on self-tests** (**POSTs**) and for configuration settings to be saved to the **complementary metal-oxide semiconductor** (**CMOS**), which needs a power supply or battery to retain settings. It offers little in the way of security, apart from allowing for passwords to protect the BIOS settings.

Attestation services

Attestation services allow for secure values to be forwarded from a hardware device to an attestation service. Microsoft supports a service called the **Host Attestation Service** within **Azure Cloud Services**. Once a device has been registered, the host TPM can be used to store values that cannot be tampered with. An example use of this service is ensuring that host operating systems are not running debugging tools as part of the host operating system. This is because debugging tools could allow attackers to gain access to local system memory and therefore access to confidential data.

Hardware security modules

A **hardware security module (HSM)** is an independent hardware device that supports crypto-processing capabilities and the secure storage of encryption keys. This can be a valuable addition to security when hosting applications that will need access to valuable private keys. E-commerce and banking websites will typically need to deploy HSMs. Most implementations are rack mounted appliances and allow for the secure storage of server keys within the data center.

Measured Boot

With **mMeasured Boot**, PCR values can be validated from the TPM. The values themselves are stored as cryptographic hashes. The hashes form a blockchain, which means a number of values can be combined into a single hash value. *Figure 9.21* shows the hash chaining function:

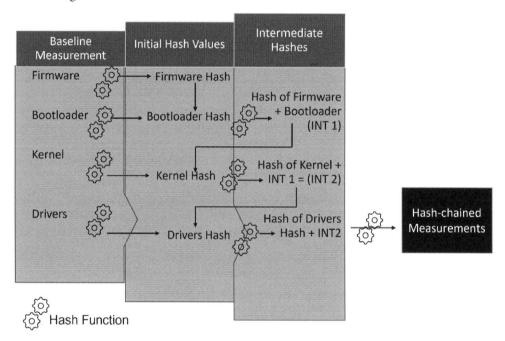

Figure 9.21 – The Measured Boot process

Hash chained measurements can be forwarded to server-based attestation services and can be used locally when unlocking BitLocker-encrypted hard drives.

Self-encrypting drives

When considering using FDE, performance may also be a goal. **Self-encrypting drives (SEDs)** use built-in hardware to provide encryption, thereby offering a performance advantage over software encryption. This is useful when incorporated into mobile computing devices.

Compensating controls

Once an organization has deployed secured/hardened computing systems, we cannot guarantee that the systems will be 100% protected. Depending on the new external threats, insider threats, and attack techniques that may develop for an organization, additional compensating controls may have to be considered. We will discuss some examples of these in the following subsections.

Antivirus tools

Antivirus tools should be deployed as a centrally managed solution for Windows operating systems. Windows is the main target for malware – there are very few examples of malware infections for Unix and Linux systems. However, Linux file servers and mail servers could pass on infected files if they are serving Windows clients. Traditional antivirus software works by identifying malware by using signature definition files. However, a virus may be programmed to change its signature, therefore defeating the signature definition approach. As a result, newer antivirus tools can look for common strings within a suspicious file. Windows comes with built-in protection with **Microsoft Windows Defender**, but additional malware detection application suites are available to further complement this.

Host-based intrusion detection systems (HIDSes) and host-based intrusion prevention systems (HIPSes)

When implementing security for your end devices, it is important to recognize where **defense in depth** (**DiD**) can be useful. A HIDS or HIPS will complement any network-based protection that is in place. Host systems will help to prevent anomalous administrator actions and any attempts to replace system files, and they will generally block any malicious actions. A HIDS or HIPS will also work alongside other anti-malware tools.

Host-based firewalls

A local firewall will complement the network firewalls by blocking unwanted connections on internal network segments also known as **east-west traffic**. To do this, host-based firewalls are frequently deployed on the most commonly used operating systems. Microsoft Windows has **Windows Defender Firewall**, which can be managed using graphical tools or with PowerShell commands. *Figure 9.22* shows a screenshot of Windows Firewall:

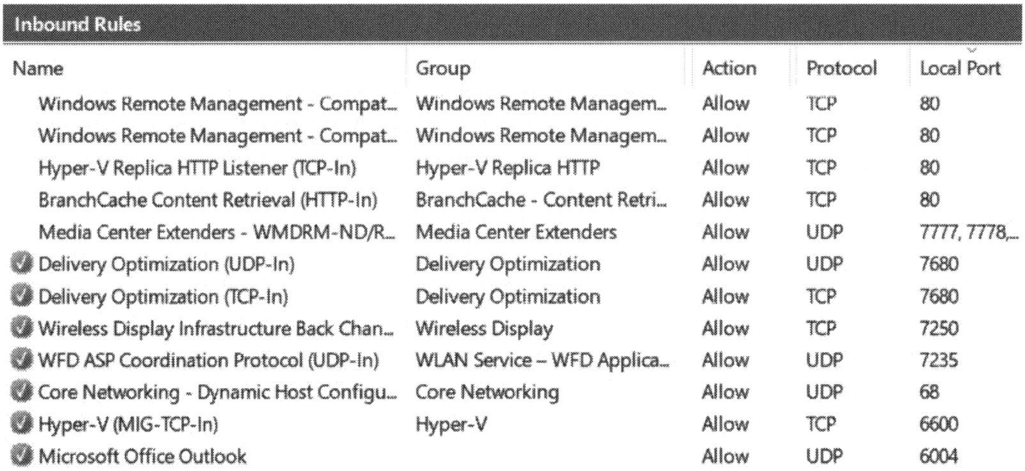

Inbound Rules

Name	Group	Action	Protocol	Local Port
Windows Remote Management - Compat...	Windows Remote Managem...	Allow	TCP	80
Windows Remote Management - Compat...	Windows Remote Managem...	Allow	TCP	80
Hyper-V Replica HTTP Listener (TCP-In)	Hyper-V Replica HTTP	Allow	TCP	80
BranchCache Content Retrieval (HTTP-In)	BranchCache - Content Retri...	Allow	TCP	80
Media Center Extenders - WMDRM-ND/R...	Media Center Extenders	Allow	UDP	7777, 7778,...
Delivery Optimization (UDP-In)	Delivery Optimization	Allow	UDP	7680
Delivery Optimization (TCP-In)	Delivery Optimization	Allow	TCP	7680
Wireless Display Infrastructure Back Chan...	Wireless Display	Allow	TCP	7250
WFD ASP Coordination Protocol (UDP-In)	WLAN Service – WFD Applica...	Allow	UDP	7235
Core Networking - Dynamic Host Configu...	Core Networking	Allow	UDP	68
Hyper-V (MIG-TCP-In)	Hyper-V	Allow	TCP	6600
Microsoft Office Outlook		Allow	UDP	6004

Figure 9.22 – Windows Defender Firewall

Linux systems can be protected by using the **iptables** service. The following command drops all packets from the `10.10.0.0/24` source network:

```
iptables -A INPUT -I eth0 -s 10.10.0.0/24 -j DROP.
```

To display the firewall rules that are currently configured, we use the `iptables -help` command.

To discard all firewall rules that are currently set, we can use the `iptables -flush` command.

Figure 9.23 shows some iptables firewall rules that are set to block traffic being received from any private network address:

```
└$ sudo iptables --list
Chain INPUT (policy ACCEPT)
target     prot opt source               destination
DROP       all  --  10.0.0.0/8           anywhere
DROP       all  --  192.168.0.0/24       anywhere
DROP       all  --  172.0.0.0/16         anywhere
```

Figure 9.23 – Some iptables firewall rules

To display rulesets (called *chains*), we use the `iptables -list` command from the Linux bash shell.

It is normal to add a rule to a security device to block source traffic originating from a private network address (like the example in *Figure 9.23*). This is done where traffic is routed from external networks, as this type of traffic normally indicates the addresses are being spoofed.

Endpoint detection and response (EDR) software

EDR software allows an agent to be deployed on endpoint devices. It will work alongside traditional anti-malware solutions but does not rely on definition files and known malware hashes. To best prepare for future threats, endpoint monitoring should be continuous, with logs being forwarded to the EDR provider. Actions can be processed in real time, with databases of **Advanced Persistent Threat (APT)** actors, TTPs, and collected baseline data from normal activity, which allows **Indicators of Compromise (IOC)** to be detected. Many security providers will offer complete managed solutions for organizations that do not have **Security Operations Center (SOC)** staff to spare (these are known as **managed security service providers (MSSPs)**). With new attacks constantly being initiated, EDR software will better protect organizations from ransomware attacks, fileless malware attacks, and zero-day exploits. Popular options for this include **CrowdStrike** and **Microsoft Defender for Endpoint**. Please see the following URLs for more details of these solutions:

- `https://tinyurl.com/crowdstrikeEDR`
- `https://tinyurl.com/defenderEDR`

Redundant hardware

When hosting important systems that may result in a disproportionate impact if they fail, we must identify ways to make them more resilient. On data center servers, it is common to deploy redundant power supplies, network interface cards, and storage. In these situations, it is important to identify where single points of failure can negatively impact a workload.

Self-healing hardware

Wherever it is possible to increase resilience, we should implement systems that can identify problematic events and where necessary, make an adjustment. One example of this is using **hardware clusters**, where a failure to send a heartbeat signal would result in a workload being hosted on another hardware node. Modern hard disk drives automatically mark out bad blocks and replace them with reserve blocks held in a *reserve pool*. On Microsoft operating systems from **Windows Server 2012** onward, the **Resilient File System** (**ReFS**) has been an available feature that allows this. The ReFS deploys an integrity scanner that constantly scans the hosted drives and initiates a repair process if needed.

User and entity behavior analytics (UEBA)

To protect valuable company data, it is becoming increasingly common to use analytics to detect patterns of behavior. If a user account was suddenly used out of context, then the system could alert administrators or block the action. So, imagine that a user, Joe, based in the United Kingdom, logs into his work email from a location identified as North Korea on December 25. He subsequently begins to delete large amounts of important manufacturing data from the engineering team's shared drive – if using UEBA, this would trigger an immediate alert to his line manager and SOC team members.

Summary

In this chapter, we have learned how to provide security for endpoint devices running a variety of operating systems. We have understood the need to harden end devices such as traditional desktop computers, laptops, tablets, and handheld and wearable technology. We have discussed how to assess the security of these devices, how to choose the appropriate technologies that the enterprise should adopt, and how to ensure we can provide the attestation that these devices are compliant with security policies. We have also understood the need for deployed images to be built from a validated secure template. We have learned that services should only be enabled if there is a business need to justify them. We investigated compensating controls, including host firewalls, EDR software, and antivirus tools. We also learned about the tools and techniques needed to secure our endpoints. We have studied technologies to support host attestation and Secure Boot options.

This information should give the reader a good baseline understanding of endpoint security, before we move on to the next chapter, where we will study how to secure critical infrastructure.

Questions

1. Some executives from an organization attend an industry conference. Using mobile devices and wireless headsets, they are able to stay in touch with colleagues back at the workplace. What may present a security concern in this situation?

   A. Tethering

   B. WPA3

   C. Device certificates

   D. Bluetooth

2. Some marketing executives from an organization attend an international trade exhibition and must connect to the company email by using their mobile devices during the event. The CISO is concerned this may represent a risk. What would best mitigate this risk?

   A. NFC

   B. A split-tunnel VPN

   C. Geofencing

   D. Always-on VPN settings

3. What function should be disabled to ensure scientists cannot use their mobile devices to bridge the corporation's network with a cellular operator's network?

   A. Tethering

   B. WPA3

   C. Device certificates

   D. Bluetooth

4. What should be implemented to ensure only company-approved applications can be installed on company devices?

   A. Containerization

   B. Token-based access

   C. A patch repository

   D. Whitelisting

5. A user calls the service desk because her Samsung smartphone is prompting her to install updates that the vendor says will offer more functionality and security. What is this an example of?

    A. MFA requirements

    B. Token-based access

    C. A patch repository

    D. Firmware over-the-air

6. An employee's company mobile device is reported as stolen 24 hours after the event. Sensitive data has been posted online by hackers. What would have mitigated this risk if the report had been made earlier?

    A. MFA requirements

    B. A remote wipe

    C. A patch repository

    D. Firmware over-the-air

7. What type of setting will ensure mobile devices will only be able to access Wi-Fi when they connect securely to the company WLAN?

    A. WPA3 SAE

    B. Device certificates

    C. Device profiles

    D. Bluetooth

8. An employee has noticed several suspicious payments made from a company debit card via Google Pay on their company smartphone. They recently attended a busy trade conference. What technology was likely used to make the payments?

    A. NFC

    B. Peripherals

    C. Geofencing

    D. VPN settings

9. How can we prevent certain mobile applications from being accessible when employees take COPE devices out of the warehouse?

    A. NFC

    B. MFA

    C.   Geofencing

    D.   VPN settings

10. The service desk receives a call from a senior manager. She is concerned that spyware may be installed on her smartphone. Recent news, traffic, and weather updates have been targeted specifically for her location. What is the most likely reason for this activity?

    A.   Airplane mode

    B.   Location services

    C.   NFC

    D.   Geofencing

11. A user is concerned that DNS lookups may be logged by government agencies. The user would like to protect their privacy. What would be the best method to protect privacy during name resolution?

    A.   Geofencing

    B.   VPN settings

    C.   DNS over HTTPS (DoH)

    D.   Containerization

12. A nation-state sends a security team to scope out a military site in California in the United States. They use mobile devices to gather images, map the locations of communications equipment, and record detailed information about troop movements. What are they performing?

    A.   Geotagging

    B.   Geofencing

    C.   Physical reconnaissance

    D.   Personal data theft

13. A personal device has many applications installed that are not available through the Apple App Store. The device subsequently fails compliance checks. What has likely made the device fail to be compliant with the security policies?

    A.   Jailbreaking

    B.   Sideloading

    C.   Containerization

    D.   An unauthorized application store

14. A senior employee has followed a QC link and installed a mobile application used to order food and beverages at a local restaurant. The application is not available on the Google Play Store. **Acceptable Use Policy (AUP)** states that applications can only be downloaded from the official vendor store. What best describes what has allowed this application to be installed?

    A.   Supply chain issues

    B.   Sideloading

    C.   Containerization

    D.   An unauthorized application store

15. Developers need to test mobile applications on a variety of hardware before making them available on official application stores. How can they install the applications locally on mobile devices?

    A.   Update the supply chain.

    B.   Use sideloading.

    C.   Use containerization.

    D.   Use an unauthorized application store.

16. A sales director would like to allow sales employees to use their personal devices for accessing company applications and data as part of an effort to reduce business costs. What would be the best control to mitigate the risk of employees co-mingling personal and company data?

    A.   Geotagging

    B.   Geofencing

    C.   Containerization

    D.   Remote wipes

17. When on a business trip, a CEO was detained for several hours at border control. When he was eventually reunited with his mobile phone, it had physical evidence of tampering. He powered on the device and input the correct pin, but found that all of the company applications and data were inaccessible. What has led to this situation?

    A.   Geofencing

    B.   Containerization

    C.   Remote wipes

    D.   An eFuse

18. A user has been able to run an unmanaged Linux operating system alongside a managed Windows 10 build on a company laptop. What actions would allow security professionals to prevent this issue from re-occurring?

    A.   Removing end-of-support devices

    B.   Using local drive encryption

    C.   Disabling CPU virtualization support

    D.   Enforcing secure encrypted enclaves and SME

19. Security administrators have deployed SELinux in enforcing mode. All unnecessary services have been removed. In a further attempt to enforce security, a number of commands – including `vmstat` and `grep` – have been blocked from some user accounts. What best describes this action?

    A.   Whitelisting

    B.   Shell restrictions

    C.   ASLR

    D.   Memory encryption

20. The CISO is meeting with software engineers to better understand some of the challenges that they face. He is asking if there are any settings that can be incorporated into build images that will help to prevent attacks against the system memory. What two features should be chosen?

    A.   ASLR

    B.   Patching

    C.   Firmware

    D.   NX/XN

21. What is deployed to mitigate the risk of privilege elevation and the misuse of applications on Android mobile devices?

    A.   SELinux

    B.   TPM technology

    C.   SEAndroid

    D.   Attestation services

22. What built-in module stores PCR values and enforces integrity on a hardware platform?

    A.   The TPM module

    B.   Secure Boot mode

    C.   UEFI

    D.   The BIOS

23. What would be the best choice of technical control to block a fast-spreading worm that targets a well-known **NetBIOS** port?

    A.   UEBA

    B.   A host-based firewall

    C.   A HIDS

    D.   Redundant hardware

24. A reporting tool has alerted the administrator that Joe Smith, who is leaving the company in 4 weeks, has uploaded a large number of PDF documents to his personal cloud storage. What has likely triggered this event?

    A.   UEBA

    B.   A host-based firewall

    C.   EDR software

    D.   Self-healing hardware

25. A system administrator needs to ensure the root account cannot be used to gain access to user data on a Linux **Network File System** (**NFS**) server. What actions would allow security professionals to prevent this issue from occurring?

    A.   Ensuring passwords are stored in a shadow file

    B.   Running SELinux in enforcing mode

    C.   Disabling CPU virtualization support

    D.   Enforcing secure encrypted enclaves and SME

Answers

1. D
2. D
3. A
4. D
5. D
6. B
7. C
8. A
9. C
10. B
11. C
12. C
13. A
14. D
15. B
16. C
17. D
18. C
19. B
20. A and D
21. C
22. A
23. B
24. A
25. B

10
Security Considerations Impacting Specific Sectors and Operational Technologies

An enterprise may operate in a diverse environment. When considering the operation of the plant and equipment within operational technologies, it is important to fully investigate legal and regulatory responsibilities. Many countries have different laws and regulatory requirements; in some cases, we may even see regulations differing between different states. Fines can be significant when it is proven that a company has broken laws or safety protocols. The technology used to deliver automation and supervisory control can be complicated and, in some cases, lacks the strict security that may be available on the business network. It is important that senior leadership within the organization understands the importance of cyber security and maintaining a strong security posture. They should sponsor and drive the enterprise to ensure it performs the appropriate risk assessments. This is especially important when diversifying into new markets or business sectors. In this chapter, we will study the following topics:

- Identifying regulated business sectors
- Supporting embedded systems

- Understanding **industrial control systems (ICSes)/supervisory control and data acquisition (SCADA)**
- Understanding **operational technology (OT)** protocols

Identifying regulated business sectors

Regulated industries are required to adhere to rules and regulations set by a regulatory or legal authority. There are many examples of regulated industries, and the regulations can be challenging as they may be region-specific. **Health and safety** (**H&S**) regulations are enforced across many business sectors, with strict penalties for non-compliance. Providers of services and utilities may be regulated to ensure they set fair pricing tariffs and may be penalized for unfair practices. One of the most important considerations must be safety, both to the workforce and to the public. There have been well-documented industrial disasters that have resulted in major loss of life both to the workforce and the surrounding population. In 1984, a chemical plant in Bhopal, India leaked highly toxic gas into the surrounding towns. The disaster exposed over 500,000 people to toxic gas, with more than 8,000 dead. **Union Carbide India Limited** (**UCIL**) paid out $470 million in settlements following the disaster. It is important when a company operates in diverse industries, often globally, that the appropriate risk assessments are performed and controls put into place.

Energy sector

Energy suppliers must adhere to regulatory authorities that may be international standards and may include country-specific requirements. In the US, electric utility companies must comply with laws and regulations relating to air pollution, greenhouse gas reporting, and industrial waste production. Agencies oversee these providers, and a lack of compliance may result in a substantial fine. The US **Environmental Protection Agency** (**EPA**) has successfully prosecuted companies through civil enforcement, resulting in significant financial loss for non-compliance. The nuclear power regulations are country-specific—for example, **United Kingdom** (**UK**) regulations are overseen by the **Office for Nuclear Regulation** (**ONR**), which is responsible for the regulation of 36 nuclear facilities, including security and safety requirements. Failure to comply with the ONR can result in a site losing the authority to operate or facing substantial monetary outlay in fines and retrospective provisions. In April 2019, Sellafield Ltd. was fined nearly £500,000 for an H&S violation that resulted in an employee receiving mild plutonium poisoning. For details, see the following link: `https://tinyurl.com/ONRnuclearfines`.

Energy suppliers have been targeted by nation-state adversaries in increasing numbers. To counter some of the threats presented by these threat actors, there is a non-profit regulatory authority named **North American Electric Reliability Corporation (NERC)**. The mission of NERC is to safeguard the electrical supply industry, and it applies to **bulk electric systems (BES)** providers in the US, Canada, and Baja California, Mexico. NERC sponsors a security initiative and compliance program named **Critical Infrastructure Protection (CIP)**. To read more about the work of NERC and CIP, you can access the following link: `https://tinyurl.com/nercstandards`.

Manufacturing

Manufacturers must prove to their customers that they can be trusted to deliver quality products and have sound business practices. Accreditation can be obtained to indicate a level of competency, such as the **International Organization for Standardization (ISO) 9001**. These standards cover **quality control (QC)** for manufacturing companies. Many other standards may need to be considered when a company is looking to produce particular goods. Some standards may be enforced nationally and internationally to ensure product compliance. In the UK, certain standards must be observed when operating plants and equipment in a manufacturing environment. Some of these requirements are quite complicated and require appropriate policies and procedures to be created to ensure compliance. Within the UK, standards are covered by the following bodies:

- ISO
- **International Electrotechnical Commission (IEC)** and **International Telecommunication Union (ITU)**
- **British Standards Institution (BSI)**
- **European Committee for Standardization (CEN)**
- **European Committee for Electrotechnical Standardization (CENELEC)**
- **European Telecommunications Standards Institute (ETSI)**

To sell products within a particular country, a manufacturer must follow these standards. Plant and equipment must be operated within strict safety guidelines. Of greater importance is the risk of **intellectual property (IP)** being stolen by an adversary. Patents can be applied for in countries where there is a threat from a competitor who may steal your inventions. In Europe, the **European Patent Convention (EPC)** covers 30 European countries. To protect your IP in other parts of the world, individual patents must be registered in each country.

Healthcare

There are many regulatory requirements for providers of healthcare, and this will differ between countries. In the US, the **Health Insurance Portability and Accountability Act (HIPAA)** requires strict control of **protected health information (PHI)** records stored and transmitted electronically. HIPAA compliance is regulated by the **Department of Health and Human Services (HHS)**. If a healthcare provider fails to implement the appropriate due diligence and due care, they may be prosecuted and fined for transgressions. Protected information includes names, addresses, medical records, social security numbers, and much more. There are strict reporting requirements for data breaches; affected individuals must be notified within 60 days and HHS must also be notified within 60 days for data breaches involving more than 500 records. Enforcement is the responsibility of the **Office for Civil Rights (OCR)**. There are different violation levels—level one carries a maximum single fine of $59,522, rising to $1,785,651 for a level four violation. An employee can also be sentenced to jail for serious violations—in the most severe cases, this can be up to 10 years.

Healthcare providors such as hospitals and clinics must make significant investments in medical equipment and systems to deliver efficient healthcare. Due to the high cost of equipment it must remain in service for extended periods of time and may present a vulnerability as the technology may be outdated.

Public utilities

In the US, public utilities are regulated under the **Public Utility Regulatory Policies Act (PURPA)**. This act was passed after the energy crisis in 1973, due to an oil embargo following the Yom Kippur war, where the price of oil increased by over 300%. It is designed to promote the production of domestic energy and renewable energy. Enforcement and regulatory requirements are managed within individual states within the US. Rates charged by public utility companies must be fair and non-discriminatory. In the UK, gas and electricity providers are regulated by the **Office of Gas and Electricity Markets (Ofgem)**. There are controls in place to ensure price rises are capped to the current inflation rate. By far the most important concern for operators of public utilities is cyberattacks against their services and data breaches concerning customer records.

Public services

Public service providers (**PSPs**) include education, emergency services, healthcare, housing, waste collection, transportation, and social care (there are more). They are services that are provided by the government and are not intended to generate profits for the provider. They are provided to benefit the community. Public services are targeted by cybercriminals; healthcare organizations have been hit particularly hard by ransomware attacks. In May 2021, the **Irish Department of Health** was targeted by a group known as **Conti**, who forced the service to cancel many patient services and were forced to use pen and paper in lieu of their usual information systems. It is estimated that around 35% of ransomware victims pay criminals to gain access to their systems and data.

Facility services

Facility services can include cleaning, maintenance, security, waste management, catering, and much more. Contracting with third parties to provide facility services can result in flexibility and cost savings. It is important to consider downstream liability when contracting out any part of your daily operations.

Many regulated sectors have a requirement for OT. This environment is sometimes referred to as *IT outside of carpeted areas*. A metropolitan **transportation service provider** (**TSP**) running a subway transit system would meet this criterion. They need to monitor safety systems, subway trains, critical signaling, and passenger movements and send urgent messages across these non-business networks. We will take a look at components used within these types of environments.

Understanding embedded systems

Embedded systems are used within OT environments. They are a combination of hardware and software, designed to operate a particular operational process. Machine tools used in mechanical engineering environments would be a good example of where we might see embedded systems, but we can see these systems in almost all environments where industrial controls are used. They will be used in power stations, water treatment plants, transportation systems, and much more. Embedded systems may rely on hardware that was designed over 50 years ago, and the software may have been written in low-level machine code.

In many cases, there is no cost-effective way to upgrade a legacy embedded system. It may be operating a nuclear facility or a coal-fired power station that is due to be decommissioned in the near future. Network segmentation is often the only way to mitigate risks when supporting these environments.

Internet of things

Internet of things (**IoT**) covers many technologies, including home automation, building control systems, and many other areas where automation of hardware is required. Many IoT devices operate wirelessly, making them potential targets if we do not harden our wireless networks. Consumer products include lightbulbs, smart speakers, televisions, refrigerators, and much more. IoT does not define a standard—it relies on standards provided by other protocols. We will compare these protocols and standards later in the chapter.

System on a chip

A **system on a chip** (**SoC**) is a single piece of silicon that contains a **central processing unit** (**CPU**), memory, storage, and **input/output** (**I/O**) port. Tablets and smartphones would be good examples of where SoC technology is used. By integrating all the components required on a compute node, power consumption is much reduced. Examples of SoCs would include **Qualcomm Snapdragon**, **Advanced RISC Machines** (**ARM**), **Apple's M1**, and **Intel Core Consumer Ultra-Low Voltage** (**CULV**).

Application-specific integrated circuits

Application-specific integrated circuits (**ASICs**) are designed for a specific application, such as bitcoin mining or taking care of a complex repetitive function on an ICS. ASICs cannot be reprogrammed, meaning a vulnerability cannot be remediated if it is found to be within the ASIC chip.

Field-programmable gate array

A **field-programmable gate array** (**FPGA**) is an example of an integrated circuit that can be configured by the end user (the customer) after the chip has left the fabrication plant (in the field). It is integrated as a semiconductor device, consisting of logic blocks that can be reprogrammed, and is basically a circuit board that can be customized. This design allows for changes in design that can accommodate new processes. This capability to be reprogrammed is why the device may be targeted and may be vulnerable to attack. There have been documented attacks against this type of chip. These types of chips are common in both enterprise networks and ICS. One example of a vulnerability was published and assigned **Common Vulnerabilities and Exposures** (**CVE**) *2019-1649*—this describes a logic vulnerability targeting **Cisco Secure Boot** hardware, affecting multiple networking products released by Cisco. It allows an attacker with local access to tamper with the **Secure Boot** verification process. This exploit could result in the installation and booting of a malicious image. The remediation is a vendor-supplied firmware update. Around 70% of attacks against embedded systems and ICS can be performed remotely and do not need authentication for the exploit to be successful. In September 2019, a vulnerability was discovered affecting **Xilinx 7-series** FPGA chips; this became known as **Starbleed**. The exploit allows attackers to plant backdoor access into the chip, reprogram the functionality, or cause physical damage. There is no remediation available, meaning the hardware needs to be replaced or the systems must be isolated or closely monitored. The following screenshot shows a Xilinx 7-series FPGA:

Figure 10.1 – FPGA integrated system board

In many situations when vulnerabilities are discovered, the hardware may need to be replaced.

Embedded systems are integrated into environments where OT is deployed—typically, this means anywhere outside of the enterprise business network where there may be a plant and equipment that requires supervision and control. We will now look at example OT environments.

Understanding ICS/SCADA

There are many examples of OTs that are deployed to automate the delivery of industrial processes and critical infrastructure. ICS are deployed within manufacturing and process control environments. They allow production lines to run and chemicals to be processed and delivered at the correct flow rates. It is important that information in the form of telemetry is displayed on management systems. There are many components required to manage complex processing environments. *Figure 10.2* shows the components of a SCADA system:

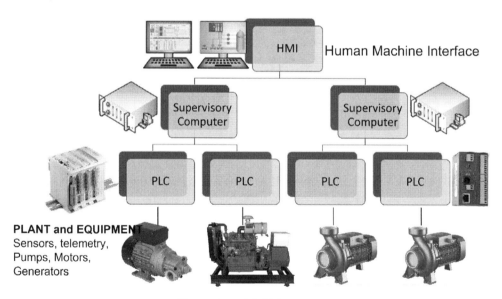

Figure 10.2 – SCADA system

Human-machine interfaces (**HMIs**) allow supervisors to oversee and control complex ICS from a control room or data center. Supervisory computing systems communicate with specialized hardware (**programmable logic controllers**, or **PLCs**) that receive information, such as telemetry, from pumps, actuators, and sensors. The plant and equipment can then be automatically controlled by the PLC, while the HMIs in the data center allow for the overall management of the plant.

PLCs

OT relies on specialist ICS, designed to operate in hostile or challenging environments. PLCs are designed to operate in factories, processing plants, and many other industrial settings. PLCs are used to automate a physical process such as a luggage conveyor belt at an airport, or a traffic light system in a mine. Unlike information systems hosted in a business environment, PLCs do not use commercial **operating systems** (**OSes**). They will run specialist embedded OSes designed to deliver specialist instructions to control industrial equipment. The first example of a PLC was used by General Motors on their car assembly plant in 1968; this PLC was named the **Modicon 084**. PLCs need to process instructions in real time in order to accurately control or adjust critical processes. The following screenshot shows an array of available PLCs used in industrial environments:

Figure 10.3 – Siemens PLC models

A PLC is essentially a dedicated computer that is also able to operate in hazardous environments.

Historian

Industrial control environments use a database logging system known as an operational historian. The data collected will be gathered from process controls such as sensors, instrumentation, and other types of controls. This allows for the capture of data that can be interpreted to show trends and allow engineers to analyze the data and adjust processes where necessary. A Historian system is composed of three main components:

- Data collectors for interfacing with the data sources such as a PLC, and networked devices.

- Server software that processes and stores the data from the data collectors.

- Client applications that allow for analysis, reporting, and visualizations.

Ladder logic

This is a simple programming language based upon relay-based logic, used originally in electromechanical relays. The program will process multiple inputs or signals and can perform a function if all the expected inputs are received while processing the logic. Engineers originally used ladder logic to design circuit boards to activate mechanical relays; now, this same approach is used in a visual programming language. Ladder logic processes instructions using rungs (like a ladder) from top to bottom and from left to right. The following screenshot shows an example of ladder logic:

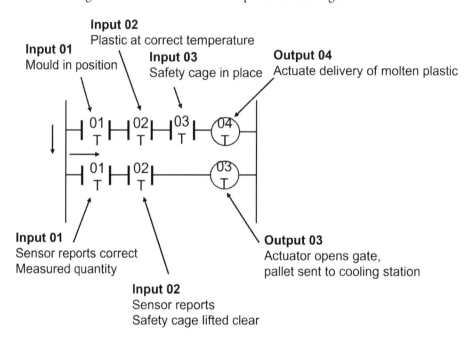

Figure 10.4 – Ladder logic processing

The logic runs from top to bottom and from left to right. If all inputs are reporting true, then the output will also be true. In the preceding example, we are showing a logical process for hot plastic to be injected into a mold on an automated assembly line. If any of the inputs are false, then the output will also result in a false value. For more information, see the following link: https://tinyurl.com/ladderlogicplc.

Safety instrumented system

A **safety instrumented system** (**SIS**) is primarily intended as a failsafe when threatening conditions are detected in critical industrial environments. SISs run independently of a **process control network** (**PCN**) and are used to shut off the process if a critical condition is detected. Industrial environments where this type of control would be commonly used include nuclear power stations, petrochemical refineries, gas production, mining, and many more. There is an international standard covering controls, for operators of plants and equipment, that are considered hazardous. **International Society of Automation** (**ISA-84**)/**International Electrotechnical Commission** (**IEC-61511**) are standards that are recognized in the US and Europe. The SIS will function in addition to a basic **process control system** (**PCS**). Its sole purpose is to take a system that has violated preset conditions into a safe state. It will consist of sensors and controls managed by a PLC. The resulting actions could be to open a relief valve or activate fire suppression systems.

Heating, ventilation, and air conditioning

In large complex industrial environments, **heating, ventilation, and air conditioning** (**HVAC**) is typically controlled using **building automation systems** (**BAS**). It is vitally important to monitor and adjust temperature and humidity to protect sensitive equipment. Environments protected by HVAC could include hospitals, data centers, silicon chip fabrication, chemical processing, power plants, and many more. Modern HVAC systems will be controlled digitally using dedicated networks.

Understanding OT protocols

Many supported protocols can be found in ICS and OT environments. Some protocols have been in existence for over 50 years and lack controls to encrypt data or provide integrity. Newer protocols have robust security built in. We will take a look at examples of these protocols.

Controller area network bus

This protocol was originally designed for the automobile industry, intended to minimize the amount of cabling deployed within a vehicle. It is able to allow devices on the bus to communicate within the requirement of a centralized host computer. The design is based upon multiplexing, where multiple signals can be transmitted on a single shared bus. In order to share the bus, each device can be assigned a priority. If two nodes transmit on the bus at the same time, then the highest-priority device will have precedence.

The **controller area network** (**CAN**) specification does not support any native security or encryption; it is intended as a specification for reliable transmission of data frames across a shared bus. CAN is a standard documented within the **ISO11898-1** standard, CAN defines the data link and physical layer of the **Open Systems Interconnection** (**OSI**) model. Vendor implementations can include provisions for security, but this is not part of the CAN specification. *Figure 10.5* depicts a CAN bus model used in a vehicle.

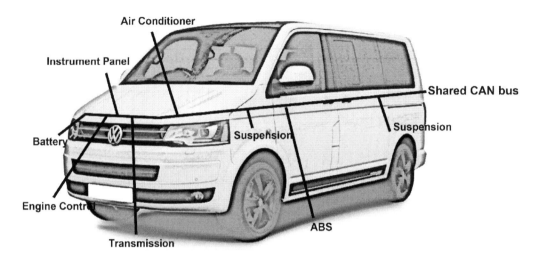

Figure 10.5 – CAN bus architecture

Given the nature of this technology, it is now deployed in many environments including ICS, agricultural equipment, lighting systems, building automation, medical instruments, and many more.

The potential for **man-in-the-middle** (**MITM**) attacks and other types of tampering could have serious security implications when considering its use.

Modbus

Modbus is a messaging protocol used in ICS to provide serial communication over different cable types, including Ethernet. It is popular as it is royalty-free and has become a de facto standard within OT environments. Modbus is typically deployed on SCADA networks where it can relay telemetry back to monitoring computers from **remote terminal units** (**RTUs**) in an industrial environment. Modbus was designed in the 1970s to service industrial communication requirements. Modbus has become the de facto standard in industrial environments. Modbus offers no security against tampering with message integrity and is therefore vulnerable to MITM attacks if an attacker gains access to the network. There are many examples of vulnerabilities posted for the Modbus protocol. See the following URL for current known vulnerabilities concering the Modbus protocol. `https://tinyurl.com/modbus-cves`.

Distributed Network Protocol 3

This protocol is intended to support ICS including power distribution and water treatment companies. It was designed and gained widespread use in the early 1990s. As with some of the aforementioned technologies, it is intended to relay messages between supervisory and management systems through to PLCs/RTUs (*RTU* is sometimes interchanged with the term *PLC*). **Distributed Network Protocol 3** (**DNP3**) is normally used to transfer and maintain synchronization between large sets of tags from one point to another (that is, a terminal server and a SCADA system). One of its major strengths is its resistance to **electromagnetic inference** (**EMI**) distortion, particularly useful when controlling electrical plants and equipment. The protocol is now covered by the **Institute of Electrical and Electronics Engineers** (**IEEE**) *1815-2012* standard. The standard is now recommended for organizations that operate any **electric power systems** (**EPS**) communications. DNP3 fully supports encrypted communications using **Transport Layer Security** (**TLS**) and **public key infrastructure** (**PKI**).

Zigbee

Zigbee is a wireless protocol intended primarily for home automation. It allows for communication with low-power devices over distances varying between 10 and 100 meters, making it an ideal candidate for **personal area networks** (**PANs**). It is covered by the IEEE *802.15.4* standard and operates over 2.4 **gigahertz** (**GHz**) radiofrequency. Zigbee has wide support from many vendors, including Samsung, Amazon, and Ikea. It is not intended as a data transport but more for control messages, as the data rate only allows for 250 kilobits/second. The network architecture supports star and tree networks, based upon a central hub acting as the coordinator. Amazon supports many products that are capable of acting as a central hub for home automation. With a central hub device, users can control lighting, central heating thermostats, home security, washing machines, and many more household appliances. *Figure 10.6* shows a typical home automation network, with a central controller:

Figure 10.6 – Zigbee network

Zigbee supports encryption of traffic using 128-bit symmetric keys based upon **Advanced Encryption Standard** (**AES**). Zigbee also supports anti-replay using a frame counter mechanism and frequency hopping to prevent jamming attacks.

Common Industrial Protocol

Common Industrial Protocol (**CIP**) is a protocol specification for the transmission of messages on industrial networks. It is used to carry messages in order to manage objects used to control plants and equipment. Typical objects will include sensors, switches, valves, and actuators. It is managed by **Open DeviceNet Vendors Association** (**ODVA**); membership comprises manufacturers of industrial automation controls.

CIP supports the transmission of messages over **Transmission Control Protocol** (**TCP**) and **User Datagram Protocol** (**UDP**), where UDP is used to deliver smaller messages, resulting in more efficiency and speed on networks. The protocol is based on a producer-consumer model—the producer submits a multicast message processed by nodes that match a network identifier.

There are four types of CIP networks, outlined as follows:

- **EtherNet/IP**—This is based on standard Ethernet IEEE 802.3 and uses the TCP/IP protocol suite.

- **CompoNet**—This implementation is designed for optimum delivery of small messages between controllers and industrial endpoints (switches, sensors, valves, and so on).

- **ControlNet**—This is used when time criticality is important, such as **safety control systems** (**SCS**). It uses a deterministic model, which means a message will be delivered within a predictable amount of time.

- **DeviceNet**—This implementation uses CAN for the datalink layer. It supports **direct current** (**DC**) power delivery over the connection, supporting devices up to 24 volts (drawing up to 8 amps).

Figure 10.7 shows the layers and relationships between CIP and the OSI model.

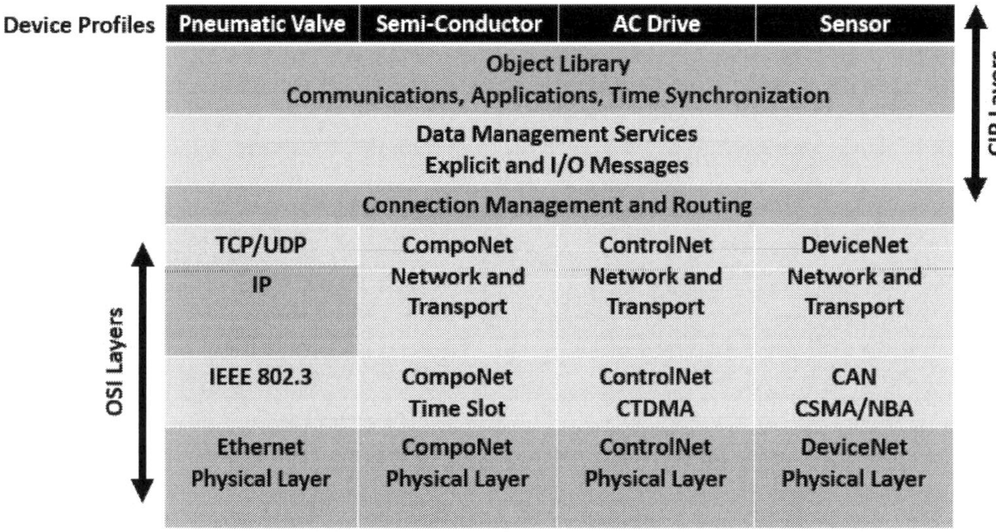

Device Profiles	Pneumatic Valve	Semi-Conductor	AC Drive	Sensor
	Object Library Communications, Applications, Time Synchronization			
	Data Management Services Explicit and I/O Messages			
	Connection Management and Routing			
	TCP/UDP IP	CompoNet Network and Transport	ControlNet Network and Transport	DeviceNet Network and Transport
	IEEE 802.3	CompoNet Time Slot	ControlNet CTDMA	CAN CSMA/NBA
	Ethernet Physical Layer	CompoNet Physical Layer	ControlNet Physical Layer	DeviceNet Physical Layer

Figure 10.7 – CIP communication model

When supporting industrial control networks using Ethernet/IP, we can use **X.509 certificates** for authentication of endpoints and **TLS** for message **encryption** and **integrity**.

Data Distribution Service

Data Distribution Service (**DDS**) is classed as networking middleware and is aimed at publishing messages to subscribers. This is known as a **publish/subscribe** (**pub/sub**) model. The specification is defined and published by the **Object Management Group** (**OMG**); membership is through a consortium of commercial companies and universities. DDS is used by many diverse industries including aerospace, military, healthcare, government, and many more.

DDS is **middleware,** meaning it is the software layer that sits between the operating system and applications. It allows various components within a system to more easily communicate and share data. It is designed to simplify development of distributed systems by allowing software developers to focus on the functionallity of their applications rather than the complexities of passing information between applications and systems. *Figure 10.8* shows the layers that are important for DDS.

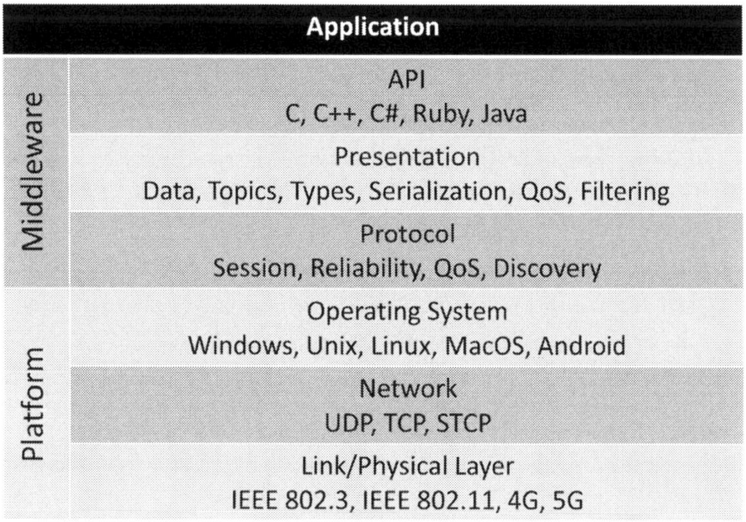

Application		
Middleware	API C, C++, C#, Ruby, Java	
	Presentation Data, Topics, Types, Serialization, QoS, Filtering	
	Protocol Session, Reliability, QoS, Discovery	
Platform	Operating System Windows, Unix, Linux, MacOS, Android	
	Network UDP, TCP, STCP	
	Link/Physical Layer IEEE 802.3, IEEE 802.11, 4G, 5G	

Figure 10.8 – DDS layers

The DDS specification covers the middleware layers.

DDS allows for the exchange of messages using **DDS, DDS-JavaScript Object Notation (DDS-JSON), DDS-Extensible Markup Language (DDS-XML), DDS-eXtremely Resource-Constrained Environments (DDS-XRCE), DDS4 CORBA Component Model (DDS4CCM),** and **Data-Distribution Service Inoperability-Real-Time Publish-Subscribe (DDSI-RTPS).**

DDS also defines a set of security controls including authentication, encryption, message authentication, digital signing, and data logging/tagging. These can be implemented as a series of plugins. This specification is covered in DDS-Security. For more information regarding DDS-Security please see the following URL: `https://tinyurl.com/ dds-security`.

Summary

In this chapter, we have taken a look at the challenges when supporting operational technologies. We have looked at examples of ICS where plant and equipment must be controlled using SCADA networks. We have studied the importance of adhering to legal and regulatory responsibilities. We have discussed that countries have different laws and regulatory requirements. We have seen examples of some significant fines that can be levied when it is proven that a company has broken laws or safety protocols. We have looked at the technology used to deliver automation and supervisory control and have taken a look at popular protocols used on these networks. We have looked at examples of embedded systems and the challenges that they may bring when networking these devices.

The skills learned in this chapter will be useful as we move on to the next chapter, where we will take a look in more depth at securing data using cryptography and PKI.

Questions

1. Which regulated business sector is intended to benefit citizens and generate no commercial profit?

    A.   Energy

    B.   Manufacturing

    C.   Healthcare

    D.   Public services

2. Which regulated business sector would typically involve the processing and storage of PHI?

    A.   Energy

    B.   Manufacturing

    C.   Healthcare

    D.   Public utilities

3. Which regulated business sector may be targeted by competitors who want to steal a company's IP?

    A.   Energy

    B.   Manufacturing

    C.   Healthcare

    D.   Public utilities

4. What type of network would likely include legacy vulnerable components?

    A.   SCADA

    B.   Zigbee

    C.   IoT

    D.   LAN

5. What risk mitigation would be used when supporting SCADA and business networks for an energy provider?

    A.   Segment vulnerable systems

    B.   Virtual LANs (VLANs)

    C.   Deploy to the DMZ

    D.   Upgrade all systems

6. What is a type of processor chip that performs a dedicated task and may be used for bitcoin mining?

    A.   IoT

    B.   SoC

    C.   ASIC

    D.   FPGA

7. What is a specialist hardened computer that will control actuators, valves, and pumps in an industrial environment?

    A.   Desktop computer

    B.   PLC

    C.   Mainframe computer

    D.   Sensor

8. What is a type of processor chip that can be reprogrammed in the field?

   A.   IoT

   B.   SoC

   C.   ASIC

   D.   FPGA

9. This term covers many technologies including home automation, building control systems, and many other areas where automation of hardware is required.

   A.   IoT

   B.   SoC

   C.   ASIC

   D.   FPGA

10. What is the database logging system known as that will collect data from process controls such as sensors, instrumentation, and other types of controls?

   A.   Historian

   B.   Ladder logic

   C.   SIS

   D.   HVAC

11. This is a simple programming language based upon relay-based logic, used originally in electromechanical relays.

   A.   Historian

   B.   Ladder logic

   C.   Zigbee

   D.   Modbus

12. What is the de facto standard message transport protocol used in industrial environments that offers no security against tampering with message integrity and is therefore vulnerable to MITM attacks?

    A.   CAN

    B.   Modbus

    C.   DNP3

    D.   Zigbee

13. What is the networking middleware known as a pub-sub model that is aimed at publishing messages to subscribers?

    A.   CAN

    B.   DDS

    C.   DNP3

    D.   Zigbee

14. Which wireless protocol intended primarily for home automation allows communication with low-power devices over distances varying between 10 and 100 meters?

    A.   CAN

    B.   CIP

    C.   DNP3

    D.   Zigbee

15. What is a protocol used for the transmission of messages on industrial networks? There are four types of networks offering different transport and network models, including 802.3 Ethernet.

    A.   CAN

    B.   CIP

    C.   DNP3

    D.   Zigbee

Answers

1. D
2. C
3. B
4. A
5. A
6. C
7. B
8. D
9. A
10. A
11. B
12. B
13. B
14. D
15. B

11
Implementing Cryptographic Protocols and Algorithms

Securing enterprise networks relies on a strategy called **defense in depth**. One very important part of defense in depth is protecting data in many different states, primarily at rest, in transit, and in use. When confidentiality is required, we can apply encryption to sensitive data to ensure we can protect that data. In some cases, we must be able to verify the integrity of the data using hashing and signing.

Cryptography can be a daunting subject area for IT professionals, with algorithms consisting of highly complex mathematical ciphers. The job of IT professionals and management is to ask the right questions and ensure the correct standards and protocols have been enabled. Regulatory authorities may have very strict requirements when using cryptographic ciphers to protect data that an enterprise will store, process, and transmit. It is the job of security professionals to ensure the correct configuration and deployment is provided for the appropriate technology.

In this chapter, we will cover the following topics:

- Understanding hashing algorithms
- Understanding symmetric encryption algorithms
- Understanding asymmetric encryption algorithms
- Understanding encryption protocols
- Understanding emerging security technologies

Understanding hashing algorithms

Hashing algorithms are primarily used to validate the integrity of data, though they can also be used to prove that you know something, such as a password secret. Hashing is a one-way process (it is unfeasible to reverse a hash) and does not provide confidentiality for the data. It is important to understand that the original data is not changed in any way. Think of hashing as a way to create a unique digital checksum for a particular document, file, or data payload. Hashing is used for **File Integrity Monitoring** (**FIM**), where we can detect if a protected operating system file has been altered. Hashing can be used in digital forensics to capture a unique checksum of a copy image, to match it with the original (this is useful to do before analysts begin the forensic investigation). For security professionals, it is important to understand what would be considered strong and what would represent weak implementations of hashing algorithms. Strong or resilient hashing will generate a larger digest (hash) output, while weak algorithms will generate a small digest (hash) output. Now, let's look at some examples.

Secure Hashing Algorithm (SHA)

SHA is the standard that's used by most commercial and government departments. It is a family of hash functions that was originally published by the **National Institute of Standards and Technology** (**NIST**) in 1993. This was approved for use and is documented in **Federal Information Processing Standards** (**FIPS**) **PUB 180-1**.

SHA-1 is a 160-bit cryptographic hash function that creates the same fixed-size output of 40 bytes (or characters). SHA-1 was deprecated in most cryptographic suites around 2010.

SHA-2 is a family of cryptographic hash functions that was approved under **FIPS PUB 180-2**. It covers the following hash functions:

- SHA-224
- SHA-256

- SHA-384
- SHA-512

It is worth noting that SHA-2 is still the preferred option for most operating systems. Windows operating systems, default tools, and utilities are based around SHA-2

SHA-3 is a family of cryptographic hash functions defined in **FIPS PUB 202**. The output size in bits is the same as SHA-2 (224, 256, 384, and 512) but uses a SHA-3 descriptor before the hash function. Most Linux/Unix distributions come with hashing utilities. In the following command, we have used a Linux Bash shell command to generate a hash to verify whether the bootstrap log has been tampered with:

```
sha256sum bootstrap.log
```

The output of this command is as follows:

```
1709de6f628968c14d3eed2f306bef4f39e4ab036e51386a59a487ec0
e4213fe bootstrap.log
```

Windows comes with a Command Prompt utility called CERTUTIL -HASHFILE <Filename>.

We can use this command to capture a hash value for the Windows operating system's kernel file:

```
certutil -hashfile ntoskrnl.exe sha256
```

The output of this command is as follows:

```
SHA256 hash of ntoskrnl.exe:
4ffa3d9c8a12bf45c4de8540f42d460bc2f55320e63caac4fdfabb
b384720b40
```

Windows PowerShell can also be used to generate hash values. The format is Get-Filehash <Filename> -Algorithm <hashtype>:

```
Get-FileHash ntoskrnl.exe -Algorithm SHA256
```

The output of this command is as follows:

```
Algorithm       Hash
---------       ----
SHA256          4FFA3D9C8A12BF45C4DE8540F42D460BC2F55320E6
3CAAC4FDFABBB384720B40
```

To address both integrity and authentication for a packet, we can use hash functions and a shared secret.

Hash-Based Message Authentication Code (HMAC)

HMAC, often referred to as simply MAC, allows a packet to be authenticated as well as checked for integrity. It will use a secret key, known by both the sender and the receiver, to be used with a hash function to create a unique MAC. The following flowchart shows the process of generating an HMAC and verifying it on the receiving host:

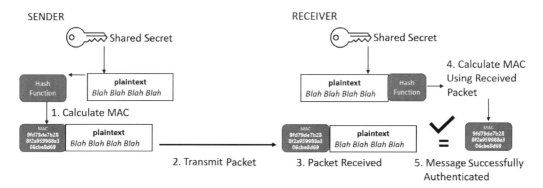

Figure 11.1 – HMAC

Please note that an HMAC provides no confidentiality for the payload; it only authenticates the packets. It does not replace a digital signature, which is used for non-repudiation.

Message Digest (MD)

The **Message Digest** (**MD**) hash function was originally published in 1989 as MD2 and was developed by Ronald Rivest. There were several updates, culminating in MD5. It has been in common use up until around 2008. It is now considered vulnerable to exploitation, including hash collisions. A hash collision is where two different inputs create an identical hash output. An attacker may replace a genuine file or document with a modified substitute that exhibits the same hash output.

RACE integrity primitives evaluation message digest (RIPEMD)

RIPEMD provides a family of hash functions. The supported functions include RIPEMD, RIPEMD-128, RIPEMD-160, RIPEMD-256, and RIPEMD-320.

RIPEMD is not used in government or many commercial applications but can be found within academic environments and some products where government approval is not important.

Hashing is very useful for providing integrity but does not allow you to protect data through confidentiality. For confidentiality, we must use symmetric and asymmetric encryption.

Understanding symmetric encryption algorithms

Symmetric encryption provides confidentiality by provisioning bulk encryption. It is highly efficient at encrypting data at rest and data in transit. Due to the relatively small key sizes that are used, it is very fast (in comparison to asymmetric encryption). Symmetric encryption uses a single key to encrypt (or lock) the data and the same key is used to decrypt (unlock) the data.

 Symmetric algorithms are divided into two main categories: block and stream ciphers.

Block ciphers

These ciphers are used to encrypt data in blocks, typically 64 or 128 bits. They offer the most robust security but lack the outright speed that's offered by stream ciphers. The following are some examples of block ciphers:

- **Triple Digital Encryption Standard** (**3DES**): 3DES replaced the original **Data Encryption Standard** (**DES**), which was designed and adopted in the 1970s. DES offered a key size of only 64 bits (56 bits for the key itself). In 1999, 3DES became the new standard, while an alternative was being developed. 3DES can be implemented in several different ways, but the most secure is by using three separate keys. 3DES has an effective key size of 168 bits. NIST guidance stipulates that 3DES will be retired by 2023.

- **Advanced Encryption Standard** (**AES**): AES is the official standard that's used in government and military environments; it is also widely adopted in the commercial world. It was approved for use in 2001 after being accepted as the best candidate from several alternate ciphers (including Blowfish and Twofish). It meets government standards as it is **FIPS-140 PUB** compliant, which describes software and hardware security implementations. **FIPS PUB 197** documents the actual details of the AES protocol standard. AES can be implemented with key sizes of 128, 192, and 256. There are additional recommendations when using AES, specifically the block cipher modes that should be implemented. When used for **BitLocker Drive Encryption**, NIST recommends using **XTS-AES** cipher mode. For more information, please see `https://tinyurl.com/nist800-38e`.

Block ciphers are the mainstay of symmetric encryption algorithms, but we must also look at fine-tuning when using these algorithms. Symmetric ciphers can be deployed using specific modes of operation.

Block cipher modes of operation

Block ciphers can be deployed using specific modes of operation. It is important for security professionals to understand the security implications of these different modes. There are also performance considerations we must respect when selecting a block cipher mode. Let's look at the available choices.

Electronic Code Book (ECB)

ECB is the oldest example of a block cipher mode and originates from the original DES implementation. ECB uses the same cipher for each block of data. The following diagram shows the process of encrypting plaintext with the same cipher to generate ciphertext:

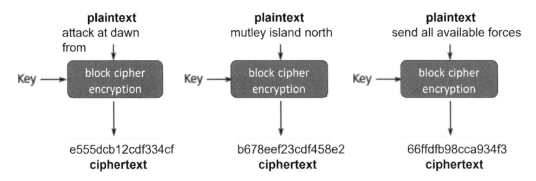

Figure 11.2 – ECB mode

Imagine that you are encrypting a 1,000-page document and that each line on every page is encrypted using the same key. If the ciphertext is subjected to scrutiny using statistical analysis, then patterns can be seen.

In the following figure, we can see an example of an image that has been encrypted using ECB mode. Discernable color patterns are evident due to the repeated use of the same cipher:

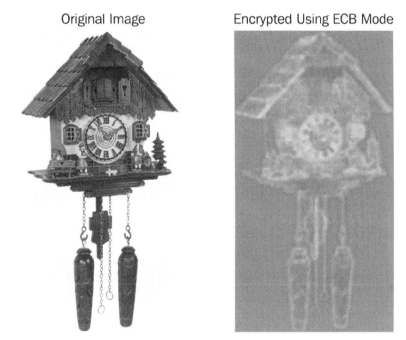

Figure 11.3 – ECB cipher weakness

In this example, if there is a discernable pattern, it will be identified by cryptanalysts.

Cipher block chaining (CBC)

CBC dates back to the mid-1970s, so it is fairly mature. By using CBC mode, every plaintext block is encrypted using a unique cipher. The first block is encrypted using a random **Initialization Vector** (**IV**), along with the key. The ciphertext becomes the IV for the next block of plaintext data. The following diagram shows the CBC process:

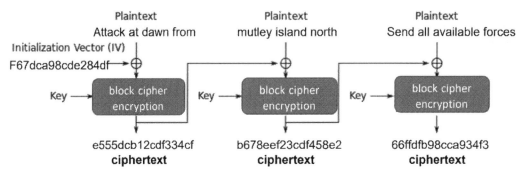

Figure 11.4 – CBC mode

CBC mode operates sequentially, which means it offers no options to improve performance by using parallel processing. Newer block ciphers offer better performance

Output feedback (OFB)

OFB enables a block cipher to behave like a stream cipher. As the cipher can be calculated before the next plaintext is encrypted, it allows the next step to run in parallel. This offers performance advantages over older block ciphers. The following diagram shows how OFB mode operates:

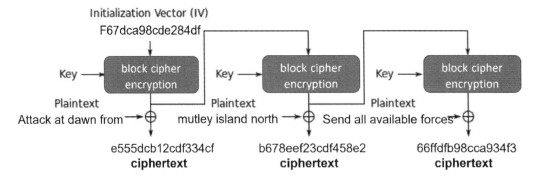

Figure 11.5 – OFB mode

Note that OFB is unlikely to be selected as there are newer blockchain ciphers that offer better performance.

Counter (CTR)

CTR mode also offers a performance advantage over legacy blockchain ciphers. It allows a block cipher to act as a stream cipher by preparing the cipher before the plaintext is encrypted. As there is no need to wait for each block of plaintext to be encrypted (it plays no part in the following cipher), then powerful multi-processor systems can take advantage of the parallel processing of blocks.

The following diagram shows an example of CTR mode:

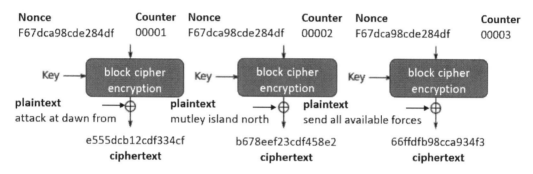

Figure 11.6 – CTR mode

CTR mode has been largely superseded by block ciphers, which offer this performance advantage along with authenticity.

Galois Counter Mode (GCM)

GCM is the default block cipher mode for many implementations of SSL/TLS. It combines the advantages of CTR mode with additional authentication of the packets that are sent using **Message Authentication Code** (**MAC**). This is one of the recommended block cipher modes to support **Authenticated Encryption with Associated Data** (**AEAD**). This protects against attacks using the chosen ciphertext, where the attacker will forward the ciphertext to a server, which will attempt to decrypt the ciphertext and send a reply. The attacker will use these responses to gain access to the encryption key. AEAD will ensure that the ciphertext will only be trusted if it has the correct MAC value. While AEAD uses a hashing algorithm, this description is included along with cipher mode descriptions, as it is a primary function of GCM mode.

The following diagram shows an example of **Mac-then-Encrypt** (**MtE**) being used for SSL/TLS packets:

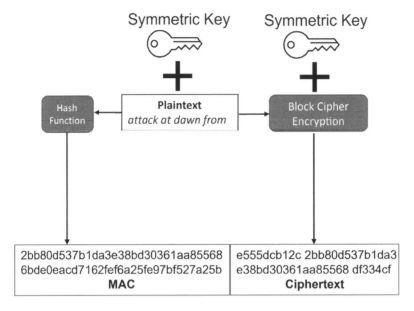

Figure 11.7 – GCM using AEAD

In the preceding example, the plaintext is processed twice; it is used as partial input to create the MAC (along with the key) and is then encrypted using the symmetric key.

Poly1305

Poly1305 is another popular cryptographic-based MAC that's commonly used along with AES (Poly1305-AES), though is also used with ChaCha. Poly1305 is popular with e-commerce providers due to its high speed on standard CPU architectures. This also supports the protocol for AEAD.

In addition to block ciphers, there are use cases where stream ciphers are considered a better option, particularly when considering data in transit.

Stream ciphers

Stream ciphers are optimized for real-time traffic. They are fast and as they process the data as a stream of bits, fewer errors are generated. The previous standard for stream ciphers was RC4, though this is no longer considered a secure cipher and was withdrawn from widespread use in 2015. The following are two popular modern stream ciphers:

- **ChaCha**: ChaCha was designed for high performance. As a stream cipher, it has many advantages over block ciphers when deployed with real-time applications such as streaming media or VoIP. It was designed as an alternative to AES when deploying SSL/TLS security. It is a refined version of Salsa20. The ChaCha cipher is based on 20 rounds of encryption using a 256-bit key size. One of its major strengths is its speed and resistance to side-channel analysis. ChaCha has been adopted by **Cloudflare** and **Google** as its preferred option for TLS 1.3 SSL/TLS connections.

- **Salsa20**: Salsa20 was developed by the same person (Daniel J. Bernstein) that developed the ChaCha cipher. It is closely related to the ChaCha cipher and offers choices of 128-bit and 256-bit key sizes. It was superseded by the newer ChaCha cipher.

Symmetric ciphers are fast and efficient but do not provide a mechanism for secure symmetric key exchanges, nor do they support concepts that are used within digital signatures. For this, we need asymmetric encryption.

Understanding asymmetric encryption algorithms

Asymmetric encryption has two main goals – one is to support a secure key exchange/agreement process, while the other is to support non-repudiation through the use of digital signatures. It is not used for bulk encryption as the key sizes (compared to symmetric encryption) are large. This would mean that it could be thousands of times slower to encrypt large amounts of data. Asymmetric encryption uses a key pair that is mathematically related; there is a public key and a private key. You can think of the public key as your bank details that you can share with a customer (who wants to make a payment). Your private key is used to securely access your funds. In this analogy, your *bank card + pin + CVC code* would be your private key. You would not share your private key with anyone.

Rivest, Shamir, and Adleman (RSA)

RSA is used for secure key exchange and digital signatures. It was developed and published in 1977, so it is one of the oldest asymmetric algorithms. It consists of a public and private key that are mathematically related. You can publish your public key but must keep the private key secure. The typical key size for RSA is between 2,048 to 4,096 bits, although current guidance is for keys of 3,072 bits to meet more stringent security standards.

Digital Signature Algorithm (DSA)

DSA is a government standard for digital signatures and is documented in FIPS PUB 186-4 (the current standard). Digital signatures are used for non-repudiation when you're sending a document by email or to validate a certificate hosted by a website. The following diagram shows the signing process when using a key pair:

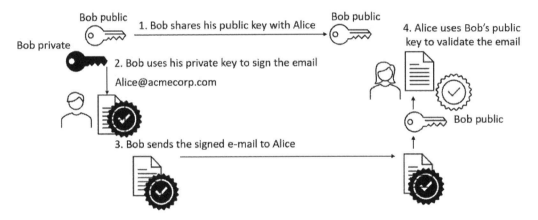

Figure 11.8 – Digital signature algorithm (DSA)

FIPS standards are used to enforce strong signature algorithms. Signing is a combination of hashing and asymmetric encryption. The public key is used to sign the hash of the document (the email body in the preceding diagram).

The signing process is a little bit more complicated than what's shown in the preceding diagram. We have broken the process down into more granular steps in the following diagram:

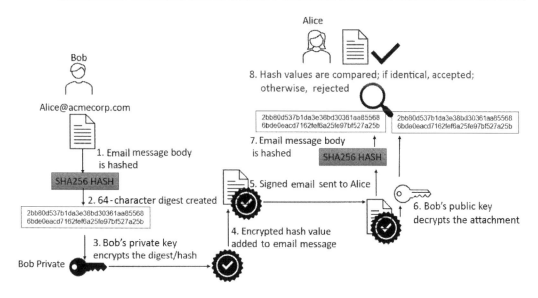

Figure 11.9 – Detailed signing process

The correct cipher suite must be selected. In this example, a cipher suite of RSA-3072 and SHA-256 would be considered a good choice. MD5 would not meet the requirements of FIPS compliance as it is weak and vulnerable to hash collisions. A **man-in-the-middle** (**MITM**) attack could allow the document to be intercepted and modified if we use a weak hashing algorithm. If the document is modified and it then matches the original hash value, then the signature will appear valid.

Elliptic-curve Digital Signature Algorithm (ECDSA)

ECDSA uses the same process as DSA by using standard keys, such as RSA keys. The advantage is that the key size is roughly a tenth (1/10) of the size of the equivalent RSA key. This results in a verifiable signature being generated, but with a vast reduction in CPU activity when using these types of keys.

Diffie-Hellman (DH)

DH is a key agreement protocol that's typically used to exchange a secret/session key for IPSec or SSL/TLS. It is not used to exchange a key but allows two parties to generate a secret/session key independently. This is useful as it means the session key was never transmitted, so any MITM attack would be unsuccessful.

Elliptic-curve Cryptography (ECC)

ECC allows key pairs to be generated using algebraic equations to draw an ellipse. Points can be plotted on this ellipse to generate keys (this is a simple description of a complex mathematical process). ECC is used for key agreements and digital signatures. The strength of ECC is in its suitability for low-powered devices. A key size of 256 bits using ECC is equivalent to an RSA key size of around 2,048 bits. ECC's key strengths are measured using **p256**, **p384**, and **p521**. A key size of 384 bits (p384) meets the **NSA suite B** security standard for top secret classification. Due to concerns about attacks from highly sophisticated threat actors using quantum computing, a new standard has replaced NSA suite B called **Commercial National Security Algorithm Suite** (**CNSA**). Check out the following URL for more information: `https://tinyurl.com/nsa-cnsa-standards`.

Elliptic-curve Diffie-Hellman (ECDH)

ECDH is a key agreement protocol where the actual public/private key pairs are based on ECC. This key exchange protocol is further enhanced by the use of **ephemeral keys** (also known as temporary keys), which makes this become ECDHE. **ECDHE** is one example of a method that's referred to as **forward secrecy** or **perfect forward secrecy**. This ensures long-term key pairs are not used during the key exchange. If an attacker managed to gain a master key (such as a server private key), they could decrypt sessions in the future until the keys were changed or rotated. When you're using forward secrecy, this is not possible.

Now that we've looked at all the individual encryption algorithms, we will look at some common implementation methods.

Understanding encryption protocols

Hashing, symmetric, and asymmetric encryption are building blocks that are used to support applications and protocols that need to secure how data is stored and transmitted. Many processes will use a cipher suite, drawing on the strengths of the different types of encryption. We depend on these protocols to protect users when we're accessing online banking, remotely accessing the workplace, protecting information systems when they must be administered across a network, and ensuring that emails that are sent and received can be trusted. We will look at some of these common protocols in the following subsections.

Secure Sockets Layer (SSL)/Transport Layer Security (TLS)

SSL/TLS is used to encrypt many application layer protocols, such as HTTP, SMTP, IMAP, LDAP, and many more. It provides confidentiality (through encryption) and integrity (through HMAC). It uses hybrid cryptography through a suite of protocols. SSL is no longer used as it is considered insecure; TLS 1.2 and TLS 1.3 are the current standards. An example of SSL/TLS can be seen in the following diagram:

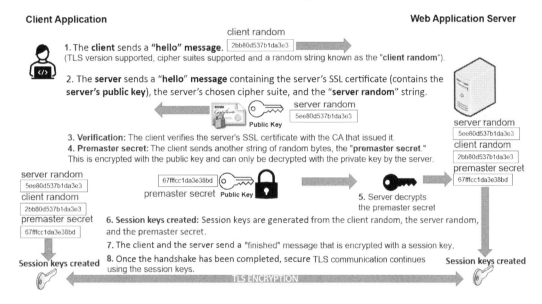

Figure 11.10 – SSL/TLS session handshake

During the SSL/TLS handshake, the client and server must agree upon a cipher suite. If there is no common cipher suite that suits both parties, then a **cipher mismatch** will occur. If there is a cipher mismatch, the connection will be refused. This may be a result of the client or server proposing a **weak cipher suite**.

Secure/Multipurpose Internet Mail Extensions (S/MIME)

MIME is the standard for emails and allows for a common protocol. This allows users to choose a mail client so that the enterprise can run an SMTP server from any vendor. To ensure that emails are protected from inbox to inbox, we can encrypt the payload using a combination of the recipient's public key and a session key. The recipient can decrypt the message using their private key.

The following diagram shows the S/MIME process:

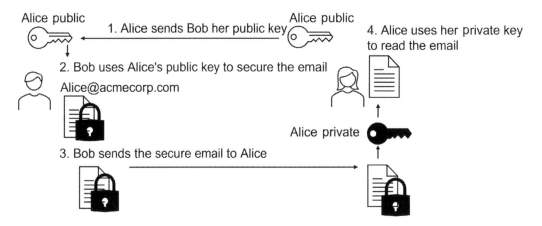

Figure 11.11 – S/MIME

This is a simplified version; in reality, the public key is used to protect the bulk encryption key (the symmetric key); the private key can decrypt the symmetric key.

Internet Protocol Security (IPSec)

IPSec is a mechanism for securing data in transit, typically when supporting **Virtual Private Networks** (**VPNs**). This can be used to secure site-to-site links or allow mobile users to secure access to the enterprise network. IPSec will use a cipher suite consisting of hashing (HMAC), symmetric for bulk encryption, and asymmetric for secure key exchange.

Secure Shell (SSH)

SSH is used to manage servers and equipment using a secure shell (or secure console). SSH uses hybrid encryption to secure the connection. A common tool for connecting to a remote device securely is PuTTY. The following screenshot shows the configuration for PuTTY when preparing for an SSH connection:

Figure 11.12 – PuTTY SSH configuration

Note that the configuration allows for a secure key exchange (asymmetric) and the session key (symmetric). It is common to rotate the keys that are used for secure connections. If the asymmetric key pair is rotated (changed) on the server, then the client device will need to download and trust the new public key.

Key stretching

Key stretching is used to protect weak keys. Examples of such keys include the passwords stored in a database. If an attacker gains access to the weak passwords that have been hashed in a database, then they can use offline techniques to crack these passwords. As they will not use the live login option, they will not lock the accounts out. Offline tools/techniques could include dictionary attacks, rainbow tables, and brute-force attacks. When we harden a password using key stretching, the original password is passed through multiple rounds of encryption. An attacker will now need to guess a password string and subject it to multiple rounds of encryption (just like the key stretching algorithm) in an attempt to crack the password. Key stretching will slow down the attacker's attempts to a considerable degree while allowing the legitimate users to access their accounts with little overhead.

Password salting

This is the most basic way to protect a password against offline attacks while using tables and brute-force techniques. A pseudo-random string of characters is generated. This **salt** is now mixed with the password string and hashed. The following diagram shows the password salting process:

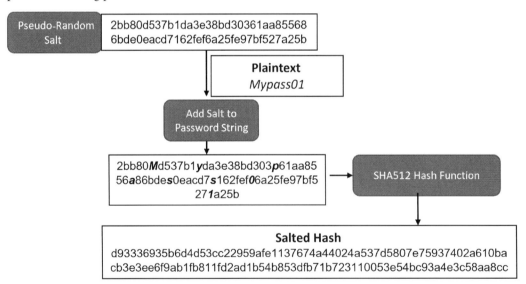

Figure 11.13 – Password salting

This salted password is now stored in the password database. This offers a useful level of protection for passwords that are stored, though can be improved upon by using key stretching techniques.

Password-based key derivation function 2 (PBKDF2)

PBKDF2 uses SHA-2 hashing and a salt of at least 64 characters to protect passwords. NIST recommends a series of 10,000 rounds/cycles of hashing to be applied to the password after the salt has been added. The following diagram shows the principle of key stretching:

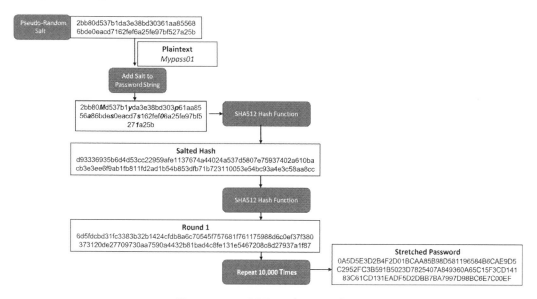

Figure 11.14 – PBKDF2 key stretching

bcrypt is similar to PBKDF2, in the sense that it also allows for key stretching, though it uses a different cipher. bcrypt is based on the Blowfish cipher, although it can also use SHA-2 to encrypt a password using multiple rounds.

Many additional technologies can be used to protect an enterprise from attacks when data, intellectual property, and the integrity of the data may be at risk. Let's learn about some of these emerging technologies.

Understanding emerging security technologies

To maintain a strong security posture, organizations must be willing to adopt new technologies and be aware of these technologies to protect the organization. Increases in computing power may allow adversaries to gain access to data that's protected using weak encryption algorithms. Newer technologies will allow for innovative solutions to address cybersecurity requirements.

Quantum computing

Quantum computing is designed to solve complex problems more efficiently than existing supercomputers. Supercomputers harness the traditional processing capabilities of compute nodes hosting thousands of CPU and GPU cores. Solving a problem using quantum processing may be thousands of times faster than using the existing computing models. A regular computer (or supercomputer) processes 0s and 1s and generates answers to problems using 0s and 1s – this is a solid approach and works well to solve many different computational problems. Let's compare this to a simple problem where a freight company needs to deliver goods to 10 different customers. There are 10 different truck types and 10 different routes to the customer sites, and each customer has a specific payload to be delivered. There may be over 3 million solutions when it comes to optimizing the use of trucks, fuel, and routes. One example quantum algorithm is called **Grover's search**, which can process the problem on a quantum computer and generate the results in a much more efficient manner (compared to traditional computers). Instead of searching through all 3 million possible solutions, Grover's search will find the solution by checking various solutions – in this case, around 1,732 calculations. For complex computational models, this may mean that an answer is available within seconds rather than weeks.

The adoption of quantum computing and efficient algorithms to harness this technology presents a major cybersecurity threat. At the time of writing, Google has a quantum computer rated at 50 qubits (qubits describe quantum bits). A qubit can represent multiple states. It is estimated that around 20 million qubits would be required to crack existing cryptographic keys. For examples of quantum computing and the threats to cryptography, go to `https://tinyurl.com/quantumthreats`.

Blockchain

A blockchain is a secure digital ledger that's supported by a public peer-to-peer network. A blockchain is a robust tamper-proof mechanism that's used to protect the **integrity** and **authenticity** of data.

Records or transactions are added as a new block and the hash is calculated and added to the chain. The following diagram shows a blockchain:

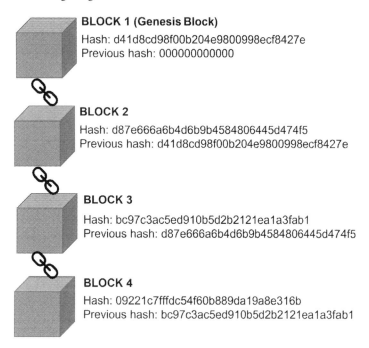

BLOCK 1 (Genesis Block)
Hash: d41d8cd98f00b204e9800998ecf8427e
Previous hash: 000000000000

BLOCK 2
Hash: d87e666a6b4d6b9b4584806445d474f5
Previous hash: d41d8cd98f00b204e9800998ecf8427e

BLOCK 3
Hash: bc97c3ac5ed910b5d2b2121ea1a3fab1
Previous hash: d87e666a6b4d6b9b4584806445d474f5

BLOCK 4
Hash: 09221c7fffdc54f60b889da19a8e316b
Previous hash: bc97c3ac5ed910b5d2b2121ea1a3fab1

Figure 11.15 – Blockchain

The first block is referred to as the genesis block; there is no previous hash calculation as there is no preceding block.

For the new transactions to be accepted, they must be approved by the majority of the nodes on a **Peer-to-Peer** (**P2P**) network. The new transaction (or block) can now be added to the public ledger. We can see the process of approving a new transaction in the following diagram:

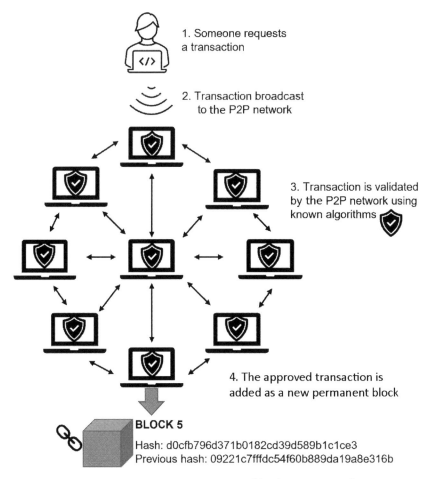

Figure 11.16 – Transaction approved by the P2P network

To tamper with transactions in a blockchain, it would be necessary to recalculate the hashes for all of the blocks (as each is dependent on the preceding block) and be able to take control of more than 50% of the nodes on the P2P network. Aside from cryptocurrencies, there are many practical implementations of blockchains, including secure voting machines, healthcare, financial ledgers, and many more. **Spotify** uses a decentralized blockchain to store information about artists, tracks, and licensing agreements.

Homomorphic encryption

This type of encryption is used to protect data in use. When sensitive data must be accessed by an application or service, then homomorphic encryption should be considered.

Private Information Retrieval (PIR)

This protocol allows you to retrieve data from a database, without the receiver accessing any sensitive data in the database. A researcher working for a medical company needs to evaluate the effectiveness of drug trials. Rather than send the researcher the entire database of information, with any sensitive data encrypted, PIR will run the query against the secure encrypted database and only return the results that are authorized for the researcher to access.

Secure Function Evaluation (SFE)

This protocol allows a function to be computed on two separate inputs, without revealing the inputs to any party. For example, let's say that Mallory would like to perform statistical analysis on customers' purchasing habits. The values that will be analyzed are held by Acme bank and Home Depot. Acme and Home Depot do not want to share sensitive PII or intellectual property with each other or Mallory. Mallory submits the query/function to the two organizations and can retrieve useful statistical information, without gaining access to any protected data from either party.

Private Function Evaluation (PFE)

This is also known as **Multi-party Computation** (**MPC**), which allows multiple parties to submit data (or inputs) to a secure enclave where the function or calculation will be performed. In this case, the function will be kept secret and the data owners will be sent the encrypted results. This protects the intellectual property of all parties, including the program owner.

Biometric impersonation

When considering security within large, complex enterprises, it is important to protect identities with robust authentication schemes. Biometrics has been very useful in providing **Multi-factor Authentication** (**MFA**), including facial recognition, gait analysis, and voice patterns. The adoption of very powerful compute nodes has also made biometric impersonation using **deep fakes** possible.

In 2020, a United Arab Emirates-based bank manager took a phone call from a company director, who instructed him to make a large transfer totaling $35 million. It later transpired that criminals had used **deep learning** computing techniques to create realistic renditions of the company director's speech patterns. To read more about this story, go to `https://tinyurl.com/deepfakeheist`.

Deep learning uses **Artificial Intelligence (AI)** and **neural networks** to extract distinct traits or features from raw information. This technology can be used to generate deep fakes.

There have been many instances of deep fakes being used to steal the identities of victims. Computer-generated deep fake audio and videos are very difficult to distinguish from the real thing. Deep fakes can also be referred to as **synthetic media**.

To mitigate the threats posed by deep fakes, there needs to be a robust way to verify that the digital media, images, or voice are original. Blockchains may be a useful solution to verify whether the media is original. The following URL provides an interesting news article on deep fakes: `https://tinyurl.com/deepfakereport`.

3D printing

This technology is widely adopted and is used by many diverse industries, from motor manufacturers to aircraft production. 3D printing uses a **Computer-aided Design (CAD)** process to create a blueprint for the printer to use. The printer can lay multiple layers of materials to create prototypes, as well as production components.

The wide adoption of this technology means it is relatively easy for a competitor to recreate designs based on the enterprise's intellectual property. Other risks may involve a hacker gaining access to a network-connected 3D printer and introducing defects into the printing process. However, it may be a useful security mitigation when we would otherwise rely on third-party manufacturers to produce prototypes and early design models. It is of paramount importance to secure the blueprints and manufacturing data that are used by this process. Some 3D printing manufacturers are incorporating technology that allows for digital fingerprinting, allowing a printed component to be traced back to the source.

Summary

In this chapter, we learned about the protocols and technologies that are used to protect data in many different states, primarily at rest, in transit, and in use. We gained an understanding of hashing algorithms, primarily to support integrity. These hashing algorithms include SHA, SHA-2, SHA-3, MD, and RIPE. We also looked at message integrity using HMAC and AEAD.

We then studied the options for ensuring confidentiality using symmetric encryption, including block ciphers such as AES and 3DES. We also identified cipher block modes, including GCM, ECB, CBC, CTR, and OFB. We then looked at common stream ciphers such as ChaCha and Salsa20, where real-time applications must be considered.

After that, we looked at asymmetric encryption, which is used for S/MIME, digital signatures, and key exchange. These asymmetric algorithms include ECC, ECHDE, RSA, and DSA.

We now understand how to deploy secure protocols, including SSL, TLS, S/MIME, IPSec, and SSH.

We also gained an understanding of key stretching using PBKDF2 and bcrypt.

We also looked at new and emerging technologies that can help protect sensitive data and intellectual property. Emerging technologies include blockchains, homomorphic encryption, biometric impersonation, and deep fakes. We then looked at some of the risks to be considered when deploying 3D printing.

These skills will be useful when we study additional security concepts using **Public Key Infrastructure** (**PKI**) as this is primarily deployed to support the authenticity of our asymmetric key pairs.

In the next chapter, we will look at how public keys can be trusted by generating digital certificates, as well as how certificates can be revoked and managed within an enterprise.

Questions

Answer the following questions to test your knowledge of this chapter:

1. Recent log analysis has revealed that archived documents have been tampered with, even though the hash-matching database shows that the values have not changed. What could have caused this?

    A. A weak symmetric cipher

    B. Hash collision

    C. An asymmetric algorithm with a small key size

    D. A poor choice of block cipher

2. Recent log analysis has revealed that archived documents have been tampered with. To mitigate this vulnerability, which of the following should *not* be used?

    A. RACE-320

    B. MD5

    C. SHA-384

    D. SHA3-256

3. Developers are creating a **File Integrity Monitoring** (**FIM**) solution to market to government agencies. What would be a good choice, considering FIPS compliance?

    A. RACE-256

    B. MD5

    C. SHA-512

    D. ECC

4. Google engineers are configuring security for a new regional data center. They are looking to implement SSL/TLS for customer-facing application servers. What would be a good choice, considering the need for speed and security?

    A. ChaCha256 and Poly1305

    B. 3DES and CBC

    C. AES256 and CBC

    D. Salsa256 and CBC

5. What is used to authenticate packets that are sent over a secure SSL/TLS connection?

    A. SHA

    B. HMAC

    C. MD

    D. Key exchange

6. Hackers can gain access to encrypted data transmissions. Log analysis shows that some application servers have different blockchain cipher configurations. Which log entries would cause the most concern?

    A. GCM

    B. ECB

    C. CBC

    D. CTR

7. When you're choosing a symmetric algorithm for real-time media streaming applications, what would be the best choice?

    A. 3DES

    B. AES

    C. ChaCha

    D. RC4

Implementing Cryptographic Protocols and Algorithms

8. A government department is configuring a VPN connection. They are looking for a highly secure key exchange protocol due to the threats that are being posed by nation state threat actors. What would be a good choice?

    A. AES

    B. ECDHE p521

    C. ChaCha-256

    D. SHA-512

9. What type of key agreement would *most* likely be used on IPSec tunnels?

    A. Diffie-Hellman

    B. DSA

    C. RSA

    D. Salsa

10. What is a good choice regarding a signing algorithm that will work well on low-powered mobile devices?

    A. DSA

    B. RSA

    C. ECDSA

    D. HMAC

11. What is the first step in the handshake for a secure web session that's using SSL/TLS?

    A. Server hello

    B. Session key created

    C. Client hello

    D. Pre-master secret

12. A government agency needs to ensure that email messages are secure from mailbox to mailbox. It cannot be guaranteed that all SMTP connections are secure. What is the *best* choice?

    A. SSL/TLS

    B. S/MIME

    C. IPSec

    D. SSH

13. An engineer sees the following output while connecting to a router:

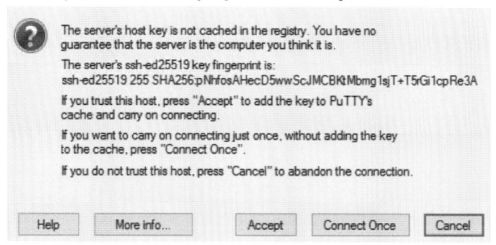

Figure 11.17 – SSH warning

The engineer logged onto the device using SSH the same day earlier. What is the most likely cause of this message?

    A. Weak ciphers

    B. Key rotation

    C. Incorrect password

    D. Incompatible cipher suite

14. While setting up a commercial customer-facing web application server, what would be a good choice regarding a key exchange that will support forward secrecy?

    A. DH

    B. RSA

    C. ChaCha

    D. ECDHE

15. What term is used to describe the message integrity that's provided by protocols such as Poly1305 and GCM?

    A. Non-repudiation

    B. Authenticated encryption with associated data

    C. Perfect forward secrecy

    D. Collision resistance

16. What would be used to provide non-repudiation when you're sending a business associate an email message?

    A. TLS/SSL

    B. AES-256

    C. S/MIME

    D. IPSec

17. A developer is protecting the password field when they're storing customer profiles in a database. What would be a good choice for protecting this data from offline attacks? Choose two.

    A. PBKDF2

    B. AES

    C. bcrypt

    D. ChaCha

18. What do Alice and Bob need to exchange before they send signed email messages to each other?

    A. Private keys

    B. Cipher suite

    C. Public keys

    D. Pre-shared keys

19. What will be used when Alice needs to sign an important business document to her colleague, Bob?

    A. Alice's public key

    B. Alice's private key

    C. Bobs public key

    D. Bobs private key

20. What encryption protocol will be used to encrypt emails while in transit, across untrusted networks, when the client has no encryption keys?

    A. SSL/TLS

    B. IPSecC

    C. SSH

    D. S/MIME

Answers

1. B
2. B
3. C
4. A
5. B
6. B
7. C
8. B
9. A
10. C
11. C
12. B
13. B
14. D
15. B
16. C
17. A and C
18. C
19. B
20. A

12

Implementing Appropriate PKI Solutions, Cryptographic Protocols, and Algorithms for Business Needs

Public key infrastructure (**PKI**) is of vital importance to any size organization and becomes a necessity for a large enterprise. PKI gives an organization the tools to verify and provide authentication for keys that will be used to secure the data. Without PKI we cannot use encryption keys, as the authenticity of keys cannot be verified. When a key pair is generated, we need to assign a trustworthy signed certificate to the unique public key, in a similar fashion to a passport that is generated for a trustworthy citizen. Without PKI, we cannot use online banking, e-commerce, smart cards, or **virtual private networks** (**VPNs**) with any assurance.

It is important to understand how the entire process works and potential problem areas that may need to be managed using troubleshooting skills. In this chapter, we will take a look at the following topics:

- Understanding the PKI hierarchy
- Understanding certificate types
- Understanding PKI security and interoperability
- Troubleshooting issues with cryptographic implementations

Understanding the PKI hierarchy

A PKI hierarchy describes the main components needed to process **certificate signing requests** (**CSRs**), authorize requests, and perform the signing process. Each component of the PKI plays an important role. In *Figure 12.1*, we can see an overview of the PKI hierarchy:

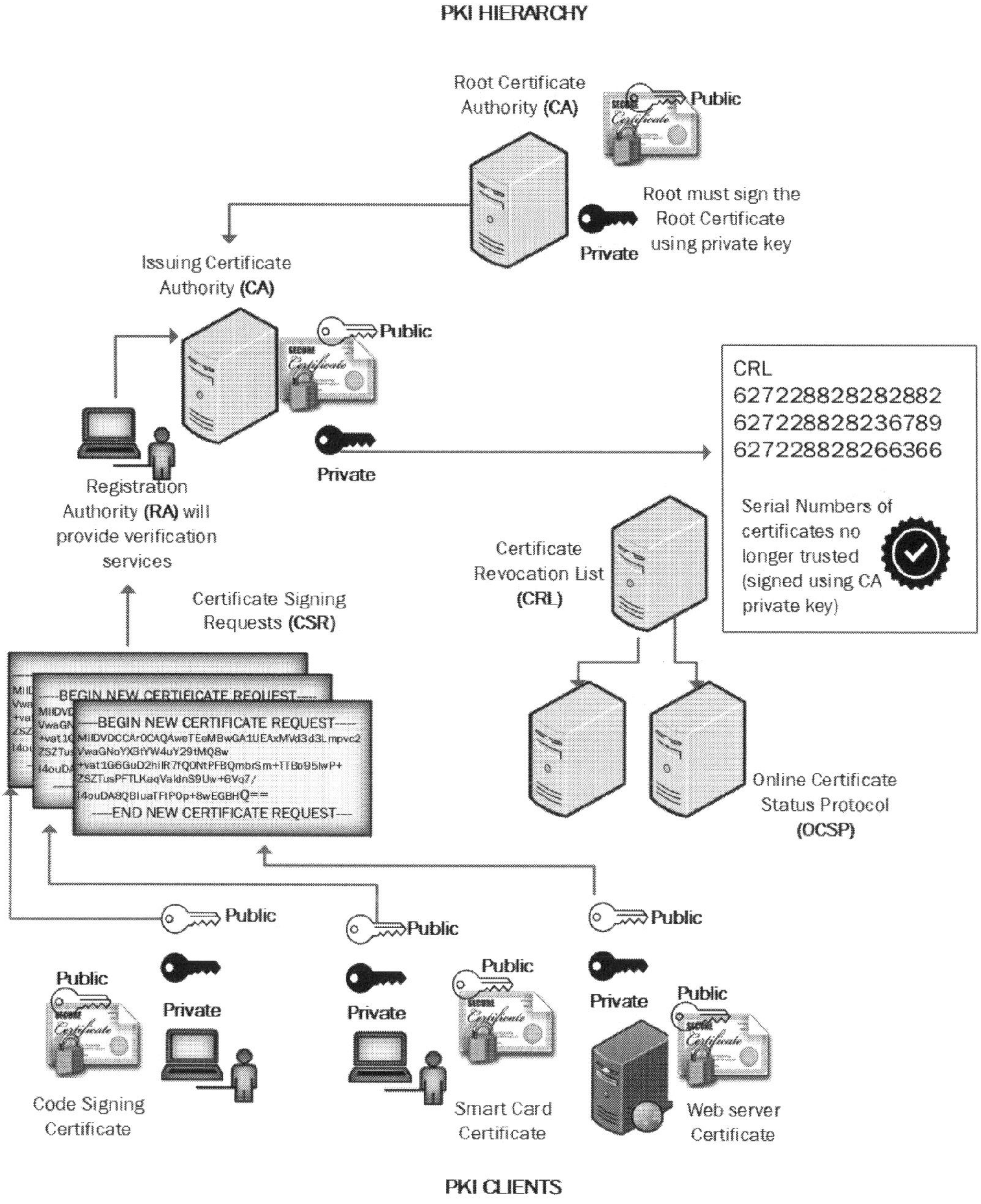

Figure 12.1 – Common components of PKI

We will now learn about these components.

Certificate authority

A **certificate authority** (**CA**) consists of an application server running a service called Certificate Services (or Linux/Unix equivalent daemon). There may be multiple levels of CAs; there will always be a **root CA**. In addition, there will normally be at least one more layer. This is known as the **subordinate** or **intermediate CA**. The root CA will typically be kept in a secure location, in many cases isolated (or air-gapped). The root CA only needs to be powered up and available to sign intermediate CA signing requests. For redundancy, an enterprise may have several issuing CAs. The issuing CA must be powered up and available to sign the client CSR; it will need to be highly available. Certificates follow a standard. The current standard is **X509.v3**, and this dictates the formatting and included information that is present on a **digital certificate**.

Registration authority

When a request is received from a client entity, there will be policies that dictate whether a request will be approved. To issue a certificate that validates a domain name or some other identity, verification checks must be done. You can compare the **registration authority** (**RA**) role to that of an auditor. If you wanted to apply for a passport, then identity verification would need to be done; otherwise, somebody could steal your identity. In the PKI hierarchy, the passport would be the digital certificate and the RA would be the government agency/department responsible for issuing passports.

Certificate revocation list

A **certificate revocation list** (**CRL**) is published by the CA and is a means of revoking certificates that should no longer be used or trusted. If a certificate is issued with a validity date of 1 year and there is a key compromise during that period, then the CA can revoke the certificate and publish the status on a publicly accessible list. *Figure 12.2* shows a typical CRL:

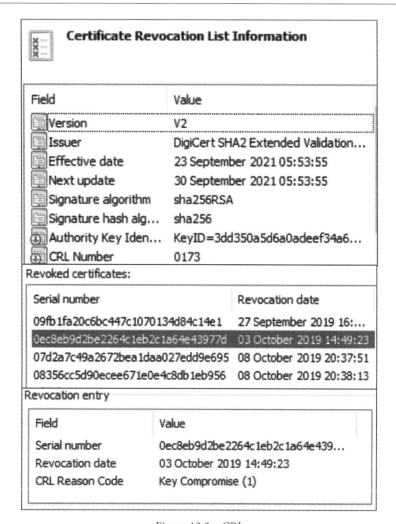

Figure 12.2 – CRL

Certificates can be revoked for a variety of reasons, including cessation of operation, change of affiliation, or key compromise (there are more options).

Online Certificate Status Protocol

In order to support a timelier response to a client request for revoked certificates, the **Online Certificate Standard Protocol** (**OCSP**) has become the standard approach to deliver a speedy response. Using only a CRL, a client must connect to the CA's CRL server and retrieve updated CRL entries. If there is an availability problem or a temporary outage on the CRL network, then a client cannot validate the status of the public key certificate. With OCSP, however, the OCSP service can cache results and respond to client requests even when the CRL is temporarily offline. The OCSP is also a far simpler protocol, as the serial number of the public key certificate is all that needs to be verified.

Once the PKI hierarchy is established, we will need to provide certificates for a wide variety of uses.

Understanding certificate types

Large enterprises have very specific needs when enrolling for certificates; sometimes, the goal may be ease of administration or flexibility to add additional sites to an e-commerce operation. In some cases, customers may need the assurance provided with highly trusted certificates. Here are some common types of certificates used.

Wildcard certificate

A wildcard certificate allows an organization to host multiple websites, using a single key pair, with a single certificate. There may be restrictions or additional costs based upon the number of sites hosted. The wildcard certificate requires all sites covered by the certificate to use the same **Domain Name System** (**DNS**) domain name. Only the hostname of each site can be different. *Figure 12.3* shows a wildcard certificate:

Certificate Information

This certificate is intended for the following purpose(s):

- Ensures the identity of a remote computer
- 2.23.140.1.2.1

Issued to: *.google.com

Issued by: GTS CA 1C3

Valid from 30/08/2021 **to** 22/11/2021

Figure 12.3 – Wildcard certificate

It is possible to host multiple sites while changing only the DNS hostname for each site.

Extended validation

An extended validation certificate is mainly used by banks and other financial institutions; it is a type of certificate that carries a high level of assurance. Customers will see a visual indicator while using their web browser, to indicate the site has an extended validation certificate. *Figure 12.4* shows Microsoft Internet Explorer connected to a site with an extended validation certificate:

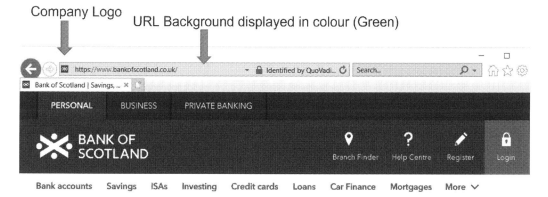

Figure 12.4 – Extended validation certificate

Sites that are enrolled for extended validation certificates benefit from additional security services and support from the CA, such as regular vulnerability scans (from the CA).

Multi-domain

If an organization needs to support multiple domains using a single certificate, then a multi-domain certificate would be appropriate. This type of certificate is different from a wildcard certificate as it allows for different subdomains, domains, and hostnames for a site. *Figure 12.5* shows the **Subject Alternative Name** (**SAN**) extension on a banking website:

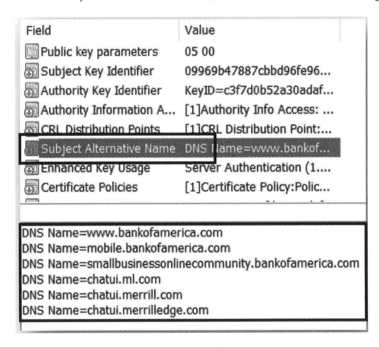

Figure 12.5 – SAN

SAN allows a high degree of flexibility when hosting multiple domain names but requires forward planning, as you will need to know all the domains that need to be added to the certificate (prior to the CSR). Multi-domain certificates will always display a primary, officially called a **Common Name** (**CN**). It is necessary to take a look at the SAN to see the other names associated with the certificate. *Figure 12.6* shows the CN extension:

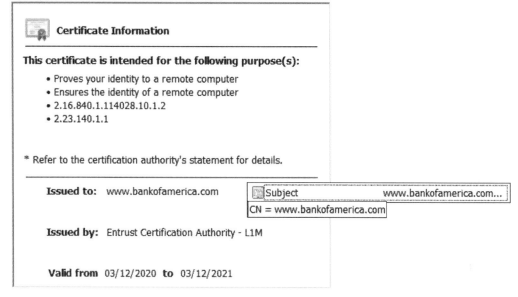

Figure 12.6 – CN extension

General-purpose

A general-purpose certificate could be issued to a user for multiple uses. A user may need to sign and encrypt email, authenticate to their Active Directory services account, and use secure VPN access. We could minimize administrative actions by providing a single certificate for the user.

Certificate usages/templates

To provide support for all the applications that are used or are being planned for, it is important to ensure the CA has the appropriate templates enabled to support user requests. Typical templates will include the following types:

- Client authentication
- Server authentication
- Digital signatures
- Code signing
- General-purpose

In *Figure 12.7*, we can see Microsoft CA templates available for client enrolment:

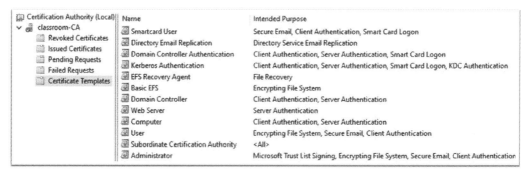

Figure 12.7 – Microsoft CA templates

Additional templates can be added from a default pool, or custom templates can be created.

It is important to support a varied set of users and entity requirements when planning for PKI. It is also important to plan for interoperability. We will now look at some of the challenges when planning for interoperability.

Understanding PKI security and interoperability

It is important to understand why a CA needs to be trusted and independently verified by third-party auditors. There are security best practices that ensure hosted e-commerce and financial sites have robust configurations. It is also important that CAs can be incorporated together using trusted certificates.

Trusted certificate providers

Commercial CAs must adhere to recognized standards; there are industry associations that govern CAs. In order to offer CA services, you must be independently audited by a recognized auditor. Microsoft recognizes the **American Institute of Certified Public Accountants (AICPA)** and the **Canadian Institute of Chartered Accountants (CICA)** as CAs that meet their stringent requirements. An annual audit must be performed to remain compliant with Microsoft policies. If a CA meets these requirements, then its root certificates can be trusted. In Europe, the recognized authority for auditing CAs is **European Telecommunications Standards Institute (ETSI)**. Many countries outside of North America and Europe have their own certification standards. India has a requirement that a commercial CA has its root public key certificate signed by the government-mandated **Root Certifying Authority of India (RCAI)** in order to be compliant. For more information, please see the following link: `https://tinyurl.com/CCA-CAAC`.

Trust models

While there are many commercial CAs who all act independently, there are also occasions where two or more CAs need to work together. Examples can be where government agencies and contracting companies need to enable trust but do not use commercial CAs. A common approach is to sign a CSR from a trusted partner.

Cross-certification certificate

When two or more CAs need to work together, they can generate a type of certificate called a cross-certification certificate. One CA will use the private key to sign a certificate containing the public key of a trusted partner. In *Figure 12.8*, we can see ACME CA signing the public key of WINGTIPS CA:

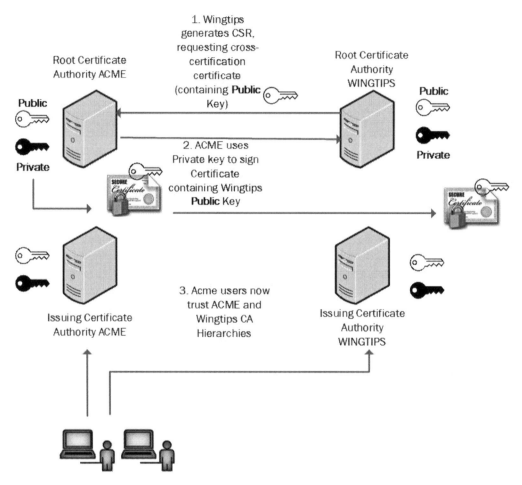

Figure 12.8 – Cross-certification certificate generation

In this example, all users who trust ACME will also trust certificates generated by the WINGTIPS CA hierarchy.

Life cycle management

It is important to recognize the risks when using long-term keys, both for the signing process and to provide encryption services. Regulatory requirements may dictate the algorithms that must be used and the key strength that must be met. In many instances, it may be a requirement that keys are changed (along with the public key certificate on an annual basis); this is referred to as **rekeying**.

Certificate pinning

HyperText Transfer Protocol (HTTP) Public Key Pinning (HPKP) headers are used to protect an organization's users or customers from **man-in-the-middle (MITM)** exploits. On the web application server, we can embed the server public key into the code so that a client application or browser will block the site/server if the certificate has changed. There are instances where the site can also pin the CA public key certificate into the code to ensure customers will only trust the site if the server certificate has been issued by a particular CA, such as GoDaddy or DigiCert.

The technology works by storing a trusted certificate value when first connecting to an application; there is a maximum age field that can be set by the application provider. The maximum age value could be anything from a few hours to several months. This is a very effective way to ensure attackers cannot create lookalike farming sites using another certificate with the same CN field.

When using this approach, you may also need to plan for an event where your server certificate may be revoked and replaced with a new one. If the HPKP is based upon the issuing CA public key certificate, then there will not be a problem. But if the public key from the web server is embedded in the code and subsequently revoked, your clients will not be able to access the web application server (until the maximum age field is reached).

In many cases, the public key is embedded into the mobile application when it is downloaded from the app store; this means when keys need to be changed, the app will need to be updated.

Certificate stapling

Stapling allows a trusted web application server to begin a secure session with a client by including both the server certificate and revocation status of the certificate. This is accomplished by sending requests to the CA OCSP service for the current status of the application server's digital certificate. This will speed up the process for the end user. *Figure 12.9* shows the certificate stapling process:

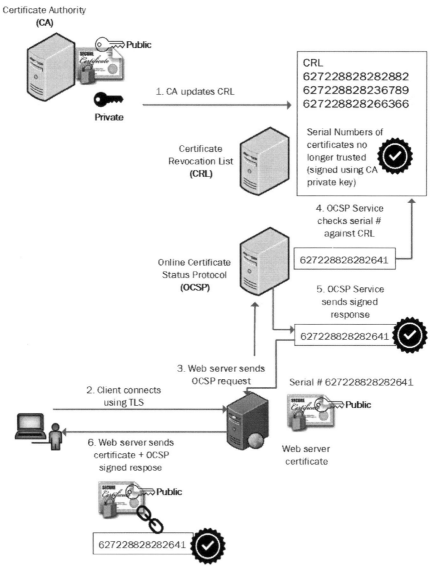

Figure 12.9 – Certificate stapling

Certificate stapling allows the client to trust the server certificate, without the need to independently contact the CA for the up-to-date CRL.

CSRs

A CSR will include the details for the creation of a certificate. Certain pieces of information will be required, along with the requester's public key. In *Figure 12.10*, we can see a typical template that must be completed to generate the CSR:

Request Certificate

 Distinguished Name Properties

Specify the required information for the certificate. State/province and City/locality must be specified as official names and they cannot contain abbreviations.

Common name:	www.classroom.local
Organization:	Digital Classrooms
Organizational unit:	Commercial
City/locality	Carlisle
State/province:	Cumbria
Country/region:	GB

Figure 12.10 – CSR template

When the request is generated, it creates a file; this is stored in **Privacy Enhanced Mail (PEM)** format and encoded using **Base64** characters. *Figure 12.11* shows a CSR file:

```
-----BEGIN NEW CERTIFICATE REQUEST-----
MIIEhDCCA2wCAQAwgYIxCzAJBgNVBAYTAkdCMRAwDgYDVQQIDAdDdW1icmlhMREw
DwYDVQQHDAhDYXJsaXNsZTEbMBkGA1UECgwSRGlnaXRhbCBDbGFzc3Jvb21zMRMw
EQYDVQQLDApDb21tZXJjaWFsMRwwGgYDVQQDDBN3d3cuY2xhc3Nyb29tLmxvY2Fs
MIIBIjANBgkqhkiG9w0BAQEFAAOCAQ8AMIIBCgKCAQEA7GdXkpYp8ofm85OFzywB
mqqJDM6v+GqIZ4YCZ+xUgC17Tseqi7upg877S6h0fggHTfXA7OkN6Nelt2p1sIr5
0r4L2ssfX0/1SQZ3pagwPAow1/sFBtW8LQEh4R1lmlt88TjS6oHKb/ia/v2B3uTA
1W8z9S2xyu9fWp5b94wARU+2Ge5dTJzPj6iqTyV/kihftJtDwVRnfZLg4f257In/
+Rq12dJe+T/2Yv8q/XfVEnDls7M6HuOBbyKFSPXBipOW7xS6vvm9G6miUpTaG31A
rrBfHu4dDjtAsXu/tGQwAhTaVQFg7uoSrvCAcnVftfyCXAAnaQrnZ9qc08lo+pxg
zQIDAQABoIIBujAcBgorBgEEAYI3DQIDMQ4WDDEwLjAuMTQzOTTMuMjBUBgkrBgEE
AYI3FRQxRzBFAgEFDBpXSU4y MDE2LURRDLmNsYXNzcm9vbS5sb2NhbbAwXY2xhc3Ny
b29tXGFkbWluaXN0cmF0b3IMC0luZXRNZ3IuZXhlMHIGCisGAQQBgjcNAgIxZDBi
AgEBHloATQBpAGMAcgBvAHMAbwBmAHQAIABSAFMAQQAgAFMAQWBoAGEBgBuAGUA
bAAgAEMAcgB5AHAAdABvAGcAcgBhAHAAaABpAGMAIABQAHIAbwB2AGkAZABlAHID
AQAwgc8GCSqGSIb3DQEJDjGBwTCBvjAOBgNVHQ8BAf8EBAMCBPAwEwYDVR0lBAww
CgYIKwYBBQUHAwEweAYJKoZIhvcNAQkPBGswaTAOBggqhkiG9w0DAgICAIAwDgYI
KoZIhvcNAwQCAgCAMAsGCWCGSAFlAwQBKjALBglghkgBZQMEAS0wCwYJYIZIAWUD
BAECMAsGCWCGSAFlAwQBBTAHBgUrDgMCBzAKBggqhkiG9w0DBzAdBgNVHQ4EFgQU
M2RG7j2BOT7X/wH0dX+UF0oI164wDQYJKoZIhvcNAQEFBQADggEBAGVl3PV6v7C+
wIM0I6u7kJVNFzXWFGOIytTw3aAWIjJKRzwmjZNlaejDtvz89rNHQS/3ETmDN439
7/MPnfqYLLe4CWDdgJiQrOllUN3Dww9JTbHUVjHxR4eKtHNAYy42xTnAitdenv06
WpxNwxLdny1QWPOBWiqgItkjzrqldfrCl1J2+eQ5Q3hFoXh8j4KmqftrZlJt2kx7
XMWRE5Fow9YyVgexOZzxAaeqVkJ9oMMftDvHHbrsdJC0NWLsa1Rz9WNoSFg6PhTy
xTYoP/H6S7ZXJfwSeUBC4rWdZWdKfbd9lwmXreQSgqDt3tJ5KIybtCMDl6RVLhJa
zg4HofIxWcA=
-----END NEW CERTIFICATE REQUEST-----
```

Figure 12.11 – CSR Base64 encoding

Once the CSR is approved, it can be forwarded to the CA and a digital certificate (containing the requester's public key) will be created and signed using the CA private key.

It is important to choose the correct certificate template when generating a CSR. If a certificate is allocated for a specific use, then this will be evident in the **Enhanced Key Usage** extension. See *Figure 12.12* for an example of this extension:

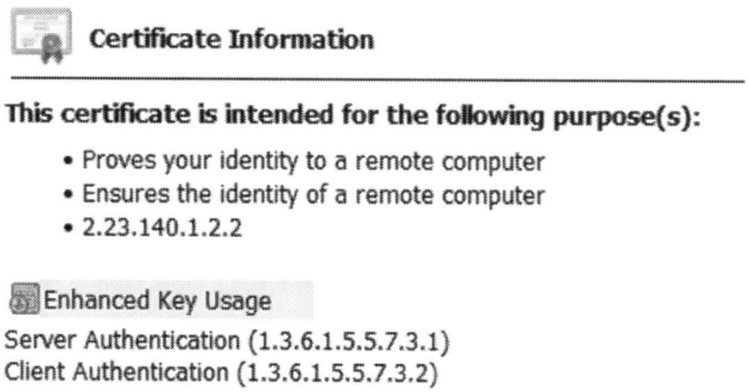

 Certificate Information

This certificate is intended for the following purpose(s):

- Proves your identity to a remote computer
- Ensures the identity of a remote computer
- 2.23.140.1.2.2

Enhanced Key Usage
Server Authentication (1.3.6.1.5.5.7.3.1)
Client Authentication (1.3.6.1.5.5.7.3.2)

Figure 12.12 – Enhanced Key Usage extension

If the certificate is presented for a different purpose, then the client will reject the certificate.

Common PKI use cases

Certificates are an important component within an enterprise; they are necessary to support everyday business processes. Here are some examples:

- Web services

- Email (**Transport Layer Security (TLS)** and **Secure/Multipurpose Internet Mail Extensions (S/MIME)**)

- Code signing

- Federation—trust models

- VPN

- Client authentication (smartcards)

- Enterprise and security automation/orchestration

In some cases, during the certificate enrolment process, there may be a requirement to capture a copy of the private key. This is not a default setting but may be required for certain types of certificate requests. Government agencies may have a policy of retaining a user's private key so that data can be recovered in the event of the loss or corruption of the original private key. It may also be a legal requirement in some countries.

Key escrow

Key escrow enables a CA to store copies of private keys for entities that have generated a CSR. Escrow is an agreement where something of value is stored securely and can only be released under strict conditions, already specified. A real-world example is when conveyancers handle the sale of a property. The conveyancers will have an escrow bank account that is separate from their own regular bank account. When contracts are signed and the buyer releases the payment, the money goes into the escrow account and is used to pay the seller. If your private key is destroyed along with a **Common Access Card** (**CAC**) or smartcard, then key escrow allows an organization to release a copy of the private key to the account holder. Key escrow requires strict security management to ensure private keys are only released in specific agreed-upon circumstances.

Troubleshooting issues with cryptographic implementations

In an enterprise-supporting PKI implementation, we can expect to see issues where there are compatibility, configurational, and operational problems that cause communication to be disrupted or executed insecurely. It is important to recognize where these problems could occur and look to mitigate them through effective policies and procedures.

Key rotation

It is important to recognize the benefits of key rotation to ensure data confidentiality is maintained. Keys can be rotated automatically or manually, based upon the organization's policies, or may be dictated by regulatory compliance. If a key is compromised, then it should be revoked immediately. The **Payment Card Industry Data Security Standard** (**PCI DSS**) requires that keys are rotated on a regular basis, based upon the number of records or transactions that have been encrypted. There are other considerations that an organization should have, including staff turnover, the strength of current encryption keys, and the value of the data. The **National Institute of Science and Technology** (**NIST**) offers guidance on suitable key rotation timelines. This guidance is documented in *NIST Special Publication (SP) 800-57 Part 1 Revision 5*, found at the following link: `https://tinyurl.com/800-57REV5`.

Mismatched keys

When considering key rotation, it is important to document all dependencies (software modules and hardware). For example, if the public key is hardcoded into the software of hardware devices and a key is rotated on a critical dependent module, then a key mismatch may occur. Documented policies and procedures should be implemented to avoid this situation.

Improper key handling

It is important to have robust policies and procedures relating to the handling of encryption keys. Specific administrators should be assigned to the roles of key generation and assignment. Where there is a possibility of fraudulent activity, then **separation of duties (SoD)** should be considered. NIST recommends a number of measures designed to improve the security of key handling, including limiting the amount of time that a private/secret key is in plaintext form, restricting the potential for personal to view plaintext keys, and storing keys as secure containers (there are more recommendations).

Embedded keys

It is possible for vendors to use embedded keys when there is a need to ship computer systems or other hardware devices with default secure configurations. An example could be Windows **operating systems (OSes)** configured for a secure boot. The Microsoft public key is embedded in **Unified Extensible Firmware Interface (UEFI) firmware**. This allows for secure boot right from first use. In some instances, the embedded key may need to be updated or changed due to the intended use of the computer. If we need to install Linux on the system and benefit from a secure boot, then we would need to change the embedded key; for the Linux distribution, this would be the public key.

Exposed private keys

It is important to secure private keys, as these will allow an attacker to decrypt sensitive data. A crypto module would be a good choice for private key storage. A **hardware security module (HSM)** is a dedicated device used to secure private keys. An HSM can be an appliance that can be secured in the data center where sensitive keys will be required for secure transactions. (Private keys should not be stored directly in the filesystem of an information system.) Where there is a business need or compliance requirements, then private keys can be stored in escrow.

Crypto shredding

Where there is a need to render confidential or sensitive data unreadable, then crypto shredding may be a good choice. This would entail encrypting the data at rest with specific encryption keys. The key used to encrypt the data could then be deleted, therefore shredding the sensitive data. This could be useful when there is no physical access to the storage device, such as when data is stored by a third-party cloud provider. Once the key has been shredded, then access to the data is not going to be possible. In the same way as physically shredding a hard drive, this is used to render the data unrecoverable. Crypto shredding is a technique that is used on Apple iPhones; when the pin number is entered incorrectly 10 times, the **Advanced Encryption Standard** (**AES**) encryption key is erased (rendering the device storage inaccessible).

Cryptographic obfuscation

Modern encryption ciphers deploy complex mathematical procedures in order to protect the keys used within a cipher. Multiple levels of confusion and diffusion are designed to make the task of a crypto-analyst very difficult. Regulatory bodies are constantly requiring additional security protocols and existing ciphers to use longer encryption keys and more complex cipher block modes. With these requirements, it is not an easy task to reverse a cipher in the event that the plaintext needs to be accessed without the encryption key.

Compromised keys

Once a key is compromised, then it should be taken out of circulation and published to the CRL. It is important this is done in a timely fashion. Depending on the value of the data and potential exposure, this may need to be performed immediately, or certainly within a few hours. Examples of compromised keys may include stolen private keys.

Summary

In this chapter, we have learned about the importance of PKI, we have taken a look at a typical PKI hierarchy. We have been able to understand the roles played by CAs and **registration authorities** (**RAs**).

We have taken a look at certificate types, including wildcard certificates, extended validation, multi-domain, and general-purpose certificates. We have gained an understanding of the common usages for certificates, including client authentication, server authentication (application servers), digital signatures, and code signing. We have taken a look at important extensions used when publishing certificates, including CN and SAN.

We have taken a look at the requirements needed to become a trusted CA, how providers are audited, and what is required to maintain trusted status.

We have looked at common trust models used when CAs need to work together and have understood the importance of the cross-certification trust model.

We have understood why is important to address certificate life cycle management, including the rekeying of credentials.

In order to mitigate common methods of attack (including MITM), we have seen how certificate pinning can be used to safeguard an organization hosting web application servers.

We have gained an understanding of the requirements to generate a CSR, and the formats and templates that are used during the process.

During this chapter, we have taken a look at the main differences between the OCSP and CRL. We have also examined how certificate stapling can speed up the secure handshaking process for a TLS connection.

We have looked at issues where there are compatibility, configuration, and operational problems that cause communication to be disrupted.

This information will be useful in the next chapter when we take a look at governance, risk, and compliance.

Questions

1. ACME needs to request a new website certificate. Where will they send the request (in the first instance)?

    A.   Root CA

    B.   Subordinate/intermediate CA

    C.   RA

    D.   CRL

2. Software engineers are developing a new **customer relationship management (CRM)** tool. They need to ensure customers will be able to verify the code is trustworthy. What type of certificate will they request?

    A.   Client authentication

    B.   Server authentication

    C.   Digital signatures

    D.   Code signing

3. Web developers have created a new customer portal for online banking. They need to ensure their corporate customers are satisfied with the security provisions when connecting to the portal. Which certificate type should they request for the portal?

    A. Wildcard certificate

    B. Extended validation

    C. Multi-domain

    D. General-purpose

4. A large e-commerce provider needs to minimize administration by allocating a single certificate to multiple sites. The sites will be country-specific, with different domain names. What would be the best choice of certificate to deliver this requirement?

    A. Wildcard certificate

    B. Extended validation

    C. General-purpose

    D. SAN

5. A multinational airline has a customer-booking portal. They need to minimize administration by allocating a single certificate to multiple sites. The sites will provide support for booking, queries, and check-in. The company-registered domain name (`WingTip.com`) will be used in each case. What would be the best choice of certificate to deliver this requirement?

    A. Wildcard certificate

    B. Extended validation

    C. General-purpose

    D. SAN

6. Wingtip Aerospace needs to ensure that certificates can be trusted by government agencies as part of an ongoing collaboration project. What allows the Wingtip Aerospace certificates to be trusted by government employees?

    A. Cross-certification

    B. Chaining

    C. Wildcard certificate

    D. Extended validation

7. Which key is embedded in an X.509.v3 digital certificate?

    A. Public

    B. Private

    C. Digital signature

    D. Symmetric

8. A **chief information security officer** (**CISO**) for a large financial company is concerned that criminals may create certificates with the same CN as the company, leading to fraudulent activity. What would best protect against this threat?

    A. Wildcard certificate

    B. Extended validation

    C. Certificate pinning

    D. Certificate stapling

9. A large online retailer would like the customer web browsing experience to be low latency, with a speedy secure handshake and verification of the website certificate. What would best meet this requirement?

    A. Extended validation

    B. Certificate pinning

    C. Certificate stapling

    D. CSR

10. A user discovers that a colleague has accessed their secure password key and may have made a copy of the private key (stored on the device). What action should security professionals take to mitigate the threat of a key compromise?

    A. Publish the public key on the CRL

    B. Delete the public and private keys

    C. Interview the work colleague

    D. Implement disciplinary proceedings against the colleague

11. Which HTTP extension will ensure that all connections to the bank's e-commerce site will always also be encrypted using the assigned X.509 certificate?

    A.   HTTP X-Frame headers

    B.   HTTP Strict Transport Security (HSTS)

    C.   HTTP Secure (HTTPS) Secure Sockets Layer (SSL) 3.0 Cipher Block Chaining (CBC)

    D.   Extended validation

12. When a public key is bundled within the UEFI firmware on a new Windows laptop, what is this termed as?

    A.   Exposed private keys

    B.   Crypto shredding

    C.   Improper key handling

    D.   Embedded keys

13. A cybercriminal has stolen the smartphone of the **chief executive officer (CEO)** from ACME bank. They have attempted to guess the **personal identification number (PIN)** code several times, eventually locking the device. After mounting the storage in a lab environment, it is not possible to access the stored data. What has likely prevented a data breach?

    A.   Embedded keys

    B.   Exposed private keys

    C.   Crypto shredding

    D.   Improper key handling

14. Several employees are required to bring their laptops into the office in order to obtain new encryption keys, due to a suspected breach within the department. What is taking place?

    A.   Rekeying

    B.   Crypto shredding

    C.   Certificate pinning

    D.   Cryptographic obfuscation

15. When an engineer connects to a switch using a **Secure Shell** (**SSH**) connection, there is a request to download and trust a new public key certificate. There was no such request when connecting from the same computer the previous day. What is the likely cause of this request?

    A.   Compromised keys

    B.   Exposed private keys

    C.   Extended validation

    D.   Key rotation

Answers

1. C
2. D
3. B
4. D
5. A
6. A
7. A
8. C
9. C
10. A
11. B
12. D
13. C
14. A
15. D

Section 4: Governance, Risk, and Compliance

In this section, you will learn the different approaches for assessing enterprise risk, including quantitative and qualitative techniques. You will study different risk response strategies and learn why regulatory and legal considerations are important during this response. Finally, you will learn about creating effective business continuity and disaster recovery plans.

This part of the book comprises the following chapters:

- *Chapter 13, Applying Appropriate Risk Strategies*
- *Chapter 14, Compliance Frameworks, Legal Considerations and Their Organizational Impact*
- *Chapter 15, Business Continuity and Disaster Recovery Concepts*

13
Applying Appropriate Risk Strategies

Enterprise risk is a major consideration for organizations and can have a significant impact on them. Risks must be understood at a strategic level to ensure long-term goals are achieved and must also be addressed for more short-term or tactical business goals. An enterprise should employ security professionals who have expertise in conducting appropriate risk assessments or engage qualified assessors to assist the enterprise. Once risks are identified, the business must have a strategy for responding to risks; these responses may be dictated by regulatory compliance or business drivers. Risk is a constant threat to a business and must be managed on a continuous cycle. In order to understand if we have deployed effective controls, we need to have monitoring and reporting in place to ensure we are operating within the enterprise's targets, for risk tolerance.

A strong security posture will provide a strong foundation for managing risk within the enterprise. This can be achieved with cybersecurity policies and practices, in order to ensure day-to-day operations are handled securely.

Supply chains add additional complexity to an enterprise's overall security footprint; lack of visibility of who is handling enterprise data or processing enterprise data can add to risk. Vendor management and assessments must be addressed by risk management teams. In this chapter, we will learn about the following topics:

- Understanding risk assessments
- Implementing risk-handling techniques
- Understanding the risk management life cycle
- Understanding risk tracking
- Managing risk with policies and security practices
- Explaining the importance of managing and mitigating vendor risk

Understanding risk assessments

When assessing risk, there are typically two approaches; one approach involves qualitative techniques. The metrics used within this approach will include likelihood and impact and may include other metrics such as speed of onset. This is considered a basic form of risk assessment and will include background knowledge from the assessor. It is often considered a subjective method, meaning two different risk assessors may not agree exactly when delivering a qualitative risk assessment. A common approach to risk management is to break the process down into steps or phases. *Figure 13.1* shows a five-step approach:

Figure 13.1 – Risk management steps

To understand risk, we must be able to quantify a level of risk as a measurement. In all cases, we will have assets that must be protected, so we then need to calculate the level of risk using likelihood and impact.

One of the accepted approaches to risk assessments is to use a qualitative method. We will now take a look at this type of assessment.

Qualitative risk assessments

In order to perform a qualitative assessment, we must adopt a step-by-step approach using likelihood versus impact. This can be a fairly simple risk matrix, as illustrated here:

Asset Customer Marketing Database			
Threat	Likelihood	Impact	Risk
Data Breach	6	9	54
Ransomware	8	9	72
Corruption	2	5	10

Figure 13.2 – Qualitative risk assessment matrix

It is important to highlight the greatest risks in order to prioritize risk responses.

There are more specific qualitative risk assessments when we are assessing risks against particular assets. When there is a requirement to host different data types on a shared information system, (often requiring different classification labels), then we can use the **Canadian Institute of Actuaries (CIA)** aggregate matrix. *Figure 13.3* shows an example of the **CIA aggregate method** of risk assessment:

POWERPLANT SCADA SYSTEM			
Data	Confidentiality	Integrity	Availability
Admin Information	LOW	LOW	LOW
Telemetry Data	MED	HIGH	MED
Scada Alerts	LOW	HIGH	HIGH
Aggregate score	MED	HIGH	HIGH

Figure 13.3 – CIA aggregate scoring

This approach is used to ensure we identify the greatest risks for the overall system and use this as a baseline to apply the controls. When calculating the aggregate values, we track the **high-water mark** in each column (this is a simplistic description where we look for the highest single value in each column). In the preceding screenshot, the impact value for admin information is **LOW**. We must, however, ensure that the potential impact for **supervisory control and data acquisition** (**SCADA**) alert data is mitigated with the appropriate control. As this is a shared information system, we may choose to implement a **high availability** (**HA**) failover solution.

One of the benefits of using a qualitative method is the fact that it can be easier to perform. However, it does not produce outputs that convey the level of risk from a financial perspective. To present risks to decision-makers, it may be necessary to use a quantitative approach in order to present monetary values. We will now take a look at this type of assessment.

Quantitative risk assessments

When risks must be conveyed to company leadership, it is important that risks are presented in a way that is easy to understand. To present risks to decision-makers, it is useful to illustrate the monetary impacts of risks. This can be achieved by using quantitative risk assessments.

Asset value (AV)

When using a quantitative approach, it is important to understand the value of an asset. This could be the purchase price of a commodity or, perhaps, the invested costs associated with creating a customer marketing database.

Exposure factor (EF)

When assessing risks, it is uncommon when an event occurs that there will be a total 100% loss in monetary terms. If my building is flooded, then it is likely the costs to repair the damage will not be equal to the total original cost of the building. This value is normally presented as a percentage figure.

Single-loss expectancy (SLE)

The amount of loss during a single event is calculated using the **Asset Value** (**AV**) x **Exposure Factor** (**EF**).

Annualized loss expectancy (ALE)

If there are multiple incidents, then we need to understand how many events will occur in a single year.

Annualized rate of occurrence (ARO)

The total loss during the year is calculated using **SLE x ARO**.

We will take a look at a simplistic example of quantitative risk.

The enterprise has a production facility, and the risk management team must assess all risks that could cause a loss to the business. The plant has a nominal value of **United States dollars** (**USD**) $10,000,000, and historical data—as well as studies in climate change (projected into the future)— is used to give a realistic likelihood value. The data calculates those floods will occur twice in 100 years, so, the ARO=.02 or 2%. It is expected that damage will result in a cost of $2,000,000 or 20% of the total value. The calculation of SLE x ARO (2,000,000 x .02) will result in a loss of $40,000, which is the ALE. *Figure 13.4* illustrates the process to determine the ALE:

Production Plant Value $10,000,000				
Threat	Exposure Factor (EF)	Single Loss Expectancy (SLE)	Annual Rate of Occurrence (ARO)	Annual Loss Expectancy (ALE)
Flood	20%	$2,000,000	2%	$40,000

Figure 13.4 – Quantitative risk assessment

As this is a low likelihood, the enterprise may choose to accept the risk. Alternatively, they may consider flood insurance if the annual cost is no greater than $40,000.

Gap analysis

A gap analysis is undertaken in order to understand where there may be missing controls. In order to perform this analysis, we must be able to assess the current state of controls and compare this to where we want the organization to be (the desired state). *Figure 13.5* shows the steps required to perform a gap analysis:

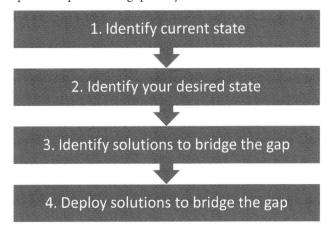

Figure 13.5 – Gap analysis

The results can be shared with senior management in order to facilitate a response.

Total cost of ownership (TCO)

When assessing solutions to control or mitigate risks, it is important to factor in all costs, not just the initial purchase price. Many solutions may require maintenance, software licensing, additional staff, or other costs that will need to be calculated over the lifetime of the solution.

Return on investment (ROI)

An ROI is an important metric as it can be used to highlight the benefits of a proposed control in monetary terms. When presenting recommendations to senior management, a positive ROI for a proposed risk mitigation solution is an effective way to get your point across.

It is normal to present an ROI as a purely monetary value, although it can also be presented as a percentage figure.

An example would be ALE based upon ransomware attacks of $100,000. So, we purchase **endpoint detection and response** (**EDR**) solution and **network-attached storage** (**NAS**) for backing up important data. The cost is $10,000 and will save the company $100,000, so the ROI is $90,000. *Figure 13.6* shows this formula used to calculate ROI:

$$\text{ROI} = \text{(reduction in risk} - \text{cost of control)}\quad = \$$$

Figure 13.6 – ROI calculation

We could use another example of phishing attacks, costing the company $100,000 annually. In this case, we invest $10,000 in EDR and security awareness training. We expect this control to be 90% effective in preventing this type of attack. So, the reduction in risk will be $90,000 - $10,000 (cost of control) = **$80,000 ROI**. If we wanted to present the benefits as a percentage figure, we would use the following calculation:

$$\text{ROI} = \frac{\text{(reduction in risk} - \text{cost of control)}}{\text{cost of control}}\quad X\,100 = \%$$

Figure 13.7 – ROI calculation displays a percentage value

In the example using the phishing attack, the ROI would be $80,000/$10,000 = **800%**.

Mean time to recovery (MTTR)

When security professionals are assessing more than one proposed solution, it is important to research the performance of the proposed solutions. MTTR could be an important metric when choosing a mitigation solution. We could use the example of the NAS to protect our data from ransomware attacks. To restore backed-up data from the NAS to a server may take 2 hours, whereas a restore from tape-based media could take 4 hours. A lower value is the desired outcome with this metric.

For systems that cannot be recovered, we would use the **mean time to fail** (**MTTF**) metric.

Mean time between failure (MTBF)

The reliability of a system can be calculated by using the MTBF metric; this is the average amount of time between each event. A higher value is desired. So, if my server is hit by crypto-malware (ransomware) on two occasions during a 24-hour period requiring data restoration from the NAS, the server will have 4 hours of downtime—20 hours' worth of uptime divided by 2 = 10 hours. So, the MTBF would be 10 hours.

Once we have identified suitable metrics to assess the risks, we can take a look at approaches to control these risks.

Implementing risk-handling techniques

Once we have identified risks, it is important to formulate a response. Approaches will differ, depending on a number of factors, including the organization's risk appetite and regulatory requirements. There are four main types of risk response, as shown in *Figure 13.8*:

Figure 13.8 – Risk response types

An enterprise should consider the following risk response approaches.

Transfer

When an organization wants to control or mitigate risk but does not have the resources (personnel or finances) to implement a response, then transference may be an appropriate strategy. If the organization cannot afford to rebuild the warehouse in case of fire, then they should consider fire insurance. If the organization does not have the personnel or infrastructure to support secure card payments, they may consider engaging a third party to process these payments.

Accept

When a risk is accepted, it is normally because the risk is considered to be acceptable to the organization based upon the risk tolerance/appetite. An example of risk acceptance would be a low likelihood event, such as earthquakes or floods in an arid location with no prior history of earthquakes or floods.

Avoid

To avoid an identified risk, the organization should cease the activity that is identified to be outside of the acceptable risk tolerance. If the risk is deemed to be extreme, such as loss of life, then the risk avoidance will be justified.

Mitigate

In many cases, the response to risk will be to mitigate risks with controls. These controls may be managerial, technical, or physical. Mitigation will not avoid risks completely but should bring the risks down to an acceptable level. Mitigation could involve an **acceptable use policy** (**AUP**) for use of mobile equipment; in addition, **mobile device management** (**MDM**) would allow the organization to encrypt company data.

As well as formulating effective risk responses, it is important to recognize risks that will have to be absorbed in some way.

Risk types

When performing risk assessments, it is important to understand that risk cannot be completely eliminated, unless we choose risk avoidance. Certain risk types will always be present.

Inherent risk

This is the risk that exists prior to any controls being applied. An example could be a financial institution that employs staff with no background checks or formal interviews. At the same time, there are no locks or barriers safeguarding the bank vault. Some organizations will have to accept a much higher level of inherent risk when choosing a particular area of operation or business sector. There is an inherent risk when considering operating in a hostile geographic region, both from an environmental and political nature.

Residual risk

This is the risk that remains after controls have been applied. There will always be some *remaining* risk, but it will be reduced to a level that falls within the corporation's risk tolerance. For banks, a solution might be background checks for employees, biometric locks, and **closed-circuit television** (**CCTV**) for the vault.

Risk exceptions

An exception is where a corporation cannot comply with regulatory requirements of corporate policy. There may be circumstances beyond the control of the organization, or perhaps a technical constraint that requires a risk exemption. A common requirement for a risk exemption may be legacy equipment or applications. Exemptions should be formally documented and signed off by the appropriate business owners or stakeholders.

Managing risk is a continuous process, so frameworks, controls, and effective management are important for an enterprise.

Understanding the risk management life cycle

The risk management process is cyclical, and risks need to be identified on an ongoing/constant basis. Business practices may change and regulatory compliance may place fresh demands on security professionals. These changing practices will mean the organization must constantly assess the security posture to ensure controls and best practices are put into place. *Figure 13.9* shows the stages of the risk management life cycle:

Figure 13.9 – Risk management life cycle

Within the risk management life cycle, an enterprise will perform the following activities:

- **Identify**—The business process, people, technology, and **intellectual property** (**IP**) are just some items that may constitute enterprise risk.

- **Assess**—In this phase, we must identify potential threats, vulnerabilities, and the level of risk that they pose to the enterprise.

- **Control**—During this phase, we identify controls that will meet the enterprise requirements, as far as the levels that they are willing to accept.

- **Review**—In this phase, we must understand that there will be changes within the industry, regulatory changes, and changes to the threat landscape. When there are changes, then the enterprise must assess these new risks. Are the controls still adequate within this changing threat landscape?

There are many frameworks adopted by organizations, and depending on the business sector or operational requirements, a particular model usually gains widespread acceptance. We'll now take a look at some risk management frameworks.

Department of Defense Risk Management Framework

The US **Department of Defense (DoD)** has adopted the DoD **Risk Management Framework (RMF)**. This is based upon a six-stage model. Each stage can be accomplished using guidance and documentation published by the **National Institute of Science and Technology (NIST)**. The exact details for this framework can be seen in *DoDI 8510.01*, available at the following link: `https://tinyurl.com/DoDRMF`.

See *Figure 13.10* for steps in the DoD RMF model:

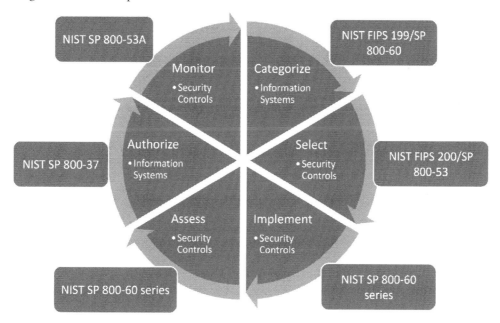

Figure 13.10 – DoD RMF

In the preceding example, we have linked each step to corresponding NIST guidance that can be used as a reference for each step.

NIST Cybersecurity Framework (CSF)

This was created in order to provide organizations with guidance on how to prevent, detect, and respond to cyberattacks. It is intended as general cybersecurity guidance for various business sectors. *Figure 13.11* shows a typical five-stage life cycle:

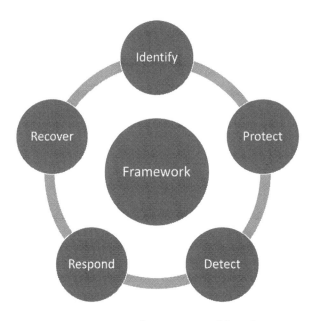

Figure 13.11 – Risk management life cycle

To understand in more detail how an enterprise can implement this framework, see the downloadable document at `https://tinyurl.com/NISTCyberSecFramework`. The stages are documented next.

Identify

In this stage, the organization must identify all assets that may be subject to cybersecurity risk. Assets may well include people, systems, data, and business operational capabilities—in other words, any element of risk. Without this identification stage, we cannot effectively focus efforts on the critical parts of the business.

Protect

Once we have identified all critical assets, we can move on to the next stage, which is to protect. We will mitigate and minimize the potential for damage arising from a cybersecurity incident.

Detect

It is important that the organization is able to detect when a cybersecurity incident is taking place. To be successful within this phase, we will need a combination of security professionals, well-trained personnel, and automated detection.

Respond

It is important to have appropriate plans in place to respond to cybersecurity incidents. We must be able to contain cybersecurity incidents while maintaining business operations. It is important to focus on response planning, communication, and tools and techniques to perform analysis, mitigation, and continuous improvements.

Recover

In the recovery phase, an enterprise should maintain plans that enable the organization to recover from significant events (**business continuity** (**BC**); incident response plans). It is important to focus on resiliency at this stage.

Understanding risk controls

There are many challenges when we consider all the potential risks that need to be managed by an enterprise. It is a fine balancing act, where we have employees, business processes, and technology that are all interwoven. *Figure 13.12* shows the relationship between people, processes, and technology:

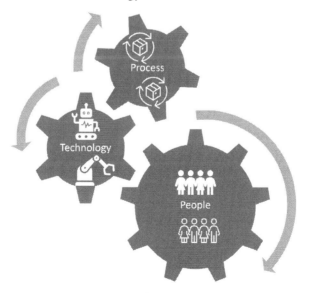

Figure 13.12 – Risk control relationship

It is important for all these elements to be considered to ensure they will work well together.

People

The controls that we choose must be effective and accepted by our staff. If they are overly complex or poorly implemented, then they may try to work around the obstruction. Imposing strict password policies on users may result in workarounds such as password reuse or writing complex passwords down.

Processes

It is important to formalize processes that will be used within the enterprise. A business process should ensure that goals are achieved in a safe and secure way. The standards and policies that the organization adopts will help to ensure that processes are performed in an efficient but secure manner. **Single points of failure** (**SPOFs**) should be identified and eliminated, and processes that have the potential for fraudulent activities should also be changed.

Technology

Technology can be useful when considering risk controls. Innovation can be an important business driver in many ways. Automation can help solve or speed up complex processing problems. **Artificial intelligence** (**AI**) and **machine learning** (**ML**) are helping to protect our information systems from ever-increasing sophisticated threats. We must, however, harness this technology to ensure it makes the right decisions; many systems still require humans in the loop.

In order to understand if the controls are effective, we must monitor risk activities. We will now look at techniques used to track risks.

Understanding risk tracking

It is important for enterprise risk to be understood and managed by the appropriate stakeholders within the organization. All risks should be documented, along with actions taken and the business owner impacted by the risk. This should be documented in a risk register. *Figure 13.13* shows a typical risk register:

Risk ref No.	Division	Department	Activity	Risk	Control Rating	Risk Level
1.0	IT	IT Helpdesk	User technical support	Understaffed dept cannot respond to user requests	Medium	Low
2.0	Sales	Online Sales	Process customer card payments	Inadequate security for payment card details, not PCI DSS compliant	Weak	High
3.0	HR	HR Staff	Health & Safety	Failure to comply with government safe working practices	Weak	High
4.0	Finance	Payroll	Salary payments	Incorrect employee payslips due to lack of training	Weak	Med

Figure 13.13 – Sample risk register

To ensure the organization is able to comply with regulatory requirements, we must have an effective method to monitor risk. By monitoring risk, we can see reports on potential risks and understand where the business may be unduly exposed.

In order to monitor and respond to risks, we must have effective metrics that allow an enterprise to track performance regarding risk.

Key performance indicators

A **key performance indicator** (**KPI**) is a measurable value, allowing the business to identify important activities in the company that contribute to a positive security posture. KPIs can be used to log the performance of activities, such as the percentage of endpoints patched to date, the number of unresolved security incidents, MTTR from a security event, or the percentage of staff having completed security awareness training.

Key risk indicators

Key risk indicators (**KRIs**) are directly related to KPIs. They are developed together in order to identify the processes that contribute to strategic objectives. If we can identify key business processes that can contribute to risk, we need a way to measure the performance, and then we can set thresholds that indicate the activity is now creating a risk to the enterprise. With proper reporting, KRIs should give early warnings to ensure the risk does not get out of hand and exceed our risk tolerance. If the business has identified a KPI, then there needs to be agreement about when this measurement quantifies a risk to the business. If we consider patching of workstations to be important, then a KPI reporting the number currently patched to be less than 90% could indicate a significant risk to the business. Ransomware is one of the biggest cybersecurity risks, targeting vulnerable unpatched systems.

Risk appetite

Risk appetite defines the amount of risk that an organization is prepared to accept when pursuing business objectives. This will differ between different business sectors and industries and will also be very dependent on company culture, competitors, objectives, and the financial wellbeing of the company. It is difficult to define an exact value when describing risk appetite. Risk appetite is usually expressed as low, medium, or high. There is usually a sweet spot that is acceptable in many industries. An energy provider with a large customer base may be content to operate gas-fired power stations. It is a well-proven technology, and if the technology is mature and relatively safe, they do not want to change the model or target new customers. Their appetite for risk is low.

Risk tolerance

This is the deviation that the enterprise will accept in relation to the risk appetite. This metric can be expressed as a number or percentage value. The energy supplier negotiates for future deliveries of gas from global suppliers. If reserves of gas, for unexpected cold weather, drop to less than 5% then we must act, as the company has set this as its risk tolerance.

Trade-off analysis

When considering enterprise risk for a large organization, there may be many risks and response strategies that should be evaluated. There may be differing views based on stakeholder priorities, and the strategic goals of the enterprise may need to be considered. If an organization decides that customer satisfaction is the main priority, they may decide to commit more resources into customer-facing support teams, taking personnel away from the sales team. This may mean fewer sales in the short term, but the long-term strategy may mean more customers.

Managing risk with policies and security practices

In order to mitigate risk, there are many approaches. Policies are one effective way to meet corporate goals. While they do not guarantee all security goals are met, they are an important layer when we implement **defense in depth** (**DiD**). Implementing more layers of security means that if one control fails, we have compensating controls.

Separation of duties (SoD)

When an employee has privileges that enable them to make high-level decisions without needing the consent of another employee, then we are missing essential checks and balances. Consider a **chief financial officer** (**CFO**) who approves new suppliers, approves supplier invoices for services, and signs paychecks. This example would allow for fraudulent activities and would be mitigated by establishing accounts receivable and accounts payable business functions.

Job rotation

When employees are in the same job role for a significant amount of time, there is the likelihood that they become complacent and burnt out. A change in job role means the enterprise has redundancy in skill sets and motivated employees. Another benefit is the fact that fraudulent activity will be less likely, as employees do not have the option to establish long-term hidden practices, and the new job holder may uncover fraudulent activities.

Mandatory vacation

In certain industries, it is common practice for the staff to be away from their job for a period of time on an annual basis. The duration may vary; in finance, the recommended mandatory vacation is 2 weeks. This period of vacation ensures that their position can be audited while they are on vacation. Another benefit is that mandatory vacation serves as a deterrent. An unauthorized activity may be difficult to hide from the company if the employee is not around to *fix* potential problems.

Least privilege

This is a good practice that involves identifying business functions and having robust account management policies to ensure the user has the privileges they need for their job. It may seem obvious, but it can be easy to overlook this basic control. It is common practice to add an employee to a role group that has privileges far in excess of the actual privileges they need. Take the example of the administrator group on a Windows server; this role allows the user to perform any administrative function on the server. A technician may need certain privileges to install software and hardware drivers; if they are added to the administrator group, they would gain privileges beyond their requirements.

Employment and termination procedures

Many risks may be overlooked without the adoption of policies for new employees and employees who leave the organization. New employees should be vetted and background checks should be performed. New employees should be onboarded, which involves mandatory security training, assignment of credentials and equipment (including sign-off), signing of an AUP, and, where applicable, **non-disclosure agreements** (**NDAs**).

When the employee leaves the company, they should be offboarded. Offboarding involves exit interviews, which will allow the organization to understand why an employee may be leaving and help with future employee retention. Exit interviews may encourage whistleblowers; the employee may be leaving because of poor attitudes and practices of their work colleagues. During offboarding, it is important to recover all company assets and disable user account credentials.

Training and awareness for users

Security awareness training is an important process, as the users are the most important asset within an organization. Users can also be considered the weakest link; over 50% of data breaches are caused by insider threats. Poorly trained users can be one of the biggest factors to consider when dealing with data breaches. Baseline security training should be implemented for all staff, with more specialized training for job roles.

Auditing requirements and frequency

It is important for the enterprise to perform regular audits to ensure the enterprise meets regulatory requirements and mitigates risks of fraudulent or malicious actions. The **Federal Information Security Management Act (FISMA)** requires government agencies and suppliers to be audited on an annual basis. To be FISMA-compliant, the following steps need to be taken:

- Maintain an information system inventory

- Categorize information systems (**Federal Information Processing Standard Publication (FIPS)** *199*)

- Maintain a system security plan

- Utilize security controls (NIST *SP800-53*)

- Conduct risk assessments (NIST *SP800-30*)

- Certification and accreditation (NIST *SP800-37*)

- Continuous monitoring

Once all the controls are in place, it is important that compliance is constantly monitored. There are vendors offering solutions to monitor, report, and alert when systems deviate from the baseline.

As an enterprise will rely on third-party vendors to perform essential business functions on its behalf, it is important that there are controls in place to assess and mitigate risks. We will now explain these techniques.

Explaining the importance of managing and mitigating vendor risk

An enterprise will need to assess risk whenever significant business changes are undertaken. There are many activities that will require an enterprise risk to be evaluated. A large enterprise may be engaged in outsourcing services to third-party vendors, often cloud-based. Maybe the enterprise will consider a merger or acquisition with a company operating within a different regulated industry.

There are many examples of attacks that have been launched, exploiting supply chains, often relying on a lack of visibility on the part of the enterprise. It is important to assess all risks that may be present when we work with third parties. When performing **vendor assessments**, we need to ensure they meet the expected levels of compliance required by the enterprise. To ensure a vendor meets the expectations of the business, we may audit the vendor or use third-party assessments. The following topics should be considered during an assessment.

Vendor lock-in

It is important to assess all available options when bringing in external providers or technology solutions. **Cloud service providers** (**CSPs**) would be a good example of potential lock-in, where the provider can impose strict financial penalties if the customer decides to switch CSP before the end of a specific contracted period. If the service is not adequate and cannot be improved due to a lack of defined **service-level agreements** (**SLAs**), then the customer may have to accept an inferior service. Technology may also be a contributor to lock-in, when bleeding-edge technology may be adopted. Later, the customer realizes the solution locks them into an incompatible database format. This could result in a solution that would be very difficult to migrate to another platform. **Vendor lock-out** could also be considered; this is when the vendor makes it difficult to work with third parties as their service may be incompatible.

Vendor viability

It is important to choose SPs that have a provable track record in delivering services that the enterprise would like to adopt. A sound financial analysis should also be conducted, as a major provider of services would present a large risk to BC if they went out of business.

Merger or acquisition risk

When an enterprise is considering a merger or acquisition, it is important to consider all risks that may transpire. Merging with a company in another geographical region may introduce practical problems such as language barriers, cultural differences, and different working practices. When considering mergers, it is important to assess the risks of co-joining networks, as there may be different regulatory requirements. When moving into a new industry or business sector, regulatory compliance or legal requirements should be considered. Data may need to be segmented and classified to ensure correct data handling is observed. When considering demergers, it is also imperative to plan for correct handling and access of business data.

Meeting client requirements

The enterprise may have very strict requirements when engaging with third-party vendors. The enterprise may have strict legal requirements that must be addressed. Major changes that may impact the customer should be agreed upon in advance using an effective **change management** process. If there are any significant changes in staffing levels that may impact the business, then there should be a clear communication channel for this event. When the vendor supplies staff directly to the business, then it is important that any staff changes are communicated to the business. Staff changes will require an **onboarding** and **offboarding** process. The client may also have very strict requirements concerning technology and the security configuration of information systems.

Support availability

It is important to agree upon levels of service; these agreements must be realistic and will be negotiated between both parties. Clear reporting metrics and agreed response times must be set. There should be a legally binding document generated; this is known as an SLA.

Geographical considerations

Data sovereignty is an important consideration for many organizations, including government agencies, critical infrastructure, and regulated industries. There is a legal requirement in some areas of operations that may require strict adherence to the storage and transmission of certain data types. It is important that the vendor service is compatible with these requirements.

Supply chain visibility

When working with third-party vendors, it is important to identify all potential risks that may be within the supply chain. Regulatory authorities have strict rules concerning data processors (**General Data Protection Regulation** (**GDPR**) is a good example). A data processor is any entity that would handle customer records or other sensitive data on behalf of the data controller (the company that is responsible for the data). A data processor can expose an enterprise to additional risks. This is often referred to as **downstream liability**.

Incident reporting requirements

If the vendor suffers an incident such as a data breach, then we must be informed in a timely manner. As the business will be the data controller, then the business is liable for subsequent actions. A large company such as a bank, may work with a vendor to offer additional services to its customers (maybe insurance). If the vendor processes the customer records/data then any breach, whilst they process the data will impact the bank.

Source code escrows

When external development teams are engaged to write applications for the business, it is important to address risks associated with the potential failure of that external supplier. If time and money are invested in the development of tools and systems, it is imperative that the source code can be retrieved by the customer. In normal circumstances, source code would remain the property of the external developer; the customer may have paid for the development of functioning code only. Future bug fixes and security patches will be difficult without future-proofing the availability of the original uncompiled source code. A third party would hold a copy of the source code, only releasing it to the customer in the event of the developers going out of business.

Ongoing vendor assessment tools

When a third-party vendor is offering services to government agencies or commercial customers, then it is important that they meet the legal and regulatory requirements of their intended customer. Common examples of third-party assessments are discussed next.

US government FEDRAMP program

Cloud providers offering services to the US government must be accredited through the **Federal Risk and Authorization Management (FedRAMP)** program before they can be given the **authority to operate (ATO)**. More information can be found at the following link: `https://www.fedramp.gov/`.

Cloud Security Alliance

To prove compliance to commercial customers, organizations can be audited to meet the **CSA Cloud Controls Matrix (CCM)**. This is a cybersecurity control framework for cloud computing, covering 197 measured controls. Vendors who meet these standards can offer their services through the **Cloud Security Alliance (CSA)**. More information can be found at the following links:

- `https://tinyurl.com/cloudCSA`
- `https://tinyurl.com/cloudccmatrix`

International Organization for Standardization

There are various security standards defined by **International Organization for Standardization (ISO)**. Standards of most interest to vendors looking to assure clients of their adherence to security would include the ones detailed next.

ISO/IEC 27000:2018

This is a series of standards published by both ISO and the **International Electrotechnical Commission (IEC)**. The standard is broad in scope, covering the main security controls for information management systems. It is a framework intended to secure IP, customer records, third-party information, employee details, and financial information.

ISO/IEC 27001:2013

This standard focuses on information security; it allows an organization to adopt a framework and prove to its customers that it has a strong security posture. Third-party assessments will ensure that an organization has adopted all the necessary controls. The standard focuses on the confidentiality, integrity, and availability of information systems. *ISO/IEC 27001* is a certifiable standard, meaning the organization and staff can be certified.

ISO/IEC 27002:2013

This standard covers all the key controls that should be included to ensure secure operations when hosting information systems. This standard is for guidance only and does not allow an organization to be accredited or certified. It allows an organization to follow guidelines, leading to the adoption of *27001* compliance.

More information can be found at the following link: `https://tinyurl.com/27000iso`.

Technical testing

It is important that the vendor provides the necessary technology to fulfill the customers' requirements. The vendor may be a manufacturing subcontractor where **quality assurance (QA)** is of the utmost importance, requiring regular on-site inspections.

Network segmentation

It is a common requirement that networks be segregated in order for the business to be compliant with regulatory bodies. Therefore, the vendor should also follow these requirements. When considering **operational technology (OT)**, **industrial control systems (ICS)**, and **SCADA**, then these types of networks should not be connected to the same network as the business users. Segmentation for some sectors may require airgaps, while in other situations **virtual local area networks (VLANs)** should be adequate.

Transmission control

When data must be sent between the customer and the vendor, all efforts must be made to ensure confidentiality is maintained. Confidentiality is also important where the vendor will act on behalf of the customer and exchange data with outside entities. The vendor may be providing monitoring and support for the customer's SCADA network. In this case. they should use **Internet Protocol security** (**IPsec**) tunnels and consider the deployments of jump servers (for jump servers, see *Chapter 1, Designing a Secure Network Architecture*).

Shared credentials

The use of shared credentials should be avoided, as it is difficult to have an effective audit trail if we do not have individual accounts. Default credentials, such as the administrator account on Windows or the root account in Linux, allow a user to obtain all privileges for a system. It is standard practice to assign a user privilege by adding them to a role group; then, we can have a proper audit trail.

Summary

In this chapter, we have been able to understand that enterprise risk is a major consideration for an organization and will have a significant impact on the organization. We have gained an understanding that an enterprise should employ security professionals who have expertise in conducting appropriate risk assessments or engage qualified assessors to assist the enterprise. We have taken a look at strategies for responding to risks.

We were able to understand why we should deploy effective controls, and the need to have monitoring and reporting. We were able to understand why an enterprise must have targets, for risk tolerance.

Supply chains add additional complexity to an enterprise. We have addressed the need for visibility of who is handling enterprise data or processing enterprise data.

An understanding of vendor management and assessments is a key takeaway in this chapter, as well as the importance of risk management teams.

We have gained an understanding of appropriate risk assessment methods, and we have been able to implement risk-handling techniques.

We have gained an understanding of the risk management life cycle and now understand risk tracking.

During the chapter, we have gained knowledge of how to manage risk with policy and security practices and managing and mitigating vendor risk.

These skills will be useful in the next chapter, where we look at regulatory compliance and legal compliance for enterprise activities. We will also take a look at managing enterprise risks through BC planning.

Questions

Answer the following questions to test your knowledge of this chapter:

1. What type of risk assessment would use likelihood and impact to produce a numerical risk rating?

    A.   Qualitative assessment

    B.   Gap assessment

    C.   Quantitative risk assessment

    D.   Impact assessment

2. What type of risk assessment would use metrics including asset value, monetary loss during an event, and a value that could be expected to be lost during the course of a year?

    A.   Qualitative assessment

    B.   Gap assessment

    C.   Quantitative risk assessment

    D.   Impact assessment

3. What is the metric that is used to calculate the loss during a single event?

    A.   Efficiency factor (EF)

    B.   ALE

    C.   SLE

    D.   ARO

4. If my database is worth $100,000 and a competitor steals 10% of the records during a breach of the network and this happens twice in a year, what is the SLE?

    A. $100,000

    B. $1,000

    C. $20,000

    D. $10,000

5. If my database is worth $100,000 and a competitor steals 10% of the records during a breach of the network and this happens twice in a year, what is the ALE?

    A. $200,000

    B. $1,000

    C. $20,000

    D. $10,000

6. A company currently loses $20,000 each year due to IP breaches. A **managed security service provider** (**MSSP**) guarantees to provide 100% protection for the database over a 5-year contract at an annual cost of $15,000 per annum. What is the ROI in $?

    A. $75,000

    B. $25,000

    C. $125,000

    D. $2,500

7. If my risk management team need to understand where the business may be lacking security controls, what should they perform?

    A. Qualitative assessment

    B. Gap assessment

    C. Quantitative risk assessment

    D. Impact assessment

8. What type of risk response would purchasing cyber liability insurance be classed as?

    A. Transfer

    B. Accept

    C. Avoid

    D. Mitigate

9. What would be considered both a deterrent and useful security practice to ensure employees' job performance can be audited when they are not present?

    A. Job rotation

    B. Mandatory vacation

    C. Least privilege

    D. Auditing

10. What is the term for risk that is present within an industry, prior to any controls?

    A.   Remaining

    B.   Residual

    C.   Inherent

    D.   Acceptance

11. What is the term for risk that remains within an industry, after the deployment of security controls?

    A.   Remaining

    B.   Residual

    C.   Inherent

    D.   Acceptance

12. What is the metric that an organization can use to measure the amount of time that was taken to restore services?

    A.   MTTR

    B.   MTBF

    C.   ALE

    D.   ARO

13. What is the metric that an organization can use to measure the reliability of a service?

    A.   MTTR

    B.   MTBF

    C.   ALE

    D.   ARO

14. What type of risk response may be considered by a financial start-up company with a high-risk appetite if the potential rewards are significant and the risk is minimal?

    A.   Transfer

    B.   Accept

    C.   Avoid

    D.   Reject

15. What is a good practice when assigning users privileges to reduce the risk of overprivileged accounts?

    A.   SoD

    B.   Job rotation

    C.   Mandatory vacation

    D.   Least privilege

16. What is an organizational policy that would make it less likely that a user will insert a **Universal Serial Bus** (**USB**) storage device that they received at an exposition?

    A.   Training and awareness

    B.   Auditing

    C.   DLP controls

    D.   AUP

17. What will an enterprise use to track activities that may lead to enterprise risk?

    A.   Key risk indicators

    B.   Risk appetite

    C.   Risk tolerance

    D.   Trade-off analysis

18. What is the term that is used to describe the situation where a vendor has proprietary technology that makes it difficult for a customer to switch vendor?

    A.   Vendor risk

    B.   Vendor lock-in

    C.   Third-party liability

    D.   Vendor management plan

19. If a customer is concerned that a third-party development team may go bust during an engagement, what can they use to ensure they will have access to the source code?

    A.   Change management

    B.   Staff turnover

    C.   Peer code review

    D.   Source code escrow

20. What is the metric that an organization should use to calculate the total loss during a year?

A.   MTTR

B.   MTBF

C.   ALE

D.   ARO

Answers

1.   A

2.   C

3.   C

4.   D

5.   C

6.   B

7.   B

8.   A

9.   B

10. C

11. B

12. A

13. B

14. B

15. D

16. A

17. A

18. B

19. D

20. D

14

Compliance Frameworks, Legal Considerations, and Their Organizational Impact

When an enterprise engages in business operations, it is important to consider many factors that are important for success. Operating within diverse industries may require compliance and the adoption of standards to satisfy legal or regulatory compliance. Regulations may be strict and, to be granted the authority to operate and to show compliance, controls and policy must be put into place. Legal compliance is often a complex area and will differ from country to country and, in some cases, may differ between states or regions within the same country. There are many relationships that an enterprise maintains in order to function.

These relationships require formal agreements, mostly legal agreements to ensure that the enterprise is protected. In this chapter, we will look at the following topics:

- Security concerns associated with integrating diverse industries
- Understanding regulations, accreditations, and standards
- Understanding legal considerations
- Application of contract and agreement types

Security concerns associated with integrating diverse industries

A challenge for large multinational organizations is understating the risks that may affect operations when supporting different business sectors and geographical locations. Country-specific laws and regulations can be complex, as can cultural differences between countries. Manufacturing, construction, oil exploration, and medical services could be some of the varied business sectors undertaken by a single business. *Figure 14.1* depicts some of the challenges faced by a business when diversifying:

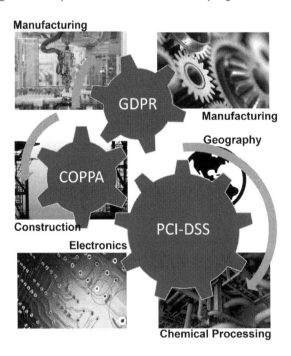

Figure 14.1 – Integrating diverse industries

In this section, we will look at some of the challenges posed by operating within diverse industries.

Data considerations

When considering the protection of data, there are many responsibilities that an enterprise must be aware of.

Data sovereignty

Data sovereignty is important when an enterprise is considering hosting data that may be subject to laws and regulations relating to the storage of certain data types. Processed digital data will need to meet the strict requirements of the country where that data has been collected. There are often strict regulations to consider if a company stores and processes data from citizens of another country. Global cloud-based providers must take care that they do not break the laws of the country when collecting or processing certain data types.

Data ownership

Ownership implies that any data created or acquired and subsequently stored by the enterprise will now need to be handled safely and securely. Data ownership means the company is accountable for the protection of the data. It is important that the company understands the value of the data and implements the controls that are required to meet legal and regulatory requirements.

Data classifications

To ensure correct data handling, data should be classified both to reflect the value to the business and to ensure that appropriate legal and regulatory controls are put in place. *Figure 14.2* shows an example of data classification for a commercial organization:

Data Classification	Description
Public data	This data can be freely used, reused, and redistributed without repercussions. Examples include press releases and marketing bulletins.
Internal-only data	Data that is accessible to internal company employees who are assigned access. Examples include business plans and internal e-mail.
Confidential data	Data that requires specific authorization and/or clearance. Examples include cardholder data and social security numbers.
Restricted data	Loss would result in a significant business impact. Examples include research data and intellectual property.

Figure 14.2 – Data classification

If data is not accurately labeled, then the data may not be secured in line with regulatory requirements.

Data retention

It is important to ensure that laws and regulatory requirements are met when considering data retention policies. Data should be labeled and stored according to the appropriate regulations, national laws, and, in some cases, local or state laws. Different data types may have different retention requirements to meet regulatory compliance. The **Sarbanes Oxley Act** of 2002 (**SOX**) requires accounts payable and receivable ledgers to be retained for 7 years, while customer purchase orders and invoices only have to be retained for 5 years.

Data types

An enterprise operating across diverse industries will likely store and handle data with different regulatory and legal requirements. In order to apply the correct controls, it is important to identify the different data types.

Health

Protected Health Information (PHI) will be subject to strict privacy rules and regulations. Hospitals, clinics, doctors, surgeries, and healthcare insurance providers will store patient records. There are strict rules for the handling of this type of data.

Financial

Financial records may include accounts receivable, accounts payable, purchase ledgers, and corporation tax records. This type of data is sensitive and should be labeled and handled with appropriate care. Data retention must be strictly adhered to as there will be strict requirements for legal and regulatory compliance.

Intellectual property (IP)

IP is data that belongs to the organization and typically has a high value as this may also include research data, design blueprints, software source code, patented ideas, and products that the organization may manufacture. An organization must have robust safeguards to ensure that it is not compromised by having this valuable asset exposed. Strict data handling and storage are required in addition to rigorous protection through patents, copyrights, and legal redress.

Personally identifiable information (PII)

PII is data that is stored electronically on behalf of employees, customers, students, or citizens within a country (there are more examples). In general, we can say that it is the data that is associated with an identifiable person. The regulatory authorities and countries may have differences in terms of what constitutes PII. When identifiable data is linked to the individual, then it is classed as PII. Obvious PII would, therefore, include the date of birth, passport number, medical records, employment records, and educational records. Organizations that control or process data must understand the implications of privacy across diverse industries, regulatory bodies, and country-specific laws.

Data removal, destruction, and sanitization

To properly manage data during its life cycle, an enterprise should have documented policies and procedures to ensure data is only retained where necessary. The less data that is stored, the less the likelihood of data leakage. Processes such as data minimization and deduplication will help to reduce the amount of data stored. The business must understand what the requirements are with regard to effective data destruction methods. ISO 27001 covers standards for data removal and destruction. There are also industry bodies that follow a code of good practice, following official standards. For printed information, approved shredders should be used, followed by burning in some cases. **Pulping** can also be effective for paper-based records. **Degaussing** magnetic media will render the storage unusable and unrecoverable. Solid-state storage should be shredded or **pulverized**. If storage is to be repurposed within the company, then the existing storage should be **cleared** of all existing data. Programs used for clearing or erasing hard disk drives include dd (Linux/Unix command), **BleachBit**, and **CCleaner** (there are many more besides). It is important to carefully research the regulations for the industry and data type as the process may require seven or more passes of writing random data to the disk.

There are recognized companies that offer accredited data disposal/destruction services. One of the recognized bodies is the **Asset Disposal and Information Security Alliance** (**ADISA**). ADISA is recognized by the UK **National Cyber Security Center** (**NCSC**). When considering data that is not physically accessible by the enterprise, such as cloud providers, then **Crypto Erase** should be considered. Crypto Erase means the encryption key that has been used to secure the data can be deleted, making the data unrecoverable.

Understanding geographic considerations

When a data controller (the business) is hosting the data, they must ensure that regulations are adhered to regarding the types of data and where the data will be stored and processed. The business must be aware of legal and regulatory requirements in terms of when the data may be stored and processed in another country. Another factor to consider is the location of the data subject, where regulatory compliance may extend beyond the borders of the data subject.

Location of data

The location of data will be important as there may be a requirement for legal jurisdiction and, for certain types of data, sovereignty laws or regulations may be applicable.

Location of the data subject

Many laws and regulations apply to data subjects (people), no matter where the data is stored or processed. With over 100 countries having specific data processing and privacy regulations or laws, this can become very complex. In the US, there are state regulations in addition to national regulations. An example of such a regulation is the **California Consumer Privacy Act** (**CCPA**), which provides citizens the right to know what personal information companies collect about them and how it is used and shared.

Location of the cloud provider

The location of the cloud provider may be significant. Government data will normally have strict requirements as regards the processing of data. If the cloud provider is offering a service such as **Software as a Service** (**SaaS**), then the location of this hosted service could be important.

In many cases, the regulatory requirements may be very complex, meaning the enterprise may consider using third-party audits or consultants to verify that the controls deployed by the business are satisfactory. We will now take a look at some of the laws and regulations.

Third-party attestation of compliance

In many cases, there is a business need for third-party attestation. Sometimes, it may also be a mandatory requirement. There is usually a greater trust in attestation provided by a third-party audit when offering a service to a customer. For example, a business may state that they follow best practices within the **ISO 27001** standard. However, if they are independently audited to ensure that they satisfy all objectives, this will be more valuable to potential customers.

Understanding regulations, accreditations, and standards

An organization needs to demonstrate to customers and partners that they have implemented standardized and recognized business practices. This makes it clear to the partner or the customer that the product or service satisfies their requirements. In many cases, a failure to implement the appropriate controls will result in a failure to attain the appropriate accreditation. If controls and standards are not maintained, the business faces the risk of being stripped of accreditation. We will take a look at some examples of regulations, accreditation, and standards.

Payment Card Industry Data Security Standard (PCI DSS)

PCI compliance is necessary if an organization intends to process debit card or credit card transactions and intends to store cardholder data. Such activities are overseen by the **Payment Card Industry Security Standards Council** (**PCI SSC**). The main reason for this council is to oversee and govern the security associated with cardholder data and minimize the potential fraudulent use of payment card data.

The council dates back to 2006 and comprises MasterCard, Visa, American Express, Discover, and JCB International. In order for an organization to be accredited by the council, it must meet key criteria as shown in *Figure 14.3*:

Figure 14.3 – PCI DSS requirements

To meet PCI DSS compliance, assessments relevant to the business must be carried out (there are many different categories of merchants). You can get more information about the PCI DSS requirements by visiting the following link: `https://www.pcisecuritystandards.org`.

General Data Protection Regulation (GDPR)

GDPR is intended to protect the personal data of **European Union** (EU) citizens stored in information systems both within and outside the EU. If an entity intends to collect and store information, it is regulated and overseen by GDPR, and the collecting entities must ensure they are compliant. GDPR has strict regulations that apply to the classification, storage, and processing of data. In *Figure 14.4*, we can see an example of the roles that are used within GDPR compliance:

Role	Description
Data Controller	The data controller is the business or organization that is accountable for GDPR compliance.
Data Processor	The processor can be the business or a third party. An example is the payroll service.
Data Protection Officer (DPO)	A DPO is responsible for overseeing the data protection approach, strategy, and its implementation. The DPO is responsible for GDPR compliance.
Supervisory Authority	A public authority in an EU country responsible for monitoring compliance with GDPR. In the U.S., it is **the Federal Trade Commission**.

Figure 14.4 – GDPR roles

GDPR protects personal data. The GDPR definition of personal data is as follows:

'Personal data' means any information relating to an identified or identifiable natural person ('data subject'); an identifiable natural person is one who can be identified, directly or indirectly, in particular by reference to an identifier such as a name, an identification number, location data, an online identifier, or to one or more factors specific to the physical, physiological, genetic, mental, economic, cultural, or social identity of that natural person.

Data controllers who are in breach of the compliance regulations can be fined €20 million or 4% of the organization's turnover (whichever is the greater). Recent examples include Google, which was fined €57 million by the **French National Data Protection Commission**. According to the commission's report, the transgression resulting in the fine was as a result of:

> *"Lack of transparency, inadequate information, and a lack of valid consent regarding ad personalization for users."*

For more information regarding GDPR, you can visit the following URL: `https://gdpr.eu/`.

International Organization for Standardization (ISO)

The **ISO** was formed in 1947 and is dedicated to the creation of standards that allow for interoperability across globally diverse industries. The ISO is independent (non-government funded) and currently comprises around 165 standards bodies. *Figure 14.5* depicts a wide range of standards that have been developed and given ISO approval:

Figure 14.5 – ISO standards examples

To operate efficiently and work with third-party entities, it is a good practice to adopt standards. If an organization can demonstrate that they are accredited or are supporting the recognized standards, then the enterprise will be more marketable.

ISO 31000 is a standard used by organizations of any size and is designed to assist in the management of risk. It is a framework that can be adopted to help a business recognize threats and allocate resources to control risks. The standard does not, however, enable an organization to become accredited. It only offers guidance. For more information about the ISO, you can visit the following link: `https://www.iso.org/home.html`.

Capability Maturity Model Integration (CMMI)

CMMI is primarily a methodology for improving the software development process and it allows a business to develop processes that decrease risks often prevalent in software and service development. It was originally developed at the **Carnegie Mellon University (CMU)** and is now administered by the **CMMI Institute** (a subsidiary of the **Information Systems Audit and Control Association**, or **ISACA**).

CMMI is important for organizations wishing to be considered for US government contracts as it often acts as a prerequisite for this type of engagement. It is not possible to gain accreditation, but instead, a company is appraised and can be awarded a maturity level rating between 1 and 5. *Figure 14.6* demonstrates the five maturity levels:

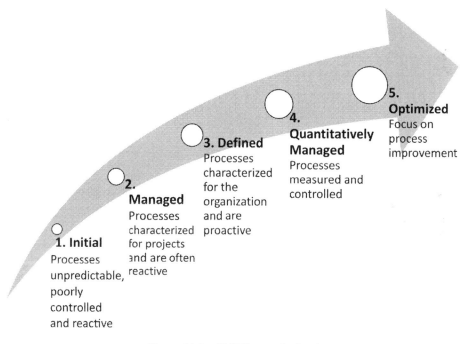

Figure 14.6 – CMMI maturity levels

The goal for the organization is to reach level 5, to ensure customers can be assured that the provider is committed to improving and maintaining standards during service and software development.

National Institute of Standards and Technology (NIST)

NIST is part of the US Department of Commerce and, hence, receives government funding. NIST dates back to 1901 and provides guidance to a diverse range of industries. See *Figure 14.7* for a sample of some of the industries that are supported by NIST guidance/publications:

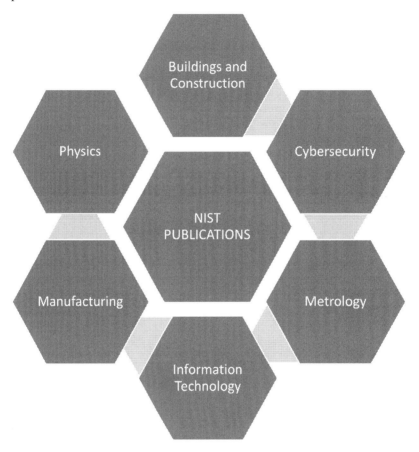

Figure 14.7 – NIST supported industries

To security professionals, the **Special Publication (SP)** series 800 will be of particular interest. SP800 covers cybersecurity publications and can be used to ensure that controls are implemented correctly. NIST publications are also important for government agencies that must adhere to **Federal Information Security Modernization Act (FISMA)** regulations. The range of publications is diverse, from deploying and managing smartcard interfaces for **Personal Identity Verification SP800-73-4** to implementing incident response planning. Incident response planning is covered in the **Computer Security Incident Handling Guide SP800-61-2**.

There are industry-specific cybersecurity publications to cover regulated industries such as healthcare, including the **HIPAA Security Rule SP800-66** (this guidance dates from 2008 and is currently being revised and updated for 2021).

Visit the following link for more details on the NIST SP800 series: `https://tinyurl.com/nist800series`.

Children's Online Privacy Protection Act (COPPA)

COPPA was enacted in the US in 1998 in an attempt to control the accumulation of PII from young persons (age 12 and under) without parental consent. Due to the proliferation of sites and content aimed at young people, this is an important consideration for online content providers and services. It applies to companies hosting content in the US and the jurisdiction also applies to children outside of the US.

There are requirements for websites to post their complete privacy policy, notify parents about the information collected, and consent must be given before any sharing of information. Courts may impose fines of up to $43,280 in civil penalties for each violation. The **Federal Trade Commission (FTC)** issued a fine of $170 million in 2019 to YouTube for COPPA violations, including tracking the viewing history of minors.

More information about the FTC and COPPA can be found by visiting the following link: `https://tinyurl.com/copparegs`.

Common Criteria (CC)

The CC are made up of members from several participating countries. 17 countries are responsible for assessing and certifying IT services and controls. 14 countries also make use of the assessments and accreditation that the CC provide. The certification for security controls and information systems falls under the **ISO/IEC15408 standard**.

Products are evaluated using an internationally agreed-upon protocol called the **Common Criteria Recognition Arrangement (CCRA)**, which ensures that devices or software are audited based upon **Protection Profiles**. A protection profile will include a criterion called **Target of Evaluation (TOE)**. An example of a protection profile is **Mobile Device Management (MDM)**, where products are assessed using multiple criteria, including support for compliance reporting, the validation of certificates, and encrypted cryptographic key storage.

Figure 14.8 shows a typical certificate of compliance awarded to a certified operating system:

National Information Assurance Partnership

Common Criteria Certificate

is awarded to

Samsung Electronics Co Ltd

for

Samsung Galaxy Devices on Android 10 - Fall

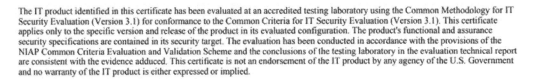

The IT product identified in this certificate has been evaluated at an accredited testing laboratory using the Common Methodology for IT Security Evaluation (Version 3.1) for conformance to the Common Criteria for IT Security Evaluation (Version 3.1). This certificate applies only to the specific version and release of the product in its evaluated configuration. The product's functional and assurance security specifications are contained in its security target. The evaluation has been conducted in accordance with the provisions of the NIAP Common Criteria Evaluation and Validation Scheme and the conclusions of the testing laboratory in the evaluation technical report are consistent with the evidence adduced. This certificate is not an endorsement of the IT product by any agency of the U.S. Government and no warranty of the IT product is either expressed or implied.

Date Issued: 2020-10-15

Validation Report Number: CCEVS-VR-VID11109-2020

CCTL: Gossamer Security Solutions

Assurance Level: PP Compliant

Protection Profile Identifier:
  PP-Module for VPN Client Version 2.1
  Protection Profile for Mobile Device Fundamentals Version 3.1
  Extended Package for Wireless LAN Client Version 1.0

Original Signed By
Director, Common Criteria Evaluation and Validation Scheme
National Information Assurance Partnership

Figure 14.8 – CC Certificate of compliance

Currently, there are over 1,500 certified products listed within the CC portal. Some examples of the categories and products can be seen in *Figure 14.9*:

Certified Products	Examples
Access Control Devices and Systems	NetIQ Access Manager, Hewlett Packard Storage Manager Software
Boundary Protection Devices and Systems	WatchGuard NGFW, SonicWall Firewall
Data Protection	Samsung Knox File Encryption, McAfee Data Loss Prevention (DLP)
Databases	Microsoft SQL Server 2019, IBM DB2
Detection Devices and Systems	Tripwire Enterprise, Trend Micro Deep Security
ICs, Smart Cards, and Smart Card-Related Devices and Systems	Samsung Microcontroller for Smart Card, NXP Secure Smart Card Controller
Key Management Systems	Fortix Security Suite, Verizon UniCERT
Mobility	MobileIron, BlackBerry Unified Endpoint Management (UEM), VMware Workspace ONE
Multi-Function Devices	HP Digital Sender, Xerox PrimeLink Copier/Printer
Network and Network-Related Devices and Systems	Cisco ASA 9.12, Dell EMC Networking SmartFabric (Storage Area Network)
Operating Systems	Red Hat Enterprise, macOS Catalina, Microsoft Windows 10
Products for Digital Signatures	Thales Luna K7 Cryptographic Module, DocuSign Signature Appliance
Trusted Computing	TPM Firmware

Figure 14.9 – CC categories and examples

To view a comprehensive list of certified products, please visit the following link:
`https://www.commoncriteriaportal.org/products/`.

Cloud Security Alliance (CSA) Security Trust Assurance and Risk (STAR)

Cloud Service Providers (**CSPs**) can showcase their products and adherence to recognized best practices by joining the CSA. Members include cloud consumers (customers), solution providers (companies that offer security or cloud services), and **SaaS** providers. The CSA also includes a large community of contributors driving forward secure cloud security and best practices in the industry. In addition to certification and accreditation for providers, there is support for personal certification for security professionals wishing to demonstrate their expertise in cloud computing. For more details on personal certification, visit the following link: `https://ccsk.cloudsecurityalliance.org/en`.

For CSPs who want to demonstrate their adherence to security standards, there are two levels for compliance. These are STAR Level 1 and Level 2.

STAR Level 1

Level 1 is a self-assessment exercise completed by the CSP. It enables the provider to document services that they offer and lets their customer know the security standards that they have implemented. The *Security Questionnaire* comprises over 263 questions. Refer to *Figure 14.10* to see examples of the controls that those members must have in place:

CCM Control ID	CCM Control Specification	CCM Control Title	CCM Domain Title
A&A-01	Establish, document, approve, communicate, apply, evaluate, and maintain, audit and assurance policies and procedures and standards. Review and update the policies and procedures at least annually.	Audit and Assurance Policy and Procedures	
A&A-02	Conduct independent audit and assurance assessments according to relevant standards at least annually.	Independent Assessments	
A&A-03	Perform independent audit and assurance assessments according to risk-based plans and policies.	Risk-Based Planning Assessment	
A&A-04	Verify compliance with all relevant standards, regulations, legal/contractual, and statutory requirements applicable to the audit.	Requirements Compliance	Audit and Assurance
A&A-05	Define and implement an audit management process to support audit planning, risk analysis, security control assessment, conclusion, remediation schedules, report generation, and a review of past reports and supporting evidence.	Audit Management Process	
A&A-06	Establish, document, approve, communicate, apply, evaluate, and maintain, a risk-based corrective action plan to remediate audit findings, and review and report remediation status to relevant stakeholders.	Remediation	

Figure 14.10 – CSA STAR Level 1 compliance

There is a separate questionnaire for CSPs who want to demonstrate their adherence to the GDPR code of conduct (this is also a self-assessment).

STAR level 2

Level 2 is assessed by a third party and allows for a more detailed audit, but, more importantly, offers the customer extra assurance due to the third-party attestation. This audit will ensure the provider meets the **ISO/IEC 27001** standards against the **Cloud Controls Matrix (CCM)**.

Regulatory compliance, legal compliance, and the adoption of industry-accepted standards are very important to an enterprise. Conformance ensures the business is able to win contracts and operate according to accepted standards. In addition, there may be very strict legal requirements required for an organization to operate.

Understanding legal considerations

One of the biggest threats to an enterprise is the risk associated with a lack of compliance with laws and regulatory authorities. Legal regulations can be complex and may need the expertise of trained legal staff knowledgeable in these matters. Litigation and fines can be a possible consequence. There may also be the risk where the regulatory authority revokes the business's **Authority to Operate** (**ATO**), certainly in areas such as nuclear power or finance. We will take a look at some important factors.

Due diligence

An organization must understand all the regulatory and legal requirements when operating within strict regulatory frameworks. Part of the responsibility is to ensure that the business takes steps to assess what mitigations and controls should be implemented to protect information systems. A simple way to remember due diligence is to think, *What are my responsibilities*? If you are storing sensitive data, you should assess all the risks associated with that activity.

Due care

Once the organization has assessed all the requirements to protect the information systems that it controls, mitigation and controls need to be implemented and maintained. When an organization has assessed all the risks, then due care would comprise the actions needed to protect the sensitive data.

Export controls

Many countries have strict laws regarding the exporting of sensitive technology, including hardware and software. It can be a criminal offense in many countries to export sensitive technologies without applying for the appropriate export licenses or ensuring that the technology is not on the government's restricted list. Obvious restricted items include military equipment or arms sales and may also include technology embedded in a mobile smartphone. For up-to-date lists of export controls concerning organizations within the US, visit the following URL: `https://www.trade.gov/us-export-controls`.

For export controls concerning the United Kingdom, visit the following link: `https://www.gov.uk/business-and-industry/export-controls`.

Legal holds

A company should be prepared to respond to an enforceable legal hold. This may be required by law enforcement or a government agency or may be obtained by a court order. Data should be preserved, failing which the company will be in contempt of the order. A legal hold will involve electronic records, paper-based records, and mobile data sources (laptops, smartphones, and external storage). It is important to suspend all normal activities, such as data retention policies (do not delete the data, even if policy dictates that it only needs to be retained for 12 months), as the legal hold will have precedence and may last for years.

E-discovery

Once the data has been *frozen*, we can begin the process of identifying relevant evidence. There needs to be a clear set of instructions on the date ranges of the required electronic documentation and the scope of the data. There needs to be agreement on the format of the data that will be provided, including the possibility that metadata may also be required.

A business must be able to respond in a timely fashion when a legal notice is served. Legal counsel will often be required for specific guidance as the law can be complex to navigate.

Application of contract and agreement types

To maintain regulatory or legal compliance, it is important to document relationships with third-party entities and, where necessary, ensure that the appropriate legal terms are agreed upon and signed off. We will now take a look at some typical documents.

Service Level Agreement (SLA)

An SLA is an important legally binding document that must be negotiated between a customer and a service provider. The terms will typically include metrics to determine the performance levels demanded by the customer and strict penalties to account for unacceptable levels of service.

Operational Level Agreement (OLA)

A service provider may have many internal dependencies that could affect the successful delivery of services to a customer. A large cloud provider may have negotiated a strict SLA (with financial penalties) to deliver a comprehensive set of information systems. If the internal storage team has a **recovery time objective** (**RTO**) of 2 hours for the **Storage Area Network** (**SAN**), in the event of an unexpected outage, but the customer has an agreement for only 30 minutes of acceptable downtime, the service provider needs to align to these expectations. An OLA will ensure all dependent internal services can support the customer (SLA). In this case, the storage team needs to look at an RTO of less than 30 minutes. OLAs are not negotiated with the external customer, they are for internal use only.

Master Service Agreement (MSA)

This type of agreement would be useful if an enterprise intends to use a third-party service provider for multiple services. It allows for an agreement between the companies where most of the terms are agreed upon in advance. Typical terms may include payment terms, dispute resolution, intellectual property ownership, and geographic operational locations.

Non-Disclosure Agreement (NDA)

Where data privacy is a requirement, it is important to have employees and service providers sign this agreement. They should be made aware of the strict terms of this agreement and the penalties that may be forthcoming if this is not followed. NDAs can be used to protect government data, intellectual property, military data, PHI, PII, and other types of sensitive data. The penalties for breaking an NDA could include civil action, resulting in significant financial penalties, while if you are working for a government agency, the outcome could be a jail term for divulging national secrets. In 2018, an NSA contractor was charged under the Espionage Act after divulging secrets about interference in the 2016 US elections. The sentence was 5 years (although this was subsequently cut to 3 years for good behavior). For more details, refer to the following URL: `https://tinyurl.com/nsawhistleblower`.

Memorandum of Understanding (MOU)

When there is a requirement for a formal process in order to define roles and responsibilities between two or more parties, a **Memorandum of Understanding** (**MOU**) may be a useful document. It is a good option when there is a requirement for something more formal than a gentleman's agreement or a handshake. It is, however, not a legal document and will not offer the same protection as a document written by lawyers.

Interconnection Security Agreement (ISA)

An ISA can be used when we need to define strict procedures when operating an interconnection between two or more parties. The agreement may stipulate a timeline for the information exchange to be supported, security requirements, data types that will be exchanged, and the actual sites that will be part of the data interchange. It can be useful when organizations need to collaborate on projects, share training data, or define requirements for the secure storage of data. There is some useful guidance on this type of agreement covered in **NIST SP800-47**. You can visit the following link for more information: `https://tinyurl.com/nist80047`.

Privacy-Level Agreement (PLA)

Cloud providers must be able to assure customers that their data will be protected when hosted by the **CSP**. A PLA ensures that the customer data will be protected by the service provider and agreed-upon steps are in place if data breaches or any adverse action were to occur. For example, CSPs who are aligned with the **CSA** can complete an assessment and prove to customers that they are compliant with the EU GDPR. More information on the CSA code of conduct can be found at the following link: `https://tinyurl.com/csagdprcompliance`.

It is very important to ensure that the correct business agreements are identified and put in place to protect the enterprise.

Summary

In this chapter, we have looked at the challenges of operating within diverse industries. We tried to understand the requirements for compliance, and the importance of standards to meet in terms of legal or regulatory compliance. We have seen where strict compliance is necessary for a business to attain the authority to operate.

We have understood why controls and policy must be put in place – to show compliance. In the chapter, we also looked at the complexities of legal compliance and understood how it differs from one country to another. We have looked at formalizing agreements to ensure the enterprise is protected.

We will find the knowledge gained to be useful in the next chapter, where we will take a look at **Business Continuity Planning** (**BCP**), **Disaster Recovery Planning** (**DRP**), high availability, incident response planning, and the use of the cloud for business continuity.

Questions

Here are a few questions to test your understanding of the chapter:

1. What must a government agency consider when planning to store sensitive data with a global **CSP**?

    A. Data sovereignty

    B. Data ownership

    C. Data classification

    D. Data retention

2. Who is accountable for the storage and protection of customer data? They must ensure that they implement controls to meet legal and regulatory requirements.

    A. Data controller

    B. Data protection officer

    C. Data processor

    D. Supervisory authority

3. A CISO is assessing regulatory requirements for hospital employees and patient data (within Europe). What type of information will need to be protected and which regulation will be most important? (Choose two)

    A. GDPR

    B. Financial records

    C. Intellectual property

    D. PII

    E. COPPA

4. A multinational company wants the assurance that data will not be accessible when their contract with a **CSP** expires. What technology may be applicable?

    A. Crypto Erase

    B. Pulping

    C. Shredding

    D. Degaussing

5. A global automobile manufacturer must ensure that its products are compatible with its worldwide customer base. What regulations or standards will be most important?

    A. Export control regulations

    B. General Data Protection Regulation (GDPR)

    C. International Organization for Standardization (ISO)

    D. National Institute of Standards and Technology (NIST)

6. A SaaS provider has several products designed to attract a young audience, while revenue is generated by advertising and subscriptions within the US. What regulations will be the most important for the provider?

    A. Capability Maturity Model Integration (CMMI)

    B. National Institute of Standards and Technology (NIST)

    C. Children's Online Privacy Protection Act (COPPA)

    D. Cloud Security Alliance (CSA) Security Trust Assurance and Risk (STAR)

7. A SaaS provider has several commercial products to assist with an automobile manufacturer. They must assure potential customers that the cloud provider is secure and trustworthy. What accreditation can the SaaS provider attain to appeal to its customers?

    A. International Organization for Standardization (ISO)

    B. Capability Maturity Model Integration (CMMI)

    C. National Institute of Standards and Technology (NIST)

    D. Cloud Security Alliance (CSA) Security Trust Assurance and Risk (STAR)

8. A software development company is trying to win a contract for a US. Federal Government agency. They must assure the customer that they have a robust security framework for the delivery of software and services. What is the most relevant?

    A. International Organization for Standardization (ISO)

    B. Capability Maturity Model Integration (CMMI)

    C. National Institute of Standards and Technology (NIST)

    D. Cloud Security Alliance (CSA) Security Trust Assurance and Risk (STAR)

9. What compliance will be most important to a US-based e-commerce retailer with respect to the storage of cardholder data and electronic transactions?

    A. Payment Card Industry Data Security Standard (PCI DSS)

    B. International Organization for Standardization (ISO)

    C. Interconnection security agreement (ISA)

    D. Non-disclosure agreement (NDA)

10. A smartcard manufacturer needs to sell products to a global market. They need to show compliance using internationally agreed-upon protocols. What would be a useful accreditation or assurance that their products have been evaluated and will meet the security requirements of their customers?

    A. International Organization for Standardization (ISO)

    B. Capability Maturity Model Integration (CMMI)

    C. National Institute of Standards and Technology (NIST)

    D. Common Criteria (CC)

11. What regulatory body is intended to protect the personal data of **EU** citizens?

    A. General Data Protection Regulation (GDPR)

    B. National Institute of Standards and Technology (NIST)

    C. International Organization for Standardization (ISO)

    D. Common Criteria (CC)

12. A US smartcard manufacturer needs to sell its products in a global market. They need to ensure that the technology is not sold to countries or governments hostile to the US. What guidance or regulations should they consult?

    A. Due care

    B. Export controls

    C. Legal holds

    D. E-discovery

13. A government department has data privacy requirements, and they need to have employees and service providers sign this agreement. They should be made aware of the strict terms of this agreement and the penalties that may be forthcoming. What type of agreement will be important?

    A.   Service level agreement (SLA)

    B.   Master service agreement (MSA)

    C.   Non-disclosure agreement (NDA)

    D.   Memorandum of understanding (MOU)

14. A large multinational company intends to purchase multiple products on a rolling contract from a **CSP**. They need to document payment terms, dispute resolution, intellectual property ownership, and geographic operational locations within the scope of the contract. What type of contract would be most suitable?

    A.   Service level agreement (SLA)

    B.   Master service agreement (MSA)

    C.   Memorandum of understanding (MOU)

    D.   Operational-level agreement (OLA)

15. Wingtips Corporation would like to build resiliency into its network connections. They are working with an **Internet Service Provider** (**ISP**) that proposes a highly available MPLS solution. To ensure the vendor is able to deliver the service with 99.999% uptime, what documentation will be important?

    A.   Service level agreement (SLA)

    B.   Memorandum of understanding (MOU)

    C.   Interconnection security agreement (ISA)

    D.   Operational level agreement (OLA)

16. What agreement should be used when business partners need to share data? This agreement may stipulate a timeline for the information exchange to be supported, security requirements, data types that will be exchanged, and the actual sites that will be part of the data interchange.

    A.   Service level agreement (SLA)

    B.   Master service agreement (MSA)

C. Memorandum of understanding (MOU)

D. Interconnection security agreement (ISA)

17. What agreement ensures that the customer data will be protected by the service provider and that agreed-upon steps are in place if data breaches or any adverse action were to occur?

A. Non-disclosure agreement (NDA)

B. Memorandum of understanding (MOU)

C. Interconnection security agreement (ISA)

D. Operational level agreement (OLA)

E. Privacy level agreement (PLA)

18. An investigation is to be performed on an employee suspected of stealing company **Intellectual Property** (**IP**). What must be done first to ensure that the data is not deleted?

A. Due care

B. Export controls

C. Legal holds

D. E-discovery

19. An investigation is to be performed on an employee suspected of stealing company **Intellectual Property** (**IP**). There are over 10 gigabytes of data stored across several information systems. What must be done to ensure that the relevant data is collected?

A. Due care

B. Export controls

C. Legal holds

D. E-discovery

20. What document may be used when business partners need to document responsibilities? This document will not be written by lawyers and is intended to formalize a verbal agreement or a handshake.

A. Service level agreement (SLA)

B. Master service agreement (MSA)

C. Memorandum of understanding (MOU)

D. Interconnection security agreement (ISA)

Answers

1. A
2. A
3. A, D
4. A
5. C
6. C
7. D
8. B
9. A
10. D
11. A
12. B
13. C
14. B
15. A
16. D
17. E
18. C
19. D
20. C

15
Business Continuity and Disaster Recovery Concepts

In order for an organization to conduct business operations in challenging and diverse environments, high-level planning and mitigation controls should be undertaken to ensure the enterprise is resilient. When the business delivers high-value services, plans must be developed for business continuity. In the event that a significant disruption may impact delivered services, plans should be created to allow the business to remain functional. Plans should be developed to ensure business operations can be resumed quickly and efficiently in the event of a disaster. High availability, redundancy, and fault tolerance are important considerations to ensure that services are available. Alternative sites may need to be identified, to allow for business continuity. Automation should be used where there is an opportunity to become more resilient, while bootstrapping can be used for the rapid deployment of workloads, using scripting for custom configuration. Autoscaling allows an enterprise to deploy workloads on demand to satisfy customer demands. When the enterprise has to deliver services to a global customer base, it may be appropriate to investigate the use of content delivery networks for low latency and the increased availability of services.

In this chapter, we will cover the following topics:

- Conducting a business impact analysis
- Preparing a **Disaster Recovery Plan (DRP)/Business Continuity Plan (BCP)**
- Planning for high availability and automation
- Explaining how cloud technology aids enterprise resilience

Conducting a business impact analysis

One of the most important things for an organization is to ensure that contingency plans are in place to protect the business from adverse events and conditions. Business leaders must ensure that a **Business Impact Analysis (BIA)** is performed to determine critical systems and services that will have a disproportionate effect on the enterprise if they are not available. Stakeholder involvement is important, enabling the business to identify key business processes.

The first step in the assessment should be the purpose. This can be performed in three steps. See *Figure 15.1* for more information:

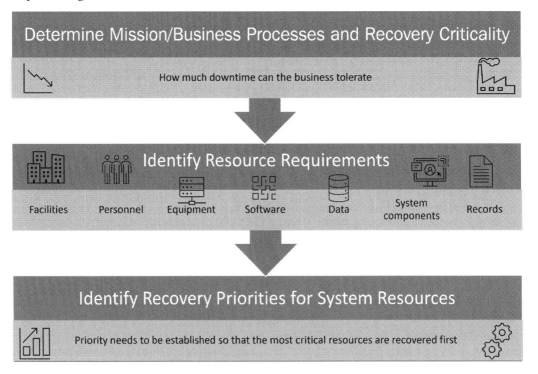

Figure 15.1 – BIA purpose

The initial purpose document can be used to build the contingency plan, while it can also be used as the basis for a **DRP**. Once key systems are identified, this information can also be used to document an effective cyber incident response plan.

The purpose of a BIA is to identify critical services that the business delivers and understand the potential impacts that may be caused by a lack of service. The goal of the exercise is enterprise resilience, with the creation of our contingency plans.

Business leaders must identify the critical resources needed for the business and agree upon acceptable downtime, using the following metrics.

Maximum Tolerable Downtime (MTD)

This metric allows stakeholders and planners to agree upon a point in time where the lack of a critical resource would cause severe adverse effects for the enterprise. For example, if an airline cannot fly planes for 6 months, then they will burn through their cash reserves and may go bankrupt. The MTD, therefore, becomes the line in the sand that cannot be crossed.

Recovery Time Objective (RTO)

The RTO metric is a goal set by the enterprise and will be agreed upon within the planning team. A critical service that has a high value to the business will be assigned a value based upon its criticality. A critical service may be an e-commerce site, used for an airline seat reservation service, for customers. If the site cannot be reached, the business will lose significant revenue. When this planning objective is used, it is important to reference the MTD value, as the RTO must be a value less than the MTD.

Recovery Point Objective (RPO)

The RPO metric is used when the restoration of a critical service will also require data to be restored. When considering the timely restoration of services, this will not always be relevant. If the customer reservation site needs to be operational within 4 hours, we must also ensure that the relevant data is available for the reservation system. As the data may contain already purchased tickets and reservation information, it may mean we cannot afford to be without this data. An RPO of 60 mins may be acceptable, although some customers will be inconvenienced as they will have lost their seat reservations. The RPO represents the amount of time between the disruption and the last backup created.

Figure 15.2 represents the RPO objective:

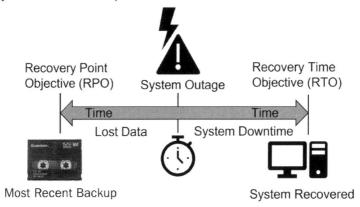

Figure 15.2 – Recovery Point Objective

Critical services will be identified, and the metrics defined by business leaders will reflect the importance of the service.

Recovery service level

The critical services required to deliver a business function must be recovered first. In the case of the airline booking system, it is vital that revenue can be generated by bringing the service back online immediately. There may be other functional elements, such as printing customer tickets, that can be addressed once the critical services are recovered.

Mission-essential functions

Mission-essential functions need to be identified by the planning team. Senior business leaders and key stakeholders must contribute to this plan. A mission-essential function would typically represent a single point of failure to the business. Documentation would be created to highlight these functions and the agreed-upon objectives to mitigate these single points of failure. *Figure 15.3* shows an example of mission-essential planning:

Mission-Essential Function	MTD	RTO	RPO
Customer booking system	24 hours	4 hours	1 hour
Invoice payment system	96 hours	24 hours	1 hour

Figure 15.3 – Mission-essential functions

Mission-essential functions are potential single points of failure and appropriate planning objectives ensure that goals can be achieved.

Privacy Impact Assessment (PIA)

A PIA should be undertaken by any organization that stores, transmits, or processes data that contains private information. Data types will vary but can include documents, database records, media such as CCTV footage, and voice recordings.

Under GDPR, this process is known as **Data Protection Impact Assessments (DPIA)** and is a mandatory requirement for any project that may expose subjects' private data. *Figure 15.4* shows a typical process for assessing risks when handling private data. There is a useful planning document that can be downloaded, for use in this type of assessment, at the following URL: `https://tinyurl.com/GDPR-DPIA`:

Figure 15.4 – PIA

As regulatory compliance is often a complex process, an enterprise needs to put procedures in place to ensure the enterprise does not fall out of alignment. The risk to the business could be significant; the fines alone may be substantial.

Preparing a Disaster Recovery Plan/Business Continuity Plan

As a result of the BIA, the business should be able to identify mitigation techniques and plan for the restoration of business functions in the event of serious disruptions.

Organizations that require guidance on the effective creation and management of BCPs should reference **ISO 22301** for an overview of the standard. The following publication may be useful: `https://tinyurl.com/isopub22301`.

NIST SP800-34 Contingency Planning Guide for Federal Information Systems offers guidance for federal government agencies. More information can be found at this URL: `https://tinyurl.com/nistsp80034`. *Figure 15.5* shows the seven stages of the NIST contingency plan:

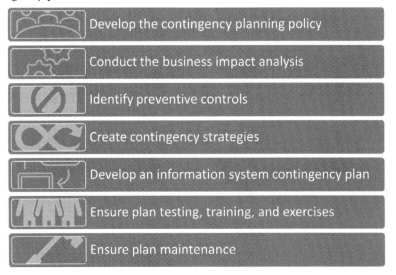

Figure 15.5 – NIST-recommended contingency plan

The contingency plan does not include planning for mission-essential functions; this is covered by a **Continuity-of-Operations Plan (COOP)**.

An important outcome for US government agencies is the creation of a **COOP**. A COOP focuses on restoring the organization's **Mission-Essential Functions (MEF)**, using alternative sites. The COOP is required to support operations for up to 30 days. Some of the elements of a COOP are shown in *Figure 15.6*:

Program plans and procedures

Risk management

Budgeting and acquisition of resources

Essential functions

Order of succession

Delegation of authority

Continuity facilities

Continuity communications

Test training and exercise

Figure 15.6 – Elements of a COOP

The COOP is designed to address mission-essential functions, so disruptions by minor threats will not be covered by the COOP.

One important consideration is where the business will operate from if the primary site is unusable. Facilities need to be identified that will meet the requirements for the organization to operate.

Cold site

When planning for alternative sites to run the business, this is the least costly. However, it is the least effective if the business must be operational within a short time frame. An example of a cold site could be leased office space and suitable facilities for computing equipment. The time to relocate personnel and systems and become operational could result in a significant delay for the organization.

Warm site

If the enterprise needs to switch operations over to an alternative site within hours rather than days, then a good choice may be a warm site. A warm site has equipment and facilities ready for the business to use. Personnel and data will need to be moved to the site to become operational.

Hot site

A hot site normally consists of all the equipment and data needed for the business to continue operations. The site should allow the organization to switch operations within a short time frame. If the business runs critical infrastructure or e-commerce, then the site would be fully replicated with all required data and information systems. Many solutions are designed to failover to the hot site within a matter of seconds. If your business is guaranteeing an SLA of 99.9999% to customers, then your site cannot be offline for more than 31.56 seconds per year.

Figure 15.7 shows the differences between alternate sites:

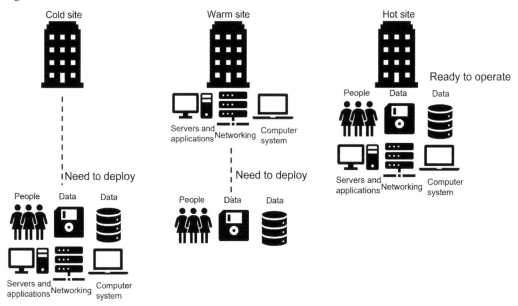

Figure 15.7 – Cold, warm, and hot sites

The correct type of site must be identified that suits the needs of the business.

Mobile site

A mobile recovery site is typically delivered on the back of a trailer. It can be in the form of a cold, warm, or hot site. It can be shipped close to the location of the staff, removing one major logistical challenge. If the business needs a solution that can be operational within seconds, then a mobile site will not be a good choice. Examples of mobile sites are military solutions, where organizational resilience is important. The US military is able to deploy mobile data centers containing sufficient facilities to house 90 units of computing equipment. The unit incorporates pop-out tents, with space for 20 people. *Figure 15.8* shows a mobile data center:

Figure 15.8 – Mobile data center (© Todd Huffman – Flickr images)

The unit can be made operational, with secure communications established, within 15 minutes.

Backup and recovery methods

When an organization needs to host a failover site for business operations, one choice it should consider is a cloud-based provider. The enterprise can choose a solution that meets with business needs for regulatory compliance or for data sovereignty.

Cloud as business continuity and disaster recovery (BCDR)

With many organizations running critical services and workloads in the cloud, it is important to assess the capabilities of the provider to provide redundancy and be resilient to geographic disruptions. An enterprise may want to consider a multi-cloud solution, where data and services may be available from more than one cloud provider. This offers a higher degree of resilience as the business can still maintain core services with more than one provider.

Primary BCDR provider

The primary **Cloud Service Provider** (CSP) chosen by the enterprise should be able to demonstrate the ability to maintain operations under adverse conditions. The main provider should have geographically dispersed data centers and be able to maintain operations during significant environmental or man-made disasters. There have been many instances of CSPs suffering significant outages that have impacted their customers.

Alternative BCDR provider

To ensure critical services can be delivered by the enterprise, it is useful to have the ability to activate workloads with alternative cloud providers. Many cloud providers offer their customers solutions that are charged according to the amount of processing performed. This allows the enterprise to use services on demand and only pay while the workloads are operational. US Federal Government has awarded large multi-billion contracts to **Microsoft** for **Azure cloud services** and also to **Amazon** for **Amazon Web Services** (**AWS**).

Planning for high availability and automation

When planning for enterprise resilience, it is important to identify systems and services that are important for business continuity. There are ways to deal with unexpected outages or to recover from an event. It is also vitally important that tools and techniques are identified to ensure that services remain available.

Scalability

Scalability is defined as the system's ability to increase and decrease performance levels in response to the demands placed upon the system. An example could be a database server. As database queries are processed, there will be a point where it cannot simultaneously handle any more requests.

Vertical scaling

In order to allow critical services to handle additional user requests, we can add more compute resources to the platform. To vertically scale an information system, we can add additional **Central Processing Units** (**CPUs**), **Random Access Memory** (**RAM**), faster disk **input/output** (**I/O**), and additional network connections. This approach poses a higher risk of downtime and outages compared to other approaches.

Horizontal scaling

Horizontal scaling is achieved by adding more workloads in the form of additional computers or platforms. This is often achieved by deploying additional compute nodes in the form of **Virtual Machines** (**VMs**). This can work well if the resources can be deployed on-demand using autoscaling.

Resiliency

Computing solutions must be resilient. This will mean that downtime is reduced and that business services can be delivered with more reliability.

High availability

High availability can be achieved by clustering important business applications or using network load balancing to efficiently distribute the workload.

Diversity/heterogeneity

Too much reliance on a single vendor solution could adversely impact an organization. Supply problems may impact systems that require spares and maintenance, while a critical unpatched vulnerability could impact all of your network infrastructure appliances. Reliance on a single vendor operating solution could result in downtime due to zero-day exploits.

Course of action orchestration

Wherever possible, it is important to create automated responses to avoid unnecessary outages. Examples can be scripted responses to certain events, such as a DDoS attack against the company network being thwarted by triggering a **BGP** route update. This would implement what is known as a **Remote Triggered Black Hole** (**RTBH**). See *Chapter 1, Designing a Secure Network Architecture*, for more details on this remediation.

Distributed allocation

When we are supporting high availability, we may need to distribute workloads across multiple nodes. An accurate algorithm must be able to best distribute workloads, thereby optimizing the computing platforms. This system is typically used for large server farms handling high numbers of client requests. To ensure that adequate compute nodes are always available, geo-redundancy and scalability are important factors.

Redundancy

Redundancy can be achieved by duplicating systems or processes. Data redundancy can eliminate outages due to disk failure by creating a mirror of a data drive.

Replication

The availability of data is often critical. Information systems can grind to a halt without reliable access to data. Critical transactions may need access to data that is time-critical. Therefore, a decision must be made about how to replicate the data. Asymmetric replication allows for a time tag. When inputting data, there is a background process copying the data to the replica storage system. Symmetric replication allows for no time lag; the data is written or committed to both systems at the same time (this is the more costly solution).

Clustering

High availability can be achieved by clustering important business applications or using network load balancing to efficiently distribute the workload. *Figure 15.9* shows a failover cluster:

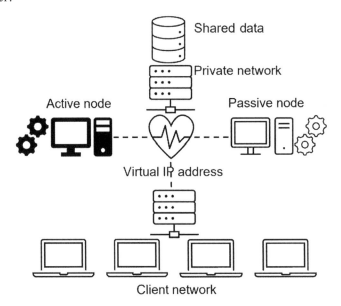

Figure 15.9 – Failover cluster

In a failover cluster, the primary server (active node) has exclusive access to the data and can service client requests. The cluster relies upon nodes generating heartbeat messages to establish the current status. In the event that the primary server is unavailable, then the secondary server (passive node) will take control of data storage and service client requests.

Automation

It is important for capacity planning to be performed in order to identify the computing needs of an enterprise. There must be provision for workloads to be deployed on-demand to service enterprise and customer requirements. In a modern cloud environment, a high degree of automation will be required to support the needs of the business.

Autoscaling

When an enterprise supports critical services, it is important that workloads can be deployed on demand. Autoscaling allows the customer to work with the **CSP** to define expected day-to-day compute needs. The customer can then choose a plan where spikes in demand result in the automatic provisioning of additional compute resources. *Figure 15.10* shows an example of autoscaling:

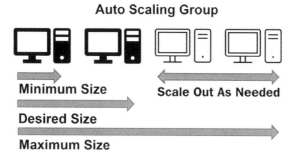

Figure 15.10 – Autoscaling

When a customer uses autoscaling, they can work with a CSP to offer highly scalable solutions to meet customer demand.

Security Orchestration, Automation, and Response (SOAR)

To assist the **Security Operations Center** (**SOC**), while dealing with ever-increasing demands to manage and monitor security-related events, Playbooks can enable staff to make quicker responses concerning security incidents, while Runbooks allow for the automation of common tasks and security-related responses.

Bootstrapping

When automating the creation and deployment of virtual machines to support workloads, bootstrapping allows for configuration files to be created to simplify the deployment of these virtual computers or appliances. Bootstrapping allows for the rapid deployment of virtualized infrastructure and supports autoscaling. It is common to apply the configuration to a compute node or cluster as it boots up from a standard image (such as Linux, Unix, or Windows).

Content Delivery Network (CDN)

CDNs are geographically dispersed servers delivering content in the form of web pages, media, and images to worldwide consumers. A large proportion of all web traffic is delivered by CDNs. Sites such as YouTube, Netflix, and Amazon depend upon this service to deliver reliable low latency content to their customers. As the data is dispersed, it also offers an effective defense against DDoS attacks.

CDNs use **caching** to ensure data is available on the edge of the network, where users or customers will benefit from lower latency and improved responses. *Figure 15.11* shows a CDN:

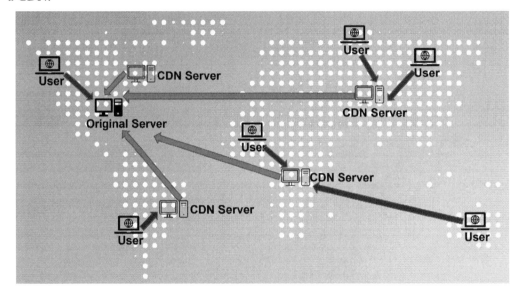

Figure 15.11 – CDN

This type of design will allow an enterprise to be very resilient, offering customers a reliable low-latency experience over a large geographic area.

Testing plans

To ensure that enterprise BCP and DRP will be effective, thorough testing will need to be performed. Without testing, there is no guarantee that the plan will be effective.

Checklist

A checklist test is a detailed examination of BCP/DRP documentation, performed by stakeholders and team members on their own. This will entail sharing the plan with the appropriate people and organizing a communication channel for feedback. This type of test intends to pinpoint any inaccuracies or errors in the documents.

Tabletop exercises

It is important to gather representation from within the company to effectively understand if there are any potential problems with a proposed plan. Stakeholder involvement is important when assessing the effectiveness of the plan. Scenarios can be discussed and actions that need to be performed can be evaluated. A tabletop exercise ensures that the **Disaster Recovery Team (DRT)** or **Cyber Security Incident Response Team (CSIRT)** do not need to perform exhaustive testing until the plans are *fine-tuned*.

Walk-through

When particular elements of a plan are being scrutinized, this is called paper-based testing, or a walk-through. It allows the architects of the plan to discuss a particular process within the overall plan. A walk-through may also include input from stakeholders who would be impacted by this part of the plan.

Parallel test/simulation test

When the plan has reached a mature stage, we can evaluate the effectiveness by performing parallel or simulation testing. These tests will not impact the production environment, but can be performed on duplicate systems.

Full interruption test

In cases where it is vital that the enterprise can be assured that BCPs or DRPs will be fully effective, then full interruption or cutover testing should be used. It can disrupt business operations, so should only be used when all other types of tests have been successfully executed.

Explaining how cloud technology aids enterprise resilience

There are many services offered by **CSPs** that enable an organization to be resilient. If the business cannot afford to build a data center to support business continuity, then they can use cloud services instead. When choosing solutions to meet the needs of the business, it is important to focus on resiliency and security.

Using cloud solutions for business continuity and disaster recovery (BCDR)

For many organizations, CSPs represent a useful alternative when hosting disaster recovery sites. With a CSP hosting workloads and virtual desktops, the business can remain operational when dealing with catastrophic events at the main business site. Many CSPs offer a cloud service, called **Desktop as a Service** (**DaaS**). The cost to the business may be minimal. *Figure 15.12* shows a DaaS solution:

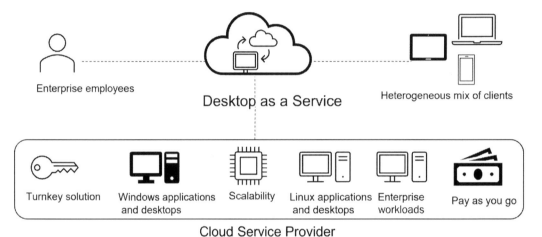

Figure 15.12 – Desktop as a Service

When assessing solutions to support business continuity, CSPs can provide highly available solutions.

Infrastructure versus serverless computing

One consideration for an organization wanting to host applications and data in the cloud is whether to host their own infrastructure in the cloud or to pay for serverless computing. In traditional cloud-based models, the company can pay for **Infrastructure as a Service** (**IaaS**) and provision a number of compute nodes to service the organization's needs. With serverless models, the organization just focuses on the applications. If the customer needs to host e-commerce applications, then they simply deploy the applications to the cloud, leaving the backend to the CSP. The customer only pays for computing time and does not need to worry about maintaining servers or reserving network bandwidth. Serverless computing makes better use of the cloud resources as the customer only pays for what they use.

Collaboration tools

Cloud-based collaboration tools can be very useful in enabling teams to work together. Common cloud-based collaboration tools allow an enterprise to work effectively with partners and remote workers and to engage with their customers. Common tools include web-based conferencing, chat, **Voice over IP** (**VOIP**), and many more. These tools have proven very useful where businesses have had to adapt to a remote working model. When considering online collaboration tools, resilience and security need to be addressed. Collaboration tools can also be useful as a failover when a primary service is unavailable. If a cellular network is unavailable due to disruption or other outages, then we can use tools such as **Microsoft Teams** or **Zoom** conferencing to communicate with partners, team members, or customers.

Storage configurations

When an organization makes use of CSP, to host critical services or to offer redundancy in the event that the enterprise needs to use the CSP for BCDR, then the security of the data is of paramount importance. To secure the data, there are methods available that can both secure the data and also offer redundancy.

Bit splitting

Bit splitting is intended to protect data stored with cloud providers. Data blocks are first encrypted using the AES 256-bit symmetric algorithm, and the encrypted block is then split and distributed across multiple data stores. The stored *split* blocks are hashed when they are written to the filesystem in order to accurately retrieve the data using data maps.

Data dispersion

Data dispersion is intended to operate much like RAID solutions that utilize parity. The data blocks are dispersed across multiple storage systems or cloud providers. If one provider is unavailable, then we can still access the data, as the algorithm used is similar to RAID5 or RAID6.

Cloud Access Security Broker (CASB)

When an enterprise uses CSPs to store data, adequate protection must be in place to protect the enterprise. Data may be subject to regulatory or legal compliance and may, in addition, contain intellectual property or sensitive information. The data may be accessed by employees, partners, or customers. This means the internal security controls will not be effective. When the enterprise uses multiple cloud providers, then security becomes difficult to monitor and enforce. A CASB can include authentication services, such as single sign-on, authorization, credential mapping, device management, encryption services, data loss prevention, malware detection/prevention, logging, alerting, and many more security services besides. A CASB is often referred to as a gatekeeper, protecting the enterprise data from inbound threats into the cloud and outbound threats such as data exfiltration. Another benefit of CASB is ensuring regulatory compliance by labeling and monitoring the use of the data, so as to ensure compliance. *Figure 15.13* shows the services provided by the CASB:

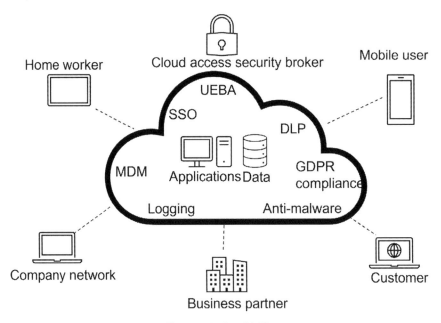

Figure 15.13 – CASB

Traditional security controls such as **Secure Web Gateways** (**SWGs**) and **Next-Generation Firewalls** (**NGFWs**) are not enough to protect the data hosted with a CSP. The connections to the cloud do not always pass through the company network. Many of the connections will be made from remote users directly into the cloud.

Summary

In this chapter, we have understood why an organization needs to conduct high-level planning to ensure appropriate mitigation controls are deployed. We have learned about why plans are developed for business continuity. We have understood what is needed in a **DRP**. We have looked at high availability, redundancy, and fault tolerance, when critical services need to be available. We have looked at the business need for alternate sites, as well as physical locations and the services delivered by CSPs. We have learned why automation should be used in an effort to become more resilient. Knowledge has been acquired about bootstrapping, which can be used for the rapid deployment of workloads using scripting for custom configuration. We have looked at cloud-based autoscaling, allowing an enterprise to deploy workloads on demand to satisfy customer demands. We have looked at CDNs for low latency and the increased availability of services. We have looked at the need for the thorough testing of plans, including checklists, walk-throughs, tabletops, and parallel and full interruption tests.

We have studied cloud-based security and collaboration tools that can protect enterprise data and enable a business to be resilient when using **CSPs**.

Questions

Here are a few questions to test your understanding of the chapter:

1. What metric is used by planners for a critical resource that would cause severe adverse effects for the enterprise? This metric forms the line in the sand that cannot be crossed.

    A. Recovery point objective

    B. Recovery time objective

    C. Recovery service level

    D. Maximum tolerable downtime

2. What metric is a goal set by the enterprise to ensure a critical service will be operational within a specified timeframe?

    A. Recovery point objective

    B. Recovery time objective

    C. Recovery service level

    D. Mission-essential functions

3. What is a planning objective used when the restoration of a critical service will also require data to be restored?

    A. Recovery point objective

    B. Recovery time objective

    C. Recovery service level

    D. Mission-essential functions

4. What planning objectives ensure that critical services are recovered first, while other functional elements, such as printing customer tickets, are given a lower priority?

    A. Recovery point objective

    B. Recovery time objective

    C. Recovery service level

    D. Mission-essential functions

5. What type of assessment should be performed by an organization that stores, transmits, or processes data that contains private information?

    A. Business impact assessment

    B. Privacy impact assessment

    C. RISK assessment

    D. Safety assessment

6. An organization has leased office space and suitable facilities for computing equipment. The intention is to relocate personnel and systems and become operational in the event that the main office location is unavailable. What have they used?

    A. A cold site

    B. A warm site

    C. A hot site

    D. A mobile site

7. A planning team has identified a requirement for a site, housing equipment and facilities ready for the business to use. Personnel and data will need to be moved to the site to become operational. What have they identified?

    A. A cold site

    B. A warm site

    C. A hot site

    D. A mobile site

8. An e-commerce site needs a failover location that has all the equipment and data needed for the business to continue operations. The site should allow the organization to switch operations within a short time frame. What should they use?

    A. A cold site

    B. A warm site

    C. A hot site

    D. A mobile site

9. What kind of scalability have we identified when we add additional **Central Processing Units (CPUs)**, **Random Access Memory (RAM)**, faster disk **input/output (I/O)**, and additional network connections?

    A. Vertically scalability

    B. Replication

    C. Performance scalability

    D. Horizontally scalability

10. What type of scalability is achieved by adding more workloads in the form of additional computers or compute nodes? This can work well if the resources can be deployed on demand using autoscaling.

    A. Vertically scalability

    B. Replication

    C. Performance scalability

    D. Horizontally scalability

11. What type of data replication will be needed where there can be no time lag, where the data is written or committed to both systems at the same time (this is the more costly solution)?

    A. Symmetric

    B. Cloud-based

    C. Asymmetric

    D. CDN

12. What is used when the customer works with the **CSP** to define expected day-to-day compute needs? The customer can then choose a plan where spikes in demand result in the automatic provisioning of additional compute resources.

    A. Autoscaling

    B. Caching

    C. Bootstrapping

    D. Clustering

13. Select the cloud service, where the service provider is often referred to as a gatekeeper. This service will protect the enterprise data from inbound threats (into the cloud) and outbound threats such as data exfiltration.

    A. IaaS

    B. CASB

    C. PaaS

    D. SWG

14. What is a cloud platform where the customer only pays for computing time and does not need to worry about maintaining servers or reserving network bandwidth? This type of computing makes better use of cloud resources as the customer only pays for what they use.

    A. Infrastructure computing

    B. Cloud access security broker

    C. Serverless computing

    D. Virtual computing

15. What cloud storage solution is intended to protect data stored with cloud providers? Data blocks are first encrypted using the AES 256-bit symmetric algorithm and the encrypted block is then split and distributed across multiple data stores.

    A. Bit splitting

    B. Data dispersion

    C. Availability

    D. Collection

16. What is a cloud storage solution where data blocks are dispersed across multiple storage systems or cloud providers? If one provider is unavailable, then we can still access the data as the algorithm used is similar to RAID5 or RAID6.

    A. Bit splitting

    B. Data dispersion

    C. Availability

    D. Collection

17. What is the testing that uses stakeholder involvement to assess the effectiveness of the plan? Scenarios can be discussed and actions that need to be performed can be evaluated. This exercise ensures that the **Disaster Recovery Team** (**DRT**) or **Cyber Security Incident Response Team** (**CSIRT**) do not need to perform exhaustive testing until the plans are *fine-tuned*.

    A. Checklist

    B. Walk-through

    C. Tabletop exercises

    D. Full interruption test

18. What is the final stage in the testing of BCP/DRP plans? This can disrupt business operations, so should only be used when all other types of tests have been successfully executed.

    A. Checklist

    B. Tabletop exercises

    C. Full interruption test

    D. Parallel test/simulation test

19. What technology is offered by CSPs to allow for the rapid deployment of virtualized infrastructure? It is common to apply the configuration to a compute node or cluster as it boots up from a standard image (such as Linux, Unix, or Windows).

    A. Autoscaling

    B. Distributed allocation

    C. Bootstrapping

    D. Replication

20. What type of network allows for geographically dispersed servers delivering content in the form of web pages, media, and images to worldwide consumers? This network uses caching to ensure that data is available on the edge of the network, where users or customers will benefit from lower latency.

    A. Autoscaling

    B. Distributed network

    C. Content delivery network

    D. Replicated network

Answers

1. D
2. B
3. A
4. C
5. B
6. A
7. B
8. C
9. A
10. D
11. A
12. A
13. B
14. C
15. A
16. B
17. C
18. C
19. C
20. C

16
Mock Exam 1

Welcome to the study guide assessment test! These test questions are designed to resemble real-world **CASP 004** exam questions. To make this test as realistic as possible, you should attempt to answer these questions *closed book* and allocate the correct amount of time. You can use some paper or a scratchpad to jot down notes, although this will be different in a real test environment. If you wish to look at the PearsonVue candidate testing rules, check out the following URL: `https://home.pearsonvue.com/comptia/onvue`.

- End of Study Assessment Test
- Number of Questions: 50
- Passing Score: 83% (Estimated)

Questions

1. Developers are building sensitive references and account details into the application code. Security engineers need to ensure that the organization can secure the **continuous integration/continuous delivery (CI/CD)** pipeline. What would be the best choice?

    A.   Perform dynamic application security testing.

    B.   Use a centralized trusted secrets manager service.

    C.   Use interactive application security testing.

    D.   Ensure the developers are using version control.

2. What type of assessment should be performed by an organization that stores, transmits, or processes data that contains private information?

    A.   Business Impact Assessment

    B.   Privacy Impact Assessment

    C.   Risk assessment

    D.   Safety assessment

3. The ACME corporation has recently run an annual risk assessment as part of its regulatory compliance. The risk management team has identified a high-level risk that could lead to fraudulent activities. The team has recommended that certain privileged tasks must be performed by more than one person for the task to be validated. What is this an example of?

    A.   Job rotation

    B.   Least privilege

    C.   Separation of duties

    D.   Multi-factor authentication

4. Security professionals are analyzing logs that have been collected from MDM software. The following log entries are available:

Device	Date/Time	Location	Event	Description
Android_2975	08NOV21 1720	57°20'22.0"N 5°39'04.0"W	Push	App 1022 install
Android_2975	08NOV21 1830	57°20'22.0"N 5°39'04.0"W	Inventory	App 1022 added
Android_2975	08NOV21 1920	57°20'00.0"N 5°39'08.0"W	Check-in	Normal
Android_2975	08NOV21 1922	28°43'25.0"N 13°50'30.0"W	Check-in	Normal
Android_2975	08NOV21 2041	28°43'25.0"N 13°50'30.0"W	Check-in	Normal
Android_2975	08NOV21 2055	57°20'22.0"N 5°39'04.0"W	Status	Storage 60% usage

Figure 16.1 – MDM audit log

What is the security concern and what response would best mitigate the risks of the mobile device?

    A.   An application was installed maliciously; change the MDM configuration to remove application ID 1022.

    B.   Sensitive data exposure; recover the device for analysis and clean up the local storage.

C.   Impossible time travel; disable the device's account and carry out further investigation.

D.   Anomalous status reporting; initiate a remote wipe of the device.

5.   An e-commerce site has recently upgraded its web application servers to use TLS 1.3, though some customers are calling the service desk as they can no longer access the services. After analyzing the logs that had been generated on the client's devices, the following was observed:

ERROR_SSL_VERSION_OR_CIPHER_MISMATCH

What is the most likely cause of the reported error?

A.   Clients are configured to use ECDHE.

B.   Clients are configured to use RC4.

C.   Clients are configured to use PFS.

D.   Clients are configured to use AES-256 GCM.

6.   The security professionals are reviewing all the servers in the company and discover that a server is missing crucial patches that would mitigate a recent exploit that could gain root access. Which of the following describes the teams' discovery?

A.   A vulnerability

B.   A threat

C.   A breach

D.   A risk

7.   ACME bank has a compliance requirement. They require a third-party penetration test of the customer-facing banking application to be conducted annually. What type of penetration testing would ensure the lowest resource usage?

A.   Black-box testing

B.   Gray-box testing

C.   Red-team exercises

D.   White-box testing

E.   Blue-team exercises

8. Recently, the ACME corporation has merged with a similar-sized organization. The SOC staff now have an increased workload and are failing to respond to all alerts. What is the likely cause of this behavior?

    A.   False positive

    B.   Alert fatigue

    C.   False negative

    D.   True positive

9. A small regional bank, with no dedicated security team, must deploy security at the edge of the network. They will need a solution that will offer protection from multiple threats that may target the bank's network. What would be the best solution for the bank?

    A.   Router

    B.   WAF

    C.   UTM

    D.   DLP

10. During baseline security training for new developers, attention must be focused on the use of third-party libraries. What is the most important aspect for a commercial development team that's considering the use of third-party libraries? Choose two.

    A.   Third-party libraries may have vulnerabilities.

    B.   Third-party libraries may be incompatible.

    C.   Third-party libraries may not support DNSSEC.

    D.   Third-party libraries may have licensing restrictions.

11. A CISO wants to change the culture of the organization to strengthen the company's security posture. The initiative will bring the development and operations teams together when code is released to the production environment. What is the best description of this initiative?

    A.   DevOps

    B.   A team-building exercise

    C.   A tabletop exercise

    D.   SecDevOps

12. A development team is working with a customer to develop a mobile application. The customer has already defined all the requirements upfront and wants the application to be developed using very strict timelines. It is not anticipated that any changes will be made to the initial definition. What software development approach would be the most suitable for this engagement?

   A.   Agile

   B.   Waterfall

   C.   Spiral

   D.   Build and Fix

13. A CISO for a large multinational bank would like to address security concerns regarding the use and auditing of local administrator credentials on end devices. Currently, users are given local administrator privileges when access is required. This current practice has resulted in undocumented changes, a lack of accountability, and account lockouts. What could be implemented to address these issues?

   A.   Use **Privileged Access Management** (**PAM**) to maintain user accounts in the local admin group.

   B.   Deploy EDR to remove users from local admins group and enable audit logs.

   C.   Use **Privileged Access Management** (**PAM**) to remove user accounts from the local admin group and prompt the user for explicit approval when elevation is required.

   D.   Deploy EDR to remove users from the local admins group and enable UEBA.

14. The ACME corporation has been suffering from increasing numbers of service outages on the endpoints due to ever-increasing instances of new malware. The Chief Financial Officer's laptop was impacted while working remotely from a hotel. The objective is to prevent further instances of endpoint disruption. Currently, the company has deployed a web proxy at the edge of the network. What should the company deploy to mitigate these threats?

   A.   Replace the current antivirus with an EDR solution.

   B.   Remove the web proxy and install a UTM appliance.

   C.   Implement application blacklisting on the endpoints.

   D.   Add a firewall module to the current antivirus solution.

15. A company has been testing its **Disaster Recovery Plan** (**DRP**) while team members have been assessing challenges that had been encountered while testing in parallel. Computing resources ran out at 65% of the restoration process for critical services. What documentation should be modified to address this issue?

    A.   Recovery point objective

    B.   Business Impact Assessment

    C.   Mission-essential functions

    D.   Recovery service level

16. A security professional is performing a system penetration test. They successfully gain access to a shell on a Linux host as a standard user and want to elevate their privilege levels. What would be the most effective way to perform privilege escalation?

    A.   Spawn a shell using sudo and use a text editor to update the sudoer's file.

    B.   Perform ASIC password cracking on the host.

    C.   Access the `/etc/passwd` file to extract the usernames.

    D.   Use the `UNION` operator to extract the database schema.

17. A security analyst is concerned that a malicious piece of code was downloaded on a Linux system. After running various diagnostics tools, the analyst determines that the suspect code is performing a lot of **input/output** (**I/O**) on the disk drive. The following screenshot shows the output from one of the diagnostics tools:

```
procs -----------memory---------- ---swap-- -----io---- -system-- ------cpu-----
 r  b   swpd   free   buff  cache   si   so    bi    bo   in   cs us sy id wa st
 3  0      0 799732   2116 1768564   0    0     2     3   20   41  0  0 99  0  0
 7  0      0 776620   2116 1764604   0    0     0    42   52 2619 53  8 40  0  0
 5  0      0 352824   2116 1805164   0    0     0   791   84 2361 76 11 12  0  0
 0  0      0 173924   2116 1870360   0    0     0   171   84 4231 62 18 20  0  0
11  0    520 160120   2104 1864472   0   90     0   133   84 4227 57 17 26  0  0
 9  0    520 492232   2104 1917992   0    0 27000 32222  117 3616 62 16 22  0  0
 4  0    520 699960   2104 1707728   0    0     0  1795   44 2646 66  8 25  0  0
```

Figure 16.2 – Diagnostic output

Based on this output, which ID should the analyst focus their attention on?

    A.   ID 99

    B.   ID 40

    C.   ID 22

    D.   ID 12

18. A CISO needs to ensure there is an effective incident response plan. As part of the plan, a CSIRT team needs to be identified, including leadership with a clear reporting and escalation process. At what part of the incident response process should this be done?

    A.   Preparation

    B.   Detection

    C.   Analysis

    D.   Containment

19. The ACME corporation's CSIRT team responded to an incident where several routers failed at the same time. The cause of the failure is unknown, and the routers have been reconfigured and restored to operational condition. The integrity of the router's configuration has also been verified. Which of the following should the team perform to understand the failure and prevent it in the future?

    A.   Root cause analysis

    B.   Continuity of operations plan

    C.   After-action report

    D.   Lessons learned

20. Jeff, a developer with the ACME corporation, is concerned about the impact of new malware on an **ARM** CPU. He knows that the malware can insert itself in another process memory location. Which of the following technologies can the developer enable on the ARM architecture to prevent this type of malware?

    A.   Execute-never (XN)

    B.   EDR software

    C.   Total memory encryption

    D.   Virtual memory encryption

21. Security professionals have detected anomalous activity on the edge network. To investigate the activity further, they intend to examine the contents of the `pcap` file. They are looking for evidence of data exfiltration from a suspect host computer. To minimize disruption, they need to identify a command-line tool that will provide this functionality. What should they use?

    A. `netcat`

    B. `tcpdump`

    C. `Aircrack-ng`

    D. Wireshark

22. Ann, a security analyst, is investigating anomalous activity within syslog files. She is looking for evidence of unusual activity based on reports from **User Entity Behavior Analytics** (**UEBA**). Several events may be indicators of compromise. Which of the following requires further investigation?

    A. `Netstat -bn`

    B. `vmstat -a 5`

    C. `nc -w 180 -p 12345 -l < shadow.txt`

    D. `Exiftool companylogo.jpg`

23. UEBA has generated alerts relating to significant amounts of PNG image uploads to a social networking site. The account that has generated the reports is a recent hire in the Research and Development division. A rival manufacturer is selling products that appear to be based on the company's sensitive designs.

    The payloads are now being analyzed by forensics investigators. What tool will allow them to search for evidence in the PNG files?

    A. Steganalysis tool

    B. Cryptanalysis tool

    C. Binary analysis tool

    D. Memory analysis tool

24. Marketing executives are attending an international trade exhibition and must connect to their company's email using their mobile devices during the event. The CISO is concerned that this may present a risk. What would best mitigate this risk?

    A. Near-field communication (NFC)

    B. Split-tunnel VPN

C. Geofencing

D. Always-on VPN settings

25. A company employee has followed a QC link and installed a mobile application that's used to book and schedule activities at a vacation resort. The application is not available on Google Play Store. Company policy states that applications can only be downloaded from the official vendor store or company portal. What best describes what has allowed this app to be installed?

A. Supply chain issues

B. Side loading

C. Containerization

D. Unauthorized application stores

26. A company has deployed a hardened Linux image to mobile devices. The restrictions are as follows:

- All unnecessary services must be removed.

- Only company-deployed apps can be run.

- The runtime code is protected against memory exploits.

The CISO is concerned that an attacker may be able to launch attacks using common utilities and command-line tools. What could be deployed to mitigate the CISO's concerns?

A. Whitelisting

B. Shell restrictions

C. ASLR

D. Memory encryption

27. A regional **Internet Service Provider** (**ISP**) is experiencing outages and poor service levels over some of its copper-based infrastructure. These faults are due to the reliance on legacy hardware and software. Several times during the month, a contracted company must follow a checklist of 12 different commands that must be run in serial to restore performance to an acceptable level. The ISP would like to make this an automated process. Which of the following techniques would be *best* suited for this requirement?

A. Deploy SOAR utilities and runbooks.

B. Replace the associated hardware.

C.   Provide the contractors with direct access to syslog data.

D.   Switch the copper-based infrastructure to fiber.

28. A security analyst is investigating a possible buffer overflow attack. The attack seems to be attempting to load a program file. Analysis of the live memory reveals that the following string is being run:

```
code.linux_access.prg
```

Which of the following technologies would *best* mitigate the manipulation of memory segments?

A.   NX bit

B.   ASLR

C.   DEP

D.   HSM

29. A CISO at a regional power supply company is performing a risk assessment. The CISO must consider what the *most* important security objective is when applying cryptography to control messages. The control messages are critical and enable the operational technology to ensure the generators are outputting the correct electrical power levels. What is the most important consideration here?

A.   Importing the availability of messages

B.   Ensuring the non-repudiation of messages

C.   Enforcing protocol conformance for messages

D.   Ensuring the integrity of messages

30. Alan, a CISO for an online retailer, is performing a quantitative risk assessment. The assessment is based on the public-facing web application server. Current figures show that the application server experiences 80 attempted breaches per day. In the past 4 years, the company's data has been breached two times. Which of the following represents the ARO for successful breaches?

A.   50

B.   0.8

C.   0.5

D.   29,200

31. Security engineers are assessing the capabilities and vulnerabilities of a widely used mobile operating system. The company intends to deploy a secure image to mobile phones and tablets. The mobile devices mustn't be vulnerable to the risk of privilege elevation and the misuse of applications. What would be the *most* beneficial to the company for addressing these concerns?

    A.   Security-Enhanced Linux (SELinux)

    B.   Trusted Platform Module (TPM)

    C.   Security-Enhanced Android (SEAndroid)

    D.   Attestation services

32. Gerry, a CISO for a national healthcare provider, is assessing proposals for network storage solutions. The proposal is for NAS to be deployed to all regional hospitals and clinics. As the data that will be stored will be sensitive and subject to strict regulatory compliance, security is the most important consideration. The proposal is for appliances running a Linux kernel and providing secure access to authenticated users through NFS. One major concern is ensuring that the root account cannot be used to gain access to user data on the Linux NFS appliances. What would *best* prevent this issue from occurring?

    A.   Ensure passwords are stored in a shadow file.

    B.   Run SELinux in enforced mode.

    C.   Disable **central processing unit** (**CPU**) virtualization support.

    D.   Enforce secure encrypted enclaves/memory encryption.

33. ACME chemicals is conducting a risk assessment for its legacy operational technology. One of their major concerns is the widespread use of a standard message transport protocol that's used in industrial environments. After performing a vulnerability assessment, several CVEs are discovered with high CVSS values. The findings describe the following vulnerabilities:

    - CVE-2018-11452: Denial-of-service of the affected device

    - CVE-2018-7842: Elevation of privilege by conducting a brute-force attack on the parameters that were sent to the controller

    - CVE-2017-6034: An attacker can replay the `run`, `stop`, `upload`, and `download` commands

Additional CVEs report multiple vulnerabilities, including no security against message integrity being tampered with and being vulnerable to MITM attacks. What is the network/protocol that has most likely been assessed?

A.   Ethernet

B.   Modbus

C.   Distributed Network Protocol 3 (DNP3)

D.   Zigbee

34.   Mechanical engineers are using a simple programming language based on relay-based logic, as shown in the following diagram:

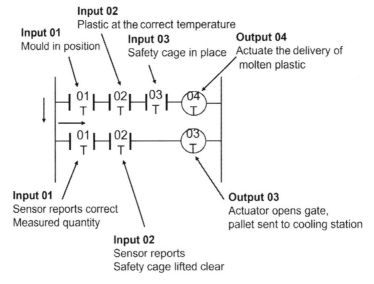

Figure 16.3 – Relay-based logic

What language/protocol are the engineers are using?

A.   Historian

B.   Ladder logic

C.   Zigbee

D.   Modbus

35. A small water treatment plant is being controlled by a SCADA system. There are four main treatment tanks, each being serviced by an input pump and an output pump. The design of the plant offers redundancy as the plant can operate without all the tanks being available. The plant is comprised of a standard SCADA mix of operational technology, including PLCs and a supervisory computer.

    What system failure will cause the biggest outage?

    A.   Loss of a treatment tank

    B.   Loss of supervisory computer

    C.   Failure of an input pump

    D.   Failure of a PLC

36. A development team is implementing a customer-facing API that uses a database backend. Before the deployment, the team is concerned about attacks, such as XSS, XSRF, and injection attacks. To mitigate these types of attacks, the team needs to identify security controls that could be implemented. Which of the following sources could the team consult to address these security concerns?

    A.   SDLC

    B.   OVAL

    C.   IEEE

    D.   OWASP

37. The customers of a large online retailer are reporting high levels of latency when they are searching for products on the e-commerce site. The site consists of an array of load-balanced APIs that do not require authentication. The application servers that host the APIs are showing heavy CPU utilization. WAFs that have been placed in front of the APIs are not generating any alerts.

    Which of the following should a security engineer recommend to *best* remedy these performance issues promptly?

    A.   Implement rate limiting on the API.

    B.   Implement geo-blocking on the WAF.

    C.   Implement OAuth 2.0 on the API.

    D.   Implement input validation on the API.

38. ACME bank engineers are configuring security for a new data center. They are looking to implement SSL/TLS for customer-facing application servers. Customers will connect to the bank API through a deployed mobile application. They must now choose a symmetric algorithm that offers the greatest speed and security. Which should they choose?

    A.   ChaCha256 + poly1305

    B.   3DES + CBC

    C.   AES256 + CBC

    D.   Salsa256 + CBC

39. Hackers can gain access to encrypted data transmissions. After performing vulnerability assessments on the application servers, several cipher suites are available for backward compatibility. Which of the following would represent the *greatest* risk?

    A.   TLS_RSA_WITH_AES_128_CBC_SHA

    B.   TLS_RSA_WITH_RC4_40_MD5

    C.   TLS_DHE_RSA_WITH_AES_256_CBC_SHA

    D.   TLS_RSA_WITH_3DES_EDE_CBC_SHA

40. A company is deploying an online streaming service for customers. The content needs to be protected; only the paid subscribers should be able to view the streams. The company wants to choose the *best* solution for low latency and security. What would be the best choice?

    A.   3DES

    B.   AES

    C.   ChaCha

    D.   RC4

41. A government agency is configuring a VPN connection between Fort Meade and a field office in New York. Of primary importance is having a highly secure key exchange protocol due to the threats posed by nation state threat actors. Which encryption protocol would be a good choice?

    A.   Advanced Encryption Standard (AES)

    B.   ECDHE p521

C.   ChaCha-256

D.   SHA-512

42. Software developers are deploying a new customer-facing CRM tool. The deployment will require the customers to download an application on their system. Customers must be able to verify that the application is trustworthy. What type of certificate will the software developers request to fulfill this requirement?

A.   Client authentication

B.   Server authentication

C.   Digital signatures

D.   Code signing

43. A large insurance provider has grown in size and now supports customers in many different countries. Due to this increased footprint, they are looking to minimize administration by allocating a single certificate to multiple sites. The sites will be country-specific, with different domain names. What would be the best choice for delivering this requirement?

A.   Wildcard certificate

B.   Extended validation

C.   General-purpose

D.   Subject Alternate Name (SAN)

44. The CISO is delivering a security briefing to senior members of staff. One of the topics of conversation concerns the current e-commerce site. During a Q&A session, the CISO is asked questions about PKI and certificates. A rudimentary question is asked – what key is stored on a certificate? What should the CISO answer?

A.   Public key

B.   Private key

C.   Public and private keys

D.   Signing key

45. A large online bank would like to ensure that customers can quickly validate that the bank's certificates are not part of a CRL. What would best meet this requirement?

A.   Extended validation

B.   Certificate pinning

C.   OCSP

D.   CRL

46. Website engineers are configuring security extensions to be deployed to all customer-facing web application servers. What HTTP extension will ensure that all the connections to the application servers will also be encrypted using the assigned X.509 certificate?

A.   HTTP X-FRAME headers

B.   HTTP Strict Transport Security (HSTS)

C.   HTTPS SSL 3.0 CBC

D.   Extended validation

47. Nation state-sponsored actors have stolen the smartphone of a government official. They have attempted to guess the PIN code several times, eventually locking the device. They are attempting to gain access to the data using forensic tools and techniques but the data cannot be accessed. What has likely prevented a data breach from occurring?

A.   Hardware write blocker

B.   USB data blocker

C.   Crypto shredding

D.   Improper key handling

48. A small startup energy company has built up a database of clients. It is estimated that this database is worth $100,000. During a data breach, a cyber-criminal (working for a competitor) steals 10% of the records. The company fails to put adequate controls in place and a second breach occurs within 12 months.

What is the **Annual Loss Expectancy (ALE)**?

A. $200,000

B. $1,000

C. $20,000

D. $10,000

49. A defense contractor currently loses an estimated $2,000,000 each year due to intellectual property theft. The company has a solid reputation for R&D and manufacturing but has no dedicated security staff. A **Managed Security Service Provider** (**MSSP**) guarantees that they will provide 90% protection for the data over a 5-year contract at an annual cost of $250,000 per annum. What is the ROI in dollars?

    A. $10,000,000

    B. $9,000,000

    C. $750,000

    D. $7,750,000

50. An automobile manufacturer suffers a power outage at one of its foundries. The facility supplies critical components for the company. The COOP designated the foundry as a mission-essential service, and it was agreed that the foundry must be operational within 24 hours. The energy supplier has struggled to repair severe storm-damaged cables. As a result, the facility is without power for 72 hours. What is the metric that describes this 72-hour outage?

    A.   Mean time to recovery (MTTR)

    B.   Mean time between failure (MTBF)

    C.   Recovery Time Objective (RTO)

    D.   Annualized rate of occurrence (ARO)

Assessment test answers

1.   **B**. Use a centralized trusted secrets manager service. Secrets can include user or auto-generated passwords, APIs, and other application keys/credentials, SSH keys, databases, and other system-to-system passwords. You should use private certificates for secure communication and private encryption keys.

    External reference: `https://www.beyondtrust.com/resources/glossary/secrets-management`.

    See *Chapter 4, Deploying Enterprise Authentication and Authorization Controls*, for more details on secure account management concepts.

2. **B**. Privacy Impact Assessment. A PIA should be undertaken by any organization that stores, transmits, or processes data that contains private information. Data types will vary but can include documents, database records, and media such as CCTV footage and voice recordings. See *Chapter 15, Business Continuity and Disaster Recovery Concepts*.

3. **C**. Separation of duties. When an employee has privileges that enable them to make high-level decisions without needing the consent of another employee, then we are missing essential checks and balances. Consider a **Chief Financial Officer** (**CFO**), who approves new suppliers, approves the suppliers' invoices for services, and signs their paychecks. This example would allow for fraudulent activities and would be mitigated by establishing accounts receivable and accounts payable business functions. See *Chapter 13, Applying Appropriate Risk Strategies*.

4. **C**. Impossible time travel. Disable the device's account and carry out further investigations.

   See *Chapter 9, Enterprise Mobility and Endpoint Security Controls* (covers location services and **user and entity behavior analytics** (**UEBA**)).

5. **B**. Clients are configured to use RC4. RC4 is considered weak encryption and would not be supported while using TLS 1.3. See *Chapter 11, Implementing Cryptographic Protocols and Algorithms*.

6. **A**. A vulnerability. When a system is missing patches, it is vulnerable to attacks. During a risk assessment, we need to assess vulnerabilities and potential threats that could target the vulnerability. See *Chapter 6, Vulnerability Assessment and Penetration Testing Methods and Tools*.

7. **A**. Black-box testing will take the least amount of time but may not discover all vulnerabilities. See *Chapter 6, Vulnerability Assessment and Penetration Testing Methods and Tools*.

8. **B**. Alert fatigue. This is when the staff are overwhelmed with too many alerts. See *Chapter 1, Designing a Secure Network Architecture*.

9. **C**. **Unified Threat Management** (**UTM**). This can combine multiple security functions into a single appliance. See *Chapter 1, Designing a Secure Network Architecture*.

10. **A** and **D**. Third-party libraries may have vulnerabilities and Third-party libraries may have licensing restrictions. See *Chapter 2, Integrating Software Applications into the Enterprise*.

11. **D**. SecDevOps. The development team and operations teams work together to ensure code is delivered error-free. See *Chapter 2, Integrating Software Applications into the Enterprise*.

12. **B.** The waterfall methodology means that we must have defined all the requirements at the start of the process and that no changes will be made during the development cycle. See *Chapter 2, Integrating Software Applications into the Enterprise.*

13. **C.** Use **Privileged Access Management (PAM)** to remove user accounts from the local admin group and prompt the user for explicit approval when elevation is required. This solution allows accounts to elevate their privileges and that these actions will be audited. See *Chapter 4, Deploying Enterprise Authentication and Authorization Controls.*

14. **A.** Replace the current antivirus with an EDR solution. The end devices must be protected when they are not on the company network. The other solutions will not adequately fulfill the requirements. See *Chapter 9, Enterprise Mobility and Endpoint Security Controls.*

15. **D.** Recovery Service Level. See *Chapter 15, Business Continuity and Disaster Recovery Concepts.*

16. **C.** Access the `/etc/passwd` file to extract the usernames. As the account is a standard user, they will not have the right to edit configuration files (sudoers), so the best option is to access the `passwd` file (you do not need any privileges to do this). See *Chapter 7, Risk Mitigation Controls.*

17. **C.** ID22 shows a high amount of disk I/O using the `vmstat` command. See *Chapter 8, Implementing Incident Response and Forensics Procedures.*

18. **A.** Preparation. For details on creating an incident response plan, see *Chapter 8, Implementing Incident Response and Forensics Procedures.*

19. **A.** Root cause analysis. This would be performed as a result of lessons learned/AAR. See *Chapter 8, Implementing Incident Response and Forensics Procedures.*

20. **A. Execute-never** (**XN**). CPU chips support memory protection within the hardware. See *Chapter 9, Enterprise Mobility and Endpoint Security Controls.*

21. **B.** `tcpdump`. This is a command-line protocol analyzer that's capable of capturing traffic and can be used to analyze previous captures. pcap is a standard packet capture file format. See *Chapter 8, Implementing Incident Response and Forensics Procedures.*

22. **C.** `nc -w 180 -p 12345 -l < shadow.txt`. Netcat can be used to run remote commands on a target system, allowing for files to be transferred. See *Chapter 8, Implementing Incident Response and Forensics Procedures.*

23. **A.** Steganalysis tool. This tool would search for data hidden within the graphics file. See *Chapter 8, Implementing Incident Response and Forensics Procedures.*

24. **D**. Always-on VPN settings. They will always have an encrypted connection that's routed through the company network. See *Chapter 9, Enterprise Mobility and Endpoint Security Controls*.

25. **D**. Unauthorized application stores. See *Chapter 9, Enterprise Mobility and Endpoint Security Controls*.

26. **B**. Shell restrictions. The current settings mitigate the main threats but do not prevent built-in commands from being run. See *Chapter 9, Enterprise Mobility and Endpoint Security Controls*.

27. **A**. Deploy SOAR utilities and runbooks. This will automate this repetitive process and take some of the workload off the technicians. See *Chapter 8, Implementing Incident Response and Forensics Procedures*.

28. **B**. ASLR. This mitigation is built into the operating system and is considered a better option (NX+DEP is hardware-based and less effective).

29. **D**. Ensuring the integrity of messages. Control messages will not normally be confidential but must be tamper-proof. This is the best solution. See *Chapter 10, Security Considerations Impacting Specific Sectors and Operational Technologies*.

30. **C**. 0.5. The ARO over 4 years is 0.5 as there were only two successful breaches. See *Chapter 13, Applying Appropriate Risk Strategies*.

31. **C. Security-Enhanced Android** (**SEAndroid**). This is SELinux for mobile devices. See *Chapter 9, Enterprise Mobility and Endpoint Security Controls*.

32. **B**. Run SELinux in enforced mode. This will enforce **Mandatory Access Control** (**MAC**). See *Chapter 9, Enterprise Mobility and Endpoint Security Controls*.

33. **B**. Modbus. This is a well-used control protocol that's used within industrial controlled environments. It is vulnerable to many different threats. See *Chapter 10, Security Considerations Impacting Specific Sectors and Operational Technologies*.

34. **B**. Ladder logic. See *Chapter 10, Security Considerations Impacting Specific Sectors and Operational Technologies*.

35. **B**. Loss of a supervisory computer. See *Chapter 10, Security Considerations Impacting Specific Sectors and Operational Technologies*. This can also be seen in the following diagram:

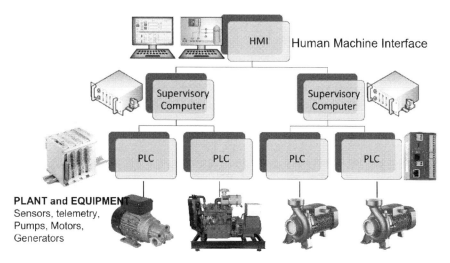

Figure 16.4 – The hierarchy of and dependencies within a SCADA system

36. **D**. OWASP. This will be the best source of reference when securing web applications.

37. **A**. Implement rate limiting on the API. This will allow for the number of connections that are forwarded to the web servers to be *throttled*.

38. **A**. ChaCha256 + poly1305. This offers a major performance advantage over existing technologies. See *Chapter 11, Implementing Cryptographic Protocols and Algorithms*.

39. **B**. TLS_RSA_WITH_RC4_40_MD5. RC4 (symmetric encryption) should not be used and will cause systems to be out of compliance. MD5 (hashing algorithm) is also weak and should not be used. See *Chapter 11, Implementing Cryptographic Protocols and Algorithms*.

40. **C**. ChaCha. This is a stream cipher and will offer very good performance for streaming media. See *Chapter 11, Implementing Cryptographic Protocols and Algorithms*.

41. **B**. ECDHE p521. This is currently the strongest form of key exchange. The other answers refer to symmetric encryption or hashing. See *Chapter 11, Implementing Cryptographic Protocols and Algorithms*.

42. **D**. Code signing. The application code needs to be digitally signed. See *Chapter 12, Implementing Appropriate PKI Solutions, Cryptographic Protocols, and Algorithms for Business Needs*.

43. **D**. **Subject Alternate Name** (**SAN**). This will allow a single certificate to be issued for multiple sites. A wildcard would not be suitable as the domain names will be different. See *Chapter 12, Implementing Appropriate PKI Solutions, Cryptographic Protocols, and Algorithms for Business Needs*.

44. **A**. Public key. A digital certificate validates the public key. Private keys are not shared but can be stored in escrow if a copy needs to be made. See *Chapter 12, Implementing Appropriate PKI Solutions, Cryptographic Protocols, and Algorithms for Business Needs*.

45. **C**. OCSP. This allows a quick response to be provided when a CRL check is required. See *Chapter 12, Implementing Appropriate PKI Solutions, Cryptographic Protocols, and Algorithms for Business Needs*.

46. **B**. **HTTP Strict Transport Security** (**HSTS**). This will ensure that all the connections are forced to use HTTPS/TLS. See *Chapter 2, Integrating Software Applications into the Enterprise*.

47. **C**. Crypto shredding. The symmetric key that was used to encrypt the data is destroyed, making data recovery ineffective. See *Chapter 12, Implementing Appropriate PKI Solutions, Cryptographic Protocols, and Algorithms for Business Needs*.

48. **C**. $20,000.

    Asset Value (**AV**) = 100,000

    Exposure Factor (**EF**) = 10%

    Single Loss Expectancy (**SLE**) = 10,000

    Annual Rate of Occurrence (**ARO**) = 2

    Annual Loss Expectancy (**ALO**) = 20,000 (SLE x ARO)

    See *Chapter 13, Applying Appropriate Risk Strategies*.

49. **D**. $7,750,000. ROI= (9,000,000 Reduction in risk – 750,000 cost of control). The contract is for 5 years, so the potential loss would be 10,000,000. As we mitigate 90% of the loss, we have saved 9,000,000 but must pay 5 x 250,000 = 1,250,000. See *Chapter 13, Applying Appropriate Risk Strategies*.

50. **A**. **Mean time to recovery** (**MTTR**). See *Chapter 13, Applying Appropriate Risk Strategies*.

Hopefully, you have enjoyed testing yourself via a typical mix of CASP questions. For more exam resources, please visit `https://www.casp.training`.

17
Mock Exam 2

Welcome to the study guide assessment test! These test questions are designed to resemble real-world **CASP 004** exam questions. To make the test as realistic as possible, you should attempt these questions *closed book* and allocate the appropriate amount of time. You can use some notepaper or a scratchpad to jot down notes, although this will be different in a real test environment. To find the PearsonVue candidate testing rules, check out `https://home.pearsonvue.com/comptia/onvue`.

End of Study Assessment Test

Number of Questions: 50

Passing Score: 83% (Estimated)

Questions

1. A company works with a **cloud service provider** (**CSP**) that provides *bleeding-edge* technology to perform data analytics and deep learning techniques on the company's data. As the technology becomes more widespread, it appears that a rival CSP can offer the same solutions for a 50% cost saving. However, it seems that the database format and rule sets that have been created can't be transferred to the rival CSP. What term would best describe this situation?

   A. Vendor risk

   B. Vendor lock-in

   C. Third-party liability

   D. Vendor management plan

2. A major retailer works with a small, highly regarded, third-party development team. They intend to invest significant resources into a new customer-facing set of APIs. The retailer is concerned about the financial stability of the development company and worries that they may need to start the development project from scratch if the developers go bust. What could be used to allay the fears of the retailer?

   A. Change management

   B. Staff turnover

   C. Peer code review

   D. Source code escrow

3. Andy is the CSO within a department of the *United Kingdom's* **HM Revenue and Customs** (**HMRC**). All new systems that will require government funding must be assessed concerning cost savings by working with a CSP. Andy is overseeing a proposed new system that will reduce the workload of the Inland Revenue HMRC employees. What must a government agency consider when planning to store sensitive data with a global CSP?

   A. Data sovereignty

   B. Data ownership

   C. Data classifications

   D. Data retention

4.   A Privacy Impact Assessment is being conducted on behalf of a private healthcare provider. A consultant is assessing regulatory requirements for the hospital's employee and patient data (within Europe). The data that is currently being held includes the following:

   - Patient's address

   - Patient's bank account details

   - Patient's medical history

   - Patient's X-ray records

   - Employee bank account details

   What type of information will need to be protected and which regulations are the most important? (Choose *two*)

   A.   COPPA

   B.   **Personally identifiable information (PII)**

   C.   Financial records

   D.   Intellectual property

   E.   GDPR

5.   A regional bank intends to work with a CSP to harness some of the benefits associated with cloud computing. The bank wants the assurance that data will not be accessible when their contract with a CSP expires. What technology would be most applicable?

   A.   Crypto erase

   B.   Pulping

   C.   Shredding

   D.   Degaussing

6.   A company manufactures medical devices, including instruments and scanners. The company intends to sell and market its devices to a global customer base. The company must ensure its products are compatible with its worldwide customer base. What regulations or standards will be the *most* important?

   A.   Export Control Regulations

   B.   **General Data Protection Regulation (GDPR)**

   C.   **International Organization for Standardization (ISO)**

   D.   **National Institute of Standards and Technology (NIST)**

7. A startup software development company is trying to win a US Federal Government contract to provision an **Enterprise Resource Planning** (**ERP**) application. They must assure the customer that they have a robust security framework for delivering software and services. What is the most relevant accreditation?

    A.   **Open Web Application Security Project (OWASP)**

    B.   **Capability Maturity Model Integration (CMMI)**

    C.   **National Institute of Standards and Technology (NIST)**

    D.   **Cloud Security Alliance (CSA) Security Trust Assurance and Risk (STAR)**

8. A large US-based retailer is transitioning toward an online selling platform. While customer details and payment card details will be stored in-house, a CSP will be used to host the e-commerce site, including the online shop. What compliance will be most important to the retailer concerning storing cardholder data and electronic transactions?

    A.   **Payment Card Industry Data Security Standard (PCI DSS)**

    B.   **General Data Protection Regulation (GDPR)**

    C.   **Interconnection security agreement (ISA)**

    D.   **Non-disclosure agreement (NDA)**

9. Eva is the CISO for a global stocks and shares trading site. She is performing a risk assessment that focuses on customer data being stored and transmitted. Customers are mainly based in North America with a small percentage based globally, including Europe. When it comes to considering regulatory and legal requirements, which of the following will be the most important?

    A.   **General Data Protection Regulation (GDPR)**

    B.   **Payment Card Industry Data Security Standard (PCI DSS)**

    C.   **International Organization for Standardization (ISO)**

    D.   **Federal Information Security Management Act (FISMA)**

10. A US smartcard manufacturer needs to sell its products in a global market. They need to ensure that the technology is not sold to countries or governments that are hostile to the US. What guidance or regulations should they consult?

    A.   Due care

    B.   Export controls

    C.   Legal holds

    D.   E-discovery

11. A government department has data privacy requirements and they need to have employees and service providers sign this agreement. They should be made aware of the strict terms of this agreement and the penalties that may be forthcoming if these requirements/standards are not met. What type of agreement will be important?

    A.   **Service-level agreement (SLA)**

    B.   **Master service agreement (MSA)**

    C.   **Non-disclosure agreement (NDA)**

    D.   **Memorandum of understanding (MOU)**

12. A large multinational company intends to purchase multiple products on a rolling contract from a CSP. They need to document, payment terms, dispute resolution, intellectual property ownership, and geographic operational locations within the scope of the contract. What type of contract would be the most suitable?

    A.   **Service-level agreement (SLA)**

    B.   **Master service agreement (MSA)**

    C.   **Memorandum of understanding (MOU)**

    D.   **Operational-level agreement (OLA)**

13. A global pharmaceutical company would like to build resiliency into its network connections. They are working with an ISP, who proposes a highly available MPLS solution. To ensure the vendor can deliver the service at 99.999% uptime, what documentation will be important?

    A.   **Service-level agreement (SLA)**

    B.   **Memorandum of understanding (MOU)**

    C.   **Interconnection security agreement (ISA)**

    D.   **Operational-level agreement (OLA)**

14. A software development company and a mobile phone manufacturer have entered a business partnership. The business partners need to share data during a series of upcoming projects. This agreement will stipulate a timeline for the information exchange to be supported, security requirements, data types that will be exchanged, and the actual sites that will be part of the data interchange. What documentation best details these requirements?

    A.   SLA

    B.   MSA

    C.   MOU

    D.   ISA

15. A regional healthcare provider needs to address ever-escalating costs. They propose to host some of the information systems with a CSP. The healthcare provider needs assurances that any sensitive data will be protected by the service provider, and that agreed-upon steps are in place if data breaches or any adverse action were to occur. What document would address these requirements?

    A.   **Non-disclosure agreement (NDA)**

    B.   **Memorandum of understanding (MOU)**

    C.   **Interconnection security agreement (ISA)**

    D.   **Operational-level agreement (OLA)**

    E.   **Privacy-level agreement (PLA)**

16. A government agency begins an investigation on an employee suspected of stealing company **intellectual property (IP)**. What must be done first to ensure the data is not deleted?

    A.   Due care

    B.   Export controls

    C.   Legal holds

    D.   E-discovery

17. A company has several internal business units. The business units are semi-autonomous but need to support each other for the business to be efficient. To ensure the business units can work together, it is important to document responsibilities for each business unit. This document will not be written by lawyers and is intended to formalize previous verbal agreements. What documentation would best suit this requirement?

   A. **Service-level agreement (SLA)**

   B. **Master service agreement (MSA)**

   C. **Memorandum of understanding (MOU)**

   D. **Interconnection security agreement (ISA)**

18. An aerospace sub-contractor supplies parts to a major commercial aircraft manufacturer. The SLAs are very strict, with financial penalties for transgressions. Mission-critical processes must be identified within the subcontractor's plant to avoid any lengthy production delays. What metric can be used by the company to ensure a critical service will be operational within the specified timeframe?

   A. Recovery point objective

   B. Recovery time objective

   C. Recovery service level

   D. Mission essential functions

19. A public transportation provider has recently completed a BIA and has determined that the **Continuity of Operations Plan (COOP)** will require an alternative site to be available in the event of a major incident at the main operational site. The planning team has identified a requirement for a site, housing equipment, and facilities ready for the business to use. Personnel and data will need to be moved to the site to become operational. What have they identified?

   A. Cold site

   B. Warm site

   C. Hot site

   D. Mobile site

20. A CISO for a cellular telephony provider is working with a **Cloud Service Provider** (**CSP**) to define expected day-to-day computing needs. The company wants to be able to choose a plan where spikes in demand result in additional compute resources being automatically provisioned. What technology would *best* meet this requirement?

    A.   Autoscaling

    B.   Caching

    C.   Bootstrapping

    D.   Clustering

21. A company wants to be more flexible concerning employee work/life balance. To allow for this cultural change, remote access and working from home will become widespread. Senior management has concerns about data security, as most of the company information systems are now cloud-based. The concerns that were discussed include the following:

    - Data loss prevention

    - Control over native features of cloud services, such as collaboration and sharing

    - **User and entity behavior analytics** (**UEBA**)

    - Configuration auditing

    - Malware detection

    - Data encryption and key management

    - Context-based access control

    As employees will not be connected to the company network, various management concerns must be addressed. What solution would *best* address these concerns?

    A.   NGFW

    B.   CASB

    C.   DLP

    D.   SWG

22. What form of testing uses stakeholder involvement to assess the effectiveness of the plan? Scenarios can be discussed and actions that need to be performed can be evaluated. This exercise ensures the **Disaster Recovery Team (DRT)** or **Cyber Security Incident Response Team (CSIRT)** do not need to perform exhaustive testing until the plans are *fine-tuned*.

    A.   Checklist

    B.   Walk-through

    C.   Tabletop exercises

    D.   Full interruption test

23. A cloud customer needs workloads to be rapidly deployed to support a large and diverse customer base. One important requirement is to allow virtualized infrastructure to be deployed, where configuration is applied to a compute node or cluster as it boots up from a standard image (such as Linux, Unix, or Windows). What technology would *best* suit this requirement?

    A.   Autoscaling

    B.   Distributed allocation

    C.   Bootstrapping

    D.   Replication

24. A news delivery platform provider needs to deliver content in the form of web pages, media, and images to worldwide consumers. The requirement is for geographically dispersed servers using caching to ensure that data is available on the edge of the network, where users or customers will benefit from lower latency. What technology would best suit this requirement?

    A.   Autoscaling

    B.   Distributed network

    C.   Content delivery network

    D.   Replicated network

25. A medical instrument manufacturer is currently experiencing problems in the production plant. The company is using a mix of **Industrial Control Systems (ICS)** on a common network backbone to operate the plant. Some of the manufacturing processes are time-critical and occasionally, bottlenecks occur at peak times during the day. To ensure that the time-critical processes are not impacted by bottlenecks, what technology would most likely mitigate these problems?

   A.   **Safety Instrumented System (SIS)**

   B.   **Data Distribution Service (DDS)**

   C.   **Operational Technology (OT)**

   D.   **Controller Area Network (CAN)**

26. A utility company is following industry guidelines to harden its server systems. One of the first steps that the guidelines suggest is to identify all the available and unneeded services. What tool would *best* suit this requirement?

   A.   Binary analysis tools

   B.   Port scanner

   C.   HTTP interceptor

   D.   Protocol analyzer

27. A well-known developer's content sharing portal has been targeted by a DDoS attack. Although it's the web application servers that are being targeted, the effect of all the traffic flooding the network has made all the services unavailable. Security experts are looking to implement protection methods and implement blackhole routing for the web application servers. What has this mitigation achieved?

   A.   Traffic is inspected for malicious payloads

   B.   Traffic intended for the systems is dropped

   C.   Traffic to the systems is inspected before it reaches the destination

   D.   Rules restrict the amount of traffic throughput

28. Security analysts are responding to SIEM alerts that are showing a high number of IOC events. The analysts have a reason to suspect that there may be APT activity in the network. Which of the following threat management frameworks should the team implement to better understand the TTPs of the potential threat actor?

    A.   NIST SP 800-53

    B.   MITRE ATT&CK

    C.   The Cyber Kill Chain

    D.   The Diamond Model of Intrusion Analysis

29. National Dynamics, an aerospace company, is looking to strengthen its cybersecurity posture by focusing on its network defenses. The company is concerned about the availability of the company's services to its B2B partners. Many manufacturing processes use JIT techniques to optimize production and false positives mustn't drop legitimate traffic. Which of the following would satisfy this requirement?

    A.   NIDS

    B.   NIPS

    C.   WAF

    D.   Reverse proxy

30. A small law firm is looking to reduce its operating costs. Currently, vendors are proposing solutions where the CSP will host and manage the company's website and services. Due to legal and regulatory requirements, the company requires that all the available resources in the proposal must be dedicated. Due to cost constraints, the company does not want to fund a private cloud. Given the company requirements, which of the following is the *best* solution for this company?

    A.   Community cloud service model

    B.   Multi-tenancy SaaS

    C.   Single-tenancy SaaS

    D.   An on-premises cloud service model

31. A company that uses **Active Directory Services** (**ADS**) is migrating services from LDAP to secure LDAP (LDAPS). During the pilot phase, the server team has been troubleshooting connectivity issues from several different client systems. Initially, the clients would not connect as the LDAP server had been assigned a wildcard certificate, `*.classroom.local`. To fix these problems, the team replaced the wildcard certificate with a specific named certificate, `win2016-dc.classroom.local`. Further problems are causing the connections to fail. The following screenshot shows the output from a troubleshooting session:

```
[root@cent07 ~]# openssl s_client -host win2016-dc.classroom.local -port 636
CONNECTED(00000003)
Server certificate
-----BEGIN CERTIFICATE-----
MIIFTzCCBDegAwIBAgITHwAAAAQ0pZcvscL82QAAAAABDANBgkqhkiG9w0BAQsF
ADBJMRUwEwYKCZImiZPyLGQBGRYFbG9jYWwxGTAXBgoJkiaJk/IsZAEZFgljbGFz
c3Jvb20xFTATBgNVBAMTDGNsYXNzcm9vbS1DOTAeFw0vMTA3MiEwNTOwNDDVaFw0v
u2THpmYtUB038Qd3+Ob/nXCUseV+YPoNtnu1n9TpemdpTc0qzw/cP37TVrQnKwy5
6v0b0TMjabbB0i+35CocagPMnaEZQuPN0T/nyI4ttdQgBsAc8Kg4HB3p9MtEN2mG
haDcOg+WfXrc5erGr/NSKPaNzEDPjGSnKDWTyZJuBR3nmrauogJjranrDHNY8nJx
8SJSP2CnF9sJtzIn+lNDcIwDrg==
-----END CERTIFICATE-----
subject=/CN=WIN2016-DC.classroom.local
issuer=/DC=local/DC=classroom/CN=classroom-CA
```

Figure 17.1 – LDAPS client troubleshooting session

Which of the following *best* explains why the LDAPS service failed initially and still fails client connection attempts? (Select *two*)

A.   The clients do not support the LDAP protocol by default.

B.   The LDAPS service has not been started, so the connections will fail.

C.   `Classroom.local` is under a DDoS attack and cannot respond to OCSP requests.

D.   The clients may not trust the issuing `CA-classroom.classroom.local` by default.

E.   LDAPS should be running on UDP rather than TCP.

F.   The company is using the wrong port. It should be using port 389 for LDAPS.

G.   LDAPS does not support wildcard certificates.

32. A sales team relies on a CRM application to generate leads and maintain customer engagement. The tool is considered a mission-essential function to the company. During a business impact assessment, the risk management team indicated that data, when restored, cannot be older than 2 hours before a system failure. What planning objective should be used when the restoration will also require data to be restored?

    A. Recovery point objective

    B. Recovery time objective

    C. Recovery service level

    D. Mission-essential functions

33. A large defense contractor has recently received a security advisory documenting the activities of highly skilled nation-state threat actors. The company's hunt team believes they have identified activity consistent with the advisory. Which of the following techniques would be *best* for the hunt team to use to entice the adversary to generate malicious activity?

    A. Perform audits on all firewall logs.

    B. Implement a bug bounty program.

    C. Increase security using isolation and segmentation schemes.

    D. Deploy decoy files on the host's systems on the same network segment.

34. A new online retailer must ensure that all the new web servers are secured in advance of a PCI DSS security audit. PCI DSS requirements are strict and define acceptable cipher suites. Deprecated cipher suites should not be used as they offer weak encryption and are vulnerable to on-path attacks. In preparation for the audit, a security professional should disable which of the following cipher suites?

    A. TLS_RSA_WITH_AES_128_CCM_8_SHA256

    B. TLS_RSA_WITH_RC4_128_SHA

    C. TLS_RSA_WITH_AES_128_CBC_SHA256

    D. TLS_ECDHE_ECDSA_WITH_CHACHA20_POLY1305_SHA256

35. A distribution company is attempting to harden its security posture regarding mobile devices. To secure the dedicated Android devices that are used in the warehouse, the company has developed SELinux policies. Security engineers have compiled and implemented the policy. Before deploying the Android devices to the warehouse staff, which mode should the devices be configured for?

   A.   Disabled

   B.   Permissive

   C.   Enforcing

   D.   Preventing

36. A software development company is concerned as it has discovered that company intellectual property is circulating on social media. The CISO wants to implement a solution that will allow the company to determine the source of these leaks. Which of the following should be implemented to identify the internal source for any future exposures?

   A.   Digital rights management

   B.   Hashing

   C.   Watermarking

   D.   Identity proofing

37. A company has recently undertaken a project to move several services into the cloud. A cloud service provider now hosts the following services:

   - Corporate intranet site

   - Online storage application

   - Email and collaboration suite

   The company must ensure that the data is protected from common threats, including malware infections, exfiltration of PII and healthcare data.

   To be more proactive, an additional requirement is that SOC staff must receive alerts when there are any large transfers of corporate data from the company's hosted storage. Which of the following would best address the company's cyber-security requirements?

   A.   NIDS

   B.   CASB

   C.   DLP agent

D.   Containers

E.   Vulnerability scanner

38. A CISO is reviewing the current security of an electricity supply company. The company has many operational sites and must connect the sites securely to the company headquarters, which is where the company's data center is located. The technology that's supported within these sites includes industrial control systems and PLCs. The technology is legacy and uses the Modbus protocol across the networks. A VPN solution is being proposed to securely connect all the sites to the company's data center.

The CISO is concerned that a recent security advisory, concerning certain asymmetric algorithms, may impact the company's operations. Which of the following will be most likely impacted by weak asymmetric encryption?

A.   Modbus

B.   VPN links

C.   Industrial control systems

D.   Datacenter equipment

39. Security administrators have run a scan on a network segment to detect vulnerabilities. They are trying to discover any protocols that may be running on host computers that may expose user passwords or sensitive data. The following screenshot shows the output from the scan:

```
Starting Nmap 7.91 ( https://nmap.org ) at 2021-12-11 17:57 GMT
Nmap scan report for 10.10.0.4
Host is up (0.63s latency).
Not shown: 98 filtered ports
PORT    STATE SERVICE
22/tcp open  ssh
23/tcp open  telnet
Nmap scan report for 10.10.0.50
Host is up (0.00056s latency).
Not shown: 98 closed ports
PORT     STATE SERVICE
80/tcp  open  http
443/tcp open  https

Nmap scan report for 10.10.0.1
Host is up (0.0010s latency).
Not shown: 91 filtered ports
PORT     STATE SERVICE
53/tcp   open  domain
88/tcp   open  kerberos-sec
3389/tcp open  ms-wbt-server
```

Figure 17.2 – Security scan output

To secure the network segment, additional rules must be enabled on the network firewall. Which rules should be added to meet this security requirement? Choose *two*.

A. SRC Any   DST 10.10.0.1   PORT 53   PROT TCP   ACTION Deny

B. SRC Any   DST 10.10.0.4   PORT 23   PROT TCP   ACTION Deny

C. SRC Any   DST 10.10.0.4   PORT 22   PROT TCP   ACTION Deny

D. SRC Any   DST 10.10.0.50   PORT 80   PROT TCP   ACTION Deny

E. SRC Any   DST 10.10.0.1   PORT 88   PROT TCP   ACTION Deny

F. SRC Any   DST 10.10.0.50   PORT 443   PROT TCP   ACTION Deny

40. A systems administrator has deployed all updated patches for Windows-based machines. However, the users on the network are experiencing exploits from various threat actors, which the patches should have corrected. Which of the following is the *most* likely scenario here?

A.   The machines were infected with malware.

B.   The users did not reboot their computers after the patches were deployed.

C.   The systems administrator used invalid credentials to deploy the patches.

D.   The patches were deployed on non-Windows-based machines.

41. A penetration tester is trying to gain access to a remote system. The tester can see the secure login page and knows one user account and email address but has not discovered a password yet. Which of the following would be the *easiest* method of obtaining a password for the known account?

A.   Man-in-the-middle

B.   Reverse engineering

C.   Social engineering

D.   Hash cracking

42. An external hacker has managed to exploit an unpatched vulnerability in a web application server. They were able to use the web application service account to download malicious software. The attacker tried (unsuccessfully) to gain root privileges to install the software and was subsequently discovered. The server admin team rebuilt and patched the server. Which of the following should the team perform to prevent a similar attack in the future?

    A.   Remove the application service account

    B.   Air gap the web application server

    C.   Configure SELinux and set it to enforcing mode

    D.   Schedule regular restarts of the service to terminate sessions

    E.   Use Nmap to perform regular uncredentialed vulnerability scans

43. A manufacturing company is deploying IoT locks, sensors, and cameras, which operate wirelessly. The devices will be used to allow physical access by locking and unlocking doors and other access points. Recent CVEs have been listed against the devices, for which the vendor has yet to provide firmware updates. Which of the following would *best* mitigate this risk?

    A.   Connect the IoT devices directly to ethernet switches and create a segmented VLAN.

    B.   Require sensors to digitally sign all transmitted control messages.

    C.   Add all the IoT devices to an isolated wireless network and use WPA2 and EAP-TLS.

    D.   Implement a wireless intrusion detection system.

44. A forensics investigator is following up on an incident where suspicious images have been stored on an employee's computer. The computer is currently powered off in the employee's workspace. Which of the following tools is *best* suited to retrieving full or partial image files from the storage device, which have been deleted so that the attacker evades detection?

    A.   memdump

    B.   foremost

    C.   dd

    D.   nc

45. An aerospace company is adding promotional material to a public-facing web application server. The server will host a website containing many images, highlighting a production plant and test facilities. The CISO is concerned that the images may contain geographic coordinates in the metadata, and some of the physical locations need to remain secret. What tool can be used to ensure that the images will not contain sensitive data within the metadata?

    A.   grep

    B.   ExifTool

    C.   Tcpdump

    D.   Wireshark

46. A critical service on a production system keeps crashing at random times. The systems administrator suspects that the code has not been adequately tested and may contain a bug. When the service crashes, a memory dump is created in the /var/log directory. Which of the following tools can the systems administrator use to reproduce these symptoms?

    A.   DAST

    B.   Vulnerability scanner

    C.   Core dump analyzer

    D.   Hex dump

47. Ontario Outdoors Inc is expecting major disruptions due to a winter weather warning. The CISO has been reviewing company policies to ensure adequate provisions are in place to deal with these environmental impacts and finds that some are missing or incomplete. The CISO must ensure that a document is immediately drafted to move various personnel and equipment to other locations to avoid downtime in operations. What is this an example of?

    A.   A disaster recovery plan

    B.   An incident response plan

    C.   A business continuity plan

    D.   A risk avoidance plan

48. Acme corporation operates a nuclear power station and relies on a legacy ICS to perform equipment monitoring functions. Regulatory compliance requires that this monitoring is mandatory. Penalties for non-compliance could be costly. The ICS has known vulnerabilities but cannot be updated or replaced. The company has been refused cyber-liability insurance. Which of the following would be the *best* option to manage this risk in the company's production environment?

    A.   Avoid the risk by removing the ICS from production

    B.   Transfer the risk associated with the ICS vulnerabilities

    C.   Mitigate the risk by restricting access to the ICS

    D.   Accept the risk and upgrade the ICS when possible

49. Following a security incident, forensics has handed over a database server to the server admin team to begin the recovery phase. The team is looking to deploy an automated build by running a script. When accessing the Bash shell, they observe the following command as the most recent entry in the server's shell history:

```
dd if=dev/sda of=dev/sdb
```

    Which of the following *most* likely occurred?

    A.   Forensics have used binary analysis tools to search the metadata.

    B.   The drive was cloned for forensic analysis.

    C.   The hard drive was formatted after the incident.

    D.   There is evidence that the forensics team may have missed.

50. A software engineer is looking to implement secure code while the code is still in the development environment. The goal is to deploy code that meets stability and security assurance goals. Which of the following code analyzers will produce the desired results?

    A.   SAST

    B.   DAST

    C.   Fuzzer

    D.   Peer code review

Answers

1. **B**. Vendor lock-in. This makes it difficult to switch providers as the technology is often proprietary. See *Chapter 13, Applying Appropriate Risk Strategies*.

2. **D**. Source code escrow. External developers represent third-party risk. This can be mitigated by storing the code with an escrow service. This protects the IP of the developers but also protects the customer. See *Chapter 13, Applying Appropriate Risk Strategies*.

3. **A**. Data sovereignty. The type of data that's stored by a government department would typically have strict regulatory controls. A global CSP may store the data offshore. *See Chapter 13, Applying Appropriate Risk Strategies*.

4. **B** and **E**. This type of data would be labeled as PII and GDPR regulatory controls would be important as the patients and employees may be EU citizens. See *Chapter 14, Compliance Frameworks, Legal Considerations, and Their Organizational Impact*.

5. **A**. Crypto erase. The customer will not have physical access to the data, so they will not be able to ensure other methods of destruction can be implemented. Crypto Erase will render the data unrecoverable. See *Chapter 13, Applying Appropriate Risk Strategies*.

6. **C. International Organization for Standardization (ISO)**. This will ensure that the products will be suitable across international boundaries. See *Chapter 14, Compliance Frameworks, Legal Considerations, and Their Organizational Impact*.

7. **B. Capability Maturity Model Integration (CMMI)**. This accreditation is required to tender for US government software contracts. See *Chapter 14, Compliance Frameworks, Legal Considerations, and Their Organizational Impact*.

8. **A. Payment Card Industry Data Security Standard (PCI DSS)**. Storage and processing of customer card details will be subject to PCI DSS compliance. See *Chapter 14, Compliance Frameworks, Legal Considerations, and Their Organizational Impact*.

9. **A. General Data Protection Regulation (GDPR)**. As this is not government or payment card data, then the focus will be on customers based in the EU. See *Chapter 14, Compliance Frameworks, Legal Considerations, and Their Organizational Impact*.

10. **B**. Export controls. This is important when you're exporting technology. See *Chapter 14, Compliance Frameworks, Legal Considerations, and Their Organizational Impact*.

11. **C. Non-disclosure agreement (NDA)**. This is legally enforceable and protects intellectual property. See *Chapter 14, Compliance Frameworks, Legal Considerations, and Their Organizational Impact*.

12. **B. Master service agreement (MSA).** This is useful when it is necessary to set baseline terms for future services. See *Chapter 14, Compliance Frameworks, Legal Considerations, and Their Organizational Impact.*

13. **A. Service-level agreement (SLA).** This will allow the customer and the service provider to agree upon delivered services and the metrics that will be used to measure performance. See *Chapter 14, Compliance Frameworks, Legal Considerations, and Their Organizational Impact.*

14. **D. Interconnection security agreement (ISA).** This is important for documenting the details when a connection is made between two or more parties. See *Chapter 14, Compliance Frameworks, Legal Considerations, and Their Organizational Impact.*

15. **E. Privacy-level agreement (PLA).** This is very important when you're looking to assure customers who must adhere to strict regulatory compliance. See *Chapter 14, Compliance Frameworks, Legal Considerations, and Their Organizational Impact.*

16. **C.** Legal holds. This ensures that the data will be retained for any legal process. See *Chapter 14, Compliance Frameworks, Legal Considerations, and Their Organizational Impact.*

17. **C. Memorandum of understanding (MOU).** This is not a legal document but it can be very useful when there needs to be co-operation between two or more parties. See *Chapter 14, Compliance Frameworks, Legal Considerations, and Their Organizational Impact.*

18. **B.** Recovery time objective. A recovery time objective is a planning objective that is set by stakeholders within the business. It may be cost-driven and requires careful consideration. See *Chapter 15, Business Continuity and Disaster Recovery Concepts.*

19. **B.** Warm site. A warm site will not be as costly as a hot site but will not be operational until data is restored and staff are available to operate the site. See *Chapter 15, Business Continuity and Disaster Recovery Concepts.*

20. **A.** Autoscaling. This allows the company to access additional computing power using automation. See *Chapter 15, Business Continuity and Disaster Recovery Concepts.*

21. **B.** CASB. The company data must be protected in the cloud. Not all users will originate from a company network, so NGFW and SWG will not work. DLP does not address all the requirements. See *Chapter 15, Business Continuity and Disaster Recovery Concepts.*

22. **C.** Tabletop exercises. Stakeholders will discuss how they will act when dealing with a presented scenario. See *Chapter 15, Business Continuity and Disaster Recovery Concepts.*

23. **C**. Bootstrapping. This allows the automated deployment of customized workloads from a standard base image. PowerShell **Desired State Configuration** (**DSC**) is an example of this technology. See *Chapter 15, Business Continuity and Disaster Recovery Concepts*.

24. **C**. Content Delivery Network. This allows the timely delivery of time-sensitive services and reduces latency. See *Chapter 15, Business Continuity and Disaster Recovery Concepts*.

25. **B**. **Data Distribution Service** (**DDS**). DDS has built-in provisions for **Quality of Service** (**QoS**). See *Chapter 10, Security Considerations Impacting Specific Sectors and Operational Technologies*.

26. **B**. Port Scanner. Nmap is a good choice for the following:

    ```
    Scanning www.comptia.org (52.165.16.154) [1000 ports]

    Discovered open port 443/tcp on 52.165.16.154

    Discovered open port 80/tcp on 52.165.16.154

    Completed SYN Stealth Scan at 15:36, 9.18s elapsed (1000
    total ports)
    ```

    See *Chapter 5, Threat and Vulnerability Management*.

27. **B**. Traffic intended for the systems is dropped. A good example of this technique is **Remote Triggered Black Hole** (**RTBH**) routing. See *Chapter 1, Designing a Secure Network Architecture*.

28. **B**. MITRE ATT&CK. MITRE receives government funding to carry out research and is well known for its published attack frameworks and tactics. The matrices are created to understand the tactics and techniques that attackers will use against operating systems, cloud network mobility, and industrial control systems. See *Chapter 5, Threat and Vulnerability Management*.

29. **A**. NIDS. Such systems protect an organization from inbound threats across the network. The technology is primarily passive, generating alerts that must be actioned by SOC staff. See *Chapter 1, Designing a Secure Network Architecture*.

30. **C**. Single-tenancy SaaS. As the CSP will be hosting and managing the company services, then the service that the customer is paying for will be **Software as a Service** (**SaaS**) to isolate the workloads. They can pay a premium to have a single tenancy. See *Chapter 3, Enterprise Data Security, Including Secure Cloud and Virtualization Solutions*.

31. **D** and **G**. The clients may not trust the issuing `CA-classroom.classroom.local` by default. LDAPS does not support wildcard certificates.

The first issue that the server team solved was the problem that LDAPS does not support wildcard certificates. The second problem is most likely that the **certificate authority** (**CA**) is not trusted. If this is an internal CA, then the root CA certificate will need to be installed in the trusted enterprise store of all client computers. See *Chapter 12, Implementing Appropriate PKI Solutions, Cryptographic Protocols, and Algorithms for Business Needs.*

32. **A**. Recovery point objective. When data must be available to service a mission-critical service, then the recovery point objective metric must be used. See *Chapter 15, Business Continuity and Disaster Recovery Concepts.*

33. **D**. Deploy decoy files on hosts systems on the same network segment. If an APT has access to the network, then a decoy file will be a good test to observe any malicious activity. See *Chapter 7, Risk Mitigation Controls.*

34. **B**. `TLS_RSA_WITH_RC4_128_SHA`. RC4 is weak encryption and will not be used in any regulated industries. See *Chapter 11, Implementing Cryptographic Protocols and Algorithms.*

35. **C**. Enforcing. To run an SElinux policy and make **Mandatory Access Control** (**MAC**) effective, the systems must be *powered* up in enforced mode. See *Chapter 9, Enterprise Mobility and Endpoint Security Controls.*

36. **C**. Watermarking. If an organization wants to detect theft or exfiltration of sensitive data, then documents can be checked out from an information system, but an automatic watermark will be applied to the document using the identity of the user who checked out the document. See *Chapter 3, Enterprise Data Security, Including Secure Cloud and Virtualization Solutions.*

37. **B**. CASB. A CASB is often referred to as a gatekeeper that protects the enterprise data from inbound threats into the cloud and outbound threats such as data exfiltration. Another benefit of CASB is to ensure regulatory compliance, by labeling and monitoring the use of the data, to ensure compliance. See *Chapter 15, Business Continuity and Disaster Recovery Concepts.*

38. **B**. VPN links. A VPN allows traffic to be secured when it's passing through untrusted networks. If the external traffic uses weak encryption, then it could be accessed by an adversary. See *Chapter 1, Designing a Secure Network Architecture.*

39. **B** and **D**.

```
SRC Any      DST 10.10.0.4    PORT 23    PROT TCP    ACTION
Deny

SRC Any      DST 10.10.0.50   PORT 80    PROT TCP    ACTION
Deny
```

Port 23 supports the telnet protocol; this allows unsecured traffic to be sent when you're configuring equipment across a network. Port 80 allows for unsecured web traffic. Port 53 is for DNS traffic; this does not transmit passwords or sensitive data. Port 88 is Kerberos; this encrypts the transmission of user login traffic. Port 22 is SSH, encrypting traffic is used to access a console session on another host system. See *Chapter 1, Designing a Secure Network Architecture*, for more information on firewall rules.

40. **B**. The users did not reboot the computer after the patches were deployed. Certain patches may not be effective until the operating system is rebooted. See *Chapter 9, Enterprise Mobility and Endpoint Security Controls*.

41. **C**. Social engineering. Once an attacker has access to credentials, the most likely exploit to reveal a password is social engineering. See *Chapter 6, Vulnerability Assessment and Penetration Testing Methods and Tools*.

42. **C**. Configure SELinux and set it to enforcing mode. SELinux enforces mandatory access control, allowing for strict enforceable policies to be deployed. This would further restrict a compromised account from accessing other resources on the system. See *Chapter 9, Enterprise Mobility and Endpoint Security Controls*.

43. **C**. Add all the IoT devices to an isolated wireless network and use WPA2 and EAP-TLS. As all the devices connect wirelessly, they must be connected to a wireless segment. It is important to separate the network as there are vulnerable systems. See *Chapter 10, Security Considerations Impacting Specific Sectors and Operational Technologies*.

44. **B**. Foremost. This is a forensics tool that can search for complete or partial files that have been deleted or hidden in some way. See *Chapter 8, Implementing Incident Response and Forensics Procedures*.

45. **B**. ExifTool. The following screenshot shows the partial output from ExifTool:

```
ExifTool Version Number      : 12.36
File Name                    : image1.jpg
Directory                    : .
File Size                    : 6.9 MiB
File Modification Date/Time  : 2021:05:02 09:07:40+01:00
File Access Date/Time        : 2021:12:12 16:47:16+00:00
File Inode Change Date/Time  : 2021:12:12 16:47:23+00:00
File Permissions             : -rw-r--r--
File Type                    : JPEG
File Type Extension          : jpg
MIME Type                    : image/jpeg
GPS Altitude                 : 297 m Above Sea Level
GPS Date/Time                : 2021:01:06 15:07:31Z
GPS Latitude                 : 56 deg 34' 14.00" N
GPS Longitude                : 3 deg 36' 39.00" W
Circle Of Confusion          : 0.005 mm
Field Of View                : 69.4 deg
Focal Length                 : 4.2 mm (35 mm equivalent: 26.0 mm)
GPS Position                 : 56 deg 34' 14.00" N, 3 deg 36' 39.00" W
Hyperfocal Distance          : 2.14 m
Light Value                  : 8.8
```

Figure 17.3 – The GPS data from an image file

Using ExifTool allows an analyst to determine the location the image was taken from.

46. **A**. DAST. DAST tools allow a tester to recreate the error. See *Chapter 2, Integrating Software Applications into the Enterprise*.

47. **C**. A business continuity plan. A business continuity plan allows the organization to identify potential problems and have alternative plans of action. See *Chapter 15, Business Continuity and Disaster Recovery Concepts*.

48. **C**. Mitigate the risk by restricting access to the ICS. The only available course of action is to segment the network that contains the legacy equipment. This is a common approach when it comes to dealing with operational technology. See *Chapter 10, Security Considerations Impacting Specific Sectors and Operational Technologies*.

49. **B**. The drive was cloned for forensic analysis. See *Chapter 8, Implementing Incident Response and Forensics Procedures*.

50. **A**. SAST. The code is still in the development environment, so SAST will be the most appropriate option here. See *Chapter 2, Integrating Software Applications into the Enterprise*.

Hopefully, you enjoyed testing yourself with a typical mix of CASP questions. For more exam resources and extra content please visit `https://www.casp.training`.

Index

Packt.com

Subscribe to our online digital library for full access to over 7,000 books and videos, as well as industry leading tools to help you plan your personal development and advance your career. For more information, please visit our website.

Why subscribe?

- Spend less time learning and more time coding with practical eBooks and Videos from over 4,000 industry professionals

- Improve your learning with Skill Plans built especially for you

- Get a free eBook or video every month

- Fully searchable for easy access to vital information

- Copy and paste, print, and bookmark content

Did you know that Packt offers eBook versions of every book published, with PDF and ePub files available? You can upgrade to the eBook version at packt.com and as a print book customer, you are entitled to a discount on the eBook copy. Get in touch with us at customercare@packtpub.com for more details.

At www.packt.com, you can also read a collection of free technical articles, sign up for a range of free newsletters, and receive exclusive discounts and offers on Packt books and eBooks.

Other Books You May Enjoy

If you enjoyed this book, you may be interested in these other books by Packt:

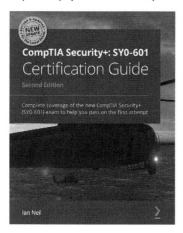

CompTIA Security+: SY0-601 Certification Guide - Second Edition

Ian Neil

ISBN: 9781800564244

- Master cybersecurity fundamentals, from the CIA triad through to IAM
- Explore cloud security and techniques used in penetration testing
- Use different authentication methods and troubleshoot security issues
- Secure the devices and applications used by your company
- Identify and protect against various types of malware and viruses
- Protect yourself against social engineering and advanced attacks
- Understand and implement PKI concepts
- Delve into secure application development, deployment, and automation

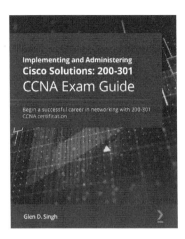

Implementing and Administering Cisco Solutions: 200-301 CCNA Exam Guide

Glen D. Singh

ISBN: 9781800208094

- Understand the benefits of creating an optimal network
- Create and implement IP schemes in an enterprise network
- Design and implement virtual local area networks (VLANs)
- Administer dynamic routing protocols, network security, and automation
- Get to grips with various IP services that are essential to every network
- Discover how to troubleshoot networking devices

Packt is searching for authors like you

If you're interested in becoming an author for Packt, please visit `authors.packtpub.com` and apply today. We have worked with thousands of developers and tech professionals, just like you, to help them share their insight with the global tech community. You can make a general application, apply for a specific hot topic that we are recruiting an author for, or submit your own idea.

Share Your Thoughts

Now you've finished *CompTIA CASP+ CAS-004 Certification Guide*, we'd love to hear your thoughts! Scan the QR code below to go straight to the Amazon review page for this book and share your feedback or leave a review on the site that you purchased it from.

`https://packt.link/r/1801816778`

Your review is important to us and the tech community and will help us make sure we're delivering excellent quality content.

Made in United States
Troutdale, OR
06/30/2024

20905151R00363